DISCARDED

EDUCATION
IN THE UNITED STATES

BY

EDGAR W. KNIGHT
THE UNIVERSITY OF NORTH CAROLINA

Lenoir Rhyne College
LIBRARY

GINN AND COMPANY
BOSTON · NEW YORK · CHICAGO · LONDON
ATLANTA · DALLAS · COLUMBUS · SAN FRANCISCO

COPYRIGHT, 1929, BY EDGAR W. KNIGHT

ALL RIGHTS RESERVED

PRINTED IN THE UNITED STATES OF AMERICA

429.6

370.9

K74e

10242

The Athenæum Press

GINN AND COMPANY · PRO-
PRIETORS · BOSTON · U.S.A.

370.9
K74e

10242

TO

ANN AND JANE

PREFACE

In the preface to "The Evolution of the Massachusetts Public School System," published in 1894, George H. Martin stated that the book was not a complete history of education in that state; the source materials for such a work were abundant, he said, but needed the approach of students with the time and inclination to make use of them.

The same obstacle which more than thirty years ago prevented Martin from preparing a complete history of education in one state has been a stubborn difficulty in the preparation of this book. The source materials for a complete history of education in the United States are now ample, as were the sources for a history of education in Massachusetts in Martin's time; but any attempt to make a fair and faithful report of the origin, progress, and problems of American education reveals at once the need for more studies of these sources. One does not proceed very far in the work before this need becomes apparent for almost any state and for every period from the colonial to the present. It is largely for this reason that this book is not a more nearly complete history of education in the United States. Until fuller and more numerous research studies are made available in the field, such a history cannot be written.

Although the lack of such research is not offered as an excuse, nevertheless it is a partial explanation of the imperfections which the book must sooner or later reveal. The fact that few researches have been made in the historical phases of American education should suggest to scholars who have the time and inclination, and to those graduate students and professors who are seeking suitable subjects for doctoral dissertations, that they should look around in this fertile field. Here the educational solutions of some problems may be found. Moreover, in this time of flux and ferment and of innumerable philosophical conflicts in education, the more remote subjects of study are safer for graduate students, even though they be a trifle less modish. Dissertations on the latest fashions in education are likely to start rows, and these are not tidy indulgences for scholars or for fledgling doctors of philosophy who would become scholars.

A wealth of untouched material bearing upon the educational history of the United States awaits the industrious and ambitious scholar. Official documentary sources are voluminous, if widely scattered and of varying quality. Although colonial and state statutes, church, local, and county records, are often so chaotic and fugitive as to defy the easy reconstruction of tendencies and practices, nevertheless they offer to students who have access to such local materials wide possibilities for useful research. Autobiographic and biographic materials, reminiscent writings, books of travel, letters, diaries, account books of obscure country stores or of individuals, wills, inventories of property, advertisements of schools and of booksellers, newspapers, children's magazines, pamphlet material of wide variety, publications of religious organizations and organizations for reform, and school textbooks (valuable collections of which are in the possession of the American Antiquarian Society at Worcester, Massachusetts, and of Wisconsin and Harvard) are of vast value to the educational historian. Studies of these and other sources can be made to throw light upon some of the educational problems of the present time.

Educational activity is one phase of the life of the American people which has not yet been as fully and as critically examined as it deserves; yet few fields of research are more fertile, and few if any promise more useful returns, than the field of American educational history or the history of social

institutions, practices, ideals, methods, customs, achievements, and traditions. Education, which is still for the most
part tradition, is often encumbered by its own inertia and
its reluctance to examine its theories, its practices, and its
claims. The veil of any myths which have grown respectable
in American education can be torn away, the danger of un-
substantiated inferences such as are so often found in this
field can be pointed out and averted, errors in accepted educational traditions can be removed, and the repetition of
mistakes prevented, only by the critical examination of present problems whose roots almost always are to be found in
the past. Only by such means can that which is be made
what it should be. Moreover, only in this way can the practical school-teacher and administrator meet sanely and safely
the new "butterfly suggestions" which, vainly and often
even gaudily adorned, flutter out increasingly into the educational world from its innovators, novices, and promoters. In
this process of critical examination historical study is a very
useful guide — one that has had only partial recognition.

This book is intended to be no more than a narrative or
historical sketch of education in this country. But in it an
attempt has been made (1) to point out some of the economic, political, and religious facts of history which seem
to have stood in the way of public education and to have retarded its growth, and seem to be doing so even now; (2) to
direct attention to some of those forces and facts of history
which seem to have encouraged its growth; and (3) to indicate some of the persistent educational problems of the
present whose roots seem to be in the past, and, whenever
possible, to suggest solutions for them. Emphasis is mainly
upon a few conspicuous movements and leaders, and less
upon theories than upon practices. Two entire chapters and
parts of others are devoted to practices. Effort has been
made throughout the book to present the material as con-
cretely as possible. The book has been developed out of

courses in the history of American education given in the
University of North Carolina for several years and in six
summer sessions in Columbia University. It is intended for
students of junior and senior grade, but some of it has been
found to be not too elementary for graduate students. The
material in the book, with the references and readings at
the end of each chapter, has proved quite satisfactory for a
twelve weeks' course of four or five meetings a week.

In teaching juniors, seniors, and graduate students, including both prospective teachers and those who have taught,
one learns how ignorant the student is apt to be of present
educational arrangements in this country. To meet this want
and to serve as a point of departure for discussion in later
chapters, the first chapter is descriptive of present conditions. This is followed by a chapter on the value of the historical approach to a study of education. Few of the chapters
adhere strictly to the chronological order; instead, an attempt is made to trace the most prominent educational principles and practices through from their beginnings in this
country. Because of the peculiar problems now found in the
Southern states a separate chapter is given to that subject.

References and readings are appended to each chapter,
and, whenever possible, new materials are used. These
references have been carefully chosen, and after each is
given a statement of its value to the student. The questions
at the end of each chapter are intended for study and class
discussion; they are made up from the material in the
chapter and from the references and readings. The selected
references and the questions should add to the teaching
value of the book.

If the criticisms are made that there is repetition in the
book and that for a historical account some of the passages
in it seem argumentative, the answer is that both repetition
and occasionally a little argument were intended. The law
of repetition is still pedagogically sound whether fashionable

this season or not; and something may perhaps be said for argument, even in a historical sketch such as this and even though a cloud of suspicion threatens to gather upon and about "indoctrination." If, for example, the political election of chief state school officers is a cardinal sin in public educational administration (as many competent authorities agree), it should not be accounted sinful to indoctrinate the public mind and consciousness against the dangers of such civic unrighteousness. If untrained and ineffective teachers and managers of schools are harmful in a democracy (as most thoughtful people probably believe), it should not be considered a pedagogical crime to indoctrinate as many people as possible against such public immoralities. And if (and this condition also does not seem contrary to fact) many of the so-called progressive movements in American education in recent years have led toward the lowering of standards and to the denial of the value of discipline, resulting in the relaxation of effort and other softening and debilitating tendencies in education, which are reflected also in adult life, it should not be improper to warn against such dangers.

Samuel Johnson's definition of *pastern* as "the knee of a horse" furnished amusement to many people and provoked a lady to ask him how the slip was made. The answer of the author of the famous dictionary is reported to have been, "Ignorance, madam, pure ignorance." The same reason for errors in this book is as frankly acknowledged, but the author will be grateful to critics, teachers, and reviewers who call attention to them.

EDGAR W. KNIGHT

THE UNIVERSITY OF NORTH CAROLINA

CONTENTS

CHAPTER PAGE

 I. PRESENT CONDITIONS 1

 II. THE HISTORY OF EDUCATION 38

 III. THE BACKGROUND 50

 IV. THE COLONIAL CLIMATE 70

 V. EARLY PRACTICES 97

 VI. THE PROMISE OF A NEW PERIOD 135

 VII. NEW FORCES 160

 VIII. THE AWAKENING 192

 IX. SECURING PUBLIC SUPPORT 241

 X. SECURING PUBLIC CONTROL 280

 XI. THE TRAINING OF TEACHERS 309

 XII. TEACHERS AND TEACHING 346

 XIII. EXTENDING THE SCHOOLS UPWARD 372

 XIV. LATER PRACTICES 411

 XV. UP FROM SLAVERY 461

 XVI. LATER DEVELOPMENTS 499

 XVII. TENDENCIES AND PROBLEMS 542

INDEX 577

EDUCATION
IN THE UNITED STATES

CHAPTER I

PRESENT CONDITIONS

Outline of the chapter. 1. The principles of American education, which is now the largest public enterprise in the United States, became accepted only after very bitter contests.

2. Each state, upon which rests the chief responsibility for education, has provided for the organization, administration, and the support of a public-school system.

3. Below the state are the local administrative units: the county, the town, the township, the city, and the district.

4. The financial support of public education is derived from many forms of taxation, the principal source being property taxes.

5. Greatly increased costs of schools in recent years constitute a difficult problem.

6. The public educational system of a typical state includes schools of elementary, secondary, and higher grade and technical and professional institutions, which require nearly a million teachers and administrators.

7. Although there are numerous agencies for the training of teachers, the changes in teaching personnel are very frequent. The average salaries of teachers vary widely among the states.

8. The problem of providing adequate educational facilities in the rural areas is very difficult.

9. In the recent phenomenal increase in college attendance new problems have arisen.

10. Many agencies and activities for adult, extension, and continuation education have recently developed, and a more extensive participation of the Federal government in general education in the states is being advocated.

11. Effort is constantly being made to increase and improve education, in which the American people have deep confidence.

Education is the largest public enterprise in the United States and the country's most important business. More money is invested in the physical plants of education than in any other public undertaking. The public-school property of the country has a valuation of nearly seven billions, and several hundred millions are required annually for school buildings. More money is annually spent by the towns, cities, counties, and states for school support than for any other public cause. Approximately three billions were provided for this purpose in 1928. Viewed also from the number of people engaged in it, the colossal proportions of public education are apparent. There are nearly a million teachers, and nearly twenty-nine million pupils are enrolled in the various types of schools. If to these are added the thousands of school-board members, janitors, and other employees of the schools, those engaged in preparing schoolbooks, school furniture, school apparatus, and other school supplies, and those engaged in the designing and construction of schoolhouses, two persons out of every seven in the United States are giving practically all their time to this large business.

The principles of American education. This large enterprise, formed and conducted as the best means of promoting the well-being and happiness of the people, is established on the theory that a democratic form of government depends for its value and effectiveness upon a citizenship educated sufficiently to understand and to direct intelligently, efficiently, and with justice all its affairs, private and personal, public and civic. The greater the political freedom of a nation, the greater also is the necessity for the proper education of its people. The people will love and serve that government whose solicitude is for their happiness and whose first great care is their improvement. Through proper education they learn that their obligation is to properly constituted government, which is all its citizens — rich and poor, high and low, strong and feeble, bright and dull.

On this foundation is established the American plan of public education, which has played in the past, still plays, and promises to continue to play in the future such a vital part in the advancement of the American people. This plan arose out of and has been built upon the so-called democratic principles of education which have come to be accepted and are now more or less practically applied in all sections of the entire United States.

Chief among these principles is that of universal education: that schools are an obligation of the state, which should provide equal educational opportunity for all the people. It is now accepted that the state has the right to make this educational provision by means of taxation, and the public support of education is now a fixed principle in all the American states. Taxation on the property of all the people for the free education of all, without regard to their economic condition, is now accepted as a sound and just method of educational support. Another important principle of public education in the United States is that of public control. All forms of public educational work, from the smallest and most remotely isolated rural school to the largest state university, are under direct or indirect public control. Compulsory attendance upon school by children between certain ages is also a principle of public education in the United States, each of which now has compulsory-education legislation. Children within the compulsory-attendance ages must go to school, although by a decision of the United States Supreme Court in the Oregon case in 1925 they cannot be compelled to attend public school. Still another principle is that public education shall be non-sectarian. Religion is not a subject of instruction in the course of study. The constitution and laws of the various states usually require that no religious or sectarian teachings of any kind can be given in any schools maintained or aided by public funds.

Bitter contests over these principles. Each of these principles of public education was contested in every state, and often rather bitterly, before it finally won acceptance in the public mind and became established in practice. Around each of these principles much controversy waged. Not all of them even now are fully and practically established in every community. How men battled over them and why these principles came so slowly to be accepted are matters for consideration in later chapters; but it should be noted here that faith in these principles and the devotion of the American people to them are exhibited in the long and laborious struggles which they have been willing to wage that these principles might be practically applied. This faith and this devotion are apparent also not only in the present organization, management, and support of schools, but in the effort that is constantly being made to improve the practical arrangements of public education.

Education a state responsibility. The Constitution of the national government makes no mention of education, but by implication in the Tenth Amendment the subject is left to the separate states. Each of these, in its constitution and by legislation, has provided for the organization, administration, and support of a public system of schools which are uniformly free and open alike to all up to the college or the university. Each state thus recognizes its responsibility for the education of its citizens and asserts the right to tax property, within the limits fixed by its constitution or laws, for school support. Numerous decisions of the courts have sustained this position. The states, in their own separate ways, have developed school systems which vary not only in details of organization and administration and in plans of taxation but also in the amount and kind of schooling provided, in educational standards, and in the ability or the willingness to provide schools. Some states acknowledge responsibility for a shorter annual school term than is acceptable in other states; some consider their educational responsibility met when they provide an elementary education for all; others consider secondary education as a legitimate part of the public-school system. The term "free education" is interpreted in some states to mean not only free tuition but free textbooks and other materials as well. In the main, however, certain characteristics of education are common to all the states. In addition to maintenance by public funds, derived from taxation levied annually or from permanent public educational endowments, it is under public control and is free, nonsectarian, and compulsory. Generally the schools are coeducational. Separate public schools for the sexes are not common. Separate schools are provided in the Southern states, however, for the children of the whites and for those of the negroes.

Organization and administrative practices. The state is now the chief administrative unit in public education in the United States and is gradually assuming larger control by granting larger financial support. It is assuming wider leadership by accepting more definite responsibility for establishing minimum standards which the smaller educational units, such as the county, the city, the town, the township, or the district must meet. Under authority of its constitution or law each state has established a central administrative organization for the support and direction of its educational arrangements. It has reserved to itself certain powers and it has delegated others to the smaller administrative units. The authority which is thus delegated to the local units varies widely among the states and often among such units within a state, but usually the general state school law regulates the educational practices in the smaller and more local units. It may permit such units to determine how they shall be organized and governed, the kind of schoolhouses that may be erected, the qualifications of the teachers, the course of study, the length of the school term, and other matters, but these powers are always subject to certain broad limitations of the state law, the purpose of which is to guide and encourage rather than to restrict the smaller units in their educational effort.

The state department of education. Each of the states administers the public elementary and secondary schools within its borders. This is accomplished by a state department of education, which is composed of a state board of education, a chief state school officer who is known as the state superintendent of public instruction or the state commissioner of education (see Chapter X), and an administrative staff whose members are expected to be specialists in the various fields of educational work. Usually also the state department has business, statistical, and clerical staffs. The state board is composed of a varying number of members, usually from seven to thirteen, who are appointed by the governor, or elected by the people, or serve ex officio. In some states the powers of this board are nominal only; in others they are large and extensive. In eight of the states this board selects the chief state school official.

In most of the states this official is elected by the people; in a few he is appointed by the governor. He serves as the executive head of the state school system and is looked upon as the leader of the state department of education. His duties and those of the department of which he is the head are numerous and varied. They relate to the initiation of educational reforms and improvements, to the preparation of courses of study, to the establishment and maintenance of educational standards and of regulations concerning textbooks, the certification of teachers, standards for school buildings, the distribution of state funds for public-school purposes, and to many other matters. Often he serves as a member of important boards of control for state educational institutions, and in some states he has judicial authority.

Local units of educational control. Below the state unit and as parts of it are the local units of educational administration : the county, the New England town, the township, the city, and the district, each of which has educational powers delegated by the state through the general school law or by special legislation.

The county. The county, which is a subdivision of each of the states for purposes of local administration, is an important unit for local educational administration. It is perhaps least important as an educational unit in New England ; but it is very important in the Western and Southern states, where it serves also as an important unit of civil administration. As a unit of school administration the county has spread rapidly and is now displacing the district system in many of the states. In some of the states city schools come under the administration of the county. Under the county plan of school organization there is a county board of education, elected by the people of the county or appointed by some other authority. There is also a county superintendent of schools, who in most of the states serves as a supervisory official for schools outside of independent cities. In some cases this official also has important executive and administrative responsibilities. In about half the states he is elected by the people of the county in which he serves ; in other states he is appointed by the county boards of education or by officials of the state.

The town. Although in many states the county has been made the unit for educational administration, in some of them this unit is still further divided into smaller units for the administration of the public-school system of the state. Among these smaller units are the towns in New England. The town system of school administration includes under one taxation unit and one board of control all the schools in the civil-town unit. This type of school administration originated in Massachusetts and is a peculiarly New England institution, although the term is also applied to similar units in New Jersey. The area embraced in the town includes not only a natural center, which may be a village or even a small city, but also rural and suburban places. The educational affairs of this unit are under the control of a town school committee which is elected by the people of the entire town. This committee has control of all the schools of the town whether they are city schools, village schools, or rural schools. All towns in Massachusetts and, to some extent, all towns in the other New England states employ superintendents of schools separately or in connection with one or more towns which are more or less contiguous. This official serves in a supervisory capacity and as executive officer of the town school committee or committees under whom he works. In Massachusetts, for example, many of the towns employ a separate superintendent of schools, and some of them often unite and employ such an officer. In some cases two towns will unite; in other cases three, or four, or more. As a rule the New England towns report their educational affairs directly to the state department rather than to some intermediate educational authorities. The town unit of school administration has been substituted in large part for the old district system.

The township. The township comprises an area larger than that of the district and sometimes larger than that of the New England town, but it does not often include large villages or cities. Wherever this unit is found the township is usually also a unit of government in the construction and maintenance of roads and bridges, the control of poor relief, and the management of other civil matters. The township system, somewhat strong in the north-central group of states, is a less effective form of school organization than the present New England town system. Its purpose, however, is to provide for the systematic organization and direction of the educational affairs of an entire township under a

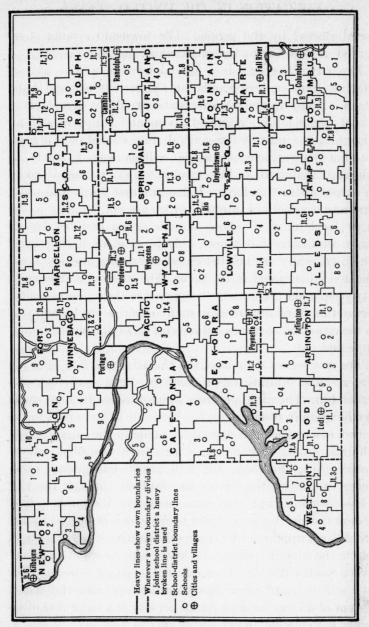

A COUNTY DIVIDED INTO TOWNS AND SCHOOL DISTRICTS

Heavy lines show town boundaries
Wherever a town boundary divides a joint school district a heavy broken line is used
School-district boundary lines
○ Schools
⊕ Cities and villages

board elected by the people. The township system is regarded as superior to the small school district system.

The city. The city is a special form of school district which is more or less popular in all sections of the United States. It enjoys special powers and privileges in matters of school organization, administration, and support, and although it is a part of the general state educational organization it is nevertheless somewhat independent. It meets the minimum standards of the state, but is given large freedom to exceed those standards. It has peculiar needs and problems and a variety of interests which are not common to the other local units of school administration and because of these conditions it has been able to gain for itself powers which generally are not delegated to smaller and less complicated educational institutions. The interdependencies of city people led them early to appreciate the value of collective action in education as in many other interests, and it is in the cities that educational reforms and improvements first appeared.

The city school systems of the United States now offer the largest opportunities for progressive educational work and leadership. The rapid progress which this country has made in education in recent years has been due in large part to the improvement that the cities have made in the organization, administration, direction, and extension of public educational effort. Probably the best public educational experience of the United States has evolved through the city school system. For the management of its public-school system the city has a separate board which is elected by the people or is appointed by some other authority. This board selects the superintendent of schools, who serves in an executive capacity for the direction of the city's schools. The city school board often has large powers, and the school system of a large modern American city is a large and often somewhat complicated organization.

The small district. The smallest unit of public-school administration in the United States is the district. It is also the oldest unit. It was the original educational organization in New England, where it arose as the natural, most simple, and seemingly most democratic unit. Because it was simple and democratic the district system spread and became more or less strong in every state. In many states it is even now strongly entrenched, and is especially dominating in the rural areas, where it is a stubborn obstacle to educational progress. The district is under the control of a local board of trustees, or committeemen, who are generally elected by the people of the district or appointed by some larger unit above it. This board is often clothed with large financial and educational powers, and sometimes it enjoys corporate rights. In the earlier days it served useful purposes, and met fairly well the educational needs of the time in which it arose; but its period of usefulness has passed, and as a system for school administration it is now ineffective, expensive, and unprogressive and makes for narrowness and provincialism.

Public-school support. Public education is supported in each of the states by state, county, and local funds derived from taxation. In all the states public funds are contributed to the support of public elementary and secondary schools under local administrative control. Public funds are also used in the support of public normal schools and colleges for the preparation of teachers for the elementary and secondary schools; and such funds are used almost exclusively for the support of other types of public educational institutions, such as colleges, universities, agricultural colleges, and institutions for physical, mental, and moral defectives.

Variety of sources. The public funds are derived from a variety of sources. In many of the states the principal source is taxation on property. Most of them also have some form of permanent public educational endowments, which are the oldest form of state aid for public educational work in this country. Every one of the units constituting the Union, except Georgia and the District of Columbia, has one or more such endowments which are intact and genuinely productive, or it maintains a permanent state debt on which the state pays interest for the support of its schools. In some cases, however, so-called permanent school funds are not permanent at all.

Other sources of state school support are state school taxes, a general mill tax on all personal and real taxable property of the state, corporation taxes, severance taxes, income taxes, inheritance taxes, sales taxes, license and privilege taxes, taxes on stocks and bonds, and poll taxes. Often the state may make a direct appropriation of a specified sum for school support from the total revenues collected by it for general state purposes. The methods used by the state in the distribution of its funds for school purposes vary somewhat in detail. Consideration is generally given to the needs and abilities of the local units in an effort to equalize as nearly as possible educational burdens and opportunities. State funds are often distributed also upon the per capita basis of scholastic population, or of enrollment, or of average daily attendance. In nearly all the states in which the county is an important unit for purposes of civil or educational administration it also contributes substantially to school support. In some cases the obligation of the support of a minimum state educational program is placed on the county, and this unit often finances, without any state aid whatever, all the public elementary and secondary schools within its boundary. This is generally the case in the wealthier counties. In a recent year 10 per cent of the total receipts for public-school purposes came from county sources. In the main the burden of supporting public schools throughout the United States falls upon and is borne by local units including the county. About three fourths of the total costs of public schools come from local sources, and the tendency is toward a diminishing state support.

Increasing costs of schools. The cost of public education increased more than 440 per cent between 1890 and 1918, and if a longer period is considered the increased cost is even more conspicuous. In the decade from 1910 to 1920 the cost of education for each inhabitant of the United States increased from $4.62 to $9.90, and teachers' salaries increased from $100,000,000 to nearly $450,000,000. In the decade from 1916 to 1926 the per capita cost for public schools rose from $6.26 to $16.25, and the cost per pupil in average daily attendance from $41.72 to $96.17. In the decade from 1913 to 1923 the cost of public education increased from about $521,000,000 to more than $1,250,000,-000. In 1913 Akron, Ohio, had a school budget of less than $500,000, and ten years later it had increased to $2,250,000. In the corresponding period the budget of Denver's schools jumped from $1,300,000 to about $3,500,000. A quarter of a century ago all the public-school property of North Carolina had a value of only $1,000,000; today it is nearly a hundred times greater. The total annual public-school fund of that state in 1900 was only $1,000,000; in 1928 it was nearly forty times larger. Ten years ago the sum of $83,000,000 was expended in New York State for public education; in 1927 this amount had increased to nearly $300,000,000.

Causes of increased costs. These increases in school costs, which constitute one of the largest problems facing taxpayers today, are due to many causes. In addition to the decreased purchasing power of the dollar, which has diminished nearly one third since 1918, the cost of public education has been greatly increased by the increased number of pupils now found in the schools. Between 1890 and 1920 the enrollment of pupils in public elementary and secondary schools increased from approximately 13,000,000 to more than 21,000,000, and the enrollment in the public colleges and universities increased from about 65,000 to 341,000 during the same period. This increase in enrollment of pupils produced an increase in the number of teachers and a consequent increase in salaries. During the three decades from 1890 to 1920 the number of teachers increased from about 364,000 to nearly 680,000.

Expanded courses of study. Another cause of the increased cost of education is the expansion of the courses of study, which in recent years have undergone many changes. Neither the elementary school nor the high school is today confining its work to the narrow and restricted subjects which were formerly found in these types of schools. The old fundamental subjects have been greatly enlarged. In addition to the fundamental subjects, there may now be found in well-organized and well-conducted elementary schools many of the newer subjects, such as nature study, history, composition and literature, physiology and hygiene, music, art, manual training, home economics, and physical education, some of which require larger and more expensive equipment than was necessary for teaching the old conventional subjects. Moreover, better school buildings are being erected. They are more substantially built and are more nearly adequate for educational purposes and for the health, safety, comfort, and æsthetic development of the children and community.

Expensive administration. Furthermore, educational administration is more expensive now than formerly, on account of both the increased number of pupils and the enlargement of the courses of study. The administration of public education has copied from the management of industrial plants and has drawn to its aid many new educational workers, such as supervisors, assistant superintendents, assistant principals, personnel advisers, psychologists, research workers, librarians, accountants, secretaries, and the like. Provision of salaries for these specialists has greatly added to the cost of education. The up-to-date and properly administered school system today exhibits an enlarged and somewhat complicated system of administration, especially when it is compared with the simpler arrangements of early days. In such a system may be found the psychologist and his staff of workers, who undertake, through the use of intelligence tests and educational measurements, to indicate more definitely than formerly the progress which each student is making or is failing to make, or to measure each student's fitness to advance from grade to grade, from the elementary school to the high school, and from the high school to college. Modern educational administration also requires numerous reports from teacher to principal, from principal to superintendent, from superintendent to school board and the public, and from the school of the smaller administrative unit to the larger unit of the state. The collection, classification, publication, and use of educational statistics are evidences of the constant effort to understand and to improve public educational work.

Other factors. The cost of public education has also been increased greatly in recent years by the lengthening of the legal school year, by the extension and more effective enforcement of compulsory-attendance legislation, and by the establishment of systems of pensions for public-school teachers and administrators. Pensions are now provided in many cities and in several of the states. In some places the teachers' retirement fund reaches large amounts. The fuller use of the school plant also adds a new element in public-school expenditures. The schoolhouse of the present is becoming more and more the center for community and neighborhood activities, both social and civil in nature. Societies of all kinds hold their meetings in it, extension courses from the university or agricultural college are conducted in it, and it is often used for numerous community purposes. The public school today belongs more than ever before to and is being used more fully by the entire community. With the enlargement of the function of public education more people are to be educated by a larger number of teachers, in a larger number of subjects, in better and safer houses, under more wholesome conditions, and through a better type of administration and direction.

Types of schools. The public-school system of an American state consists of elementary schools, high schools, normal schools or teachers' colleges, and other forms of higher education, generally including an agricultural and mechanical college and a university. The elementary schools contain more pupils, employ more teachers, and have more money annually expended on them than all other types of public educational institutions within the state. Many states compel attendance on the elementary school until its work is completed, and all of them view an elementary education as the minimum essential for all the people. Kindergartens are also found in some states as parts of the regular public-school system.

The elementary school. In most of the states the work of the elementary school comprises eight grades; in others (chiefly within the Southern area of the United States) it consists of only seven grades. The objectives for the work of these grades generally include the attainment of skill in the fundamental processes of reading, arithmetic, spelling, the graphic arts, and handwriting as preparation for intelligent citizenship, good health, and proper living. An attempt is also made to give the pupils some understanding of industrial processes and of civic organizations in preparation for their proper participation in the social, economic, and political life of the communities in which they are likely to live. Definite courses of study for the elementary grades are generally prepared and published by the state departments of education under the authority of the school law. In such courses of study each subject to be taught is generally named and described and its objectives are defined, the purpose being to relate the work of each grade to the other grades in a unified way. City school systems generally enjoy a wider measure of freedom in the selection and adaptation of the subjects in the prescribed state courses of study than is allowed other educational units.

The school day in most of the elementary schools is divided into two sessions, one in the morning and one in the afternoon, with usually an intermission of about an hour at noon, the length of the school day being generally defined by law. The children of the first few grades usually attend for a shorter daily period than is required of the older children. The elementary grades, and often the high schools as well, often receive helpful coöperation from the parents of the children through organized clubs and associations of parents and teachers, in the periodic meetings of which the problems of the school and of the home are presented and discussed. It is estimated that a million and a half mothers of school children are enrolled in classes designed for the purpose of studying the abilities and interests of children.

The high school. The development of public high schools in recent years has been a most remarkable phenomenon. Since 1890 the rate of increase of public high-school enrollment has been twenty times greater than the rate of increase in population. Nearly four million children from all social and economic groups are now enrolled in high schools, which usually give four years of work above the elementary grades. Standards of work done in these schools have been formulated by state departments of education, by colleges and universities, by associations formed voluntarily by the high schools themselves, and by the work of voluntary accrediting agencies, such as the New England College Entrance Examination Board, the Association of

Colleges and Preparatory Schools of the Middle States and Maryland, the Southern Association of Colleges and Secondary Schools, the North Central Association of Colleges and Secondary Schools, and the Northwest Association of Secondary and Higher Schools. Many of the high schools prescribe certain subjects which must be successfully completed for graduation, although many of them follow broad policies of allowing comparative freedom in the choice of subjects. A definite number of units in such subjects as English, mathematics, foreign languages, the natural sciences, and the social sciences is usually required. The junior high school, the purpose of which is to give training suitable to children in early adolescence and to facilitate the change from the elementary to the secondary studies, has appeared in comparatively recent years and is attracting wide attention.

Enrollment, attendance, and terms. Of the total enrollment of pupils in public schools of elementary grade about 20 per cent are found in the first grade, 14 per cent in the second, 13 per cent in the third, 13 per cent in the fourth, about 12 per cent in the fifth, about 11 per cent in the sixth, a little more than 9 per cent in the seventh, and about $7\frac{1}{2}$ per cent in the eighth. Of the total enrollment in the high-school grades nearly 38 per cent is in the first year, nearly 27 per cent in the second, 20 per cent in the third, and about 16 per cent in the fourth. Although the schools are now holding proportionately more pupils until graduation year than formerly, retardation and elimination and nonattendance are still persistent problems in public educational administration. These are expensive problems also. It is estimated that waste resulting from irregular attendance costs annually about $175,000,000.

The average number of days all public elementary and secondary schools were in session in the country as a whole in 1926 (the latest year for which official statistics are available) was about 169.3. The average number of days attended by each pupil enrolled was about 140; the average daily attendance of the enrollment was about 80.3 per cent. The facts for the various states and the District of Columbia for 1926 appear in the table on page 20.

In the table on page 21 appear statistics showing the percentage of the total pupil enrollment in high school and the percentage of annual school term not attended in the United States as a whole and in each of the states and the District of Columbia, according to official reports for 1926.

The teachers. As noted at the beginning of this chapter there are in the entire country now almost a million school teachers and administrators. About 20 per cent of these educational workers are men. Nearly 618,000 of them are employed in the elementary schools, and more than half that number are serving in rural schools. The salaries of the teachers amount to about 75 per cent of the total public expenditure for elementary and secondary schools; but in the institutions of higher grades — colleges, universities, normal schools, and teachers' colleges — this item of cost is somewhat smaller. The lowest salaries are generally found in the small schools in rural communities, and the highest in the largest city systems. As a rule the highest salaries are paid for administrative service, and the lowest for teaching service. Often the salaries in the secondary schools are higher than those in the elementary schools, and this condition frequently moves teachers with special fitness and preparation and perhaps fondness for elementary-school work to accept positions in high schools for which they are not so well qualified. To remove the evils of this practice, a so-called "single salary schedule" — an attempt to base salaries on training, professional improvement, successful experience, and teaching effectiveness — has been adopted in many school systems. The theory of this plan is that teachers with the same qualifications should receive the

State	Term in Days	Days Attended by Each Pupil Enrolled	Percentage Attendance of Enrollment
Alabama	137.5	97.0	70.6
Arizona	165.5	125.3	75.7
Arkansas	146.4	103.0	70.4
California	180.6	138.2	76.5
Colorado	178.0	137.0	77.0
Connecticut	181.6	150.7	83.0
Delaware	184.3	154.1	83.6
District of Columbia	180.6	149.7	82.9
Florida	150.1	109.7	73.1
Georgia	144.8	107.8	74.4
Idaho	165.0	138.3	80.0
Illinois	184.9	153.4	83.0
Indiana	173.8	160.4	92.3
Iowa	176.0	141.1	80.2
Kansas	175.0	147.0	84.0
Kentucky	164.3	109.0	66.3
Louisiana	148.4	112.1	75.6
Maine	176.3	156.0	88.5
Maryland	186.0	151.2	81.3
Massachusetts	179.6	156.3	87.0
Michigan	188.5	152.3	80.8
Minnesota	178.3	144.4	81.0
Mississippi	141.0	102.4	72.6
Missouri	167.5	138.9	82.9
Montana	174.1	146.8	84.3
Nebraska	183.0	149.9	81.9
Nevada	173.0	146.5	84.6
New Hampshire	174.2	151.8	87.2
New Jersey	186.5	149.6	80.2
New Mexico	175.0	135.2	77.2
New York	185.6	159.4	85.9
North Carolina	146.1	108.1	74.0
North Dakota	166.8	138.5	83.1
Ohio	171.2	146.3	85.5
Oklahoma	148.9	102.0	68.5
Oregon	171.4	150.1	87.6
Pennsylvania	180.7	151.5	83.8
Rhode Island	190.0	158.8	83.6
South Carolina	144.0	102.9	71.5
South Dakota	168.7	141.9	84.1
Tennessee	152.2	105.5	69.3
Texas	134.7	114.9	85.3
Utah	173.8	141.2	81.2
Vermont	171.3	146.3	85.4
Virginia	159.4	122.7	77.0
Washington	178.8	142.7	79.8
West Virginia	164.7	132.2	80.3
Wisconsin	178.2	156.0	87.5
Wyoming	170.2	143.0	84.1

STATE	PERCENTAGE OF TOTAL ENROLLMENT IN HIGH SCHOOL	PERCENTAGE OF ANNUAL SCHOOL TERM NOT ATTENDED
United States	15.2	19.7
Alabama	8.7	29.4
Arizona	12.7	24.3
Arkansas	7.0	29.6
California	25.3	23.5
Colorado	17.6	23.0
Connecticut	12.9	17.0
Delaware	14.5	16.4
District of Columbia	18.3	17.1
Florida	10.2	26.9
Georgia	9.5	25.6
Idaho	18.6	20.0
Illinois	17.7	17.0
Indiana	23.1	7.7
Iowa	20.1	19.8
Kansas	19.9	16.0
Kentucky	7.9	33.7
Louisiana	11.5	24.4
Maine	18.2	11.5
Maryland	12.6	18.7
Massachusetts	18.4	13.0
Michigan	14.6	19.2
Minnesota	15.3	19.0
Mississippi	7.5	27.4
Missouri	15.3	17.1
Montana	17.9	15.7
Nebraska	18.4	18.1
Nevada	18.0	15.4
New Hampshire	16.9	12.8
New Jersey	14.3	19.8
New Mexico	9.3	22.8
New York	16.5	14.1
North Carolina	10.3	26.0
North Dakota	13.5	16.9
Ohio	17.8	14.5
Oklahoma	12.8	31.5
Oregon	21.5	12.4
Pennsylvania	14.5	16.2
Rhode Island	13.4	16.4
South Carolina	9.9	28.5
South Dakota	16.0	15.9
Tennessee	8.2	30.7
Texas	16.1	14.7
Utah	21.9	18.8
Vermont	16.4	14.6
Virginia	12.6	23.0
Washington	21.4	20.2
West Virginia	9.4	19.7
Wisconsin	23.4	12.5
Wyoming	19.3	15.9

same salaries whether they engage in teaching service in the elementary schools or in the high schools.

Licenses or certificates required. All teachers in public elementary and high schools must hold appropriate licenses, or certificates, which are issued by the state or by some other authority under the general school law. Such certificates are generally issued on examination or on evidence of successful study in normal schools, teachers' colleges, teacher-training classes in high school, or on diplomas of graduation or other accepted credentials from institutions of higher learning. Public funds are generally not paid to persons who do not hold legal licenses to teach. The various kinds and grades of certificates are either fixed by the general state law or by the regulations of the state department of education under the authority of law. As a rule the power to grant such certificates is vested in the state department of education, although in some states permission is given to smaller units of educational administration, such as cities and counties, to issue teaching certificates.

Age and other requirements. All applicants to teach in the public schools usually must have reached a minimum age and, if required to do so, must furnish evidence of good moral character. They must have attained also to some definite educational standard. A large number of the states set graduation from the high school as the minimum standard; others require, in addition, some professional training as prerequisites for teaching certificates. The requirement for high-school teachers is often higher than that demanded of teachers in the elementary schools. The tendency today is for governing educational authority to issue certificates on the basis of a minimum academic and professional training rather than on examinations; more than a third of the states have now eliminated examinations as a method of certificating teachers. Some states, moreover, are beginning in a modest way to issue certificates so as to limit the teachers in high school to those subjects in which they have had special preparation. Although most of the teachers are fairly well trained and competent, fully half a million of the school children are still being taught by teachers who have not advanced beyond the elementary school, and three millions of them are taught by teachers who have not studied beyond the high school.

Standards for college teachers. Teachers in colleges, universities, teachers' colleges, and normal schools are usually not certificated by the state. Standards for teachers in such institutions are generally set by the institutions themselves or by voluntary accrediting agencies, such as the American Association of Teachers Colleges, the North Central Association of Colleges and Secondary Schools, the Northwest Association of Secondary and Higher Schools, the Southern Association of Colleges and Secondary Schools, the Association of Colleges and Preparatory Schools of the Middle States and Maryland, and the Association of American Universities, which usually require teachers in member institutions to present evidence of appropriate training.

The training of teachers. The professional training of teachers for the public schools of the United States is usually given in normal schools, teachers' colleges, schools of education in colleges and universities, teacher-training classes in connection with high schools, summer schools, and through work done by correspondence and in extension classes. Two years of study above high-school graduation is the commonly accepted standard for the professional training of teachers in the elementary schools. The courses pursued by the prospective teachers during these two years are planned to give them the proper perspective of subject matter and of teaching technique. As already noted, not all teachers attain to these standards. The minimum academic preparation commonly accepted as the standard for prospective high-school teachers is graduation from high school and from a college, and many colleges have introduced professional courses in education in addition to the subject-matter courses. Again, not all teachers in the high schools have attained to these commonly accepted standards, though the tendency is increasingly toward the maintenance of such standards.

Numerous teacher-training agencies. There are now almost 400 normal schools and teachers' colleges in the United States, with an enrollment of nearly 250,000 students. In other types of teacher-training agencies there are approximately 175,000 students who are preparing to teach. Approximately 78 per cent of all persons preparing to teach are enrolled in institutions that are under public control. Elementary teachers, as a rule, are prepared principally in normal schools and teachers' colleges; schools of education in colleges and universities confine their efforts in teacher-training work chiefly to the preparation of teachers for the high schools. Many thousands of teachers are studying through extension courses, and tens of thousands of them attend summer sessions every year. In 1927 more than 377,000 were enrolled in summer schools in all parts of the country.

Frequent changes in the teaching personnel. Although the agencies and opportunities for teacher-training are numerous, one of the difficult problems in the public schools of the United States is involved in the frequent changes among the teachers. Probably 16 per cent of the teachers in public elementary and high schools leave the work annually, and the percentage of those who move from one school to another is even larger. This evil is the result of certain conditions which have developed within the teaching profession rather recently. In many states free tuition is granted in normal schools, teachers' colleges, and in schools of education in colleges and universities to persons agreeing to teach in the public schools of the state for a specified but generally brief period. Many young people who intend to enter other occupations later seek teaching as temporary employment and thus escape the payment of tuition fees for their higher education. In many states also low certification requirements invite numerous persons into teaching who later discover their unfitness for it, but use it as a stepping-stone to other kinds of work. Positions in other occupations often offer larger initial salaries and better opportunities for advancement for beginners than are generally found in teaching. Moreover, the "hire and fire" policy adds to the difficulty of this condition. In some states the governing school authorities are not permitted to make contracts with teachers for more than one year at a time. Only a few of the states have enacted teaching tenure laws providing for a period of probation before permanent appointment. Laws concerning the certification of teachers and enacted by the individual states do not generally recognize reciprocity or coöperation with other states. These conditions, and perhaps others including low salaries, operate against the stability of the teaching profession.

Salaries of teachers. The average annual salaries of all public-school teachers, principals, and supervisors in the country as a whole in 1926, the latest year for which official statistics are available, were $1277. The average salaries in each of the states and in the District of Columbia appear in the table on page 26.

The rural schools. The task of equalizing educational opportunity in the remotely rural areas of the United States has become increasingly difficult, because of the depletion of rural life and the concentration of population and wealth in the industrial and municipal centers. Approximately 12,000,000 of the school children of the United States are in schools in the open country or in rural villages and towns of a thousand or fewer people. It is very difficult to supply these children with adequate instruction in the elementary

State	Average Annual Salaries	State	Average Annual Salaries
Alabama	$678	Nebraska	$1047
Arizona	1575	Nevada	1479
Arkansas	686	New Hampshire	1164
California	1905	New Jersey	1930
Colorado	1290	New Mexico	1028
Connecticut	1572	New York	2025
Delaware	1356	North Carolina	781
District of Columbia	2068	North Dakota	905
Florida	831	Ohio	1411
Georgia	684	Oklahoma	979
Idaho	1134	Oregon	1267
Illinois	1515	Pennsylvania	1468
Indiana	1361	Rhode Island	1478
Iowa	1241	South Carolina	761
Kansas	1114	South Dakota	923
Kentucky	777	Tennessee	778
Louisiana	892	Texas	837
Maine	844	Utah	1204
Maryland	1353	Vermont	899
Massachusetts	1618	Virginia	746
Michigan	1510	Washington	1515
Minnesota	1215	West Virginia	1072
Mississippi	582	Wisconsin	1237
Missouri	1153	Wyoming	1143
Montana	1096		

and secondary schools. The problem baffles the state and the smaller administrative units. More than 4,000,000 of these rural children are in the old-fashioned and primitive one-teacher schools, which still number more than 150,000. Probably 1,500,000 more children are in two-teacher, three-teacher, and four-teacher schools of the unconsolidated and unprogressive type. Consolidation of these small, weak, and ineffective schools and the transportation of the children to stronger and better schools offer the only relief. The consolidated movement is gaining rapidly. This better type of rural school is being established at the rate of about one thousand a year, and transportation items in the annual public-school budgets of the entire country now amount to more than $30,000,000. More than a million rural children are annually transported to school by public motor busses, horse-drawn vehicles, and private conveyances.

Higher education. Above the elementary and secondary schools are the colleges, the universities, the professional and technological schools, and the junior colleges, the last of which undertake to offer the first two years of standard college work. Although most of the elementary schools and high schools of the United States are under public control and support, the state does not have a monopoly in higher education. The private and denominational colleges, universities, and professional schools are more numerous than those under public direction. Almost eight hundred of these institutions of higher education receive their support from endowments, private gifts, tuition and other fees of students, and contributions from religious denominations. The public institutions of higher education are supported by revenue from taxation by cities, states, and the national government, by tuition and other fees, by endowments, and by private donations. The state, however, is the largest supporter of higher education under public control.

Educational foundations. Higher education is generously aided also by numerous educational trusts or foundations which have developed in recent years. Among the largest and most influential of these foundations are the General Education Board, the Rockefeller Foundation, the Rockefeller Institute for Medical Research, the Laura Spelman Rockefeller Memorial, the Carnegie Institution of Washington, the Carnegie Foundation for the Advancement of Teaching, the Carnegie Corporation of New York, the Russell Sage Foundation, the Commonwealth Fund, the Duke Endowment, and the John Simon Guggenheim Memorial Foundation (see Chapter XVII). Approximately eight hundred millions of private wealth are represented in these foundations, and all except about eight millions has been set up since 1900 for purposes of education and public welfare.

Types of higher institutions. Most of the states have at least one university or college under public support and control, some of them have more than one, and each of them has one or more public teachers' colleges or normal schools, or both. In the United States and the dependencies of Alaska, Hawaii, and Porto Rico there are one hundred and five public colleges and universities. Sixty-nine of these are colleges of agriculture and mechanic arts, commonly known as "land-grant colleges"; of this number seventeen, in as many states, are maintained exclusively for negro students. These agricultural colleges were established under legislation enacted by Congress in 1862 "to promote the liberal and practical education of the industrial classes in the several pursuits and professions of life." The Federal government annually appropriates to each state the sum of $50,000 for the support of these colleges and gives them other sums for certain specified purposes, such as experiment stations and scientific investigations. The total annual appropriations by the national government for these schools were about $12,000,000 in 1926.

A new problem of higher education. The requirements for admission to the freshman, or entering, class of most of the higher educational institutions, in courses leading to degrees, are usually those attained through the completion of the work given in a standard, accredited four-year high school, or satisfactory evidence of the equivalent of such work. Students are now admitted less than formerly through entrance examinations and more generally upon the certification of the high schools. The tendency, however, is more and more toward the selection of students from among those of best records in the high schools, which are every year graduating many more students, technically prepared for college and desirous of admission to it, than can be accommodated. One of the increasingly numerous problems of higher education in the United States arises out of this condition. The increased college and university attendance is a marked tendency of recent years. Although the population of the country has increased somewhat more than 80 per cent since 1890, college enrollments have increased about 500 per cent. Today there are nearly seven times as many college students in proportion to the population of the country as there were half a century ago.

Some characteristics of higher education. A period of nine months usually constitutes the academic year in these higher institutions. In most of them this is divided into two semesters or three terms, of about equal length. Some institutions, however, continue operation for the entire year, on the basis of four terms, or quarters; and most of those not on the quarter basis maintain a summer session of one or two terms of six weeks each.

Degrees. The so-called colleges of liberal arts and sciences are the oldest and are more numerous than all other institutions of higher education. They are either independent institutions or parts of universities which are generally formed round the college of liberal arts as the central unit. The degree of bachelor of arts, bachelor of science, or some other similar degree is conferred upon those students who complete the four-year course of study of the college. A well-developed and modern university is composed of the college of arts and sciences and of professional schools and a graduate school, each with its own faculty. A bachelor's degree is usually required for admission to the graduate school, which confers advanced degrees — master of arts, master of science, and the doctorate — in arts and sciences and in the other fields of learning. The right to confer degrees is granted to the college or the university by the state in its general laws of incorporation or by special acts of the

legislature. Some states have thrown safeguards around the
privilege to confer degrees by establishing well-defined
educational and financial requirements for the institutions
which are given this power. Most of the higher educational
institutions also confer honorary degrees.

Technological and professional schools. Technological and
professional schools are also numerous in the United States.
In addition to the schools and colleges of agriculture and engineering, there are schools of law, of medicine, of dentistry,
of pharmacy, of architecture, of journalism, of education,
and of other subjects. Many of these schools are parts of the
organization of well-developed universities. Voluntary associations throughout the country have undertaken to establish
definite standards for accrediting the schools which provide
technological and professional education. This action is taken
in the interest both of uniformity and of improving standards.

Adult education. The general term "adult education"
is used to designate many agencies and activities that provide for voluntary study during the leisure time of those
people who are beyond the compulsory school age. One of
the first purposes of adult education was the reduction and
eradication of adult illiteracy. The latest census of the
national government showed nearly five million people ten
years of age and above, or approximately 6 per cent of the
total population of that age, who could not write in any
language. Illiteracy ranges in the various states from 1.1 per
cent to nearly 22 per cent. Statistics show that although
illiteracy has been greatly reduced during the last half-
century and is being still further reduced, it still remains
one of the serious blights on the prosperity and well-being
of the American people. It is particularly prevalent in the
large cities, and in the rural areas in those states which have
a large negro population. In some of these states there is a
high percentage of illiteracy among the native-born whites
as well as negroes. Illiteracy is being reduced through com-

pulsory educational laws and a more wholesome attitude toward their enforcement, and by the legally constituted agencies which some of the states are providing to teach adult illiterates. Nearly half the states are aiding adult classes from public funds, and these are also expended for teaching foreign-born illiterates, who are most numerous in the cities. The early voluntary efforts to reduce adult illiteracy proved unsatisfactory, however, and are rapidly being replaced by better-organized and better-supported efforts. In some states evening schools have been made a part of the regular school program.

Extension and continuation education. Other efforts in adult education appear in the university-extension movement, which has developed widely in recent years. Courses offered by correspondence and in classes conducted away from the institutions are now provided by state universities and colleges and by private institutions. Work done by correspondence is now being supplemented by talks and instruction over the radio, and the motion picture is being used. Many institutions offer by correspondence or extension classes most of the subjects offered in residence. Correspondence schools, established and operated for profit, are also numerous, Chautauqua and lyceum courses are popular, and schools and classes are conducted by the Young Women's Christian Association, the Young Men's Christian Association, the Knights of Columbus, and the Young Men's Hebrew Association. The United States Bureau of Education and the American Library Association are encouraging home study by the preparation of reading courses. Adult education is being promoted also by the National Congress of Parents and Teachers, which now has a membership of more than a million people. The organized library is serving as an essential part of public educational systems for the encouragement of adult education and continuation study. More than half the people of the United

States now live in areas having access to public-library service. Thirty-one states have enacted legislation which permits counties to provide county library service, and in other states this service is provided under general powers.

The national government and education. Although the Federal government has never assumed responsibility for general education in the states, nevertheless it has given direct or indirect aid practically from the beginning. In addition to maintaining the United States Military Academy at West Point, the Naval Academy at Annapolis, and the Coast Guard School, for the training of men for military, naval, and coast-guard service, it participates in many other forms of educational work. The United States Bureau of Education, maintained under the Department of the Interior, collects statistics concerning the condition and progress of education in the several states and diffuses them in an effort to promote better school systems and the cause of education throughout the country. It is primarily an agency of educational research and promotion through field service, investigation, surveys, and the dissemination of information. In addition to the public lands given for common schools, universities, agricultural schools, and other educational purposes, the Federal government has given aid under the Smith-Lever Bill of 1914 to the states for instruction and practical demonstrations in agriculture and home economics. It also coöperates with the states in paying the salaries of teachers, supervisors, and directors of agricultural subjects, industrial subjects, trade subjects, and home economics. This work was begun in 1917 under the Smith-Hughes Law, through the Federal Board for Vocational Education. In 1918 the Smith-Sears Vocational Rehabilitation Act was passed to provide for vocational reëducation and the medical, surgical, and mental treatment of soldiers and sailors disabled by the World War. Three years later, with the passage of the Sheppard-Towner Maternity-Aid Act, the national government began to aid the states in the promotion of "the welfare and hygiene of maternity and infancy." Interest in a more extensive participation of the Federal government in general education appears in proposed legislation now before Congress and known as the Curtis-Reed Bill.

Efforts to improve education. Although public education — elementary, secondary, higher, and professional — falls short of its ideals and purposes, increased effort is being made by the several states to improve educational facilities and to enlarge the opportunities of the people. Through administrative devices, special, or "opportunity," rooms, and special teachers an attempt is being made to adjust the work of the school to the needs and abilities of the individual students. The scientific study of educational administration and of methods of teaching is leading to reorganizations of educational arrangements. "School-surveying" is being used as a method of determining points of weakness and points of strength, and more and more are school workers employing approximately scientific measurements of educational results through the use of standard intelligence and educational tests and scales. Moreover, the well-organized and properly directed state school system now embraces schools for its inert and unprogressive members — its physical, moral, and mental defectives. There are schools and other institutions for the deaf, the blind, and the crippled, for the weak of will, and for truants and incorrigibles. The public is gaining a more humane attitude toward its dependents and defectives and the delinquent members of society. In some cases much that is being done in this direction is doubtless largely a work of patching up and repairing. But many branches of science are now joining hands in a patient effort to solve human problems by examining and facing all the facts which bear upon them.

The outlook. The people of this country are settled in the conviction that provision for a liberal system of free education for all the people is the state's most important duty. Under this conviction they have assumed larger educational responsibilities than any democracy has ever undertaken. The magnitude of the task is almost bewildering. Can this task ever be completely achieved? The future holds the answer. Whatever the ultimate answer, the doctrine of educational equality and the principles of universal, free, public, compulsory, and secular education have already been justified in the diffusion of knowledge and in the moral uplift, the heightened civic virtue, and the improved economic and social conditions of the masses. But not even the most zealous advocates claim perfection for the American school system. Its principles have not yet been practically applied in every community. Its reach still exceeds its grasp. But in the sacrifices and struggles that have been made and waged for these principles and for the enlargement of educational opportunity there is hope for the future.

The story of those sacrifices and struggles is the major theme of the chapters which follow. But before the story is taken up the next chapter calls attention to some of the values which should come to teachers, school administrators, and the public generally from the historical approach to the subject.

REFERENCES AND READINGS

AYRES, L. P. An Index Number for State School Systems. New York, 1920.

> A study of educational progress by states from 1890 to 1918, based on an index number.

CUBBERLEY, E. P. An Introduction to the Study of Education. Boston, 1925.

> An elementary but suggestive and helpful treatment. Chapter IV gives a fairly clear description of the organization of education in the United States. Chapter XVIII discusses adult, vocational, and extension education; Chapter XIX deals with college and university education, Chapters XXII and XXIII with the problems of public-school finance and the increasing costs of schools, and Chapter XXIV with the progress and problems of present-day educational organization and administration.

CUBBERLEY, E. P. State and County Educational Reorganization. New York, 1914.

> Contains the constitution and school laws of the hypothetical state of Osceola, and is intended to present ideal constitutional and statutory foundations for a state school system.

CUBBERLEY, E. P. State School Administration. Boston, 1927.

> A more advanced and exhaustive treatment of the topics treated in "An Introduction to the Study of Education." Detailed attention is paid to national and state educational policies; to state administrative organization; to the scope of the school system; to financing the schools and to materials and equipment; to the training, certification, tenure, pay and pensions of the teachers; and to other subjects. Chapter XXVII discusses private and denominational effort in education and the court decision in the Oregon case. Contains very valuable lists of carefully selected references.

DUTTON, S. T., and SNEDDEN, D. The Administration of Public Education in the United States (Revised Edition). New York, 1913.

> The introduction and Chapters I–X, inclusive, supplement the material of this chapter.

KEITH, JOHN A. H., and BAGLEY, W. C. The Nation and the Schools. New York, 1920.

> Discusses the application of the principle of national aid for education.

Education in the United States of America. Washington, 1927.

> One of the best brief descriptions of present-day local, county, and state educational organization and administration. Prepared under the direction of John J. Tigert, who was at that time United States Commissioner of Education, for the Pan-Pacific Conference on Education, Rehabilitation, Reclamation, and Recreation, held at Honolulu in April, 1927.

The Educational Finance Inquiry Reports (13 vols.; New York, 1923–1924) and the reports of the United States Commissioner of Education contain descriptions of recent progress, present conditions, and other material bearing on the subject of this chapter.

Reports of the chief state school officers.

Reports of state educational-survey commissions, which many of the states have had.

The school laws of the different states, usually available as separate publications from state departments of education.

QUESTIONS FOR STUDY AND DISCUSSION

1. Compare the cost of public education in your county, city, and state with the cost of other public enterprises.

2. Consider the so-called democratic principles of education as they are now accepted in the United States and list arguments for and against each of these principles:

> *a.* Universal education.
> *b.* Free education.
> *c.* Public support.
> *d.* Public control.
> *e.* Nonsectarian education.
> *f.* Compulsory education.

3. Find out what you can about the Oregon case (1925), in which the Supreme Court of the United States held that children within compulsory school-attendance ages cannot be compelled to attend *public schools*. Upon what grounds was this decision given?

4. Consider the principle of "free education." What legitimate extensions of public educational effort not now common can the state make?

5. Point out any arguments against coeducation.

6. How is the state board of education in your state constituted? What is an ex officio board? What are the arguments against such a board?

7. Give the arguments for and against the election of the chief state school officer by popular vote.

8. Why do the cities, as a rule, have better schools than are usually found in rural sections?

9. *a.* Account for the stubborn strength of the small school district.

b. Give the arguments for and against the district system.

10. What are the various sources of public-school support in your state?

11. Add to the factors given in this chapter as causes of increased school costs any other factors which you know.

12. How can the waste from irregular attendance, nonattendance, retardation, and elimination be checked?

13. Why do the salaries of teachers vary so much among the different states?

14. Account for the instability in the teaching personnel. Indicate a solution of this problem.

15. Account for the rapid increase of students in colleges and universities in recent years.

16. Give the arguments for and against the work of educational trusts or foundations.

17. Point out the social significance of adult education, of the extension movement, and other such agencies.

18. Why do the public schools provide no religious instruction?

19. What legitimate demands can the state make upon private schools or parochial schools?

20. Show how the use of standard tests and measurements marks an advance in democratic education.

CHAPTER II

THE HISTORY OF EDUCATION

Outline of the chapter. 1. A knowledge of the history of schools and other educational agencies is an important part of the professional training of the teacher or the school administrator.

2. Much of the work of the school is traditional. The nature of the work of the teacher and the school administrator is restrictive and tends to foster prejudices in favor of familiar methods. The history of education is the "sovereign solvent" of educational prejudices.

3. The history of education enables the educational worker to detect fads and frills in whatever form they may appear, and it serves as a necessary preliminary to educational reform.

4. Only in the light of their origin and growth can the numerous educational problems of the present be viewed sympathetically and without bias by the teacher, the school administrator, or the public.

5. The history of education shows how the functions of social institutions shift and how the support and control of education have changed from very simple and local arrangements to those that are now somewhat centralized and complex.

6. The history of education is an ally in the scientific study of education rather than a competitor. It serves to present the educational ideals and standards of other times and it enables social workers to avoid the mistakes of the past.

7. It inspires respect for sound scholarship and reverence for great teachers.

The physician or psychologist, called upon to prescribe for physical or mental trouble, is apt to inquire into its cause. "How did it develop or come about?" he is likely to ask. Moreover, one of the most effective ways by which an organism and its function or purpose can be understood appears in a study of its origin and growth. This is true not only in the field of biology and botany but also in those fields which include political and social institutions, such as the state and government, the church, and the school.

Much light may be shed upon the purpose of educational institutions by a study and examination of their origins and development. A knowledge of the history of schools and other agencies of education is therefore an important part of the professional training of the teacher, school administrator, or other educational specialist, who could profitably approach their problems as the physician or the psychologist approaches his.

The conservative character of education. Few activities in American life are more conservative than education, and few are more afflicted by tradition and the dead hands of the past. Much of the work of the school is conventional or traditional. Much of it is being done in the way it is being done, for the most part, because it has been done in that way. Tradition, to a large degree, serves to explain the presence of certain subjects in the course of study. Furthermore, the nature of the teacher's work tends to limit and restrict his ideas to a narrow circle and his professional activities to a few subjects. It tends to foster prejudices in favor of familiar kinds of effort and methods of doing things. The work of teaching usually brings the teacher into contact with minds less mature than his own, and this restrictive influence often results in narrowness. Enlargement of the horizon of thought and experience is the best corrective for the condition of the narrow teacher, who is generally zealous in supporting his particular work and methods and often displays bitterness in defending them. The history of education serves to warn him against the unwillingness to reconsider and to revise his work. The work of the school administrator is limitative, often leading to a narrow view of educational principles and practices. The history of education serves as the "sovereign solvent" of his educational prejudices; it helps to emancipate his thinking about things as they are and to free him and his work from the bondage of tradition.

Education subject to fads. Although quite conservative, few activities of American life have been more subject to exaggerated movements, to waves of opinion, and to fads than education. Scheme after scheme has its day and then is heard of no more. School after school arises. Movement after movement appears. Experiments follow experiments. Old methods, often in new and attractive styles, recommend themselves and become the fashion of the time. Strange theories emerge and then cease to be. The educational worker who has a knowledge of the history of education is able to detect frills in whatever form they appear, and is likely to view the purpose and process of education in a rational manner. He is protected from a narrowness of view, which is zealous and so active in its own behalf.

Some values of the historical approach. A knowledge of the history of education is a necessary preliminary to educational reform and improvement. It leads educational workers to a willingness to revaluate and perhaps even to change their theories and practices in the light of the past, and to take broad and liberal views of educational questions when new needs are to be met and progressive educational policies are to be shaped. It helps to give perspective to education and makes for open-mindedness in teaching. It leads also to a more exalted ideal of the teacher's work. By increasing his knowledge of the history of his occupation it develops his desire for higher personal effectiveness and heightens his sense of the dignity and importance of teaching in its relations to the improvement of individuals, of society, and to the advancement of learning.

Knowledge of the origin of the school not only helps the teacher and the administrator to understand its function and purpose, but is useful also to the layman, to parents, and to the public generally. When the public knows the school better, indifference or hostility to extensions of its efforts will decrease or disappear entirely. The public will

then believe in it more thoroughly and support it more
fully and intelligently. A fuller knowledge of the origin
and purpose of the school would alter even the taxpayer's
attitude toward education and liberalize his views toward
its problems.

Educational problems numerous. Educational problems
are more numerous than ever before in history. Formerly
they were few and simple, but now they are many and
complex. And not all educational "problems" appear in
the catalogue descriptions of courses in teachers' colleges,
normal schools, and schools of education, though there is
significance in the increasing efforts of these institutions to
help teachers, principals, supervisors, superintendents, and
the so-called educational expert to meet the difficulties of
practical educational conditions. Nor are all these difficulties in the path of active school workers. Parents are
themselves becoming conscious of them; and the public is
thinking and talking more and more of school finance, of
school organization and administration, of the curriculum,
of vocational guidance, and of a multitude of other problems
which demand solution. Many of these problems of modern
education, if not all, are historical, though some are naturally
older and more stubborn than others. Only in the light of
their origin and growth, however, can they be viewed sympathetically and without prejudice or bias by the teacher,
the administrator, or the public.

The shifting of functions. The historical study of education shows the marked tendency toward the shifting of
the functions of present-day institutions. Formerly the
family performed almost all the services for the individual;
today the state, through its various agencies, performs most
or many of the functions which the family or a very small
neighborhood group performed in earlier times. Education
was once the exclusive function of the family or of the
church; today it is a function of the state, which also looks

after the health of the individual, inspects his food, furnishes him amusement and recreation, throws safeguards round his life and property, protects his investments, aids him to get employment, insures his life, and pensions his widow. The school also has assumed many of the duties that once engaged the attention of the family. It undertakes to teach manners and morals, once the peculiar obligation of home and family and church. Much of the practical education formerly given in the home has now become one of the tasks of the school. As functions which formerly belonged to one institution shift or are shifted to another, new educational problems arise. It is this social phenomenon that makes the school of today different from the school of the past. Its tasks are different. Those who are charged with the responsibility of meeting those tasks can do so intelligently and effectively only by a knowledge of their origin and the conditions of their growth.

New questions. Many thoughtful people today seriously question the ability of the American states to continue to finance their present educational arrangements. Many doubt the ability of the public to provide for additional forms of educational effort. Many questions arise concerning education. Can the period of compulsory attendance upon schools be extended? Can provision be made for adult education? How far can the state safely go in ministering to its inert and unprogressive members? Can it afford to give its citizens professional training in the law, medicine, dentistry, pharmacy, agriculture, and architecture? Must the national government come to the aid of general education in the various states?

These and other questions acquire meaning and can be understood only in the light of the conditions out of which they arise. The enormous financial burdens which education has created, rising to nearly three billions annually, have mounted as a result of changing political, social, and economic conditions which must be understood before the burdens themselves can be viewed intelligently or justified by the public. The purchasing power of the dollar has decreased. School enrollment and attendance have increased, calling for more teachers and equipment. Attendance has greatly increased in secondary schools, and the per capita cost of maintaining these is double that of the maintenance of elementary schools. Better school buildings have been erected and equipped, and newer, special, and often more expensive subjects have been added to the curriculum. Formerly the support of schools was a local and simple matter; today it is a problem of large proportions, and can be understood and solved only in the light of its history.

Localism and centralization. The management of education is a similar story. Local communities which formerly had schools or not, as they wished, are now forced by state constitution or statute to maintain schools of standards specified by the state. Often these communities are now heard to complain bitterly at some educational requirement imposed upon them by a larger administrative unit, such as the county or the state. A result is that state departments of education are frequently charged with autocracy and tyranny, and are often described as gluttons for power. Teachers chafe under the license or certification requirements imposed upon them by superior authorities whose whip hand is the pay check and the control of the tenure of teaching positions. These conditions can be understood only in the light of their development.

There are protests by localities against state curriculum and building standards, which sometimes are said to work hardships if not injustice upon smaller and weaker units. Formerly these units determined their own local educational arrangements. They fixed the length of their own school term, they passed upon the qualifications of their own teachers, they decided on the type of schoolhouse and built it without let or hindrance and often without aid from township, county, or state. The requirements for teachers were simple and simply met, often varying from locality to locality. If the teachers were orthodox in the religion of the community and bore a certificate of good moral character, they were acceptable. Educational qualifications were minor considerations. The localities also approved the subjects taught in the schools. They knew no compulsory-attendance or child-labor regulations. Localism was the rule. The school was a primitive neighborhood arrangement which seemed democratic and was therefore in high favor. It was natural that encroachments by larger units should have been resisted by the neighborhood and school district in their early days, and it is not unnatural that even now such encroachments should be resisted.

The tendency to centralization. Today these and other features of public educational work are regulated more or less by the state as the authoritative unit of school administration. Gradually the state has gained more and more control over local educational arrangements until " state school systems" have become a commonly accepted term in educational phraseology. The state now determines the length of the minimum school term, it prescribes the kind of schoolhouses that may be built, and it determines the educational qualifications of teachers. It may require them to show evidence of successful vaccination and of freedom from tuberculosis. It even attempts to require teachers to believe the Mosaic explanation of the origin of the earth and of man. The state prescribes and enforces the attendance of children at school and prohibits them from working between certain ages and in certain occupations. Generally also the course of study is fixed by state statute. In these and other ways the state has assumed a highly centralized control over matters that were once accepted as local educational functions. All these developments have been made on the background of the past; therefore the historical approach is an effective aid to an understanding of them.

History also an aid to science. Even the highly esteemed scientific method, with which the present educational age is feverish, sooner or later calls for the aid of history in the treatment of educational and other social ills. Educational magic and wizardry are found to be insufficient. Statistical data and imposing tables and graphs, though immensely valuable, are often impotent in the face of certain chronic educational diseases. Before the remedies can be found the inevitable question arises: How did these conditions develop?

The history of education is an ally of science rather than a competitor. It establishes the right of the past to be heard in the discussions of the problems of the present. It enlarges the understanding of those who are held responsible for the solution of educational problems. Its proper presentation removes the cloud of suspicion that it is a pretender in the field of teacher-training. To be successful, educational arrangements must be practical enough for an age that is busy with experimentation, the use of the statistical method, and the restless and ceaseless questioning of human nature. By forcing theorists and practitioners to face the stubbornness of facts, history can perform for education — in an age still marked by an embarrassing lack of a positive science of the subject — a service which education cannot perform for itself.

To avoid mistakes of the past. The history of education enables teachers, school administrators, and governing authorities to avoid the educational mistakes of the past; it develops and broadens the cultural interests of workers in education; it helps to focus the information and knowledge of other subjects on the work of the teacher; it serves to present ideals and standards of educational work of other times, and thus serves as a guide for the practical work of the teacher and administrator today.

The history of civilization. The history of education is in large part the history of civilization. It is the history of changing ideals, the story of the conscious and unconscious means used for the advancement of public well-being. The height of a civilization may be measured by its attitude toward child life; its effectiveness, by the extent to which social and humanitarian factors have influenced the masses of the people. It has long been manifest that the validity and the security of democratic civilizations depend upon the proper education and training of the masses. If ignorance and superstition, those twin pillars of priestcraft and demagogism, stalk in the life of a state or civilization, social or political convulsions are encouraged, and governments perish from their own limitations. The destiny of a democratic society is determined by and depends upon the increase and diffusion of knowledge and culture among the people. The influence of education upon national welfare is therefore not merely an academic subject for the professional reformer and the professor at large. The history of education exhibits evidence that whatever the teacher and school would make effective in the life of a community or state they must first make effective in the lives of the children they teach. This is no discovery of recent times. The greatest thinkers of the world knew it, and American teachers need to learn it. Plato and Aristotle noted it in their treatises on political philosophy, and despaired of the stability of states without education.

Respect for scholarship. The history of education teaches that learning has larger responsibilities than those it owes to itself; that scholarship for its own sake is not sufficient. It teaches that willful blindness to the needs of his time is an overt breach of the teacher's duty. It inspires respect for sound scholarship and is an effective answer to the baleful argument that great scholars are not great teachers, which is often perhaps a subtle argument for a cheerful educational indolence. The history of education illustrates the truth that a teacher cannot give to another what he does not himself possess; and that the test of his work is that it endures. It shows that the influence of an Abelard, an Arnold, a Mann, or an Eliot outlives that of any king, potentate, politician, or military leader of his age.

Reverence for teaching. From history come also to the teacher and the school worker today lofty views of education. In the history of education the ideal of the teacher's work is exalted. Through it come high and worthy motives for cherishing and defending all education that is thorough and excellent. The history of education is in large part the biography of great men, masters of the teaching art, and great leaders of educational reform. A knowledge of it develops reverence for the living words of the dead. Contact with great teachers of the past stimulates the teachers of the present and the future. It increases respect for sound and disciplined learning and enlarges the desire for excellence in their own work.

In the following chapters the history of education in the United States is traced in an effort to explain the system described in Chapter I. Inasmuch, however, as the theories and practices of the early period can be understood only in the light of European antecedents and influences, attention must first be given to the background of education in this country during the colonial period, which is the subject of Chapter III.

REFERENCES AND READINGS

BURNHAM, W. H., and SUZZALLO, HENRY. The History of Education as a Professional Subject. Teachers College, 1908. (Proceedings of the Society of College Teachers of Education, 1908.)

   The article by Burnham bears the title "The History of Education," and that by Suzzallo "The Professional Use of the History of Education."

CUBBERLEY, E. P. Public Education in the United States (author's preface). Boston, 1919.

KIEHLE, D. L. "The History of Education: What it Stands For," *School Review* (May, 1901), Vol. IX, pp. 310–315.

KNIGHT, EDGAR W. "Presentation to Professor Paul Monroe," *Teachers College Record*, Vol. XXIV, No. 3 (May, 1923), pp. 249–252.

KNIGHT, EDGAR W. Public School Education in North Carolina (preface). Boston, 1916.

MONROE, PAUL. "Opportunity and Need for Research Work in the History of Education," *The Pedagogical Seminary* (March, 1910), Vol. XVII, pp. 54–62.

MONROE, PAUL, and KANDEL, I. L. "The History of Education," in A Cyclopedia of Education, Vol. III, pp. 293–297.

MOORE, E. C. "The History of Education," *School Review* (May, 1903), Vol. XI, pp. 350–360.

NORTON, A. O. "Scope and Aims of the History of Education," *Educational Review* (May, 1904), Vol. XXVII, pp. 443–455.

PAYNE, W. H. "The Practical Value of the History of Education," Proceedings of the National Education Association, 1889, pp. 218–223.

WILLIAMS, S. G. "The Value of the History of Education for Teachers," Proceedings of the National Education Association, 1889, pp. 223–231.

QUESTIONS FOR STUDY AND DISCUSSION

1. Consider some of the stubborn educational problems in your state. Show how a knowledge of the history of its educational development is an aid in the solution of those problems.

2. The history of education has been defined as "essentially a phase of the history of civilization." It has been looked upon as a record of educational theories and as a record of actual educational practices, or of both. Consider these definitions of the subject, and prepare to discuss a definition of your own.

3. Consider some of the social, political, and economic facts of history which have had influence on educational theory and practice in the United States.

4. Make a list of the ways in which a knowledge of the history of education is valuable to the teacher, to the school administrator, to parents, and to governing authority (members of legislatures and of state and local boards of education).

5. Illustrate the statement that the history of education "is in large part the biography of great teachers," and show how a knowledge of it develops reverence for them.

6. Consider any fads or frills which have appeared in American education in recent years, and account for their appearance.

7. Most of the states continue to elect their chief school officers by popular vote, but the presidents of public colleges and universities are not elected by such means. Give the historical explanation.

8. Give any example that you can think of in which a knowledge of the history of education may enable educational authorities to avoid a mistake of the past.

CHAPTER III

THE BACKGROUND

Outline of the chapter. 1. The principles of public education are now generally accepted, but they can be understood only in the light of their origin and growth.

2. Economic, political, and religious conditions in England just before and during the period of colonization were disquieting, and they help to explain England's motive for colonization and the incentive which led people to become colonists. Colonial expansion was a pressing necessity for England in the seventeenth century.

3. The desire for religious and political freedom was doubtless real in a measure among some of the colonists, but the desire to escape from economic bondage made strong appeal to most of them.

4. The force of economic interest was strong, and the economic purpose of colonization and settlement was a potent element in the institutional development of the colonies.

5. English theory and practice in education were transplanted in large part to the American colonies.

As pointed out in Chapter I, education is today one of the largest public enterprises in the United States — perhaps the dominating public interest of the American people, who annually expend from sources of taxation hundreds of millions of dollars in its support and employ thousands of men and women in its management and direction. It was also pointed out there that although the so-called democratic principles of education are now generally accepted in this country, and public-school systems more or less practically established in all the states, these achievements have been made only through severe struggles. The way of the public school has been long and toilsome, often beset by most stubborn and discouraging difficulties. Even now the way toward further extensions of what may seem to be legitimate public educational effort is difficult. As one views the difficulties which have embarrassed the way of public educational development in the United States, one wonders not that public schools came to be established in this country in the nineteenth century and that the so-called democratic doctrine of education came to be accepted by the end of that century, but, considering the backgrounds of their past and the conditions out of which they developed, that such schools and such a theory could be established and accepted at all.

The historical approach. The theory of the equality of public educational opportunity, now so often proudly pointed to as a guiding principle in American life, gained its present place in the United States only after many bitter struggles. These struggles over the American principles of education were waged between the forces of aristocracy, vested privileges and interests, property rights, and conservatism on the one hand, and the forces of democracy, human rights, and liberalism on the other. Between such forces they are still waged even now, here and there in the United States. Out of these conflicts, whose roots reach back into the past, have emerged and are still emerging the theories and practices of American education today. And these can be understood only in the light of their origin and growth.

England at the time of American colonization. The American colonies, which were essentially English in origin, were established during the seventeenth century. The reign of Queen Elizabeth (1558–1603) had been rather remarkable for exploration and expedition, and during this period attempts were made to settle America. But it was during the reign of James I and the succeeding Stuarts, who left a record for autocracy and tyranny, that successful settlement and colonization were made in what is now the United States. Of the thirteen colonies which gained political independence from England in the late eighteenth century, all except one (Georgia, 1732) were established between 1607, when the plantation of Virginia was begun, and 1682, when Pennsylvania was founded.

The beginnings of this country, which started as tiny settlements, were made during a romantic period and under conditions which required energy and heroism for those who had part in the undertakings. Adventure and suffering marked the enterprise of colonization and settlement. William Bradford noted, in his account of the Plymouth Plantation, that they were too delicate and unfit to become colonists who could not endure the bite of a mosquito. These early settlements were made by small groups of adventurers after many losses and discouragements, and at great expense to merchants and noblemen who sank large sums in the expeditions, probably without receiving any substantial returns for their efforts. Fully half the seventeenth century had passed before the English colonies became an appreciable asset to the mother government.

Sturdy seamen and buccaneers of the Elizabethan period had led the way. But the colonial settlements were actually made through merchants and capitalists who, ambitious for profit for themselves or prestige for their country, saw in the New World opportunities for wealth and power. Doubtless the desire for religious and political freedom moved men to risk their lives over dangerous seas in an effort to reach a world that was unknown but in a measure promising. But the beginnings of the United States were made primarily for purposes of commerce. In colonization the spirit of trade was a powerful motive.

Colonial expansion necessary. Colonial expansion had become an economic necessity for England in the seventeenth century. Her greatest need was the restoration of her industrial life. Her forests, one of the most important of her natural resources, had become depleted, and the shortage of shipbuilding material was having an alarming effect upon England's merchant marine. The country was over-run with idle and hungry people, and it was believed that the surplus population would readily flow into colonies if these could be planted. Her writers were urging the necessity for colonies as a means of securing economic independence. Only this way lay national security. England's trade was the mother and nurse of her seamen, says Lord Haversham, her seamen the life of her fleet, which was the security of her trade, and fleet and trade were her wealth, her strength, and her glory. England turned to America as the hope of her safety.

These conditions gave meaning to the organization of the London Company, and its efforts to establish colonies in America assumed the character of a crusade. The plan appealed to patriotic Englishmen, who hoped to have a hand in the restoration of the industrial life of their country. The settlement of Jamestown was the result, therefore, not altogether of a selfish and private venture but of years of endeavor and perhaps of patriotic pleading with the English public to help break the economic bonds which were so rapidly closing on the little island. True, England wished to limit the growing domains of Spain in the New World, then monopolized by that country and Portugal, which had seized the richest parts of the prize Columbus had won. But this motive of England was economic.

The people of England at the time of colonization was made up of two classes. The self-supporting or independent class was composed of the nobility, the higher clergy, knights, country gentlemen, lawyers, the lesser clergy, freeholders and farmers, shopkeepers and tradesmen, artisans and craftmen; the dependent class consisted of journeymen, apprentices, vagrants, and "thieves and sturdy beggars," whose employment, wages, and movement from place to place were generally determined by the independent class. At the accession of James I half the population of England was dependent, and probably looked upon the independent as highly favored if not as superior beings.

The dangers of pauperism. This condition was the result of certain social and economic changes which had modified the structure of English life before the seventeenth century. One of these influences developed out of the change from the medieval to the more modern land and agricultural system. Much poverty and vagabondage followed inclosures and sheep-raising and the consequent eviction of tenants who had made a living at farming. For many years after the Black Death, which caused a scarcity of labor, the wool industry came to be very important. The price of wool increased rapidly, and by the beginning of the sixteenth century sheep-raising had become a far more profitable industry than farming had been; it also demanded fewer laborers. More and more landowners turned their attention to this industry. Vast areas which had hitherto been used for tillage and which had furnished work for many laborers were made into sheep pastures, and many people whose livelihood had hitherto depended upon arable farming were thrown out of employment. England was forced to establish colonies as means of relief from the persistent dangers of pauperism.

Those who had land or sufficient money to rent and stock land with sheep grew prosperous. But the poorer people were dispossessed and made helpless and inefficient under the new industrial system. Some of the farmers were got rid of by fraud or force. Eviction was often resorted to when other means failed. Many evicted farmers were reduced to a condition of pauperism and vagabondage and were forced to beg or steal for a living. Whole families were often driven to a life of vagrancy. The number of the poor and dependents increased, and their economic condition grew more and more intolerable. There was evidence of social unrest. The wrongs of the poor and unfortunate found indignant expression in the literature of the period, which was often full of protests against the evils of inclosures and the depletion of the rural communities.

Hard times were increased also by the destruction of the great bands of retainers, who had been lawless elements throughout the period of feudal power. Feudal armies had greatly impoverished many rural sections during the Wars of the Roses between the houses of Lancaster and York (1455–1485). During the peace of the Tudor period numerous retainers, without wages, had become marauders under the protection of their lords, and stole for a living. A law had been passed against them near the close of the fifteenth century, and as they were dismissed from the protection of their masters they became capable rogues and vagabonds and a menacing problem for the government.

The problem of the poor and of unemployment had grown very vexatious. Opportunities for work in corporate towns were decreased by the exclusive policy pursued by the guilds. Moreover, the kingdom was burdened with Henry VIII's taxation. He also debased the coinage, and the prices of necessary commodities doubled and often trebled without any corresponding advance in wages. The hard way of the poor thus became harder. The needy increased in great numbers. Meanwhile the usual means of poor relief were constantly decreasing. Even the guilds found it difficult to make provision for their sick and dependent.

Sources of relief cut off. The dissolution of the monasteries, those sure sources of definite comfort and relief, added to the miseries of the poor, the needy, and the vagrant. Henry VIII viewed these institutions as dangerous to his new ecclesiastical order. Although the monastic authorities seemed to appear obedient, it was feared that they did not approve the drastic measures Henry VIII had used to terminate the power of the Pope in England. Moreover, many of the monasteries were wealthy. They held extensive landed estates which the king coveted. It was alleged also that there were evidences of corruption and of evil living in the monasteries, and they were suspected of immoral and irreligious motives. Action by the king seemed warranted, and in 1536 Parliament suppressed nearly four hundred of the monasteries which had an annual income of less than £200. Three years later the larger ones were confiscated also and their possessions added to the revenues of the crown. In a few years monasticism, which had so long served as a means of relief to the poor and otherwise unfortunate, practically disappeared from England.

Distressing results. Finally, the Chantries Act of 1547 completed the royal confiscation and destruction of religious endowments. Many guilds had set apart funds for charitable purposes. Some of these endowments supported priests, provided loans without interest to poor guild members, supported members who were sick and infirm, cared for widows and orphans, and in many ways provided for the underprivileged. The confiscation of these means of charity, like the destruction of the monasteries, added fresh hardships to the lot of the poor. Aimless wanderers and vagrants multiplied.

But these classes of dependents were not reproached for their condition. The long practice of indiscriminate charity had respectabilized and almost dignified their ways of existence and had increased the number of the idle poor. The practice of the "open house," kept alike by clergy and baron ; the mendicant practices of the wandering friars and other religious orders ; the habits of the wandering scholars and their "ABC shooters" and of the pious pilgrim who begged his way from shrine to shrine, — all these customs and practices had served to encourage a class of beggars whose habits of life had acquired a degree of respectability. The beggars were of many kinds. A contemporary account gave two dozen varieties. They ranged from the impotent poor to the Abraham-man who, like the fool in "King Lear," feigned lunacy and begged "charity for poor Tom" in the hope of securing aid from the passers-by.

Political conditions. During the first forty years of the seventeenth century — the century of American colonization and settlement — the government of England was autocratic and tyrannical. The claims of the monarchy were more exorbitant perhaps than at any other time in English history. The people were not even allowed to question any of the many rights of the kings. The "divine right" of the rulers was accepted not only by those in authority but also by those under authority. The theory of divine right was almost a reality in the lives of all English subjects. But there were now and then some bitter contests between the king and Parliament, and the latter slowly gained a slightly larger participation in the government. Those who sympathized with Parliament relied for their cause more and more upon what came to be known as "the ancient rights and liberties of the people." Parliament appealed, through the Petition of Right (1628), to the guaranties of the Great Charter, which had been wrested from King John at Runnymede in 1215, and to other declarations of personal liberties. In 1641, the Grand Remonstrance contained such expressions as "the people," "the rights of the people," "the liberties of subjects"; and finally many rights and privileges of the people were incorporated in the Bill of Rights in 1689.

It was during these contests of the people with their rulers that American colonization was progressing. Out of these struggles emerged certain ideas of civil liberty, and these, vague and indistinct as some of them may have been, were brought by the colonists to the New World. For the most part these colonists were not of strong royalist spirit. They were generally those people who were not on comfortable terms with the king but favored the views of Parliament.

And yet even among the colonists there was not complete agreement on political matters. Strong as their interest may have been in self-government, the differences of the political views they had held in the Old World were naturally transplanted in the New.

Religious conditions. Before England became a colonizing nation the power of the Church had been questioned. The English Humanists had turned their attention to an examination of the teachings of the Church and indicated the need for religious reform. The right of interference by the Pope was boldly questioned. There was slowly developing also in the minds of the laity the desire that individuals should be free in their religious life instead of being made to obey blindly an ecclesiastical authority. Although the efforts of those in England who would reform the Church were not altogether fruitless, real religious changes came finally after the revolt which was led by Martin Luther in the early part of the sixteenth century.

When England became a colonizing nation, in the early part of the seventeenth century, there were at least four well-defined religious parties in that country. There were the members of the Established Church, which was the official state church. At the beginning of the seventeenth century this had been for a generation the only religious system in authority in England, and through the law of the land and the support of patriotic feeling it was strongly intrenched. A second religious party was the Roman Catholics, who held allegiance to the Pope as their earthly head. Even after Henry VIII had attacked the supremacy of the Pope and the practice of the Roman Catholic Church and had established the Church of England, the Roman Catholics in England had remained faithful to Rome in spite of frequent rigorous applications of harsh laws against them.

The Puritans constituted another religious class. They at first protested against certain ceremonies and the formalism of the English Church, which they believed was drifting toward Roman Catholicism, but later they turned from these considerations to more vital matters of morals. Self-control, plainness in dress, sincerity and honesty of speech, and complete faith in the Bible are said to have characterized their manner and belief, especially in the case of those Puritans who, encountering harsh persecutions at home, hastened to Holland and a decade later to Plymouth, Massachusetts. They were called Pilgrims because of the manner of their moving. *Vocantur patres, et saepe sunt,* though most of them were under the age of forty. The Separatists, or Independents, who believed in the independence of each local congregation of believers and to whom the idea of a state church seemed idolatrous, formed another religious party.

During the personal government of Charles I, from 1629 to 1640, there were no sessions of Parliament. The administration of affairs was mainly in the hands of the Star Chamber, the High Commission, and the Privy Council. These powerful instruments were in sympathy with the Established Church. The Puritans and other dissenting sects were greatly oppressed and persecuted. During this period and under these conditions of religious intolerance large Puritan migrations to America were made, and nearly twenty thousand adventurers found their way to New England.

The motives of the settlers. It was out of these economic, political, and religious conditions that many of the early colonists came. In these conditions are to be found also the incentives which led Englishmen to come to the New World. Certainly there was desire among some of them for larger political rights than they were allowed in England. It is not unreasonable to believe also that some of them desired the opportunity for larger religious freedom than they or their fathers had enjoyed before or after the days of Henry VIII. The "religious liberty" doctrine, sanctified by Bradford, the amazing historian of the Pilgrims, has been repeated, added to, and supported by scores of others since his time. It was doubtless more than a fiction among those who have taught that this country was divinely selected as the home of those who had been persecuted in Europe for their religious beliefs. Certainly it was but natural also that men, even in the seventeenth century and in the American colonies, should desire to worship as they saw fit, even though they were often unwilling for others to enjoy the same privilege.

It should not be forgotten, however, that when these same people, whose ways Bradford records, clashed with the Church of England and fled to Holland they were sorely grieved because, among other things, they could eke out a living only by the heaviest manual labor of long and tedious hours. The hardness of Holland was such, says Bradford, that few of their fellows in England would join them and fewer still would continue with them. True, their children were oppressed and were becoming Dutch in speech and ideas, and they themselves through grinding toil were growing old and decrepit before their time. But there is some significance in the fact that the economic condition of this little Scrooby group had not improved after ten or more years in Holland. At the end of that time they were without sufficient money to finance the voyage to Virginia, in which they applied for a grant in the early months of 1620. They were forced to enter into an agreement with London merchants for the means of the expedition, and these drove a hard bargain. As a guaranty the Pilgrims agreed to a bondage of seven years' collective labor, the fruits of which were to be shared in common.

The Puritans doubtless craved a place where religious liberty would be more secure than in England during the despotic and disquieting reign of Charles I. They and others who during these years left their old homes in England for new ones in America probably hoped for a place where political liberty would in a measure also be granted to them. But many of those who preferred the uncertainties of an ocean voyage and of life in a strange land to the many religious and political disadvantages in their own country must have viewed as particularly attractive the reported opportunities which the New World offered the underprivileged to escape from economic bondage.

After Charles I had lost his head — to the satisfaction of a small group of extremists — the zealot Cromwell led a compact army which, with prayers and psalms upon their lips, advanced upon their enemies, especially those of Roman Catholic persuasion. Those who supported the crown, the aristocracy, and the Established Church now found it comfortable to leave. Many of that political faction in England which cheered for the cause of Charles migrated to Virginia. There fertile land, the mildness of the climate, and the magic of the Indian plant, tobacco, opened the doors of opportunity wide to the enterprising and industrious colonists. Many of them soon gained economic strength and through it political and social power and prestige, and acquired the name of Cavaliers, which they graciously gave to their children.

The force of economic interest. Although the colonizing ventures were in large part commercial undertakings, England also wished to extend the influence of the Established Church and to bring the heathen Indians from darkness to light. To propagate the gospel, to preach, to "baptize into the Christian religion," and to snatch "out of the arms of the devil a number of poor and miserable souls wrapt up unto death in almost invincible ignorance," were the first great care of Virginians, says John Smith. The officers of the London Company made an effort to establish religious habits in the colony, and indicated in their advertisements for colonists their desire to have those of correct religious manner. Here, no less than in the colonies of New England, those of pious and devout faith in the orthodox manner of life would be less troublesome to the authorities and also make more dependable and sober workers. These were important motives, but they were not so significant alongside the pressing need for national expansion and economic independence.

So deep was this purpose of colonization that economic forces of one kind and another were to underlie much of the social and educational development of the future in those states which grew out of the tiny settlements made along the Atlantic coast in the seventeenth century. Perhaps the desire for religious and political freedom was real among not a few of the early settlers in America, and it commands admiration. But the chance which the New World offered to live under less economic pressure and anxiety must have made a strong appeal to the masses of those who came. Moreover, if the desire for religious and political freedom had been very strong among many of the colonists, religious intolerance and political restrictions, those twin difficulties in the way of public schools, could not have become and remained so fashionable.

Tobacco was the key that opened the door of opportunity in Virginia in the seventeenth century and most of the eighteenth. It determined the character of life; it helped, as perhaps did no other single force, to mold social classes and the political structure of the colony; it developed a system of labor which held until the Civil War; and it influenced religion, morals, and education. Men maddened in Virginia over the thought of tobacco, and won wealth through its growth. Economic factors were determining influences in the other colonies as well; they had deep effect upon their life, their government, and their social development. Within a few years most of the colonists, especially those who gained authority, were in better economic condition than they had enjoyed in England. Merchants grew prosperous in New

England and the middle colonies and plumed themselves as gentlemen, as prosperous men were in the habit of doing in England. They directed the economic life, and from land and sea, through industry and thrift, accumulated fortunes.

The influence of slavery. In all the colonies slavery was looked upon as respectable and proper, and was made use of so long as it seemed profitable. The Baltimores in Maryland sought to entice emigrants by praising the climate and the soil, after the fashion of real-estate dealers today, and hinted at the opportunity to make much profit out of indentured servants. The wealthy Penn offered five-thousand-acre lots at a fixed price to large investors and fifty acres additional for each indentured servant whom they would bring, though natural conditions served as obstacles to prevent Pennsylvania from becoming a semifeudal domain such as Virginia and Maryland. Georgia opened its doors to all except Roman Catholics, and forbade slavery and the sale of rum; but most of the colonists, seeing how men prospered in South Carolina through the labor of slaves, soon came to demand slaves and rum and greater economic freedom by which they could buy and sell land. All three privileges were soon gained, plantations developed, slaves multiplied, and Georgia became, like her Southern sisters, a region in which economic gain was to give direction to the course of political and social life for many years to come.

Whether the American settlements were begun as religious or political havens or as the enterprises of commercial organizations or of rich and powerful individuals, or grew out of the dream of philanthropy, all of them soon took a decided economic turn, and the force of economic interest became and remained powerful. The road to influence lay in wealth, though the many glowing accounts of the New World appealed to many classes: to the patriotic, who would promote the power of England; to the pious, who would propagate the Christian faith among the heathen;

to the impatient and restless; to the adventurous; to those of straitened economic circumstances and restricted social conditions; to those who desired land and the position of gentlemen; and to others to whom the avenues of advancement were closed at home. In the New World they saw new opportunities.

England's theory of education. The dominating influences in England during the American colonial period and even later were aristocratic. The common belief that the masses of the people were born to obey and not to govern fixed the social position of unborn generations. So strong was this belief and so well was its meaning taught and understood that the simple and humble people looked upon the privileged as superior beings. In effect the distinction between the high and the low was real and absolute. Those in authority were zealous in their efforts to preserve class distinctions, which were never suitable soil in which to plant and grow common or public schools.

It was important for the governing authority to keep the poor in ignorance. Learning among the masses would threaten the established order and lead to disobedience. This was probably the view of most of the American colonists, if they had views on the matter at all. Governor Berkeley of Virginia, in his remarkable reply to the authorities in England in 1671, thanked God that there were no free schools and no printing presses in that province, and hoped that there would be none for a hundred years. "Learning," he said, "has brought disobedience, and heresy, and sects into the world, and printing has divulged them, and libels against the best government. God keep us from both!" It should be remembered, however, that the testy governor had many years before sanctioned bequests for schools in Virginia when he approved the act which incorporated the Symms School. It was this theory that retarded the growth of public education in England and delayed its development in the United States. The attitude of most of the American colonists toward education was similar to that of the mother country.

Not a function of the state. During the sixteenth, seventeenth, and eighteenth centuries the theory persisted that education was not a responsibility of the State but the business of the family and the Church. During the Middle Ages the Church had had a monopoly on education, and after the establishment of the English Church in the sixteenth century this theory and practice continued. School-teachers were required to hold a license from the bishops or other Church authorities. The educational work of dissenters from the English Church was not permitted. With the exception of the Society for the Promotion of Christian Knowledge, the English Church made little effort before the nineteenth century to provide for the education of the masses.

THOMAS BRAY

A colonial representative of the Society for Propagation of the Gospel in Foreign Parts. (From C. K. Bolton's "Portraits of the Founders")

This society was founded in 1699 to provide schools to give instruction in the catechism and the Scriptures and the liturgy of the Church. Part of its mission was to erect schools for the instruction in reading, writing, and the catechism of any children whose parents or relatives were unable "to afford them the ordinary means of education." An auxiliary of this society, known as the Society for the Propagation of the Gospel in Foreign Parts, did missionary and religious educational work among the poor in most of the American colonies. In such agencies as these appear almost all the educational efforts of the English Church until far into the nineteenth century.

Education of the poor. The educational emphasis of the Church was upon the training of poor and otherwise underprivileged children. Education in the home and in private dame schools was the prevailing practice for those whose parents were not poor; but instruction in charity schools maintained by voluntary religious societies or by individuals of philanthropic disposition was the rule for the children of the poor. During the last quarter of the eighteenth century the Sunday school appeared in England and gave instruction not only in religious matters but also in reading and writing and probably in the elements of arithmetic. The work of this agency, whose aim was as much secular as religious, spread to the United States and served a very useful purpose in furnishing elementary education to poor people.

Monitorial schools. In the early nineteenth century (1808) the British and Foreign School Society, a nonsectarian agency, developed out of the efforts of Joseph Lancaster and his monitorial schools for poor children. Lancaster claimed for his plan no sectarian motive, and it served to arouse considerable public interest in the education of poor children. The society, which enjoyed the patronage of the king and of many of the nobility, prospered and probably aroused jealousy among extreme sectarians of the English Church. Through assistance from Dr. Andrew Bell, who was also interested in methods and means of monitorial instruction, the National Society for Promoting the Education of the Poor in the Principles of the Established Church was organized in 1811. This organization was able to secure some of the support which formerly had gone to the nonsectarian British and Foreign School Society, and the rivalry of these two agencies led to an agitation that stimulated interest in public elementary education. The contest was so long and bitter that the principles of public support and public control were not established in England until 1870.

An effort has been made in this chapter to indicate briefly the economic, political, and religious conditions in England during the period of colonization, and the more potent forces in the settlement of this country. It appears that early schools and other means of education in the American colonies were inherited from England. The character of colonial life and institutions in general was determined (1) by the purposes of English colonization and the motives which led or drove the colonists to America, (2) by the traditions and customs which the colonists inherited and brought with them from their old homes, and (3) by the "conditions of the wilderness" — the physical circumstances of the new world in which the colonists found themselves. It was natural that Englishmen would do here the same things they had been accustomed to do there, and in a similar manner. For the most part, therefore, the customs of England were adopted or adapted to the conditions of a frontier region. This transplanting of English theories and practices will be seen in Chapter V, which deals with education in the American colonies. But first in Chapter IV other aspects of colonial life will be considered.

REFERENCES AND READINGS

BEARD, CHARLES A., and MARY R. The Rise of American Civilization, Vol. I, chaps. i–iii. New York, 1927.

> Deals with conditions in England before and during the colonizing period and with the potent motives in the settlement of America.

BECKER, CARL L. Beginnings of the American People, chap. iii. Boston, 1915.

> Discusses the English migration in the seventeenth century.

BROWN, E. E. The Making of our Middle Schools. New York, 1903.

> A scholarly and standard account of American secondary education which gives the English background.

CHEYNEY, EDWARD POTTS. The European Background of American History, chaps. vii, xi–xvi. New York, 1904.

> Furnishes the necessary point of departure for a knowledge of American history and shows the English institutions which were ready for transplantation in America.

CUBBERLEY, E. P. Public Education in the United States, chap. i. Boston, 1919.

> Deals with the European background.

DORAN, ALBAN H. G. "Medicine," in Shakespeare's England, Vol. I, pp. 413–443. Oxford University Press, 1916.

EGGLESTON, EDWARD. The Transit of Civilization, chaps. i–v. New York, 1901.

> Treats of the transfer of English culture, customs, and traditions to this country.

KNIGHT, EDGAR W. Public Education in the South, chap. i. Boston, 1922.

> Describes political, economic, social, and religious conditions in England at the beginning of the colonial period.

LEACH, A. F. English Schools at the Reformation. London, 1896.

> Suggestive for the English educational background.

LITTLEDALE, H. "Folklore and Superstitions; Ghosts and Fairies; Witchcraft and Devils," in Shakespeare's England, Vol. I, pp. 516–546. Oxford University Press, 1916.

PARKER, SAMUEL CHESTER. The History of Modern Elementary Education. Boston, 1912.

> Chapter III discusses, among other subjects, the condition of elementary education in England in the sixteenth century.

PARRINGTON, V. L. The Colonial Mind, 1620–1800, Book I, chaps. i, ii. New York, 1927.

> The English background and the transplanting of ideas. Contains materials hitherto largely neglected.

SANDYS, SIR JOHN EDWIN. "Education," in Shakespeare's England, Vol. I, pp. 224–250. Oxford University Press, 1916.

STOWE, A. M. Elizabethan Grammar Schools. New York, 1908.

> English education during the last half of the sixteenth century.

TYLER, LYON G. England in America, especially chaps. i, iii–iv, vi, xi, xiii, xix. New York, 1904.

> A story of the English settlement in this country which shows "the reasons for, as well as the progress of, English colonization."

WATSON, FOSTER. English Grammar Schools to 1660. Cambridge University Press, 1909.

> Contains materials on education in England in the sixteenth and seventeenth centuries.

WERTENBAKER, THOMAS J. The Planters of Colonial Virginia, chaps. i, ii. Princeton University Press, 1922.

> Describes the critical conditions from which England sought relief through colonial expansion in the seventeenth century, and the power of tobacco in the civilization of colonial Virginia. The book dispels pleasant old illusions and disproves many a boast.

QUESTIONS FOR STUDY AND DISCUSSION

1. Describe the economic, political, religious, and social conditions in England in the sixteenth century.

2. Discuss the motives which probably led the colonists to this country.

3. If the colonists came to secure religious freedom, why was it so feebly guaranteed during the colonial period? Consider the same question with reference to political liberty.

4. What was the condition of education for the lower classes in England during the period of colonization?

5. Show why it is difficult for a common-school system to develop in countries or communities where class distinctions are marked. Point out any present-day examples.

6. What old theories are upset by Wertenbaker's study of colonial Virginia? Consider his sources of information.

7. Why were free schools and printing presses so low in the esteem of Governor Berkeley of Virginia? Was his assumption sound? What is the attitude of governing authority in the American states today toward such agencies of popular enlightenment?

8. Make a study of the monitorial schools in regard to (1) purpose, (2) organization, and (3) results.

CHAPTER IV

THE COLONIAL CLIMATE

Outline of the chapter. 1. Conditions in the American colonies were unfavorable for the development of the finer elements of civilized life among the masses.

2. Colonial culture was an inheritance from Europe, where the aristocratic theory of education was strong. Class distinctions, based for the most part upon slavery, were marked.

3. The franchise was generally restricted to property owners in all the colonies, and these restrictions were not removed in the old states until after the Revolutionary War.

4. Social distinctions were conspicuous in the earliest New England colleges until the eve of the Revolution. The rules of primogeniture and entail and the legal establishment of religions served to strengthen class distinctions.

5. Contrasts in colonial culture were probably not so striking as has commonly been supposed. Geography is the explanation of most of the differences that did develop.

6. Throughout the colonies democracy was disliked socially as well as politically. Distinctions between the well-to-do and the underprivileged helped to prevent the growth of public education.

All the American colonies except Georgia were established during the seventeenth century, under conditions described in the preceding chapter. The early settlements were scattered, the pressure of material needs upon the settlers was heavy, the means of transportation and of communication were crude and slow, and colonial life was restricted and controlled in large part by European thought and traditions. Hardships marked this pioneer period. Conditions were unfavorable for the rapid development of the finer elements of civilized life among the masses of the people. Most of the colonists lived close to the soil and had little leisure or opportunity to develop a taste for intellectual interests. The value of collective action in providing the means of education — an unknown value in Europe in the seventeenth century — was not promptly found in the New World. The colonial period is important, however (especially the latter part), because in it appeared the beginnings of the theory on which the American school system was finally to be established.

Colonial culture inherited from Europe. As noted at the end of Chapter III, schools and other means of education in the American colonies were for the most part inherited from Europe; so also was colonial culture in general. A voyage of a few weeks across the sea could not alter the theory or the practice of education with which the colonists were acquainted in their old homes. In Europe education was intended only for the upper classes. The idea of free education, available for all at public expense, was generally unknown in the countries from which the early settlers came. Rarely did such an idea occupy the minds of the most advanced educational thinkers.

It was but natural that the European traditions of education should continue in the colonies. England had her universities at Oxford and Cambridge, and in the colonies by the end of the seventeenth century there were established Harvard in Massachusetts, William and Mary in Virginia, Yale in Connecticut, and six other colleges by 1769: Princeton in New Jersey, Academy and College (now the University) of Pennsylvania, King's College (later Columbia) in New York, Brown in Rhode Island, Rutgers in New Jersey, and Dartmouth in New Hampshire. These institutions were suggested by if not set up on the pattern of the English universities. In England were the Latin grammar schools, with their emphasis upon Latin and Greek. These schools were transplanted bodily, became numerous in New England, and were found also in all the other colonies except Georgia. They served in the New World the same purpose for which they were established in the Old — to prepare the sons of the well-to-do for college. In both England and America the curriculum of the Latin grammar school was almost identical.

England had her famous Eton and Westminster, established on endowments and attended by the sons of the privileged classes; Virginia, her Symms and Eaton, established before that colony was fifty years old; and New England, her Andover and Exeter, founded in the Revolutionary period. These and numerous other academies, which had their beginnings in a proposal by Benjamin Franklin in 1743, were patterned in part on academies in England. Even the Sunday school, which began in England shortly after the middle of the eighteenth century, was brought to the United States.

Many of these different types of schools had their origin in private philanthropy, another practice inherited from Europe. The motive was generally religious and grew out of medieval church practices whose roots probably reached back to St. Paul's doctrine of good works. The endowed school was old in England when that country planted colonies in America. Generous individuals had given of their wealth to support schools, as is their habit today, through genuine interest in the cause of education or, under coercive courtesy, in an effort to square their accounts with the Church. The wills of the period testify to this practice in the colonies.

England had her dame schools, and these flourished also in the colonies, especially in Massachusetts. England had her tutorial instruction, and so had the colonies, especially those in the middle and southern parts. England made almost no provision for the education of women, and this neglect was also inherited in the colonies. The apprenticeship and poor-law practices were directly transplanted from England; so also was the charity, or pauper, elementary school, which so long stood in the way of the growth of the free, publicly supported, publicly controlled, nonsectarian school now so widely developed in the United States.

The idea of public education slow to appear. The beliefs that education should be controlled by the Church, and that instruction and training in religious doctrines and ideals were important purposes of education, were also included in the heritage transmitted by England to America. The results of the Reformation had not weakened either of these beliefs and had greatly strengthened the latter. The idea that it was the duty and function of the State to control or support education in any form was very slow to appear. When the theory finally emerged, it strengthened slowly, and the contests which have marked the long and laborious efforts made to gain its practical acceptance became quite bitter. In almost all respects the educational traditions and practices of England served as the guide to the American colonists and reflected themselves in colonial life or were actually reproduced in it.

Some parts of the educational work were inherited directly from England and were reproduced in the American colonies with little or no change. Other parts were modified by conditions of environment in the colonies. Differences in environment (the result primarily of geography), the occupational differences of the colonists, and class distinctions which grew out of prevailing economic conditions and were found in all the colonies explain for the most part the lack of uniform means and methods of educational work. The colonists inherited motives and purposes of education, types of schools, textbooks, methods of teaching, and educational machinery or forms of organization and control, such as charters, statutes, and the like, and these were somewhat similar in all the colonies. College professors were often imported from Europe. Even the New England Primer, which served to teach "millions to read and not one to sin," had its origin in England. Colonial practices in education entirely different from practices in Europe were very few.

Class distinctions marked. Colonial life, built upon the culture of Europe, could not be democratic. Class distinctions, based upon servitude — black slaves or white indentured servants — were conspicuous. The rich Boston merchants "owned slaves as house servants and bought and sold them like other merchandise," just as did prosperous planters in the South; and merchants and traders dominated life in New England just as prosperous planters directed political and social affairs in the South.

New Englanders and Virginians alike enslaved their fellow men of all colors — white and black, and even red whenever possible. If they finally showed preference for their black brothers, it was because of economic necessity. The white could serve their time, as they did in all the colonies, and turn their faces toward freedom. The high-spirited Indian, stubborn or rash under compulsion, was a poor worker and therefore an expensive servant. But the nature of the negro made him easy to control. He was somewhat inexpensive to maintain, he was tractable, and he was generally a good worker. The negro slaves increased rapidly and, by the time of the Revolution, exceeded in number the white people in the Carolinas, Georgia, Maryland, and Virginia. They constituted one fifth of the population in Delaware and Pennsylvania and one sixth in New York. Even in New England, where they were unprofitable and where the loudest protest against their condition was earliest heard, they numbered one fiftieth of the population at that time.

Among the privileged people, who were separated from the underprivileged, or servile, classes, often even by distinctions in dress, close attention was paid to the niceties of rank. Congregations in New England classified and seated their members in church according to rank. The committee on seating were expected in the interest of the peace and dignity of the neighborhood to be guided in their solemn decisions by considerations of family descent, economic wealth, social prestige, age, and military rank; but when there was controversy the facts were heard and assignments were made by a committee appointed by the town meeting. While New England was observing these rules the privileged in Virginia were asserting their right to lead by requiring their underprivileged neighbors to wait outside the church until the leaders in the congregation had found their pews.

In the American colonies one sat at table or held place in processions by regulation among those people who are so often applauded for leaving England in protest against restricted conditions there. Under the law in colonial Massachusetts a "true gentleman" could not be punished by whipping "unless the crime was very shameful and his course in life vicious and profligate." It was presumptuous for an ordinary person to dispute the opinions of his betters or to question their right to leadership. "A poor man has rarely the honor of speaking to a gentleman on any terms and never with any familiarity but for a few weeks before the election," said a spokesman of the underprivileged in Philadelphia on the eve of the Revolution. A school system designed for the education of the masses could not develop in such an atmosphere. Such a system could not even be designed under such conditions.

Restriction of the ballot. The restriction of the ballot to those who were privileged in property also retarded the growth of public education. In all the colonies the privilege of voting was fixed and permitted according to the old English theory that ownership of real estate was the correct qualification for voting. Under this theory a man's property, and not his character, nationality, residence, or educational fitness, entitled him to vote. This right to the ballot was claimed and given in much the same way as one would today claim the right to vote in a meeting of the stockholders of a corporation — ownership of stock is the requirement. Ownership of real estate was accepted as evidence of material interest in the community.

Seven of the thirteen colonies — Georgia, North Carolina, Virginia, New Jersey, New Hampshire, New York, and Rhode Island — required the ownership of landed property as a qualification of the voter. Five required the ownership of land, or as an alternative other property of a fixed value, usually forty or fifty pounds. These colonies were Pennsylvania, Delaware, Maryland, Connecticut, and Massachusetts. South Carolina required ownership of real property or the payment of taxes amounting to ten shillings a year. In all the colonies the theory prevailed that those persons who had a fixed, valuable, and permanent interest in real estate were fittest to choose and to be officers and lawmakers. They must stand or fall with their country. If the property requirement should be relaxed or removed and an uncertain requirement substituted, strangers, transients, or beggars who would have little interest in the community could easily become lawmakers and officers. They could oppress the landed people with burdensome taxes.

Moral, religious, and residential qualifications, when required at all, were confined for the most part to particular colonies. Moral and religious qualifications were practically limited to the colonies most directly under Puritan influence and during the seventeenth century. Massachusetts restricted the ballot to those having church membership. But when Massachusetts and Plymouth lost their independent status by their union in 1691, property replaced religion as the principal qualification for the right to vote. In New York the letter of the law excluded Jews and Catholics from the suffrage, though this seems not to have been strictly enforced. In Virginia free negroes and Catholics were excluded, and in South Carolina only Protestants were allowed to vote.

In all the colonies the franchise was restricted to a small fraction of the people. There were fewer voters proportionately in New England than in the other colonies. In Massachusetts and Connecticut only one person in fifty exercised the suffrage, although a larger proportion had the right. The number of church members in Massachusetts included only a very distinct minority of the population. As early as 1635 a law had been passed compelling all the inhabitants to attend church under penalty of fine and imprisonment, and three years later a law was enacted requiring every resident, whether a freeman and church member or not, to be taxed to support the ministers. But in 1640 probably three fourths of the people were outside the pale. The voters formed only 9 per cent of the population in Rhode Island. Half the men over twenty-one years of age were without any political privileges whatever in New York. Three eastern counties in Pennsylvania manipulated the franchise in the entire colony until the Revolutionary period. The proportion of voters in the other colonies was very small.

Gradual disuse of the property test. The property qualification for voting remained the dominating requirement far into the national period. During the Revolutionary period only eight of the states altered their laws on suffrage, and these changes were so slight as to indicate almost no change in the theory which had dominated during the colonial period. The most manifest tendency in the changes was toward the reduction of the amount of property required. Moral and religious qualifications soon substantially disappeared, but the exclusive property test remained the rule for half a century or longer.

It fell into disfavor slowly, especially in those states where the forces of conservatism continued intrenched. In New York, in Massachusetts, and in Virginia in the decade from 1820 to 1830 the fight on the subject was bitter, and the old practice died hard. Some of the ablest leaders of these states, including the eminent James Kent, labored to restrict the suffrage to the small group of property owners and taxpayers. But the states which entered the Union after 1800 never had the struggle of property interests against the new and growing democratic ideal. The forces of liberalism gained rapidly among the new states, where property qualifications and tax requirements for the privilege of voting were generally frowned upon by the sturdy pioneers and the insurgent spirit of frontier democracy, which denied the validity or justice of distinctions. The constitution of Indiana of 1816 admitted to suffrage white men of one year's residence in that state, in 1818 Illinois made the same provision but reduced the requirement to six months, and in 1820 Missouri provided for suffrage in the same manner and required a residence of only three months in the state.

Social distinctions in the early colleges. Perhaps nowhere in American colonial life were class, or social, distinctions and special privileges more conspicuous than in New England's earliest colleges: in Harvard, founded in 1636, and in Yale, established in 1701. In the catalogues of Harvard down to 1772 and of Yale down to 1767 the names of the students were not listed alphabetically, as democracy would presumably demand, but in an order which was supposed to indicate the social rank of their fathers or their families. This practice probably grew out of conditions with which the founders of Harvard had been accustomed at Oxford and Cambridge, where many of them had been trained. Although there was not in the English institutions the identical usage, the custom in the New England colleges was connected with certain distinctions of rank observed in the English universities. There the students defined their own status by the fees that they paid, and these were determined somewhat by their financial and social position. By their practice some sort of social precedence must have been indicated, though no attempt seems to have been made at Oxford and Cambridge to arrange the trades and professions of the students' fathers in any order of precedence.

Lists based on family pedigree. These class lists, especially at Harvard in the early period, were made principally on the basis of family pedigree. There was a conscious effort through the college roll to preserve the respect due to family names of distinction. And even at Yale, a trifle more democratic and homespun than Harvard, there was high respect for such names. The claims of family aristocracy and ancestral distinctions were protected or exalted, and it is probable that personal partiality or prejudice had influence. At both institutions a name of renown was its own justification for an unrivaled place in the college lists; though at both an ample fortune seems also to have been taken into account in estimating family rank.

The low place occupied by the son of unquestioned family claims could be explained only by "straitened paternal circumstances." The notebook of the president of Yale, within two decades of the Revolution, revealed that the parents of certain students low in the lists were "of middling estate, much impoverished." Exceptional regard was paid then, as now, to economic wealth, and slights upon some of those who failed by the test of wealth were as common in college as in the world outside. The students who ranked highest generally had the most influential friends. They were given the best living quarters and had the right to help themselves first at table. When the freshmen were notified of their rank they took their places in classes, dining rooms, and chapel in carefully graded precedence.

At Harvard and Yale the class lists were made up at the opening of the session each year and remained unchanged except upon discovery of some error in arrangement, which was probably infrequent, or when a student suffered "degradation" for misconduct, which ranked in severity next to expulsion. Even improvement in the father's social or official position during his son's college career did not always make for the rearrangement of the latter's position on the class lists.

Important relations of parents to the colleges were also considered in the ranking of their sons. Advantage was given to the sons of trustees or benefactors, and the relative status of the professions and other employments was recognized. The son of an innkeeper, to whose high public trust honorable regard was paid, was listed at the head of his class at Harvard in 1667, and his social inferiors included the sons of a minister who was a graduate of an English university. Later, however, the occupation of innkeeper failed to maintain the esteemed rank it once enjoyed.

Objections to the custom. Criticisms of the custom were heard from students and parents for some time before it was abandoned. The spirit of independence, gradually growing buoyant and defiant, helped to break down the bars of aristocratic precedence in college and to discard the recognition of superior privileges and the rights of rank and station. Moreover, the plan was increasingly difficult to administer. The highest and the lowest members of a class could be ascertained readily, perhaps; but there was chance for uncertainty and error in determining the intermediate members, especially in those cases which easily lent themselves to an indulgence of partiality by the college authorities. Much excitement followed the placing of the students, who were often enraged or chagrined by disappointment and generally settled down to an acquiescence in their lot slowly and reluctantly.

The custom stubborn. Nor did the parents always escape the effects of the practice. When Samuel Phillips, the founder of the well-known academy at Andover bearing his name, was placed below Daniel Murray in a class at Harvard, complaint was made. The father of Phillips and the father of Murray were both justices of the peace, but

Phillips had been elevated to the distinction earlier than Murray. When this startling evidence was discovered, the system at Harvard was brought to a crisis and soon collapsed. This incident led to a report of the governing body of the college, which recommended the substitution of the alphabetical arrangement of students for the old plan of placing them on the basis of the "supposed dignity of the families." This change took place about 1772. Ten years or more earlier an effort to establish another college in Massachusetts seems to have been led by a man who was humiliated if not irritated because his son had been ranked fourteenth in a class of thirty-five students at Harvard, whereas he himself had ranked tenth in the class of 1727, which contained thirty-seven students.

The practice was given up at Yale about 1767. A student there at the time indicated that a new emphasis was being placed upon scholarship and literary attainment rather than upon artificial class distinctions. "There appears to be a laudable ambition to excel in knowledge," he wrote. "It is not he that has got the finest coat or largest ruffles that is esteemed here at present. And as the class henceforward are to be placed alphabetically, the students may expect marks of distinction to be put upon the best scholars and speakers."

The custom died hard in both institutions. The practice of degradation seems to have continued at Harvard for many years. It was listed as one of the established penalties until 1820, and was used for disciplinary purposes. At Yale the practice of degradation disappeared with the custom out of which it grew.

There is no evidence of the custom of placing students on the basis of family at Brown, which had no students until 1765, or at Dartmouth, which opened a few years later. By that time the custom was in disrepute at Yale and growing in unpopularity at Harvard. Nor is there evidence of such practices at Princeton or at Pennsylvania or at Columbia or at Rutgers. There seems to have been nothing of this kind at William and Mary, the third college to be established in the colonies and the only one in the South, though the early records and memorials of this institution are very few. The available records indicate that this college was rather democratic and the students were accepted on equal terms. Although they may not have been seated at table according to social rank, they were jealous of their rights. A petition signed by James Monroe, afterwards president of the United States, and other students suggested to the faculty that the food in the dining hall be improved.

Primogeniture and entail. Class distinctions were also strengthened in the colonies by an ancient family institution brought from England — the old custom of transmitting landed property. The rule of primogeniture, which gave the landed inheritance to the eldest son to the entire exclusion of sisters and younger brothers, prevailed in all the colonies except Massachusetts, Connecticut, New Hampshire, Maryland, and Pennsylvania, and in these the eldest male generally received a double portion. The law of entail, making landed property an inalienable possession that could not be given away or sold, was widely applied also. These two rules worked against the equal distribution of inheritances and encouraged feudalistic distinctions which were not removed until the Revolutionary period, when there was an onslaught on some of the special privileges of colonial days.

Religious interests. The general distaste of the governing colonists for democracy appears in matters of religion. The English Church was established by law in Virginia, in Maryland, and in the Carolinas. In Virginia it was recognized from the beginning of the colony; in 1643 a law was passed against dissenters, and only Anglican ministers were permitted to conduct religious services. But the attempt to exclude all except those of the Anglican faith finally failed just before the Revolution. In North Carolina the English Church was less powerful than in Virginia, and the people showed widespread unwillingness to be taxed to support a religion which they did not profess.

Established churches. A similar attitude prevailed in South Carolina, though the English Church, established there in 1706, was strongly intrenched. This came to be the established church in Georgia also. Maryland, settled by Catholics, had no church establishment in its early period, and about the middle of the seventeenth century it passed a law for religious toleration, probably to enable the Baltimores to hold their property; but by 1702 the English Church was set up and severe laws were enacted against the Catholics. In New Jersey, Pennsylvania, Delaware, and New York laws could not be passed to establish and give monopoly to any form of religion, but in the last of these colonies the Anglican Church finally won a place of supremacy. Dissenters multiplied in all these colonies. "Africa is not more full of monsters than Pennsylvania is of sects," wrote a disturbed minister of the Anglican Church. The small colony of Rhode Island was tolerant in religion and became a refuge for all who sought freedom of worship. Roger Williams believed that no one should be compelled "to worship or to maintain a worship against his own consent"; that "persecution for cause of conscience" was contrary to the teachings of Christ. In the other New England colonies Puritanism was very strong, and the Congregational churches were supported by taxation.

At the opening of the Revolution nine of the thirteen colonies had legally established churches. In Virginia, Maryland, the Carolinas, Georgia, and New York, which had the right of support by public taxation, it was the Anglican Church; in Massachusetts, Connecticut, and New Hampshire the Puritan, or Congregational, Church had a similar monopoly. It was many years after the Revolution before the church was disestablished in all these states. In Massachusetts the religious monopoly was held until 1833.

Religious interests strong. Religious interests were more or less strong, however, in all the colonies. Confession of no religious belief was no more heinous in New England than it was in Virginia, where it was almost as bad as the confession of favor for the ways of Catholics or of Quakers, who were punished in the pillory for wearing hats in church. Religious fanaticism laid the penalty of death upon witches in Massachusetts, and in Virginia juries of matrons were appointed to fumble over the bodies of old women for "witch marks." Sins or delights of the flesh were condemned as severely in Virginia as in New England. So also was skepticism or atheism. Even Edward Maria Wingfield, a man of high birth and good family connections, who became the first president of the council and governor of the colony of Virginia, stood substantially accused of denying the existence of God because he failed to take a Bible with him to the New World. A candidate for speaker of the House of Burgesses accused of blasphemy and atheism seems to have had his case investigated by the general court. Virginia even mildly disciplined its blasphemous soldiers by piercing their tongues with red-hot irons.

The clergy in the South were generally devout and as exemplary as the times demanded, though, as elsewhere, there were instances among them of loose living and ungodly conversation. The Established Church bred in the South some fox-hunting parsons and perfunctory church worshipers, and in New England gloomy Puritanism grew a domineering body of clergy, witch-watchers, and heresy-hunters. The churches in the South were never crowded, and nonattendance at the unwarmed churches became a problem for New England magistrates as early as 1646, when governing authority closely scrutinized conduct and legislated "for the more effectual suppressing of immorality and irreligion and for putting in due execution sundry laws already made against vice and profaneness." It also noted the "want of Bibles in particular families, remissness and great neglect of attendance on the public worship of God," deficiency in family government, the neglect of catechizing, the prevalence of "talebearing, defamation, and intemperance," and sought to prevent the "unseasonable meetings of young people in the evenings after the Sabbath days." Even fines were ineffective on those who committed many and sundry abuses "on the Lord's day": children playing in the streets and other places; "youths, maids, and other persons, both strangers and others, uncivilly walking in the streets and fields, traveling from town to town, going on shipboard, frequenting common houses and other places to drink, sport, and otherwise to misspend that precious time."

There was now a new generation of American-born in New England who were less strict than their fathers and felt less resentment toward other religious sects. These must be called back to the old faith. Early Puritanism was weakening. Flaming youth was beginning to vex the fathers. The magistrates must now legislate in an effort to outwit the devil, and the "old deluder" act of 1647 (Chapter V) was passed by the General Court of Massachusetts. Instead of being a foundation stone upon which the American school system has been constructed, as is so often claimed for this law, it seems rather to have been an effort to restrict the influence of Catholics and adherents to the English Church and to impose the Puritan creed upon this first generation of native-born New Englanders.

Colonial contrasts. Many historians, often with the zeal and fervor of provincial patriots, have written much concerning cultural differences in the colonies — Puritan and pious New Englanders, mercenary merchants in the middle colonies, and careless Cavaliers in the South. William Bradford, sometimes called the father of American history, believed that New England was set apart as a chosen land and its early settlers as the elect. "We are the Lord's chosen people. His hand is ever guiding us," the New Englanders said humbly but proudly. "God sifted a whole nation that he might send choice grain over into the wilderness," declared the Reverend William Stroughan in a sermon in 1668. Those who (by an accident of early seventeenth-century navigation) landed in New England have been held up as deeply religious and highly respectful toward learning and its advancement. They became learned and democratic, developed devotion toward liberty and equality, and gave to America a democratic school system. Those who settled in the middle colonies are often mirrored as indifferent to education and the demands of the higher life, and interested chiefly in commerce and trade. Schools and other means of education were left largely to each religious group and to those who could pay for the privilege. And it has often been written that farther south the early settlers had come not as like-minded congregations, such as found their way to New England, but singly and alone, and intent on economic gain. Class distinctions were strong, education and religion were neglected, and popular government was frowned on.

The influence of geography. From the outset geography served as a powerful influence in the life of the American colonists. It was perhaps more powerful than motives of settlement and religious and educational attitudes. Geography, topography, climate, and occupational interests, which were determined by these conditions, had deep and lasting influence on colonial life and culture.

The climate was gentle and nature otherwise generous in the South, where the land was cheap and fertile and assured an easy living. "Plenty and a warm sun" made for a life of ease in North Carolina, according to William Byrd's notes, which he jotted down in his journal while he served as a member of the commission that ran the boundary line between Virginia and North Carolina in 1728. "Surely there is no place in the world where the inhabitants live with less labor than in North Carolina," and he believed that this condition was due principally to "the great felicity of the climate" and to "the easiness of raising provisions." And such was the entire Southern region, which became and has remained a rural and agricultural section.

The power of tobacco in Virginia. Tobacco was a strong influence in Virginia. It was highly respected not only by the colonists themselves but by the government in England as well. The custodian of the crown's purse appeared enraged when the Virginia Assembly sent to England in 1693 James Blair, a minister of high standing, to secure a charter and financial aid for the institution now known

JAMES BLAIR

Founder and first president of the College of William and Mary. (From C. K. Bolton's "Portraits of the Founders.")

as the College of William and Mary. Blair presented the order for the funds to the custodian, who complained at the extravagance. Blair then reminded him that a college was needed in Virginia to train ministers to preach the gospel to the people, who had "souls to be saved." "Souls!" exclaimed the custodian. "Damn your souls! Raise tobacco."

The road to wealth and to political and social leadership in Virginia lay in land and tobacco, a crop which could be made easily with unskilled and cheap labor. Negro slavery, introduced into that colony in 1619, promised almost from the outset to be profitable, and it was encouraged and developed until the Civil War. In the same year that unfortunate and dispossessed class known as white indentured servants were introduced. Many of these were political offenders, perhaps even condemned criminals, and some were fairly well-educated people who had fallen on evil days. Some came from jails and poorhouses and the streets of London; in vagabondage because they could get no work, or given to petty thievery because they were hungry. The servant was a person who was generally bound by the ship captain, who transported him to the planter, who paid his transportation or otherwise purchased the right to his service. The term of service for such a person varied from two to seven years, and at the end of that period he became free.

Many of these servants became renters or tenants on the plantations of their former masters, some became planters themselves, and some even attained membership in the Assembly of Virginia. Of the forty-four members of the House of Burgesses in 1629 seven were listed as servants five years earlier and were working out the cost of their passage across the ocean. Six members of that House in 1632 had been servants. It is estimated that from 30 to 40 per cent of the landowners of Virginia before and during the year 1635 had come to the colony as servants, and that as late as the middle of the century there were wide opportunities for men of this class.

Although leadership fell to the great planters, individual initiative and industry were rewarded. The white servant could become the farmer, the farmer could become the planter, and the planter could attain a place of social and political leadership in Virginia, which was not free, however, from feudalistic tendencies. But there, as in the other colonies, the main basis of distinction was the possession of wealth. Nowhere in the colonies was this frowned upon as a social grievance, but in all of them it was respected as evidence of success. And it had its own reward. Commerce, trade, and land, whether in New England, the middle colonies, or the South, furnished the foundation of political and social control.

Economic interests in other colonies. New England was adapted to no single staple crop. It had no wide-stretching areas. It developed a domestic coasting trade and trading centers, and both these and the middle colonies went from commerce to manufacturing. In them the conditions were more favorable for the Industrial Revolution, that new economic basis for educational and industrial interests. In compact village communities which early arose the value of collective action was early learned. But the influence of geography made it impossible for the common school to develop in a domain of large plantations and scattered population. In Virginia and the other Southern colonies old-field and neighborhood schools, with the migratory teachers of the time, seem to have taken the place of the town schools in New England.

The extent of education. If common schooling was somewhat less extensive in the colonies outside New England, the culture of the educated and leading class seems to have been wider and more generous. This was true in particular of Virginia, which had many private libraries of considerable size. Before 1680 Virginia had no printing press, and the large number of books found in that colony in the seventeenth century had been printed in England, Holland, and France. Private collections of books indicate wide interest among the planters in reading for information, recreation, and pleasure. New York, Charleston, Philadelphia, and Boston had small public libraries before the Revolutionary period for the "self-improvement" of the people generally. Especially useful was the library in Philadelphia, where, under the stimulus of Franklin, there was growing in the eighteenth century an eager spirit of inquiry. Before the end of the century it had "ten thousand volumes, well selected, for the information and improvement of all ranks of the citizens." Studies of wills and of inventories of personal property appraised during the seventeenth century continue to reduce the supposed differences in such means of culture between New England and the other colonies.

Democracy not in favor among the leaders. But democracy was as much disliked socially by the early colonists, whether in the North or the South, as it was scorned politically. Men who were not significant in England became so in the New World, with its isolation, its freedom from traditional restraints, and its opportunity for success with little or no capital. When they gained social and political position they guarded it jealously and were slow to admit others to it. It was natural for them to endeavor to intrench themselves in economic, political, and even legal privilege. However implicit democracy may have been in the Mayflower Compact and in other covenants of the church or the town in New England, it was not recognized for the most part by the leaders there or elsewhere in the colonies. They were miniature aristocracies based upon economic wealth, whether acquired chiefly on tobacco and rice plantations in the South or principally through commerce and trade in the North. And democracy must develop before the public school could be provided.

In the minds of the colonial leaders, of most of the early national leaders, and of many of those who later dominated in political and social matters, property rights were closely identified with natural rights. To them political liberties came to mean privileges which they themselves prescribed. Under such conditions the principle of the equality of education could have no practical meaning or application. Scores of those who did lip service to the "enlightenment of the minds of the people at large" were valiant enough in resisting any attacks upon their own liberties when the attacks came from their political or social equals; but when it came to the test of providing for the less well-favored, they were unwilling to share with their inferiors the liberty that they themselves claimed to love.

Throughout the colonial period and far down into the nineteenth century the underprivileged were taught to look upon "gentlefolk" as belonging to a superior order and to keep their humble distance. One group owned most of the property, paid most of the taxes, and monopolized the places of power. Even some of the most enlightened leaders of the early national period were slow to believe any signs pointing· to the democratic awakening which came later. The other group, generally honest and industrious and able to live creditably among their neighbors, were nevertheless unprepared for leadership and without the means of education and training. They were powerless in conditions where the distinctions between the well-to-do and the inferior were so marked. And these distinctions were the rule rather than the exception throughout the colonial period and even later in the United States. They stood as stubborn obstacles in the way of public education.

Enslaved to superstition. The intellectual life of the colonists was bottomed upon the prevailing opinions, prejudices, and notions of England of the period. The popular imagination, edged by theology, was still under the spell of medieval science: "moon-signs, zodiac-signs, horoscopes, ominous eclipses followed by devastating fires, and comets presaging disaster and the death of princes," and the active meddling of grotesque evil spirits and house-haunting demons. Belief in witchcraft was the fashion of the time, the Puritans in particular fully accepting the Biblical injunction "Thou shalt not suffer a witch to live." The penal code of the period, which was marked by Mosaic and medieval barbarity, recognized differences in rank. Punishments fell less heavily upon the well-to-do than upon the inferior.

Colonial life was not characterized by humaneness. The conditions surrounding the poor and the unfortunate, the blind and the insane, the weak of will, and the debtors in filthy prisons were horrible. The extraordinary medical notions of the time reveal to some extent the slavery of the colonists to superstition. Spider-web pills were given to cure ague, screech-owl brains were recommended for headache, fangs of wolves necklaced on children saved them from fright, and girdles of cast-off rattlesnake skins aided childbirth. An atmosphere of such savage hocus-pocus was not good for science and the advancement of learning. But history cannot condemn the colonists for errors and superstition when fully half a century after William Harvey's discovery of the circulation of the blood the orthodox medical faculty of the University of Paris asked the French king to prohibit the teaching of the theory.

This chapter shows that in almost no way was the climate of the colonies good for public schools. The right to life, liberty, and the pursuit of happiness had not yet been recognized. The rights of men as men were unknown. The only known and recognized rights were of men as members of classes and groups. "The people," to whom appeal was made as the conflict with England approached, were in fact a privileged class whose rights were rooted in the ownership of property. The poor and the unfortunate, the servant and the slave, and the underprivileged must patiently wait for relief and for opportunity from sources and forces not much in evidence in the colonial period. Such forces, later to develop, and their influence upon education are to be treated in Chapters VI and VII. Meantime a glimpse should be taken of the types of schools and other means of education that were established in the colonies.

REFERENCES AND READINGS

ADAMS, JAMES TRUSLOW. The Founding of New England. Boston, 1921.

A scholarly work which upsets some conventional views of early New England history.

ADAMS, JAMES TRUSLOW. Provincial Society, 1690–1763. New York, 1927.

Many hitherto obscure and scattered materials of social history are here brought together in a scholarly and interesting manner for rapid and summary review. Chapters on the aristocrats, the common man, the intellectual outlook, and the life of the spirit supplement the material of this chapter. Excellent bibliographical notes.

ADAMS, JAMES TRUSLOW. Revolutionary New England, 1691–1776. Boston, 1923.

Chapter III deals with the culture and ideals of the colonists.

ANDREWS, C. M. The Colonial Period, chaps. iii, iv. New York, 1912.

Discusses the political, social, and economic characteristics and influences.

ANDREWS, C. M. Colonial Folkways. Yale University Press, 1919.

Deals, among other subjects, with the everyday needs and diversions of the colonists, with travel, and with intellectual and spiritual interests.

BEARD, CHARLES A., and MARY R. The Rise of American Civilization. Vol. I, chap. iv. New York, 1927.

Seeks to show the derivative origin of colonial culture: "the whole conventional heritage, from its noblest ideals to its grossest vulgarities, was European, in a strict sense, English." Excellent as supplementary material for this chapter.

BECKER, CARL L. Beginnings of the American People, chaps. iv, v. Boston, 1915.

Good accounts of England and her colonies in the seventeenth and eighteenth centuries and the American people in the eighteenth century.

BISHOP, C. F. History of Elections in the American Colonies. New York, 1893.

A standard account of the subject.

BROWN, E. E. The Making of our Middle Schools. New York, 1903.

The early chapters contain valuable information concerning secondary education in the colonial period.

BRUCE, P. A. Economic History of Virginia in the Seventeenth Century. 2 vols. New York, 1896.

> Contains a vast amount of valuable information.

BRUCE, P. A. Institutional History of Virginia in the Seventeenth Century. 2 vols. New York, 1910.

> Contains interesting chapters on religion, schools, libraries, and illiteracy.

DEXTER, FRANKLIN D. "On Some Social Distinctions at Harvard and Yale before the Revolution," *Proceedings of the American Antiquarian Society*, New Series, Vol. IX.

> Tells of class distinctions in two colonial colleges.

EGGLESTON, EDWARD. The Transit of Civilization. New York, 1901.

> Chapter V deals chiefly with education.

HALL, BENJAMIN HOMER. A Collection of College Words and Customs. Cambridge, Massachusetts, 1856.

> A gossipy discussion of words and customs with historical significance.

HART, A. B. (Editor). American History told by Contemporaries, Vol. I. New York, 1897.

> Original documents which include, among many others, Governor William Berkeley's official report on Virginia in 1671, the "True Blue Laws of Connecticut" (1672), account of the trial of a Quaker (1661), a schoolmaster's duties (1661), the penalty for not going to church (1666), and other interesting subjects.

PARRINGTON, V. L. The Colonial Mind, 1620–1800, Book II, chaps. i–iii. New York, 1927.

> Contains, among other things, selections from the journal of Sarah Kemble Knight, on a trip from Boston to New York in 1704, and some of the breezy comments of Colonel William Byrd for his history of the dividing line between North Carolina and Virginia in 1728.

PORTER, KIRK H. A History of Suffrage in the United States, chaps. i–iv. The University of Chicago Press, 1918.

> Deals with the qualifications for voting.

WEEDEN, W. B. Economic and Social History of New England, 1620–1789. 2 vols. Boston, 1890.

> Replete with useful information. Volume II, pp. 528 ff., deals with the matter of social distinctions.

WERTENBAKER, THOMAS J. The First Americans, 1607–1690. New York, 1927.

> A fresh and valuable contribution to the social history of this country in the seventeenth century. Excellent bibliographical notes.

WERTENBAKER, THOMAS J. The Planters of Colonial Virginia. Princeton University Press, 1922.

> Chapters III–VIII, inclusive, throw new light upon economic conditions in colonial Virginia and disprove the old belief that the early founders of the colony were substantial planters and property-owners from the beginning.

QUESTIONS FOR STUDY AND DISCUSSION

1. Show how education in the American colonies was inherited from Europe.

2. List the obstacles in the way of a healthy growth of public education in the colonies.

3. Account for the fact that class distinctions were marked in the colonies.

4. What were the arguments for and against the restriction of the ballot to those who owned property?

5. If the early settlers came to this country to gain religious and political liberties, why was the ballot so restricted and Jews and Catholics usually excluded from the suffrage?

6. Explain the social distinctions which prevailed in Harvard and Yale. Indicate any survivals in higher education today of deference to family names of economic or social distinction.

7. Show how the ancient rules of primogeniture and entail were not wholesome for the growth of democracy.

8. Discuss the effect of officially established churches and their monopoly of religion upon education. How did they aid education? How did they retard it?

9. One state has better educational facilities than another, and counties in the same state often vary in educational advantages, some having good and others having inadequate facilities. Geographical location and the type or character of the people are among the factors that have influence in this matter. What factor, if any, in your opinion is most influential in determining the kind of schools or other educational agencies which a community or a state provides?

10. It is said that the location of the settlements in Virginia in 1607 and in Massachusetts in 1620 was somewhat accidental if not largely so. If those people who came to Virginia had located in Massachusetts and if those who landed at Plymouth Rock had located in Virginia, what would have been the subsequent history of education in those two states? Give reasons for your answer.

11. Offer evidence to prove the statement that civilization in Massachusetts is higher and more worthy than that in Mexico. What, in your opinion, are the most reliable measures of the height of a civilization?

12. Note any survivals today of superstition and barbarous laws the roots of which run back to the colonial period or earlier.

CHAPTER V

EARLY PRACTICES

Outline of the chapter. 1. Generally throughout all the colonies education was looked upon not as a function of the State but as a function of the Church.

2. The apprenticeship practices were established upon the act of 1601 of England and developed into a system of education for the under-privileged.

3. The first general school law (in 1647 in Massachusetts) was not, as has often been claimed, the basis of the public-school system of the United States.

4. The growing power of localism led to the random establishment of schools in most of the colonies; then came the beginnings of the district school.

5. The Latin grammar school, inherited from England, appeared in most of the colonies, if not all, but reached its fullest development in New England.

6. Nine colleges were established in the colonies, with philanthropy the mother of them all and the religious or theological purpose strong in all of them except one; Franklin's proposed course was liberal.

7. Educational endowments were numerous, the dame school appeared, and there were evening schools, but the education of women was neglected.

8. The materials of instruction were meager and the methods were wasteful.

9. Interest in cultural agencies appeared in printing presses and in newspapers.

10. Discipline was severe in school and out, the penal code was brutal, and the rights of childhood were not often respected.

When William Berkeley, Virginia's early royal governor, reported in 1671 to the authorities in England on conditions in the colony, he said, concerning educational practices, "The same course that is taken in England out of towns; every man according to his ability instructing his children." The practices to which he referred were prevalent also in the other colonies. Those who could afford the privilege of education, the dominating theory of which was aristocratic, provided it for their children by tutorial instruction or in local neighborhood schools. Education was not generally looked upon as a function of the State, but as the business of the Church, the family, or the individual.

Nearly three decades earlier the legislature of Virginia, in confirming the will of Benjamin Symms, who had still earlier founded a school in that colony, officially encouraged "others in like pious performances." Here was revealed another educational practice in the colonies. Philanthropic individuals, societies, or religious organizations established schools or other means of education and training primarily for the poor, who had been neglected and who, under the Protestant theory of personal salvation, must be able to read the Bible. The work of these agencies in the American colonies was usually very elementary and consisted chiefly of instruction in reading, writing, and arithmetic, and training in morals and religion through the Bible and the catechism.

The religious motive. Early educational efforts in the American colonies were, therefore, religious in their practice

MILK
FOR
BABES.

DRAWN
Out of the Breasts of both
TESTAMENTS.

Chiefly, for the spirituall nourishment of *Boston* Babes in either *England*: But may be of like use for any Children.

By JOHN COTTON, B.D. and *Teacher* to the *Church* of *Boston* in New-England.

LONDON,
Printed by J. Coe, for *Henry Overton*, and are to be sold at his Shop, in *Popes-head* Alley.
1646.

TITLE PAGE OF A COLONIAL BOOK WHICH ILLUSTRATES THE RELIGIOUS MOTIVE IN EDUCATION materials of instruction were religious or theological, and the teachers were chosen in the interest of orthodoxy and under its closest scrutiny. Instruction was generally marked by sectarian dogmatism, and discipline by a severity and brutality rooted in a theology which looked upon children as conceived in iniquity and born in sin. Theology gave the child a bad name, which he has found difficult to live down even with the assistance of the most accommodating and fashionable psychology.

Apprenticeship and the poor. Under the conditions described in Chapter IV nonsectarian schools, supported and controlled by the public and open alike to all, whether rich or poor, could not develop. Popular education in the modern sense was as foreign and as inappropriate to the colonists as was the idea of popular and democratic government. The education of the masses had scarcely been thought of even as an ideal. But governing authority (the Church or the State) in colonial America early gave slight educational attention to underprivileged and poor children, and thus took the initial step along the toilsome and difficult way toward a public-school system. This step was taken through legislation providing for the compulsory apprenticeship of poor and neglected children.

The custom of apprenticing beginners in crafts and trades to masters had been general throughout England as early as the fourteenth century. Until 1562 it was a local custom, however, its regulation differing somewhat in different localities. Under the Statute of Artificers enacted in that year it became in effect a national system and operated and was regulated everywhere in England in the same way. The numerous and often conflicting laws on the subject of apprentices were consolidated in an effort to banish idleness, to advance husbandry and industry, and to afford a measure of protection and reasonable wages to the apprentices, "both in time of scarcity and in time of plenty."

This legislation sought to provide adequate training in trades and to reduce unemployment, which was a serious problem in England.

The statutory foundation of apprenticeship. The wholesome effect of the Statute of Artificers led to the passage of the Poor Law of 1601, which consolidated and strengthened previous laws in an effort to "provide work for those who could work, relief for those who could not, and punishment for those who would not." This act required the churchwardens and overseers to apprentice all poor children, the boys until they were twenty-four years of age and the girls until they were twenty-one or married. Indentures, or agreements, between the master and the churchwardens and overseers were required and were publicly recorded. The essential characteristics of this practice were reproduced in the American colonies, were carried over into the national period, and remained in wide force and practice until other agencies appeared to care for underprivileged children. In this country, however, certain features of the law were modified from time to time and others of an educational nature were acquired.

Colonial statutes. The apprenticeship practices became in the colonies an educational system of considerable significance for the underprivileged. As early as 1641 the General Court of the colony of New Plymouth passed an act recognizing the principle of the English Poor Law of 1601, that the care of poor children was a public responsibility, and providing that they could be placed in families for proper maintenance and presumably also for education.

In June, 1642, the Massachusetts Bay Colony passed a similar act. Many parents and masters were greatly neglecting to train their children "in labor and learning and other employments which may be profitable to the commonwealth," and the local officers were empowered by this law to correct the evil. The officers were to find out whether

Lenoir Rhyne College
LIBRARY

parents and masters were teaching their children "to read and understand the principles of religion and the capital laws of the country" and to fine those who failed to report on these matters when required. They were also given authority to apprentice the children of those parents who were unable or unfit "to employ and bring them up." Each town was to be so divided that each officer would be responsible for a certain number of families. The provisions of this legislation, whose purpose was in part economic, were an improvement upon the English act, which sought to provide homes for poor children but not the means of their education. The Massachusetts law sought not only to promote employments profitable to the commonwealth but also the education of the children.

In March, 1643, Virginia passed similar legislation. The overseers and guardians of orphans were ordered by the county courts "to educate and instruct them according to their best endeavors in Christian religion and in rudiments of learning." The practice which developed under this legislation was popular in North Carolina also, where it appeared before the end of the seventeenth century and closely resembled the Virginia laws. Legislation on the subject was passed in South Carolina and Georgia in that century also.

In 1671 New Plymouth ordered that the officers "of every town shall have a vigilant eye from time to time over their brethren and neighbors" to see that all parents and masters "teach their children and servants as they grow capable, so much learning as through the blessing of God they may attain, at least to be able to read the Scriptures, and other profitable books printed in the English tongue and the knowledge of the capital laws." Parents and masters neglecting to "bring up their children and apprentices in some honest lawful calling" were to be fined. Apprenticeship, as thus regulated, became an educational practice and was adopted in all the colonies. Tennessee and the other states which entered the Union during the early national period adopted the same or similar practices.

Essential features of apprenticeship. In all its essential features the system of apprenticeship applied to poor children, orphans, and illegitimate children, to those whose economic competence was insufficient to maintain and educate them "according to their rank and degree," and to girls as well as boys. It sometimes applied to negro and mulatto children also, especially in the South, although the indentures did not always make it obligatory on the master to teach his negro or mulatto apprentices to read and write. There are on record, however, a few cases of free negro children who were bound out and apprenticed under indentures which gave them the benefit of the usual educational features of the system. The practices of apprenticing neglected children was very general throughout the colonies, though they were more extensive in some than in others. In the main the indentures, or agreements, were similar.

The agencies of apprenticeship. The principal agencies for putting the machinery of the apprenticeship plan into operation were the town officials or the county courts, whose powers were conferred by legislation or derived from custom or the common law. Their interest in the poor and dependent children was usually more than nominal perhaps, though the educational provisions of the indentures were not always enforced. It is not unlikely that in some cases the indentures or their interpretations were more favorable to masters than to apprentices.

Guardians or masters were required to report at stated times, and the officers were charged with the proper administration of the practices and were also required to make inquiry annually concerning the observance of the laws. Often, however, the enforcement of the agreements, or indentures, depended on whether the apprentices, through friends or the grand jury, were able to get their cases before the court. Complaints of failure to comply with the law and the indentures were not uncommon. Occasionally a master was summoned to answer the complaint of his apprentice and to "shew the court reasons why he does not teach him to read, as by indenture he is obliged." In such a case the master usually promised to "put his apprentice forthwith to school." The indentures did not always contain the educational requirements of the system, despite the directions of the law. Occasionally children were able to read and write when they were apprenticed; in such cases there was no legal necessity for including the educational requirements in the agreement.

Extent of the practices. The extent of the practices in the colonies will probably never be accurately known because of the scarcity of evidence. Moreover, it is not improbable that the children who were apprenticed often took their places in the homes of the guardians or masters on conditions of maintenance and care ordinarily granted to other members of the household, the guardians or masters giving their apprentices essentially the same attention which they gave their own children. When apprentices were ill used, the law or custom required their removal, and they were reapprenticed to other masters approved by the officials. Therefore the success of the educational feature of apprenticeship naturally depended on the interest of the masters or guardians and on the desire of the apprentices to get "book learning."

The old apprenticeship laws generally recognized first the economic, or industrial, or vocational purpose, because there was need for skilled artisans or workers. This came to be the dominating purpose, though humanitarian, religious, or philanthropic purposes were present in the practices. In the main, however, the purpose was to give poor, unfortunate, and neglected children opportunity to learn useful trades and occupations so that they might become self-supporting and not public charges. It is not unlikely, therefore, that both the officials and the masters were more interested in the industrial than in the educational features of the apprenticeship plan, and through it sought to relieve the community of the financial burden incident to caring for its dependents.

A form of compulsory education. Through the system a distinct form of compulsory education was provided, crude and defective, but containing some useful elements. At best it was haphazard in operation and probably served to delay the growth of a wholesome public attitude toward social needs. It also implanted in governmental activity in education the element of charity, which was to prove a mischievous influence. Discrimination between the children of the well-to-do and those of the poor, by giving preference to the latter, was maintained in the school laws of the various states far into the nineteenth century. In these apprenticeship practices, however, appears the germ of the important principle that it is the duty and function of governing authority to care for the poor and to prepare poor and underprivileged children for useful occupations.

The first general school law. Another step in governmental activity in education, after the colonial adaptation of the English Poor Law of 1601, was taken by Massachusetts in 1647, when the so-called "old deluder" act was passed. Educational writers have repeatedly and proudly though uncritically pointed to this law as a firm and valid assertion of the right of the state to establish and maintain schools at public expense. This was the first general school law enacted in the American colonies; it formed the basis of the earliest school plan through the effort of a colonial government. Here it is in full, the spelling modernized :

It being one chief object of that old deluder, Satan, to keep men from the knowledge of the Scriptures, as in former times by keeping them in an unknown tongue, so in these latter times by persuading from the use of tongues, that so at least the true sense and meaning of the original might be clouded by false glosses of saint-seeming deceivers, that learning may not be buried in the grave of our fathers in the Church and Commonwealth, the Lord assisting our endeavors,

It is therefore ordered, That every township in this jurisdiction, after the Lord hath increased them to the number of fifty house-holders, shall then forthwith appoint one within their town to teach all such children as shall resort to him to write and read, whose wages shall be paid either by the parents or masters of such children, or by the inhabitants in general, by way of supply, as the major part of those that order the prudentials of the town shall appoint: *Provided*, Those that send their children be not oppressed by paying much more than they can have them taught for in other towns; and

It is further ordered, That where any town shall increase to the number of one hundred families or householders, they shall set up a grammar school, the master thereof being able to instruct youth so far as they may be fitted for the university: *Provided*, That if any town neglect the performance hereof above one year, that every such town shall pay five pounds to the next school till they shall perform this order.

Not the basis of a public-school system. Into the provisions of this act, which the other New England colonies except Rhode Island copied in whole or in part and from which they built up their further educational legislation, strange meanings have been tortured. It has been claimed that here are the beginnings of those secular features which now characterize the American school system. In no American sense, however, does this appear to be a provision for public schools. The authority asserted was that of the Puritan congregation, which was identical with the state but was more powerful than it. Until 1691 no person who was not a member of that church could vote in Massachusetts, and few there were who voted. They levied taxes on all to support ministers of their own faith, and under the law of 1647 they revealed their zeal to preserve and extend that faith by imposing the Puritan creed upon the children. The devil must be outwitted, and the dangers of "saint-seeming deceivers," whether Catholic or Anglican, must be averted. The control of the schools established under this law was ecclesiastical and not secular, the teachers were ministers or were approved by the ministers under the strictest vigilance as to orthodoxy, and the materials of instruction were religious.

Probably nowhere in colonial education is the sectarian, or religious, motive for schools more clearly exhibited than in this act, which grew out of the extreme religious consciousness of Calvinism. It is difficult to see in it the beginnings of free, compulsory, and secular schools. The wages of the teacher were to be paid by the parents or the masters of the children "or by the inhabitants in general." There is significance also in the innocent word "or" in this act, as is so often the case when it is used in legislation today. The parents were not compelled to send their children to school. The word "shall" was directed not to the parents but to the towns, which were difficult to arrest and fine.

The law not popular. This law, strong in purpose but weak in execution, was not in high favor among the people. It seems to have been more largely disregarded than obeyed. Significance may be attached to the fact that the original fine of five pounds was increased in 1671 to ten and in 1683 to twenty, and that near the close of the century there was official complaint from the legislature that the law was "shamefully neglected by divers towns." The requirement for grammar schools was not generally met. In 1700, when there were twenty-seven such schools in New England, there were eighty-one towns in Massachusetts alone, though the size of their population is unknown. Seven years later the list of polls given in by twenty towns in Middlesex County showed that nine had more than a hundred families, but only five had attempted to conform with the law, and only four had succeeded in establishing grammar schools. The general unwillingness of the public to support the schools financially may help to explain in part the scarcity of schoolmasters by the end of the seventeenth century. Special favors to make up in part for low wages were often offered teachers, who in 1692 were exempted from taxes, a year later from military duty, and in the last year of the century from the watch.

The theological purpose of the law. The object of education under this legislation was theological, and theology was the principal use made of it. The devotion of New England to education under the leadership of men like Horace Mann, Henry Barnard, James G. Carter, and many others, in the nineteenth century, has been fruitful for the cause of schools and learning in the United States. Many are the educational trails which lead finally to that part of this country. But it may be seriously questioned whether the "old deluder" act was not an obstacle instead of an aid to free, universal, secular education. Its influence on the people was narrowing rather than broadening, for there were few books that were not theological and little intellectual stimulus except that which came from the severe sermons of stern Calvinists. Preoccupation with all the brutal beliefs that went to make up the epic of Calvinism extended the strength of priestcraft, which banished men for opposing the official theology of the time and made strict the censorship of the press. Sectarianism could not enlighten the minds of the masses. Instead it served to fill the way of public schools with difficulties which had to be removed two centuries later by men like Mann, who was fought by sectarian preachers and bitter ecclesiastics, and by the religious press, which tore into him because he believed in the justice of religious toleration. The dead hands of the past bore heavily upon education in Massachusetts even in his day.

Educational decline and the district school. The passage of the Massachusetts act of 1647 was followed by a period of educational decline in that colony. Before the end of the century some of the conditions which in the earlier period had forced the colonists to live in compact village communities had been removed. King Philip's War, which extended widely over New England, greatly depleted the resources of the colonists, but the victory served to remove their timidity and encouraged them to take up settlements in more remote parts of the townships. The danger of attack by the Indians was now no longer so great. In the frontier regions younger people began to make new settlements which lacked the definite centers characteristic of the older communities. Separate churches came to be established, and the new settlements came slowly to gain local self-government and other privileges somewhat similar to those of the older centers. It was natural that the control of schools by the central township authority should weaken.

The wane of Calvinistic despotism. Meantime the complete domination of the unified and bigoted Calvinism of the early period was losing its hold. Puritan churches split up into factions on questions of admission to membership or through other dissensions. Other sects began to establish places of worship; and the persecution of Baptists, Quakers, Episcopalians, and other Protestant groups was gradually abandoned under the slow and painful growth of religious toleration. The Puritan ideal was dimming. Calvinistic despotism was gradually breaking down.

Intellectual decline. During these years of change there was a gradual intellectual decline. The original settlers, many of whom had had advantages of education in England, had now passed away. Scores of graduates of English universities had settled in New England by the middle of the seventeenth century. Most of them had become ministers and had been eager to promote religion. One of their fears was that an illiterate ministry would appear when "our present ministers should lie in the dust," and to recruit the thinning ranks of the clergy was one purpose of the act of 1647. But the younger generation lacked the zeal and fervor of their fathers.

Some towns had established schools before they were ordered in 1647 to do so, but afterwards the tricks which some of them used to evade the law developed into a high art. Often the local minister was engaged to serve as the nominal schoolmaster, and not infrequently a teacher would be hired only while the legislature was in session. However, when the fine for violation became large enough to support a teacher, it was less expensive to hire one than to violate the law. Then the people living in the more distant portions of the township demanded that the school should be brought near them, and out of this demand arose the moving school, and out of this in turn grew the district school.

The growth of localism. By the middle of the eighteenth century the division of townships into districts was common in New England. In 1789 Massachusetts officially recognized the practices of a century and legalized the small school district. Nearly a decade earlier Thomas Jefferson had proposed the district system as a part of his plan "for a more general diffusion of knowledge" among the people of Virginia. There as elsewhere the local neighborhood school had already become a social convenience which fitted in well with the democratic theory of government. The district system of schools, to be controlled by the local community and to be supported as the people desired — by tuition, by "rate bills," by local taxes, or by any other means at hand — was to spread to all parts of the United

States and, from a simple neighborhood convenience, was to become a stubborn political institution in which local jealousies and disputes over the selection of school committeemen, of teachers, and even of the sites for schoolhouses were to rankle and inflame. The defiant spirit of the frontier and the assertion of local rights in education were to become an obstacle to education, and even today the ghost of the district lingers in the path of rural-school progress.

Colonial schools established at random. The more or less random establishment of schools was characteristic of most of the colonies outside Massachusetts, Connecticut, and New Hampshire, and even the attempt of these colonies to provide schools on a systematic plan was not successful. Outside New England there was little evidence of educational interest on the part of colonial legislatures. In Rhode Island, with its doctrine of religious freedom, the slow growth of the colony, and the existence of slavery, no general school legislation was enacted during the colonial period. However, it is claimed that Newport established a school by popular vote in 1640 and set aside some land to support a school for "the poorer sort"; and Providence in 1663 reserved lands for the maintenance of a town school. Parochial schools, which grew out of the social traditions of Holland and the influence of the Dutch Reformed Church, were established in New York before England took possession of that colony in 1674. These schools were supported and controlled jointly by the local church and civil authorities. After the English occupation New York made no definite advance toward a school system during the remainder of the colonial period.

A similar practice was followed in Pennsylvania, where the tolerant attitude of the Quaker government attracted Germans, Swedes, Scotch and Irish Presbyterians, Dutch, English, and Welsh, and each of these groups was naturally interested in its own denominational schools. The Quakers, through their yearly meetings, encouraged the establishment of elementary and, in some cases, secondary schools near their meetinghouses. Other religious sects, such as the Lutherans, did likewise. In New Jersey, where a similar practice developed, educational advantages came chiefly through the church or through private effort. Generally in these colonies much freedom was allowed the local communities, and each parochial group did practically as it wished.

Early educational effort in Delaware was local and was made through the encouragement of various religious bodies, such as the Swedes, the Dutch, and the English. At the beginning the Swedish authorities ordered that the patrons of the colony of Delaware should "support at all times as many ministers and schoolmasters as the number of inhabitants shall require." It seems that education, which was under private and church control, was not neglected. In 1744 the legislature of the colony confirmed the earlier gifts of lots and houses for school purposes. Here, as in other middle and Southern colonies, schools arose during the colonial period as local neighborhood and social conveniences.

Before the close of the seventeenth century Maryland made an unsuccessful legislative effort to establish schools in every county. In 1723 provision was made for a county system of free high schools, and county trustees were appointed to manage the schools, in which a certain number of poor children were to be taught free of tuition; but the plan later failed for lack of funds. During the first quarter of the eighteenth century South Carolina undertook to establish a school in each parish and also to establish a county system of schools, the cost to be assessed on the lands and slaves of each jurisdiction. Ten poor children were to be received free of charge in each school. Near the middle of the eighteenth century North Carolina authorized the town authorities in Edenton to build a schoolhouse, the expense of which was to be defrayed by money arising from the sale of town lots and from donations and subscriptions, but there, as in most of the colonies, educational effort was left largely to local community interest.

The idea of charitable education was strong in Georgia because of the philanthropic motives of its settlement. In addition to sporadic efforts here and there, schools were maintained by the Society for the Propagation of the Gospel in Foreign Parts, which promoted educational work in other Anglican colonies; and when Georgia became a royal province about 1752 the crown promised to continue the allowance which had hitherto been made by the trustees of the colony for the support of a minister and two schoolmasters. This agreement was maintained until the Revolution and seems to be the only case of educational support in the colonies by the Parliament of England.

The Latin grammar school. Among the earliest schools in most of the colonies were those of the Latin-grammar-school type, which grew out of the influence of the Renaissance and the Reformation and were patterned on the Latin grammar school of England. This type of school appeared in all the colonies except Georgia, but probably reached its greatest development in New England.

The earliest attempt to establish a school in any of the colonies was aided in 1621 by a shipload of merchants from the East Indies. The proposal was to build a Latin grammar school in Virginia, but the Indian massacre of 1622 and the collapse of the Virginia Company caused the project to fail. In 1634 or 1635 Benjamin Symms left valuable property to establish a school in Virginia, and a few years later the Symms will was confirmed by the legislature. The school founded on this endowment has been called "the earliest foundation for free education made in English America by a citizen of an English colony." Symms's example was followed shortly afterwards by Thomas Eaton, of the same county in Virginia, who gave five hundred acres of land and other property as the foundation for a free school similar to that provided by Symms. Both of these schools seem to have had creditable careers. In 1850 they were united and incorporated as Hampton Academy, and the endowment is still preserved separate from the school fund of the state. These schools became models for other communities in Virginia, and others of a similar character were established in that colony shortly after the middle of the seventeenth century.

The first successful attempt to establish a Latin grammar school in this country was made in Boston in 1635 from funds subscribed by forty-five contributors. The chief purpose of this school, which was the principal school in Boston for nearly half a century, was to prepare boys for Harvard. In it Ezekiel Cheever, with a record of seventy years of faithful teaching in New England, taught for thirty years. Latin grammar schools also appeared in other places in Massachusetts, where it is presumed the act of 1647, which required a grammar school in every town having a hundred families, stimulated their development. They appeared in other neighboring colonies, which copied the laws of Massachusetts, and by 1700 there were at least twenty-seven in New England. But the laws requiring Latin grammar schools seem not to have been fully met. The list of Harvard graduates between 1644 and 1770 shows that some New England towns which were credited with grammar schools had not sent any students to that college, though some students (presumably prepared by ministers) had entered Harvard from communities which had no such schools.

Characteristics of Latin grammar schools. The Latin grammar schools, which were exclusive, were not popular even in New England, where they were most numerous. They were generally planned, supported, and managed by the classes and not in the interest of the masses. The students paid tuition fees. The chief aim of the curriculum, which was almost exclusively narrow, in most cases confined entirely to a study of Latin and Greek, and modified but little if at all during the century and a half of the grammar-school period, was to teach boys to read and write Latin and possibly to speak it. The original purpose of these schools, preparation for college, was held to steadfastly. The growth of the grammar schools was often uncertain, however, and attendance on them gradually dwindled because they failed to meet the increasing social needs of the time. Local conditions often rendered inoperative the grammar-school requirements of such legislation as that of Massachusetts in 1647. Moreover, the district school was slowly developing and destroying the central authority, which existed or was presumed to exist when that law was enacted. Few grammar schools survived at the end of the eighteenth century, when a new type of secondary school, the academy, more democratic and more suitable to social needs, was springing up almost everywhere in the United States. The growth of the academy (Chapter XIII) was probably in part both the cause and the result of the failure of the Latin grammar school.

Colonial colleges. By 1769 there were nine colleges in the colonies. Philanthropy was the mother of all of them, and the religious motive was strong in the establishment of all except one, the College of Philadelphia, which grew out of Franklin's Academy and into the University of Pennsylvania. The others were proposed and fostered by college men (there were many graduates of Oxford and Cambridge in New England in the early colonial period, and graduates of these universities served as teachers and ministers in Virginia also), but this institution sprang from the liberal mind and labor of a man who had never bowed the knee to collegiate traditions.

Harvard, the earliest of them all, was authorized by legislative act of Massachusetts in 1636, and two years later it received money, books, and a name from John Harvard.

AFTER GOD HAD CARRIED VS SAFE TO NEW ENGLAND
AND WEE HAD BVILDED OVR HOVSES
PROVIDED NECESSARIES FOR OVR LIVELI HOOD
REARD CONVENIENT PLACES FOR GODS WORSHIP
AND SETLED THE CIVILL GOVERNMENT
ONE OF THE NEXT THINGS WE LONGED FOR
AND LOOKED AFTER WAS TO ADVANCE LEARNING
AND PERPETVATE IT TO POSTERITY
DREADING TO LEAVE AN ILLITERATE MINISTERY
TO THE CHVRCHES WHEN OVR PRESENT MINISTERS
SHALL LIE IN THE DVST.
                    NEW ENGLANDS FIRST FRVITS

BY THE GENERAL COVRT OF MASSACHVSETTS BAY
28 OCTOBER 1636 AGREED TO GIVE 400 £
TOWARDS A SCHOALE OR COLLEDGE WHEAROF 200 £
TO BEE PAID THE NEXT YEARE & 200 £
WHEN THE WORKE IS FINISHED & THE NEXT COVRT
TO APPOINT WHEARE & WT BVILDING
15 NOVEMBER 1637 THE COLLEDG IS ORDERED
TO BEE AT NEWETOWNE
2 MAY 1638 IT IS ORDERED THAT NEWETOWNE
SHALL HENCEFORWARD BE CALLED CAMBRIGE
13 MARCH 1638-9 IT IS ORDERED THAT THE COLLEDGE
AGREED VPON FORMERLY TO BEE BVILT AT CAMBRIDG.
SHALBEE CALLED HARVARD COLLEDGE.

© J. F. Olason

TABLETS ON THE GATEWAY OF HARVARD, SHOWING EARLY RECORDS
OF THE FIRST COLLEGE IN THIS COUNTRY

It opened under the auspices of the Puritan faith and for the purpose of training preachers. The College of William and Mary was established in Virginia in 1693, under the auspices of the Established (Anglican) Church, as a "seminary of ministers of the gospel." Yale, also under Puritan auspices, was founded in Connecticut in 1701 by graduates of Harvard and later received its present name from Elihu Yale, who made bequests to it. The College of New Jersey, now known as Princeton, was established in 1746 under Presbyterian influence. The work of William Tennent and his "Log College" led to its founding. Jonathan Edwards was chosen as the first president, but died shortly afterwards.

The Academy and College of Philadelphia grew out of interest created by a pamphlet by Benjamin Franklin on "Proposals Relating to the Education of Youth in Pennsylvania" (1749). Instruction began two years later, and the institution was chartered by the Penns in 1753. It owed allegiance to no religious denomination, and differed from the other colleges also in a scientific and secular instead of the classical program of studies. King's College (Columbia) was established in New York under the auspices of the Anglican Church in 1754. Its first funds came from a lottery. Brown University in Rhode Island began in 1764 under Baptist influence, Rutgers in New Jersey in 17 under the auspices of the Dutch Reformed Church, a Dartmouth in New Hampshire in 1769 under religious missionary if nonsectarian influences. The course of st in all these colleges, except Pennsylvania, was confined ma to Greek and Latin, sometimes Hebrew, logic after Arist some elementary mathematics, and bits of natural scienc

Franklin's perspective. Even Franklin's proposed lil course, with mathematics, surveying, navigation, phy chemistry, agriculture, natural history, government, tory, civics, modern languages, and the like, was force submit to compromise and revision, and it also fell (in at least) into the narrow and traditional mold. But t is significance in the fact that the idea of an enlightened advanced program of higher learning came from a educated man who loved useful learning, "truth for tru sake," and sought to find and accept it himself and to "communicate it to others." Many years were to pass before Franklin's perspective for higher education was to be gained in the United States.

Perhaps more important in the educational history of the United States than the founding of any of the colleges was the famous Dartmouth College case, which grew out of the attempt of the legislature of New Hampshire between 1815 and 1819 to discontinue the college and establish in its place another institution under different control. Out of the case, bitterly fought through the Supreme Court of the United States, came the decision that a charter is a contract the obligation of which a legislature cannot impair. The principle of law evolved in the case, notable also for the argument of Daniel Webster, a distinguished graduate of Dartmouth, gave peculiar protection to private property, guaranteed the perpetuity of endowments, and stimulated the establishment of private and denominational colleges. The decision in effect determined that higher education in this country could not become a monopoly of the state.

Educational endowments. Examples of colonial endowments for schools, which began with Symms in Virginia and with Harvard in Massachusetts, were fairly numerous in the eighteenth century, especially in the South. One of the most important of such bequests was that of Richard Beresford, who left a large sum of money in 1722 for educational purposes in St. Thomas's Parish in South Carolina. The school was continued until the Revolution, when it was interrupted and its funds lost in part, but it was later reopened and continued until the Civil War. Resuming its work still later, the school had a healthy career until near the close of the nineteenth century.

The Winyaw Indigo Society. In addition to the philanthropy of individuals, certain societies in the Southern colonies also promoted education. One of the most novel

of these was the Winyaw Indigo Society, which was founded
in South Carolina about 1740. This society, which was
formed largely as a "convivial club" by certain planters
who met in Georgetown on the first Friday in each month
to discuss the latest London news, "to hold high discourse
over the growth and prosperity of the indigo plant, and to
refresh the inner man, and so to keep up to a proper standard the endearing ties of social life by imbibing freely of the
inevitable bowl of punch," cannot be pointed to as the origin
of present-day luncheon and civic clubs. However, the
manner by which it became interested in education suggests
the youthful enthusiasms of present-day organizations.
When the exchequer from initiation fees and annual contributions "became plethoric of gold" and the "hearts of
our founders overflowed with the milk of human kindness . . .,
it became the question of the hour, to what good purpose
shall we devote our surplus funds?"

As the tale runs, at the close of the discussion (which was
very brief but pertinent and solid) the presiding officer requested the members to fill their glasses. He would close
the debate with a definite suggestion, and each member
who indorsed it would signify his approval by emptying his
glass. Then the chairman made a speech. He held that
there "may be intellectual food" which some people may
not be fit to partake of, and to set such before them would
be "as absurd as to give a quadrant to an Indian." But he
also believed that knowledge was as necessary as light and
should be as common as water and as free as air. "It has
been wisely ordered," he said, "that light should have no
color, water no taste, and air no odor; so, indeed, knowledge should be equally pure and without admixture of creed
or cant. I move, therefore, that the surplus funds in the
treasury be devoted to the establishment of an independent
charity school for the poor." The meeting rose to its feet,
and the glasses were all turned down "without soiling the

linen." In this manner began the society's school, which for more than a hundred years served all the country lying between Charleston and the North Carolina line.

From 1756 until 1861 the school had a very successful career, and twenty-five or more children were annually educated in it. The annual dues of the members of the society, private benefactions, and the proceeds of escheated lands greatly increased the available income, and many poor children were maintained as well as educated. The trustees allowed the principal to receive a certain number of pay scholars in addition to the pupils for whom the school was originally designed, and for teaching these he was allowed extra compensation. The school became well known and widely patronized, but the Civil War practically destroyed the value of the invested funds. For more than a year the school building was occupied by the Federal troops. The library was scattered, and some of the books were never recovered. When the organization was allowed possession of the building again, funds were raised as a beginning of a new endowment, and the work of the school continued from 1866 to 1886, during which time it educated ten poor children annually. At the latter date it was incorporated as one of the public graded schools of South Carolina.

Bethesda Orphan House. The most notable example of educational effort in Georgia before it acquired statehood was the work of the Bethesda Orphan House, suggested by Charles Wesley and established by George Whitefield and James Habersham in 1739. Whitefield secured a large tract of land from the trustees of the colony and was also successful in soliciting funds. His eloquent plea induced Benjamin Franklin to empty his pockets to aid the enterprise, as is learned from the "Autobiography." This institution, in which orphans and poor children were maintained and educated, served a useful purpose. After Whitefield failed in 1764 to secure the permission of the crown to change his school into a "seminary of literature and academical learning," he undertook to convert it into an academy similar to Franklin's in Philadelphia; but the plan failed, and Whitefield died without ever fully realizing the favorite ambition of his life.

The dame school. The dame school, which was transplanted to this country at the time of the early settlements, was usually taught by a woman in her kitchen or living-room. Here the young children of the neighborhood were taught the alphabet, the hornbook, the elements of reading, and moral and religious subjects. In New England this type of school prepared boys for admission to the town schools, which did not receive them until they could "stand up and read words of two syllables and keep their places." The dame school helped to suggest the idea of the moving school and probably furnished an example for the district school. It was a private and local neighborhood arrangement, or it was semipublic and recognized by the town authorities and sometimes assisted by them, or it was entirely public, especially in the summer season. It grew out of the family responsibility of teaching children the rudiments of learning. Not infrequently a woman in teaching her own children would include other

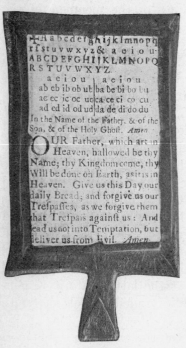

A HORNBOOK, FROM WHICH CHILDREN LEARNED THE ALPHABET AND HOW TO READ

children in the neighborhood. Tuition fees were generally charged in the private and semipublic dame schools.

The education of women neglected. It was many years after the establishment of the first school in the colonies before girls were given equal educational opportunity with boys. The domestic duties of girls demanded little instruction beyond the rudiments of reading and writing, practical

AN ENGLISH DAME SCHOOL
After a drawing by Barclay

feminine skills were acquired by imitation generally in the home, and propriety forbade the training of girls outside. Women were expected to stick to their knitting and not to meddle in "such things as are proper for men, whose minds are stronger," as Governor Winthrop declared. They received their education in the family, in the dame school, in private schools, by tutors, and later by separate instruction given by the local schoolmaster. Sometimes, by special action, girls were admitted to town schools in New England, but often only for half time. The educational rights of women were tardily recognized.

Evening schools. In the late seventeenth century and during the eighteenth century evening schools were established in some of the cities. These schools were private in support and control and were intended for those whose occupations prevented attendance upon day schools. It appears that they were open to any people who believed that they could benefit by the instruction. Advertisements

CORNER OF AN OLD SCHOOLHOUSE, SHOWING ITS MEAGER EQUIPMENT

in newspapers and the indentures of apprenticeship reveal many of these schools in New York, Boston, Philadelphia, and Charleston. More than one hundred indentures in New York City during the years 1698 and 1727 referred to the practice of sending apprentices to such schools. Evening schools were usually conducted in the winter season, but sometimes in other seasons as well, and generally through terms of three months. Some of the teachers, "respectable members of the teaching profession of the period," were graduates of the colonial colleges. Many of them taught private day schools also, and some who were engaged to teach community schools were given permission to conduct night schools as private enterprises. Some of the schools were open to girls and women only, and some to both sexes, but the students in most of them were boys and men. The courses of study ranged from the rudiments of an English education to foreign languages and higher mathematics, and included also commercial subjects, surveying, navigation, geography,

AN OLD DISTRICT SCHOOLHOUSE

astronomy, map-making, conic sections, "French quilting, knotting for bed quilts," Dresden work, flowering, and shading on "cambrick, lawn, and Holland."

Materials and methods. School sessions in the colonial period were usually long. In some communities they continued from seven o'clock in the morning until five in the afternoon in the spring and summer months; from August to December the hours were from eight to four. In New Haven in 1684 the school kept nine hours a day for six days a week in the summer season, but for a somewhat shorter period in the winter. The intermission in the middle of the day was often used in New England, especially on Monday, for the purpose of assembling the children to be examined on the sermon the day before and to enable the master to take notice of any mischief which the children may have

TEACHER'S DESK IN A COLONIAL SCHOOLHOUSE

been guilty of on the Sabbath. Colonial school-teachers were generally schoolmasters, and in many cases they were ministers. Those who taught in the Latin grammar schools were often well educated for the time, were orthodox in religious faith, and not infrequently were capable as teachers. The teachers in neighborhood schools were not always men of education, and some of them were not strong in character. Wherever they taught, all of them, except the private teachers, were licensed by the church or other authority, principally upon evidence of orthodoxy. Methods of instruction were usually individual and often very wasteful, school equipment was meager, unhygienic, and insanitary, and the materials of instruction were

SCHOOLHOUSE ERECTED IN DEDHAM, MASSACHUSETTS, ABOUT 1649

for the most part religious. Textbooks before the American Revolution were English in origin. Hornbooks, primers, the psalm book, and the Bible were most commonly used. Secular textbooks did not appear until near the Revolutionary period.

The New England Primer, the most famous of all the early books, illustrates the religious character and purpose of colonial education. This little book, which appeared about 1690, was widely used for more than a century, going through many editions. Spellers or spelling books began to make their way into the schools near the middle of the eighteenth century, and became popular with the appearance of Noah Webster's blue-backed speller, which appeared in 1783.

Printing presses and newspapers. Interest in cultural and educational agencies is somewhat reflected in the establishment of printing presses and newspapers. The printing press was permanently set up in Massachusetts, Pennsylvania, and New York before the close of the

In Adam's Fall
We finned all.

Thy Life to mend,
This Book attend.

The Cat doth play,
And after flay.

A Dog will bite
A Thief at Night.

An Eagle' flight
Is out of fight.

The idle Fool
Is whipt at School

SPECIMEN PAGE FROM THE NEW ENGLAND
PRIMER, A FAMOUS OLD TEXTBOOK

seventeenth century and in the other colonies between 1709 (Connecticut) and 1762 (Georgia). The earliest newspapers appeared as follows: the *Boston News-Letter* at Boston in 1704, the *American Weekly Mercury* at Philadelphia in 1719, the *New York Gazette* at New York in 1725, the *Maryland Gazette* at Annapolis in 1727, the *Rhode Island Gazette* at Newport in 1732, the *South Carolina Gazette* at Charleston in 1732, the *Virginia Gazette* at Williamsburg in 1736, the *Connecticut Gazette* at New Haven in 1755, the *North Carolina*

Gazette at New Bern in 1751, the *New Hampshire Gazette* at Portsmouth in 1756, the *Wilmington Courant* at Wilmington, Delaware, in 1762, the *Georgia Gazette* at Savannah in 1763, and the *New Jersey Gazette* at Burlington in 1777.

The severity of discipline. "What must become of you if you are wicked?" To this question in Isaac Watts's "Young Child's Catechism," a part of which was intended for children three or four years old, was this dismal response : "If I am wicked, I shall be sent down to everlasting fire in Hell among wicked and miserable creatures."

The prevailing colonial view of the character of children is seen also in Michael Wigglesworth's "Day of Doom," which appeared in 1662. The book went through many editions, was printed upon "broadsides and hawked about the country," and became the best seller for a century. As late as the early nineteenth century many people in New England could repeat large parts of it. In this poetical description of the last judgment and discourse about eternity, unbaptized infants who had died in babyhood are condemned. They beg for mercy, pleading that they should not be blamed for the sins of Adam, and from the judge, burlesqued by Wigglesworth into a "pettifogging country justice," they hear :

> You sinners are, and such a share
> 　　As sinners may expect,
> Such you shall have ; for I do save
> 　　None but my own elect.
> Yet to compare your sin, with their
> 　　Who lived a longer time,
> I do confess yours so much less
> 　　Tho' every sin's a crime.
> A crime it is, therefore in bliss
> 　　You may not hope to dwell ;
> But unto you, I shall allow
> 　　The easiest room in Hell.

Nothing illustrates more definitely the brutality of the time than the manner of disciplining children, both in and out of school. Cruel punishments, sanctioned by the past, were the rule everywhere. Whipping posts were not uncommon in the schoolroom or close by. Boys were looked upon as children of wrath, and old Adam must be beaten out of them. This theory was encouraged by theology and the theologians. Even Martin Luther suggested appropriate beatings as useful restraints upon impudence and as an aid to learning. The same church which blessed a union in matrimony viewed its offspring as sinful, to be regenerated by the rod of religiosity and revenge. The severity of the Mosaic law could be invoked against the disobedient child. Under the laws of New England even young people of sixteen could be put to death for striking or smiting their parents. The iron creed of Puritanism adjudged incorrigibleness "a sin of death."

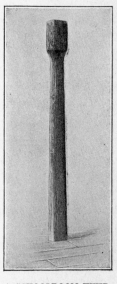

A SCHOOLROOM WHIP-
PING POST

The penal code brutal. Moreover, as noted in Chapter IV, the penal code of the time was not a model for gentleness. Branding, public whippings, the pillory, the stocks, were common penalties, and capital punishment could be inflicted for scores of crimes. Thomas Sargent, a Harvard student, convicted in 1674 of speaking blasphemous words, was publicly beaten in the library before all the scholars; but the solemn punishment was preceded and followed by prayer by the president, under whose supervision it was inflicted. He had learned to be gentle perhaps from the misfortune of the first head of Harvard, Nathaniel Eaton, who was dismissed for cruelly whipping students, "giving them twenty to thirty stripes at a time," and for beating his assistant in an inhuman manner. Ardent and narrow religionists believed that those who held heretical opinions should suffer death. If the proposed laws of that hard-headed defender of orthodoxy, John Cotton, had been adopted in 1641, any unpleasant critics of magistrates

A WHIPPING POST OUTSIDE A SCHOOLHOUSE IN SALEM, MASSACHUSETTS, ABOUT 1768

From a water color by Dr. Orne in the collection of the Essex Institute

would have settled with the hangman. Capital punishment by barbarous methods was often inflicted. Teachers were often slaves, and were advertised, bought, and sold as other commodities. Slaves could be beaten lawfully by their masters, and were not teachers the masters of the children and privileged to beat them at will?

The rights of childhood not yet established. The rights of childhood could not be held in high regard in a community which forbade joyousness, prohibited whistling on the Sabbath, and where all æsthetic pleasures were considered reprehensible. Even singing was so frowned upon in New England that only a few tunes were in general use in the seventeenth century. The laugh of the child was not allowed in the land. It should be kept in mind, however, that managing a school in those days was a difficult task which demanded much muscle. Timid masters were often turned out by the big and brawny boys who afflicted the educational life of almost every community. And when two or three had been turned out in succession the school came to be known as hard. Cases of insubordination of pupils or of teachers who were unable to get and keep the mastery were very common. Scores of schools in Massachusetts were broken up by such causes as late as 1837, and there is no reason to believe that discipline was a more difficult problem in one section of the country than in another.

The brief description which this chapter contains of early educational practices in this country shows, as was pointed out in Chapter IV, that conditions in the American colonies were generally not favorable to the development of the finer elements of civilized life among the masses. The belief that education should be controlled by the Church continued as a part of the English heritage. The religious motives for schools continued to dominate, localism remained strong, and the ideals of the leaders of the period were strongly aristocratic. The beginnings of a democratic school system are not easy to find in any educational theory or practice of the colonial period. Slight promise of such a system was made here and there, however, during the Revolution and after it; but the promise of that period was largely unfulfilled, as the following chapter indicates.

REFERENCES AND READINGS

ADAMS, JAMES TRUSLOW. The Founding of New England. Boston, 1921.

> Chapter XV deals in part with the impoverishment of intellectual life, and "The New England conscience with its pathological questionings and elaborate systems of taboos."

BEARD, CHARLES A., and MARY R. The Rise of American Civilization, Vol. I, chap. iv, especially pages 145–188.

> Deals with the intellectual interests of the colonies.

BROWN, E. E. The Making of our Middle Schools. New York, 1903.

> Chapters III–VII, inclusive, deal with topics discussed in this chapter.

BROWN, S. W. The Secularization of American Education. New York, 1912.

> The early chapters deal with the religious purposes of education and the instruction of the underprivileged.

BRUCE, P. A. Institutional History of Virginia in the Seventeenth Century. New York, 1910.

> Vol. I, Part II, is excellent supplementary material for this chapter.

CRITTENDEN, CHARLES C. North Carolina Newspapers before 1790, The James Sprunt Historical Studies (University of North Carolina), Vol. XX, No. 1. Chapel Hill, 1928.

> A very careful study of the subject.

DEXTER, E. G. A History of Education in the United States. New York, 1904.

> Chapter XV considers, among other subjects of higher and special education, the nine colonial colleges. (Separate histories of the more important institutions of higher learning, however, are available. The American College and University Series, edited by G. P. Krapp, should be consulted. A first-rate history of higher education in the United States has not yet been written.)

DRAPER, ANDREW S. "Public School Pioneering in New York and Massachusetts," *Educational Review* (April, 1892), Vol. III, pp. 313 ff.; (October, 1892), Vol. IV, pp. 241 ff.; (April, 1893), Vol. V, pp. 345 ff.

> An interesting controversy conducted with considerable ability by Draper with George H. Martin over questions of the beginnings of public educational practices in New York and Massachusetts. (See the articles by Martin referred to below.)

FORD, PAUL L. The New England Primer. New York, 1899.

> A reprint of the famous book, with an interesting historical introduction.

HEATWOLE, C. J. A History of Education in Virginia. New York, 1916.

> The early chapters deal with the colonial period.

JACKSON, G. L. The Development of School Support in Colonial Massachusetts. New York, 1909.

> Describes the various methods used for school support.

JERNEGAN, M. W. "Compulsory Education in the American Colonies," "The Educational Development of the Southern Colonies," and "Compulsory Education in the Southern Colonies," *School Review* (January, May, and June, 1919), Vol. XXVII, Nos. 1, 5, and 6.

> An excellent discussion of the apprenticeship practices, based on original sources.

JOHNSON, CLIFTON. Old-Time Schools and School-Books. New York, 1904.

> A chatty discussion of schools and their books and other practices based upon original material and dealing largely with conditions in Massachusetts.

KEMP, W. W. The Support of Schools in Colonial New York by the Society for the Propagation of the Gospel in Foreign Parts. New York, 1913.

> A thorough study of the educational work of this missionary society of the Anglican Church.

KILPATRICK, WILLIAM H. The Dutch Schools of New Netherlands and Colonial New York, *Bulletin No. 12*, United States Bureau of Education, Washington, 1912.

> A careful study of schools and school practices from original sources.

KNIGHT, EDGAR W. Public Education in the South, chaps. ii, iii. Boston, 1922.

> Theories and practices in the Southern colonies, the operation of the poor laws, and the apprenticeship system.

MADDOX, W. A. The Free School Idea in Virginia before the Civil War. New York, 1918.

> An excellent account of the subject. The first three chapters bear on the subject of this chapter. Contains a valuable bibliography.

MARTIN, GEORGE H. The Evolution of the Massachusetts Public School System. New York, 1894.

> A very good account of public education in Massachusetts. The first three chapters supplement the material of this chapter.

MARTIN, GEORGE H. "Public School Pioneering," *Educational Review* (June, 1892), Vol. IV, pp. 34 ff; (March, 1893), Vol. V, pp. 232 ff.

> An answer to the articles by Draper, referred to above. The Draper-Martin controversy contains valuable historical information. *The Educational Review*, Vol. V, pp. 406–407, contains an editorial on the merits of the controversy.

MONROE, PAUL, and KILPATRICK, WILLIAM H. "Colonial Period in American Education," in "A Cyclopedia of Education" (Paul Monroe, editor), Vol. II.

> A general historical account, with reference to various topics, and a bibliography.

SEYBOLT, ROBERT F. Apprenticeship and Apprenticeship Education in Colonial New England and New York. New York, 1917.

> A very careful study and interpretation of the old records on the subject.

SEYBOLT, ROBERT F. The Evening School in Colonial America. The University of Illinois, 1925.

> An interesting account of evening schools based largely upon advertisements in newspapers.

SMALL, W. H. Early New England Schools. Boston, 1914.

> A description of various phases of early school life based on the early records, with their quaint phraseology and construction retained.

SUZZALLO, HENRY. The Rise of Local School Supervision in Massachusetts, 1635–1827. New York, 1906.

> Traces the evolution of the powers of the school committee in Massachusetts.

THOMAS, ISAIAH. History of Printing in America (Vols. V and VI of the *Transactions and Collections of the American Antiquarian Society*). Albany, 1874.

> Contains valuable information on printing, printers, newspapers, and magazines.

THORPE, F. N. Benjamin Franklin and the University of Pennsylvania. Washington, 1892.

> A good account of Franklin's educational interests.

UPDEGRAFF, HARLAN. The Rise of the Moving School in Massachusetts.
New York, 1907.

> A first-rate account of colonial education in Massachusetts.

WEEDEN, W. B. Economic and Social History of New England, 1620–
1789. Boston, 1891.

> Pages 861 and following of Volume II bear upon this chapter, but
> the table of contents or the index of the work should be consulted.

WEEKS, STEPHEN B. The Press of North Carolina in the Eighteenth
Century. Brooklyn, 1891.

> An account of the printing presses, newspapers, and books pub-
> lished in North Carolina during that period.

WELLS, GUY F. Parish Education in Colonial Virginia. New York, 1923.

> Discusses the nature of the educational arrangements used by the
> Virginia parishes.

QUESTIONS FOR STUDY AND DISCUSSION

1. Consider any practices or problems of education today which
had their origin in colonial or earlier conditions.

2. Make a list of the evidences of interest in educational and
cultural matters in the colonies.

3. Account for the fact that the colonial assemblies, or legislatures, gave little or no attention to education.

4. Compare or contrast the Latin grammar school of the
colonial period with a modern public high school.

5. Compare or contrast education in the colonial times and now
in (1) aim, (2) curriculum, (3) methods of teaching, (4) financial
support, (5) management and control, and (6) preparation, certification, and salaries of teachers.

6. Examine the early legislation and records on apprenticeship
in your state for (1) purpose, (2) the plan of operation, and (3) the
extent of the apprenticeship practices.

7. Examine the court records of your county for any peculiar
examples of the apprenticeship system.

8. Consider the organized public agencies now in operation in
your state to do the work which was left in colonial times to the
poor-law and apprenticeship practices.

9. Analyze the Massachusetts law of 1647 and criticize the interpretation given on pages 105–107.

10. Trace the evolution of the district-school system from a simple and local neighborhood convenience of the early days to the stubborn institution which it later became and has remained.

11. Compare or contrast any one of the early colonial colleges with the same institution today.

12. Why was the education of women so long neglected in this country?

13. Make a study of (1) libraries, (2) newspapers, and (3) book-sellers in any one of the colonies.

14. Explain the severity of discipline in the early schools.

CHAPTER VI

THE PROMISE OF A NEW PERIOD

Outline of the chapter. 1. During the early national period the exacting conditions of frontier life served to lower intellectual and educational standards among the people.

2. Schools were the dreams of theorists. Interest in education as an activity of the state was not wide. The Federal Constitution was silent on the subject, and state-constitutional provisions for schools were vague.

3. Evidence of educational interest was reflected in the views of national leaders and in the Northwest Ordinances.

4. Discussions of the function of education increased after the Revolution, and plans for school systems were proposed under the influence of the American Philosophical Society. The plans by Benjamin Rush and Robert Coram are significant in American educational history, but these advanced views of public education were not caught by the governing authorities of the period.

5. The theory of education as an activity of the state probably received its strongest support in the work of Thomas Jefferson, but even his own commonwealth failed to respond to his appeal for schools.

6. There was promise in the new and strange social forces of the period; but decades were to pass and many obstacles had to be removed before the democratic theory of education could be practically and fully applied in the American states.

During the early years of the national period the people of the United States lived for the most part under rural conditions. For most of them isolation reigned, and shut off interests upon which community coöperation was essential. There were few towns and cities, and most of these were in the Northern states, Philadelphia leading in size with a population of 42,000 in 1790. New York had 32,000, Boston 18,000, and Baltimore 13,000. Richmond, the largest center in Virginia (which was the largest state of all, with a population of 747,000), had less than 4000 people.

North Carolina had not a town of 2000 people. Charleston had a population of 15,000. Savannah was still a tiny place. Next to Virginia came Pennsylvania with 434,000 people, North Carolina with 393,000, Massachusetts with 378,000, and New York with 340,000. In all the states the population numbered about 3,929,000, one fifth of whom were negroes and most of whom lived in the open country. The Potomac divided the total population into halves. Increase in population was largely by birth, for immigration had been cut off by the war. During these years the estimated annual increase by immigration was about 4000, and it did not become much larger until after the War of 1812.

Conditions unfavorable for education. Life in the United States in the last decades of the eighteenth century was full of struggles, dangers, and deprivations. Men of means had comfortable houses, but the poorer people lived in rude structures. The means of transportation and of communication were meager. Traveling was by large wagons called stagecoaches, which could do only from four to five miles an hour over the best roads, and roads were usually not good. Travelers depended for lodging and meals upon inns and taverns which were not always attractive. Religion, which had monopolized colonial thought, was slowly giving way to political discussions. But education was making little progress. The energies of the people, almost exhausted by war, were absorbed in more immediately pressing needs. Material recuperation seemed most urgent to the average American of the early national period, and material prosperity was not quick to manifest itself. Life was not full of hope and confidence. Demoralizing effects followed the war, which had left the states greatly impoverished and depleted and burdened with a debt of $75,000,000. Commercial life was deadened, and agriculture was still primitive and unpromising. There were internal disputes and conflicts which developed a "critical period." In the minds of many people there were grave doubts about the wisdom of independence and about the permanency of the new nation whose constitution, said John Quincy Adams, had been "extorted from the grinding necessities of a reluctant people." The exacting conditions of pioneer and frontier life served to lower intellectual and educational standards among the people rather than to raise them. There was but little time, opportunity, or means for schools, and education was forced into a temporary decline.

The dream of the theorist. Under such conditions schools could not flourish. Popular education was still the dream of the theorist and the reformer rather than the conviction of the great masses of the people or even of governing authorities. The need for education was not widely felt, and illiteracy was no reproach. Moreover, if there must be schools, said many thoughtful people, they should be established and maintained by the churches and by philanthropic individuals and societies, as had been the custom in colonial days. Education was still looked upon as a luxury for those who could afford it or as a charity for the poor. Free education for all at public expense was considered a visionary and impracticable undertaking. Many changes had to be made in the life of this country before a democratic school system could be established. Some of those changes were made during or shortly after the Revolutionary period, and others followed during the period which closed with the Civil War.

Before the Revolutionary War the colonists had in large part depended upon England for their laws and literature, their books and teachers, and their leaders in government and the church. After the struggle the people were thrown upon their own resources and were forced to depend on the new nation for leadership and ideals. Moreover, other influences were to appear. Democracy was to receive an impetus that had been impossible in colonial days. Those of high birth and official station, those who had enjoyed special privilege and had taught the common people reverence for rank and subordination to social superiors, were now slowly to lose some of their influence to the growing power of the "filthy democrats." Inequalities were to decrease or disappear. The development of the immense material resources of the country was to be begun, and the foundation of greater social progress was to be made. The rich lands were to be taken up, roads and other means of transportation and communication were to be built, and commerce was to be established. These things preceded, as they do now, the spiritual and educational prosperity of the people. Meantime self-government, now to be given a trial, was also to become educative in character. New demands for schools, which came slowly to be viewed as necessary, were to arise out of new problems of public welfare.

Constitutional provisions vague. Interest in schools as a public necessity was not widespread. The Federal Constitution did not declare its purpose to promote either religion or education, but "to form a more perfect union, establish justice, insure domestic tranquillity, provide for the common defense, promote the general welfare, and secure the blessings of liberty to ourselves and our posterity," — purposes which dealt with secular affairs, matters of this rather than of another world. Congress could not establish a state religion or the requirement of a religious test as a qualification for holding a Federal office. Religious qualifications for voting and for holding office were numerous, however, in state constitutions formed during this period. But in providing for religious freedom the Federal Constitution helped to lay the foundation for the later building of nonsectarian, free, publicly supported, and publicly controlled schools. A new state motive, to be substituted for the old religious motive for schools, involved state support and control of schools; the aim was education for all, to the end that liberty and political equality might be preserved. Nor did the Constitution give attention to schools, but left educational matters to the states, by implication in the Tenth Amendment. Those which made constitutional provision for schools before 1800 were Pennsylvania and North Carolina in 1776, Georgia and Vermont in 1777, Massachusetts in 1780, New Hampshire in 1784, Vermont again in 1787, Pennsylvania again in 1790, Delaware in 1792, and Georgia again in 1798.

In none of these constitutions, however, were specific instructions given to the legislature concerning the establishment of schools. The vagueness of the language has been offered as one cause of the long delay by some of the states in providing for schools. The mandates seemed not to be specific. "The legislature shall, as soon as conveniently may be, provide by law . . . for establishing schools," said the constitution of Delaware. The constitution of Vermont said:

A school or schools shall be established in every town by the legislature, for the convenient instruction of youth, with such salaries to the masters, paid by each town . . . to enable them to instruct youth at low prices. One grammar school in each county, and one university in this State ought to be established by direction of the General Assembly.

The constitution of Pennsylvania said that "a school or schools shall be established in every county by the legislature, for the convenient instruction of youth, with such salaries to the masters, paid by the public, as may enable them to instruct youth at low prices; and all useful learning shall be duly encouraged and promoted in one or more universities." North Carolina copied this provision in its first constitution and continued it unchanged in the constitution of 1835. In 1790 Pennsylvania made the following constitutional provision, which was continued in its constitution of 1838: "The legislature shall, as soon as conveniently may be, provide, by law, for the establishment of schools throughout the State in such manner that the poor may be taught gratis." Georgia in its first constitution said that "schools shall be erected in each county, and supported at the general expense of the State, as the legislature shall hereafter point out," and in its constitution of 1798 provided that "the arts and sciences shall be promoted in one or more seminaries of learning."

New Hampshire in its constitution of 1784 and again in 1792 held that "knowledge and learning generally diffused through a community being essential to the preservation of a free government, spreading the opportunities and advantages of education through the various parts of the country being highly conducive to promote this end, it shall be the duty of the legislature and magistrates, in all future periods of this government, to cherish the interest of literature and the sciences, and all seminaries and public schools." The constitution of Massachusetts of 1780 was likewise general in its provision for schools. After dwelling at length upon the activities of "our wise and pious ancestors," it declared that "wisdom and knowledge, as well as virtue, diffused generally among the body of the people, being necessary for the preservation of their rights and liberties ... it shall be the duty of the legislature and magistrates, in all future periods of this commonwealth, to cherish the interest of literature and the sciences."

High-sounding statements of leaders. Evidence of educational interest was somewhat reflected in the views of many leaders of the time. Washington, in his first message to Congress, declared "that there is nothing which can better deserve your patronage than the promotion of science and literature. Knowledge is in every country the surest basis of public happiness." The "enlightened confidence of the people" was indispensable. Men must be taught to know and to value their rights and "to discern and provide

against invasions of them." And in his Farewell Address
he urged the promotion of "institutions for the general
diffusion of knowledge" and the enlightenment of public
opinion. Jefferson had declared earlier in the preamble to
his bill for public schools in Virginia, that the most effectual
means of preventing the perversion of power into tyranny
was through the illumination "of the minds of the people
at large." That people will be happiest "whose laws are
best and best administered," and these would be "wisely
formed and honestly administered in proportion as those
who form and administer them are wise and honest." He
believed that public welfare depended upon the education
of the people without regard to "wealth, birth, or other
accidental condition or circumstance."

General Francis Marion, in a statement on the need for
popular education in South Carolina, said:

God preserve our Legislature from penny wit and pound fool-
ishness. What! Keep a nation in ignorance rather than vote a
little of their own money for education! . . . What signifies this
government, divine as it is, if it be not known and prized as it
deserves? This is best done by free schools. Men will always
fight for their government according to their sense of its value.
To value it aright they must understand it. This they cannot do
without education.

But the "Swamp Fox" could not conclude without reference
to the element of charity, which so long persisted in public
education in the United States: "And, as a large portion of
the children are poor, and can never attain that inestimable
blessing without the aid of government, it is plainly the
duty of government to bestow it freely upon them."

John Jay, the first Chief Justice of the Supreme Court of
the United States, declared "knowledge to be the soul of a
Republic." Through education the weak and the wicked
could be diminished in number, "and nothing should be

left undone to afford all ranks of people the means of obtaining a proper degree of it at a cheap and easy rate." James Madison believed that "popular government without popular information or the means of acquiring it" is the first step toward "a farce or a tragedy, or perhaps both." A people who intend to be "their own governors must arm themselves with the power which knowledge gives." John Adams declared that the instruction of the people for the proper practice of their moral duties as "men, citizens, and Christians, and of their political and civil duties as members of society and freemen" was a public responsibility which should extend to all, "of every rank and class of people, down to the lowest and the poorest." Schools for the education of all should be maintained at public expense. Before he finished his panegyric of public education he added, "Laws for the liberal education of youth, especially of the lower classes of people, are so extremely wise and useful that . . . no expense for this purpose would be thought extravagant."

The views of others. In other quarters also voices were raised in behalf of education. Tom Paine, who described the Revolutionary days as "the times that try men's souls," declared in his "Rights of Man" that in a properly governed nation none should be permitted to go uninstructed. Over in England Adam Smith, in his "Wealth of Nations" (which appeared in the year that America declared independence), held that it was a matter of State interest that the ranks of the people be instructed, to make them useful to society and to render them "less apt to be misled into any wanton or unnecessary opposition to the measures of government." He believed that an instructed and intelligent people are always more decent and orderly than those who are ignorant and stupid, and that the State had the right to provide education and make it compulsory.

Thomas Robert Malthus, English political economist, in "An Essay on the Principle of Population," argued that "an instructed and well-informed people would be less likely to be led away by inflammatory writings" and much more able than an ignorant people "to detect the false declamation of interested and ambitious demagogues." He believed that the safety of society lay in education diffused among the people. Talleyrand, the Frenchman, to meet the provision of the constitution requiring the creation of a system of public instruction common to all citizens and free "in respect to those subjects of instruction that are indispensable to all men," was proposing to his government a school plan which recognized the new attitude toward education and accepted the theory that education is a function of the State and not of the Church. Condorcet, another Frenchman, who believed in the perfectibility of the human race, proposed to his government a school plan of great significance in support of the State theory of education. He maintained that the State should offer to all its people the "means of providing for their wants, of insuring their welfare, of knowing and exercising their rights, of knowing and fulfilling their duties," and of developing in everyone "to the fullest extent the talents which he has received from nature." In these statements appeared a new theory of education and a new motive for schools arising out of the theory of government by the people. Gradually there was to grow and develop the doctrine that education is a responsibility of the State and that schools are essential in a democratic government whose direction and operation depend upon the enlightenment of the people.

The Constitution of the United States silent on the subject. But the Constitution of the United States contained no mention of education; the subject was not debated, nor was it even seriously considered by the convention. The reasons are obvious. Schools were everywhere looked upon not as activities of the State but as functions of the Church, the family, or the individual. And the men who framed the Constitution were products of the old aristocratic doctrine of education, of the theory that schools were intended for the leaders and for those who could afford the privilege of education. Moreover, weightier questions than those of schools engrossed the attention of the makers of the Constitution.

The Northwest Ordinances. But before the adoption of that document the Continental Congress had passed the Ordinance of 1785, which called for a survey of that territory lying between the Ohio and Mississippi rivers which had been surrendered to Congress by the states which had conflicting claims to it. In providing that the sixteenth lot of each township was to be reserved for the maintenance of schools, this ordinance laid the basis of land endowments which the new states, formed out of territory belonging to the Federal government, have received for education. In 1786 the Ohio Company, whose principal interest was in real estate, was organized in Boston by a group of New Englanders. Through spokesmen led by Manasseh Cutler, the company's shrewd representative, whose affable and easy manners gave him ready access to Congress, the Ohio Company bought a huge tract of the Northwest Territory. But the transaction was not easily made. The promoters met congressional indifference until they secretly agreed that influential members of Congress should share in the profits. In his personal journal Cutler wrote: "We obtained the grant of near five millions of acres, . . . one million and a half for the Ohio Company and the remainder for a private speculation, in which many of the principal characters of America are concerned," and he adds that without agreeing to the opportunity for speculation, "similar terms and advantages could not have been obtained for the Ohio Company."

Plan of administration. In the plan of administration provided by Congress in the Ordinance of 1787 for the gov-

ernment of the territory northwest of the Ohio, additional
encouragement was given to the establishment of schools
and the promotion of education. "Religion, morality, and
knowledge being necessary to good government and the
happiness of mankind," said one section of the ordinance,
"schools and the means of education shall be forever encouraged" in those states to be formed out of this domain.
It was probably believed that this declaration would encourage settlement in the Northwest.

Ohio, in 1803, was the first state admitted to the Union
from this territory. At that time Congress gave to the new
state the sixteenth section of every township for the maintenance of schools within the township, on condition that
the national lands lying within Ohio be exempted from taxation. This offer was continued in the case of other states
formed from the Northwest Territory, and in every other
state later admitted, except Texas, which owned its land, and
Maine and West Virginia, which were formed from older
states. Since 1850, when California was admitted, two sections of each township have been given for schools, except
in the cases of Utah, Arizona, and New Mexico, which were
allowed four sections because of the low value of the lands.

This early action of Congress may or may not have implied the purpose of the Federal government to participate
in and aid education in the states. It may or may not support the arguments of the advocates of the measures before
Congress in recent years which have had as their aims the
creation of an educational secretaryship in the President's
cabinet and definite aid by the national government to
general education in the various states. The educational
provision of the Northwest Ordinance may be viewed as an
act of Federal benevolence or as Federal self-interest or as
evidence of the gratitude of the national government to the
sturdy pioneers who braved hardships in settling the frontier region. It may or may not be looked upon as a trick

of adroit real-estate dealers. Whatever the motive, however, it seems clear that this provision of the ordinance stimulated sentiment for schools and may have suggested to the older states the idea of permanent public funds for school purposes at a time when taxation for schools was not yet looked upon as a legitimate public obligation.

Advanced theories and plans. Discussions of the function of education greatly increased in this country as soon as the success of the movement for independence from England seemed assured. Educational theories as important parts of political theories formed another phase of the movement of liberalism and the revolt against tyranny and improperly constituted authority. Near the middle of the century Benjamin Franklin had published a plan for education from which an academy and later a college developed in Philadelphia. The American Philosophical Society, another result of Franklin's intellectual interests, began to concern itself with the peculiar problems which had arisen as a result of the Revolution. In the view of many members of this organization education formed one of the most important of those problems, and in an effort to help in the solution of it the society offered a prize "for the best system of liberal education and literary instruction, adapted to the genius of the government of the United States; comprehending also a plan for instituting and conducting public schools in this country, on principles of the most extensive utility."

Plans were offered by prominent men of the time as well as by others who are less well known to history. The best essays were submitted by Samuel Knox, a physician, minister, and school-teacher, head of an academy in Maryland, and Samuel H. Smith of Philadelphia. Other plans were prepared and published by Benjamin Rush, Robert Coram, James Sullivan, Nathaniel Chipman, Du Pont de Nemours, Lafitte du Courteil, and Noah Webster. Some of these discussions contained descriptions of the extreme backwardness of education of the Revolutionary and post-Revolutionary periods; but their chief value in the history of American education appears in the advanced ideals and ideas and in the comprehensive plans which they suggested for education — universal and free, supported and controlled by the public, and open alike to girls and boys. The purpose and the content of education were also discussed with amazing insight at a time when neither received great attention.

Benjamin Rush, a colleague of Franklin, insisted that the youth of America have opportunity to study those things which will "increase the conveniences of life, lessen human misery, improve our country, promote population, exalt the human understanding, and establish domestic and political happiness." He expressed advanced views also on the education of women, and advocated provisions for the proper training of teachers and for liberal national support of schools. These theorists looked upon education as a function of the State, to be secured by government to every class of citizen and to every child in the State. "Education should not be left to the caprice or negligence of parents, to chance, or confined to the children of wealthy parents," declared Robert Coram. "It is a shame, a scandal to civilized society, that part only of the citizens should be sent to colleges and universities, to learn to cheat the rest of their liberties." The country districts should have as good schools as the towns. "If education is necessary for one man," he said, "my religion tells me that it is equally necessary for another." In his opinion equality of educational opportunity was a reasonable demand of democracy. But these fine views of education as a means of progress and for the service of all men were not caught by the governing authorities of the time. Owing in part to the deadliness of indifference, which has always acted upas-like upon new

suggestions for social reform, the proposals of these thinkers were to remain only the visions and theories which all
except a few people considered them to be at the time.

The work of Jefferson. The theory of education as a
function of the government, which was slow to appear and
develop in this country, probably received its strongest
support in the reform program which Thomas Jefferson
launched and in a meas-
ure achieved in Virginia
during and immediately
after the Revolutionary
period. Although at first
a movement of local char-
acter, certain phases of
Jefferson's work had wide
influence. Among the most
effective reforms which he
worked were the divorce
of the Church and the
State and the establish-
ment of the rights of
conscience, the abolition
of entail and of primo-
geniture, the revision of
the laws, and the movement for public schools.

THOMAS JEFFERSON

An early advocate of education as a
function of the State

The Established Church was weakened in Virginia by a
series of legislative enactments dealing with the religious
question. These enactments began with the bill of rights,
which contained a broad declaration of religious liberty and
pronounced a decree of absolute divorce between the Church
and the State. Within a few years the last vestige of the
Established Church in Virginia was destroyed, persecution
for religious causes ceased, and religious qualifications for
civil office were abandoned. Entail and primogeniture were
abolished, and the accumulation and perpetuation of enor-

mous wealth in the hands of a few families who had monopolized the honors of Virginia were prevented. The whole system of ancient laws and usages designed to prevent a distribution of wealth was soon to crash. With the abolition of primogeniture and the unequal distribution of inheritances, equal distribution of property among heirs was made possible, and feudalistic and dangerous tendencies were removed. A complete revision, or codification, was made of the Virginia laws, which included British usages and colonial acts from 1619 and were "a chaos of obsolete and antiquated enactments, good for lawyers, bad for clients."

Jefferson's faith in the people made him a strong supporter of public schools. He believed that the people were capable of self-government, that they meant well, and that they would act well whenever they understood. He was eager to enable them to understand through education and training, and accordingly he introduced a school bill into the legislature of Virginia.

Jefferson's school plan. This bill was one of the most definite and striking evidences of educational interest during the Revolutionary and early national periods. It was introduced two or three years after Jefferson had written the Declaration of Independence, and bore the title "A Bill for the More General Diffusion of Knowledge." Not only did it embody an advanced plan for schools for that state, but it was the first definite American proposal for a modern state school system and was prepared at a time when Jefferson saw his country shaken by one of the most important revolutions in history. He sought through this means to devise a plan to educate and prepare his countrymen for the opportunities of a new era which he believed to be dawning. In that plan he expressed the belief that, however heavy should be the sacrifices of the people to secure to their posterity the blessings of civil freedom, failure would end their efforts unless suitable provision should be made for the proper education of their children. "If a nation expects to be ignorant and free in a state of civilization," he said later, "it expects what never was and never will be." He believed that "ignorance and bigotry, like other insanities, are incapable of self-government," and that "no nation is permitted to live in ignorance with impunity." Jefferson would make Virginia great in science. "Preach, my dear sir," he wrote from France to a former teacher in Virginia, "a crusade against ignorance; establish and improve the law for educating the common people."

Provisions of the plan. The plan proposed was based on Jefferson's political theory of local self-government. It provided for a division of the counties into "hundreds," of such convenient size that all the children within each hundred could daily attend the school to be established in it. The voters of each division were to select the site for the schoolhouse, which was to be built and kept in repair by the three county aldermen, who were to be chosen by the qualified voters of the county. At each school all the free children, boys and girls, resident within the respective hundred were to receive free tuition for the term of three years "and as much longer, at their private expense, as their parents, guardians, or friends shall think proper." The subjects of reading, writing, and arithmetic were to be taught from books which would at the same time acquaint the children with Greek, Roman, English, and American history. A superintendent "eminent for his learning, integrity, and fidelity to the commonwealth" was to be appointed annually by the county aldermen to superintend every ten of these schools. His duties were to appoint teachers, to examine the pupils, and to visit and have general control over the schools. The salary of the teacher and all other expenses connected with each school were to be provided by the hundred in such manner as other county expenses were then by law directed to be provided.

In order to provide grammar or high schools convenient to the youth of every part of the state, the various counties were to be districted, two or more counties forming one district. In each district a high school was to be established and equipped with one hundred acres of land, a brick or stone house with necessary offices, "a room for the school, a hall to dine in, four rooms for a master and usher, and ten or twelve lodging rooms for the scholars." The expense of establishing and equipping these schools was also to be paid out of the public treasury. Latin and Greek, English grammar, geography, and the "higher parts of numerical arithmetic" were to constitute the curriculum. A visitor from each county composing the district was to be appointed by the overseers and to have powers over the grammar schools similar to the powers of the overseers over the primary schools.

Every overseer or superintendent of the elementary schools was to select from among the boys who had spent two years at one of the schools under his direction "one of the best and most promising in genius and disposition . . . without favor or affection," who was to be educated and boarded at the grammar school of his district for one, two, or more years, according to his "genius and disposition." Here Jefferson, as had Plato two thousand years earlier, anticipated the modern doctrine of individual differences. Those children whose parents were too poor to give them further education were to have preference. And here Jefferson voiced the prevalent view of the period and recognized the element of charity which has so long afflicted public education in the United States. The most promising ones of those who were advanced through the grammar schools were to be "educated, boarded, and clothed" three years at public expense at the College of William and Mary, which was also to be improved and enlarged. The strong features of this plan as well as its weaknesses are obvious to the student of education today; but, viewed in the large, the proposal was advanced for the eighteenth century and shows the influence of the educational ideas of certain French revolutionists whom Jefferson greatly admired.

No favorable action. The legislature received the plan with some interest, but never acted on it. The confusion of the times and the heavy expense which the proposed system would have involved led to its defeat. Moreover, the matter of providing the schools which Jefferson here proposed was in the hands of the landed gentry, who were already provided with private schools and did not keenly feel the need of schools for others; therefore they were not likely to tax themselves for schools which they would not patronize. The absence of a strong middle class to support it helped also to bring failure to the plan.

To none of the many activities in which he engaged did Jefferson attach greater importance than to education. No man of the period had greater enthusiasm for education, and none more faith in its power for promoting the public weal. In his advocacy of public schools in a period when education of all forms and degrees was viewed solely as the concern of the Church and of private effort, he urged a bold and big extension of State activity. He would have a system of general instruction put within reach of "every description of our citizen, from the richest to the poorest." Education was one of the first of all public matters in which he took interest and it was also one of the last. At a time when they were without the means of instruction Jefferson voiced a faith in the masses of the people, whom he would free from ignorance, indigence, and oppression. To his program for education his civic oath gives meaning: "I have sworn upon the altar of God eternal hostility against every form of tyranny over the mind of man." His own commonwealth failed to respond fully to his appeal for schools before 1860, but in his last years he did realize in the University of Virginia a part of his noble educational ideal. Not all American communities have yet gained Jefferson's full perspective for public education.

The significance of similar reforms elsewhere. Reforms similar to those of Jefferson in Virginia were being worked in other states also. Within a decade entails had been abolished in all the states except two (in which the practice of entails was not extensive), and within fifteen years every state had abolished the rule of primogeniture and all except four had placed girls upon an equal footing with boys in the division of inherited lands. The movement for the separation of the Church and the State and for religious freedom also gained strength. At the outbreak of the Revolution nine of the colonies had established churches, which enjoyed a religious monopoly supported by public taxation. Attacks were at once made upon these ecclesiastical establishments. Some surrendered slowly and stubbornly, but finally the disestablishment was completed in all the states; New Hampshire in 1817, Connecticut in 1818, and Massachusetts in 1833 were the last to submit to separation. Furthermore, elsewhere as well as in Virginia, the "light of reason" was turned upon the bloody and brutal legal practices which, borrowed from England, had given the colonies codes of cruelty and savagery. For twenty toilsome years Jefferson worked to soften the laws of Virginia, and similar reforms were made in the other states. However, during the Revolutionary period only slight changes were made in the qualifications for voting. The requirement of the ownership of property, which had dominated colonial theory and practice, prevailed in many states far into the national period, and survivals of it may even now be found in some of them. The absence of full manhood suffrage served to retard the growth of public education; but freedom of speech and freedom of the press were phases of the general movement of liberalism which served to place a new emphasis upon education.

The unfulfilled promise of the period. Viewed in the large, a more humane era was opening. There was promise in the new and strange social forces at work in the early national period. But for many years the noble doctrines of the Revolutionary movement were to remain theories only. Decades were to pass before the democratic theory of education was to be fully and practically applied in any American state. Many obstacles were still in the way of schools for all by public support and control. A real educational consciousness could not develop rapidly among a people sparsely settled and lacking in means of communication. The value of the principle of collective action, which has been so helpful in the development of the American school system, could not be easily learned under such conditions. Moreover, class distinctions were still strongly marked, and the pauper and parochial views of education retarded the growth of interest in public schools. The ancient doctrine that the education of the masses would be dangerous to society was still generally held in high esteem by the classes. And the poor believed that public education would stamp them as paupers. Opposition appeared also on the part of sectarian interests, which feared that their own religious schools would be replaced. Many thoughtful people viewed education by the state as an invasion of the parental and family function. But one of the most stubborn of all these difficulties was the chattel bond of their black brothers, whose slavery wore the sanction of the centuries and even of the Christian Church. A fully democratic school system could not be established in any American state while human slavery was lawful in any other.

Legislative gestures. Under the conditions of the time the principles of public education were slow to appear and slower to receive popular approval in the United States during the first half-century of national life. The idea of universal and free education for all had to be developed

gradually. Some of the states, through legislative enactments, made gestures for schools, but as the foundations of
practical public-school plans these were little more effective,
if any more, than the pious and patriotic but empty in-
junctions of the state constitutions on the necessity of pre-
serving liberty and political equality by diffusing knowledge
and learning among the people.

In most of these states partial programs of public education
were sketched; but in almost every case they were on paper
only, and in practice turned out to be only the merest frag-
ments of a democratic system. Taxation for school support
was generally local, optional, and permissive, and the rate
bill (a charge levied upon the parents according to the number of children they had in school) flourished generally until
the middle of the nineteenth century or even later. Rarely
did local schools receive state aid during the early national
period. Control of education was likewise local until far
into the century. State control or supervision was imperfectly developed and was always bitterly opposed by local
communities, which, under the movement for independence,
had quickly learned to love and respect the democratic doctrine of local self-government. When the localities finally
yielded their rights of control to the authority of the state,
they did so under the whip hand of state support, that
wonder-working power in modern American public-school
systems. Rarely also were the schools really free in any of
the states until far into the nineteenth century. The pauper-
school view of education, directly inherited from England
during the colonial period, prevailed far beyond the period
which chanted the doctrine that "all men are created equal,
and endowed by their Creator with certain unalienable
rights."

In education this doctrine did not apply fully to the
children of men in any of the states — not in Virginia, or
Pennsylvania, or New York, or even in New England. So

advanced an advocate of public education as Henry Barnard believed that part of the expense of the child's schooling should be borne by the parent, as he declared before the American Institute of Instruction at Springfield, Massachusetts, less than a decade before the close of the Civil War. "Some able men among us," declared a member of the Connecticut State Board of Education in 1867, "say the state has no right to educate any but paupers. . . . They would have 'pauper school' written over the entrance to the public school." The degrading practice of the rate bill kept "hundreds and thousands of children out of school" in Connecticut as late as 1868; and even when this charge was decreased or remitted in the case of poor parents, it nevertheless served to stamp such beneficiaries as paupers. Conditions were probably no better in any state. Free schools, by state support and state control and open to all the children without humiliation by the taint of charity, were not realities in the American states during the first half of the nineteenth century.

This chapter shows that interest in education as an activity of the state was not wide in this country during the early national period, although there were discussions of the subject, and some effort (for example, Jefferson's plan for Virginia) was made to establish public schools.

This plan probably gave to the theory of public education its strongest support during the early national period, but even Jefferson's own state failed to respond to his appeal for public schools. There was promise, however, in the new and strange social forces at work during these years, although many obstacles had to be removed before the principles of public education as a function of the state could be practically applied in the United States. Some of these forces and the obstacles which they helped to remove are discussed in the following chapter.

THE PROMISE OF A NEW PERIOD

REFERENCES AND READINGS

ADAMS, JAMES TRUSLOW. New England in the Republic, 1776–1850. Boston, 1926.

> Chapter III is a good account of the moral and intellectual effects of the Revolutionary War.

BEARD, CHARLES A., and MARY R. The Rise of American Civilization. 2 vols. New York, 1927.

> Chapter X (The Young Republic), Vol. I, is an excellent and breezy narrative of the economic and political movements which worked many changes in the cultural life of the United States.

CUBBERLEY E. P. Public Education in the United States. Boston, 1919.

> Chapter III, on early national and state attitudes, is suggestive.

CUBBERLEY, E. P., and ELLIOTT, E. C. State and County School Administration. New York, 1915.

> A source book which contains (chap. i) the state-constitutional provisions for schools before 1800 and gives also (chap. ii) information on the national land grants.

DU PONT DE NEMOURS. National Education in the United States of America (translated from the Second Edition of 1812 and with an introduction by B. G. Du Pont). University of Delaware Press, 1923.

> A plan for national education written in 1800 at the request of Jefferson, many of whose ideas are reflected in it.

FAŸ, BERNARD. The Revolutionary Spirit in France and America (translated by Ramon Guthrie). New York, 1927.

> A study of the moral and intellectual relations between France and the United States at the end of the eighteenth century. Contains considerable material on Jefferson and Franklin and voluminous notes and bibliographies.

FORD, PAUL LEICESTER (Collector and Editor). The Writings of Thomas Jefferson. 10 vols. New York, 1892–1899.

> Volume II, pp. 220–229, contains Jefferson's "Bill for the More General Diffusion of Knowledge," 1779.

HANSEN, ALLEN OSCAR. Liberalism and American Education in the Eighteenth Century. New York, 1926.

> Sets forth the influences of the liberal movement of the eighteenth century upon American life and institutions; a scholarly exposition of the sources. Contains the plans of Rush, Coram, Sullivan, Chipman, Knox, Smith, and Du Pont de Nemours.

HEATWOLE, CORNELIUS J. A History of Education in Virginia. New York, 1916.
> Chapter VII deals in part with Jefferson's work.

HENDERSON, JOHN C. Thomas Jefferson's Views on Public Education. New York, 1890.
> A fairly good account of Jefferson's interest in and labors for public education.

HINSDALE, B. A. "Documents Illustrative of American Educational History," Report of the United States Commissioner of Education, 1892–1893, Vol. II, pp. 1312 ff.
> Contains the provisions of the state constitutions concerning schools.

JEFFERSON, THOMAS. Notes on the State of Virginia. Philadelphia, 1788.
> Written in 1781, and corrected and enlarged the following year, "in answer to queries proposed to the Author, by a Foreigner of Distinction, then residing among us."

KNIGHT, EDGAR W. Public Education in the South. Boston, 1922.
> Chapter V describes briefly Jefferson's educational plan of 1779 and the early educational work of the older Southern states.

KNIGHT, EDGAR W. Public School Education in North Carolina. Boston, 1916.
> Chapter V discusses the early educational agitation in North Carolina.

MCMASTER, JOHN B. History of the People of the United States from the Revolution to the Civil War. 8 vols. New York, 1883–1913.
> An excellent life of the people which all students of American educational history should consult. Chapter I of Volume I bears on the subject of this chapter.

MADDOX, W. A. The Free School Idea in Virginia before 1860. New York, 1918.
> Chapter II is an excellent brief exposition of Jefferson's idea of the place of education in a democracy. Contains a useful bibliography.

REISNER, EDWARD H. Nationalism and Education since 1789. New York, 1922.
> Chapter XV deals, among other subjects, with the Federal government and education and the Northwest Ordinance and is good supplementary material for this chapter. Chapter II relates to the educational promise and achievement of the French Revolution, — Condorcet's report and Talleyrand's educational bill.

QUESTIONS FOR STUDY AND DISCUSSION

1. Point out any conditions of the early national period which are not mentioned in this chapter but which seem to you to have been obstacles in the way of public educational development.

2. With the constitution and laws, trace the growth of education as a concern of government in your state.

3. Show why the conception of education as a private or religious obligation persisted after the organization of the national government.

4. From a study of Jefferson's school plan of 1779 point out its strong points and its weak points.

5. Jefferson considered education a proper obligation and function of the government, but he believed in the principle of local control rather than control by the state. Explain.

6. Consider the validity of Jefferson's theory, that the intellectually superior students should be given special attention. How does his view on the subject suggest the doctrine of individual differences?

7. Compare the educational arguments of the political leaders during the early years of the national period with those advanced today for an extension of public educational effort.

8. Trace the changing conception of education as it appears in the messages of governors and in the expressions of private individuals and of the press.

9. Indicate the various conditions or factors which affected public education during the early years of the national government.

10. Why were the early constitutional provisions for schools so vague and indefinite?

11. Consider the first three words in the educational provision of the Northwest Ordinance of 1787 in the light of the fact that religious instruction is today not given in public schools.

12. Make a study of any educational leaders in your state before 1835 and note their positions on the subject of public-school support.

CHAPTER VII

NEW FORCES

Outline of the chapter. 1. Interest in education as a function of government was developed slowly by certain influences during the first half of the nineteenth century.

2. School societies, the infant-school movement, and the Lancasterian and other monitorial schools served to stimulate interest in the subject.

3. The secular Sunday school also helped to promote the idea of public schools. Sunday schools of the secular type were numerous.

4. The development of means of transportation and communication had social as well as economic effects. The movement for internal improvements helped to develop a social consciousness.

5. The growth of cities, the rise of the factory system, and the awakening of a class consciousness among the laboring people in industrial centers led to the consideration of new social problems and stimulated interest in education.

6. Some of the reforms which the labor movement advocated were achieved slowly and only after long agitation.

7. Other social as well as economic and political influences arose out of the frontier and the westward migration. The democratic movement, typified by the election of Jackson, was also helpful to the cause of schools. New conceptions of democracy slowly appeared.

8. The idea of education as a function of government was strengthened by the humanitarian movement in the first and second quarters of the nineteenth century.

Before a school system could develop and become democratic, even in theory, a consciousness of the need for education must be awakened among the people, and before it could be made democratic in practice the people must become willing to provide the means for supplying education. The opinions of the few who favored public education had to become the common sentiment of many people. Prejudice had to be overcome, religious jealousies and sectarian suspicions had to be allayed, the dead hands of tradition had to be lifted, and a new view of the function of government had to be gained by governing authorities and lawmaking bodies, by the privileged and the propertied, and by the underprivileged and the deprived. To establish a democratic and general system of schools was a task for wise statesmanship and for agencies of propaganda and publicity. The task was finally to be accomplished by these and many other forces and influences.

School societies. The practice of the philanthropic support of education, which was popular and widely used in the colonial period, continued far into the <u>nineteenth</u> century, when many societies and associations were formed primarily for the purpose of educating poor children. One of the most prominent of these was founded in New York

DeWITT CLINTON

(which did not establish a public-school system until 1842) and was known as "The Society for Establishing a Free School in the City of New York." The organization was supported by public-spirited people, among them DeWitt Clinton, who was one of its founders and for many years its president. Its chief purpose was to establish a free school "for the education of such poor children as do not belong to, or are not provided for, by any religious society."

Chartered in 1805 by the legislature of the state, this society undertook to provide educational opportunity "for all children who are the proper objects of a gratuitous education." In 1815 it received aid from the common-school fund of the state. Slightly more than a decade later it changed its name to "The Public School Society of New York" and was permitted by its new charter to accept tuition from those children who were able to pay. Immediately there was a decrease in attendance because many parents were "too poor and too proud to confess their poverty," and in 1832 the schools were again made entirely free to all. Meantime the society had had serious conflicts with religious and sectarian agencies. A decade later the legislature created the New York City Board of Education and laid the basis for a city system of public elementary schools. The society continued its work, however, until 1853, when it transferred its property to the city school board. By that time it had trained twelve hundred teachers, had built many schoolhouses, had provided schooling for more than six hundred thousand children, and had greatly increased public confidence in public education. Similar societies, though not so large or of such extensive educational service as this one in New York, were established and maintained in many cities, and served to stimulate interest in education at public expense and under public control.

The infant school. Another movement, whose roots ran into philanthropy, had influence in the early nineteenth century. This was the infant school, which appeared in New Lanark, Scotland, as early as 1816, when Robert Owen, the British socialist (known also for the later establishment of a communal colony at New Harmony on the Wabash River in Indiana) was moved by the unhappy condition of the very small children of the workers in a factory which he owned in part. The idea soon found its way to this country and led to the establishment of infant schools and of infant-school societies.

In 1818 Boston appropriated money to aid such schools for the purpose of preparing young children in the rudiments of learning for admission to the public schools of the city, which did not then admit children until they could read and write. This elementary training had previously been acquired by private instruction in the home or in the dame schools, but there were many parents who could not afford the cost of this minimum schooling. Therefore, the infant school, as a supplement to the public-school system, seemed to fill a real social need. Other cities in the East adopted the practice, and societies for its encouragement were established in New York in 1827 and in Philadelphia about the same time. In 1828 Providence, Rhode Island, established schools for children between the ages of four and eight. When the infant school was changed in name to "primary department" or "primary grade" and united with schools already regularly established, the lower level of the usual American public-school system was thus formed. The kindergarten was to appear at a much later period. Aside from this result in organization the infant school seems to have served to encourage public interest in the development of a common-school system.

The Lancasterian and the Bell monitorial schools. An early practice which was borrowed from England and which served to arouse interest in public education appeared in the monitorial school. Joseph Lancaster, a young English schoolmaster, needing additional teachers for his school and having no money to provide them, turned in the emergency to the use of monitors, a practice which Andrew Bell, another Englishman, had used a few years earlier in an orphan asylum in India, and which he had described in a published account called "An Experiment in Education" (1797). Bell's plan and Lancaster's were closely similar, though the latter seems to have been arrived at independently, and the idea of monitorial instruction was old when these two men made practical use of it.

The use of the older, more intelligent, and more competent children as monitors for the instruction of small groups of younger, less intelligent, and less competent children — to use those who knew little to teach those who knew less — was the chief principle of monitorial instruction. This device lent itself to the economical management of a school-

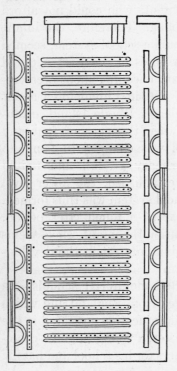

A PLAN OF A LANCASTERIAN
MONITORIAL SCHOOLROOM

room. The Lancasterian system was so elaborate that the teacher had little to do "except to organize, to reward, to punish, and to inspire. When a child was admitted, a monitor assigned him his class; while he remained, a monitor taught him (with nine other pupils); when he was absent, one monitor ascertained the fact and another found out the reason; a monitor examined him periodically, and when he made progress a monitor promoted him; a monitor ruled the writing paper, a monitor had charge of the slates or books, and a monitor-general looked after all the other monitors."

Lancasterian methods. Lancaster described in many publications his methods of organizing schools, and in his manuals he gave minute directions from the construction of the house to the conduct of the recitations. Under his plan one teacher could direct the instruction of several hundred children. The routine of school management and teaching was so organized as to save time and to keep all the pupils constantly employed. "A place for everything and everything in its place" and "Let every child at every moment have something to

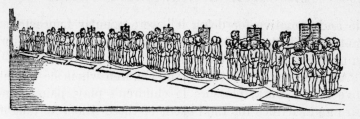

Groups of children reciting to monitors from reading charts or wall slates

Monitor leading pupils to seats. The hats are hung on the pupils' backs to save time and cloak rooms

Monitor inspecting written exercises at signal "Show slates"

LANCASTERIAN MONITORIAL SYSTEM

do and a motive for doing it" were popular Lancasterian mottoes. The teacher taught the monitors, and the monitors in turn taught their groups of children.

An affectionate interest in the children whom he taught, love of the work, pleasure in children's play, painstaking care and sacrifice for the benefit of those whom he taught, and confidence in orderly activity were among the prominent characteristics and traits of Lancaster's work and methods. And yet his plan in practical operation contained many weaknesses and defects. Among these were the formality of the routine work, the superficiality of much of the instruction, the rigid and mechanical discipline, memorization, and the absence of the psychological aspects of education. But Lancaster cannot be reproached for exercising the memory of the children, which had been and was to remain for many more years a popular and plausibly defended practice. Many decades were to pass before psychology was to appear as an aid in schoolroom practice.

But the Lancasterian method, when compared with the individual method in use in the old schools, wore the color of effectiveness. Especially did the cheapness of the monitorial plan recommend it highly in the United States, where it spread rapidly (especially in the larger towns and cities) after the first decade of the nineteenth century. The first Lancasterian school was opened in New York through the influence of the Public School Society of that city. The system spread from Massachusetts to Georgia and into some of the cities of the West. North Carolina and Maryland proposed, and the latter state actually undertook, a state system of schools upon the Lancasterian plan. In 1814 the treasurer of the Raleigh Academy announced the introduction of "the highly approved mode of teaching children the first rudiments of learning, invented by the celebrated Joseph Lancaster of London." Lancaster himself came to this country about 1818 and spent many years here, and

schools were organized on his method in various parts of
the country. The plan fell into disuse before the end of the
ante-bellum period, but before it disappeared it had served
to awaken public interest in, and sentiment for, the public-
school idea. Men like DeWitt Clinton of New York, Governor Wolcott of Connecticut, and Archibald D. Murphey
of North Carolina thought highly of the Lancasterian system. It is probable also that the monitorial method provoked
discussion on questions of education and promoted the idea
of schools at public expense. Moreover, it served to improve
the technique of classroom management and to draw attention to the necessity of special preparation for teachers.
The Lancasterian model schools were forerunners of normal
schools in the United States, and in this way the system
encouraged the development of agencies for the training of
teachers. As public opinion became aroused on the subject
of education, and as the material prosperity of the people
increased and the people became willing to contribute more
liberally to the support of schools, the Lancasterian system
disappeared; but it had served as a step, if feeble, toward
the American free-school system that was to be.

The secular Sunday school. By acquainting neighborhoods and communities with schools and by drawing the
attention of the well-to-do to the educational needs of the
underprivileged in a way, perhaps, that political theory
could never have done, the secular Sunday school also
served to promote the idea of public schools. In the name
of religion and on terms of equality it brought together
the children of all classes. Virginia seems to have been a
pioneer in the movement in this country. A Sunday school
was established in that state as early as 1786; and three
decades later this type of school was viewed by some leaders
as a substitute for the common public school, which, there
as in most of the states at that time, contained the taint of
charity.

The Sunday school was imported from England, where Robert Raikes had begun it in 1780 for the purpose of providing underprivileged factory children with instruction in reading and the church catechism by teachers who were paid for their services. From this modest beginning the movement grew and received wide support by interdenominational societies, a fact which testifies to a purpose broader than the sectarian motive or theological tone that it finally acquired in the United States. The historian Green believed that "the Sunday schools established by Mr. Raikes were the beginnings of popular education."

In the early days of the Sunday school in this country, where the need for separate schools for the very poor and destitute children was not so great as in England, the religious denominations opposed its nonsectarian character. The beginnings were generally made by voluntary effort; but by the opening of the second quarter of the nineteenth century some of the churches accepted responsibility for this type of school, which has now come to be maintained as an important phase of denominational activity. From a school with a full day of instruction in reading, writing, and ciphering, it is now an agency which gives a brief period to the teaching of religious materials.

Sunday schools of the secular type were numerous, however, during nearly half a century after the opening of the first one in Virginia. They appeared in all the Southern states and in the East, especially in the cities. A Methodist conference in session in Charleston in 1790 ordered the establishment of Sunday schools in or near the church or place of worship, and provision was to be made to secure persons "to teach gratis all who will attend and have capacity to learn, from six o'clock in the morning till ten, and from two o'clock in the afternoon till six, when it does not interfere with public worship." A year later a Sunday-school society was organized in Philadelphia to provide instruction for the poor children of the city. Schools of this type appeared during the succeeding years in Boston, in New York, in Paterson, New Jersey, in Pawtucket, Rhode Island, in Pittsburgh, in Portsmouth, New Hampshire, and in Baltimore. Sunday-school unions, combinations of local efforts, were later formed in some of the cities, and from them was organized the American Sunday School Union in 1824. Cincinnati became the headquarters of the organization in 1832, and a systematic campaign was waged to extend the movement in the Mississippi Valley. Within two years twenty-eight hundred schools were established in that region. Societies for the purpose of encouraging the work of the Sunday school were established in many of the cities.

A memorial of the Orange County Sunday School Union to the legislature of North Carolina in 1825, signed by forty substantial citizens, stated that the Sunday school was to be found at that time in almost every state in the Union, and had "been invariably attended with marked advantage to the young." That particular union, which asked for legislative aid to carry on its work, had under its care twenty-two schools in which were instructed "from eight hundred to one thousand children, many of whom, the children of the poor who would otherwise have been brought up in utter ignorance and vice, have been taught to read and trained in habits of moral reflection and conduct." The memorialists asked for the sum of twenty-five cents a year to purchase books "for every Sunday-school learner under their care, out of the public taxes," and that similar provision be made for all Sunday schools then in the state and for any which should thereafter be established. The committee to whom the memorial was referred reported "that it is inexpedient to grant the prayer of the petitioners and therefore recommend its rejection." Two years later the legislature considered, and the senate passed upon its first reading, a bill to encourage Sunday schools established "to instruct poor and indigent children in the art of reading and writing," but further action on the matter was later indefinitely postponed.

Transportation and communication. The political necessity of interstate communication had been emphasized by the Revolution when the difficulties of transporting troops had revealed the inefficiency of primitive roads. The opening of the Southwest, the development of commercial relations between that section and the older sections of the South and the East, and the rapid growth in population in the entire Western region made better means of communication necessary. The democratizing influences of the westward expansion and the development of the huge material resources of the country could be made possible only through such means. The direction of social as well as economic forces was to be changed through the building of turnpikes and the construction of canals, steamboats, and railroads.

Turnpikes, begun before the close of the eighteenth century, had been fairly well supplied in New York, Pennsylvania, and New England. There and elsewhere local roads were improved and continuous lines for through traffic were established. Much private money found its way into investments in these enterprises, and often state aid was also given to promote them. The tolls were heavy, but the cost of transportation was reduced and communication was made more speedy. The distance of more than three hundred miles from Philadelphia to Pittsburgh could be covered in less than six days, and travelers could find comfortable lodging every night while on the way.

After Gallatin, Secretary of the Treasury, in 1807, made an impressive report on roads, canals, harbors, and rivers and proposed a comprehensive plan for their improvement by aid of Congress, the national government became interested in internal improvements, and there was widespread agitation of the subject. Congress was interested for political and for economic reasons, and there was interest also in improvements by which greater speed and safety could be given to mails. The only result of this interest and agitation, however, was the construction of the Cumberland Road, or "National Pike," from the national capital to Vandalia, Illinois, which was completed in 1838 at a cost of something above $4,000,000. Meantime, doubts of the constitutionality of Federal aid to internal improvements arose, and the national plan was abandoned, but the states themselves took up the task of providing better means of communication and trade.

The mania for internal improvements. The importance of using the rivers as highways had meantime become recognized when Robert Fulton demonstrated the practicability of steam navigation by water, taking the clumsy *Clermont* the one hundred and fifty miles from New York to Albany in thirty-two hours in August, 1807. Steamboats soon came into wide use, increased the river trade, which had already become considerable through the use of barges and flatboats, helped to solve the problem of outlet for the produce of the Western sections, and served also to increase and strengthen the economic bonds in an immense country hitherto so widely separated into strongly marked sections of East, West, and South. Canals were also being built. Many small canal projects had been done earlier, the Dismal Swamp Canal, which was constructed under joint charter of Virginia and North Carolina and opened in 1794, being the first; but the Erie Canal, completed in 1825 and connecting the Hudson River with the Great Lakes (a project which George Washington had predicted), was the most important artificial waterway of them all. It formed a continuous waterway from the Atlantic seaboard to the great Middle West and served to open up vast reaches in that section of the country. A mania for canal construction and other internal improvements followed the prompt success of the Erie enterprise. Pennsylvania constructed a system of canals from Philadelphia to Pittsburgh, completing it in 1834 at a cost of more than $10,000,000. Private capital being unequal to the task, assistance was sought from the states, and the Federal government, although it had withdrawn from such work, indirectly aided the various states by the distribution of its surplus revenue in 1837.

The magnitude of the development of internal improvements appears in the rapid increase in state debts from less than $13,000,000 in 1820 to $200,000,000 two decades later, most of the money going into roads, canals, and railroads. The era of railroad-building was one of far-reaching economic and social beneficence. The sail car of Evan Thomas, built for use on the Baltimore & Ohio (the pioneer railroad in the United States, which was begun in 1828 and opened for traffic two years later) demonstrated how little power was required to propel a car on rails. Horse power was also used, and after eighteen months of experiment with it and sail power, steam was applied. In a brief period the principal cities on the coast were united by railways. By 1835 Pennsylvania had two hundred miles, by 1840 the entire country could boast of nearly three thousand miles, and by 1860 nearly thirty-one thousand miles had been constructed. The craze for railroad construction at state expense led to extravagance and waste and, in some cases, to corruption and became one of the vital causes of the panic of 1837. Easily made, the debts when due were not infrequently repudiated.

A social consciousness. Chief among the many beneficent influences of the movement for improved means of transportation and communication was the impetus given to the development of a social consciousness. Places formerly remote were brought closer together, economic interdependencies were established, isolation was in part broken down, ideas were now more readily exchanged, and men were able to take another step in their emancipation from the limitations of the primitive conditions which had so long surrounded them. The rise and spread of railroads were more than economic forces.

The awakening of labor. The democratic awakening, out of which were to come the principles of education by public support and under public control, was due in part also to the awakening of a class consciousness among the laboring classes in the industrial centers. The cities had developed somewhat rapidly during the first three or four decades of the nineteenth century, although less than 7 per cent of the people of the entire country lived in so-called urban communities in 1830. These were new classes in America, products of the introduction of machinery, of the factory system, of the rise of capitalism, and of the Industrial Revolution in general, all of which affected the daily lives of men, women, and children everywhere. Before the close of the Revolutionary War remarkable inventions by which machinery had been applied to spinning and weaving, — the spinning "jenny" of James Hargreaves, the illiterate weaver of Lancashire; the spinning "frame" of Richard Arkwright, an English peddler; the spinning "mule" of Samuel Crompton, an English weaver; and the power loom of Edmund Cartwright, an English clergyman, — had revolutionized industry in England. That country, possessing the machinery, controlled the manufacture of cotton and woolen goods, jealously guarded the monopoly, and prohibited the exportation of machines, tools, or models used in such manufacturing; but by smuggling or other artful devices many of the secrets of the English inventors soon became known, and their inventions were copied in the United States.

The factory; new social problems. American inventors also added to what they could borrow from England. In 1789, the same year that the national government began, a complete cotton machinery was set up at Pawtucket, Rhode Island, by Samuel Slater, an Englishman, who reproduced from his memory of English machines all the mechanical details of the first American cotton factory. The growth of manufactures was slow, and in 1804 there were only four cotton factories in the country; but by 1815 nearly $50,000,000 were invested in textile factories, and the consumption of raw cotton in that year reached ninety thousand bales.

About the same time (1814) Francis C. Lowell introduced the power loom and, in "the first complete factory in the world," brought under one roof at Waltham, Massachusetts, the various processes of spinning and weaving. Meantime an ingenious Connecticut school-teacher in Georgia, a year after his graduation from Yale, devised saw teeth on a revolving wheel that picked the lint from cottonseed. At that time cotton was raised only in Georgia and South Carolina; its culture now spread rapidly to other states, and slavery accompanied it and became identified with it. The factory system spread rapidly also. The age of steam and machinery had begun, and with it came towns and cities in which soon congested new and large working classes who were separated for the first time from the soil.

·Thousands of men, women, and children were drained off from the farms and firesides, and to these were added other thousands from Europe. They came into new and strange grievances. Unrest was inevitable. New social problems were inevitable. The problems of ignorance concentrated in congested communities, of pauperism, of delinquency and dependency, of vagrancy and crime, now appeared to an alarming degree for the first time in American life. Neither science nor law offered the workers protection from the destitution and disease, vermin and vice, that were certain results from long and unregulated hours of labor. Insanitary and unhygienic conditions in blocks of ugly tenements, the liability of imprisonment for debt (whose shadow still lingered in many of the states), the lack of fit water supply or sewerage system or garbage collection, the lack of law by which men could retain rights in the products of their labors as long as their wages were unpaid, and the scanty opportunities of schooling for their children, — all united to crush down this new class of workers.

Labor unions formed. Aroused by these unwholesome and unjust conditions, workingmen, as their numbers increased, sought defense and relief in associations. Local societies were formed, and agitation and campaigns begun for better working and living conditions. Labor journals and speakers and agitators appeared in behalf of the "laborin' man an' laborin' woman," as James Russell Lowell wrote it in the "Biglow Papers." Before Jackson left the White House there were fifty-three unions in Philadelphia, about the same number in New York, nearly two dozen in Baltimore, and sixteen in Boston. Attempts were made by these and other local associations to confederate in 1834, "to unite and harmonize the efforts of all the productive classes of the country," but the undertaking was not a signal success. The balance of power was not yet fully in the hands of the workers, although they were able to throw fright into the greedy and avaricious capitalists (who had already developed a keen scent for special privileges to be had from legislatures and courts) and to force politicians to pay some heed to the voice of labor. Numerous bills looking to improvement found their way into legislative halls, but the public conscience was not fully aroused to the economic and social needs of the underprivileged.

Conditions of labor. These needs were numerous and large. The factory hands were new and helpless figures in the economic and social order in America. Many of them were women and children whose meager wages and long hours of labor were arbitrarily fixed by the factory-owners.

The working day was generally from dawn to dark in foul air, poor light, and the incessant noises of machinery. Five minutes after sunrise Hope Factory in Rhode Island locked its gates against the tardy workers, not to be unlocked again until eight at night, and the charge was made that the authorities lengthened this day by manipulating the clock. During the fifteen or sixteen hours of toil the workers (more than half of whom were children) were allowed two periods of twenty-five minutes for a cold breakfast and dinner which they brought to the factory. The conditions were similar elsewhere — at Paterson in New Jersey, at Griswold in Connecticut, and at Lowell in Massachusetts. Replies to questions sent to the mayors and aldermen of all Massachusetts factory towns by a legislative committee in 1825 showed that not one town claimed less than eleven hours of toil for children — workers from six to seventeen years of age — and only two reported a day so short as that. The long working hours were for every day except Sunday. One reported an average of twelve hours a day, and the humanitarian mayor added, with the pious inflection which has been heard so often even in recent years, that "these children are better off than their neighbors."

A statement, somewhat mild and perhaps also a trifle partisan, signed by "Many Operatives" and appearing in a labor journal in 1830, described the bad conditions under which children worked in the factories in the City of Brotherly Love. The hands were boys and girls, not more than one sixth of whom could read and write. Parents there as elsewhere were deprived of the opportunity of giving their children "a trifling education" by the threats of the factory authorities that if one child should be taken out of work for school, even for a short period, all members of the family would be forced out of employment, "and we have known such threats put into execution," said the statement. At a labor convention in Boston two years later a similar report was made of the opportunities for the schooling of children who worked in factories. Very seldom were these children, who represented two fifths of all the factory employees, taken from the mills to be placed in school. The only educational opportunities allowed them were "on the Sabbath and after half-past eight o'clock of the evening of other days." These conditions were described as harmful "to the character of American freemen, and to the wives and mothers of such." The evils complained of were declared to be unjust and cruel, no less than the sacrifice of the best interests of the rising generation "to the cupidity and avarice of their employers."

Hostile attitude toward labor. Complete faith in general education was often expressed by the early spokesmen of labor interests. In equal education for all many of them seemed to see remedies for every existing evil, though such a view was, of course, not shared by all, even among the labor leaders. Thomas Skidmore in 1829 discussed the rights of man to property, and called the educational enthusiasts in New York "political dreamers." In general the propertied and so-called respectable classes gave labor no sympathy, and the newspapers were often bitterly and contemptuously hostile.

President Monroe in a message to Congress congratulated the manufacturers on the "fall in the price of labor, so favorable to the success of domestic manufactures"; and Alexander Hamilton thought it "worthy of particular remark that, in general, women and children are rendered more useful, and the latter more early useful, by manufacturing establishments than they would otherwise be." Hamilton sought to strengthen his argument by noting that four sevenths of the cotton-factory workers in Great Britain were women and children, "of whom the greater proportion are children and many of a tender age." Even the courts reflected the opposition of the classes and stood as stubborn obstacles to the cause of the workers. Not until 1842 did any court recognize that workmen had the right of collective action in seeking to improve their conditions. And upon the floor of Congress, while the factory system was in its infancy, gratitude was expressed for cotton-manufacturing machinery and its immense saving of labor. Five or six men could manage a factory, and "the other hands are mere children, whose labor is of little use in any other branch of industry." A congressional committee in 1816 estimated that of the hundred thousand persons employed in the cloth industry, only one tenth were men, nearly one fourth were boys, and sixty-six thousand were women and girls. Mathew Carey, writer and publisher, and founder of the *Columbian Magazine*, was enthusiastic over the opportunities which the factory offered young girls who were "preserved from idleness and its attendant vices and crimes — and whose wages probably average $1.50 a week." On the other hand, William Ellery Channing, Unitarian preacher and writer, crying out against slavery in another form and praying that "Providence will beat back and humble our cupidity and ambition," viewed questions of labor as essentially those of human welfare. Horace Mann and other humanitarians held similar if not such strong views. Catherine Esther Beecher, the author and lecturer, while recognizing the danger of collision with "pecuniary and party interests" in discussing the conditions of women and children in industry, pointed to the great

CATHERINE ESTHER BEECHER

danger of the manufacturing localities of our country, "which every third year are sending at least sixty thousand American women from domestic labors to toil in shops and mills, and in three years receiving back at least one in every three with impaired constitutions."

However, as opportunities increased for accumulating economic wealth through the development of factories, the Puritan's view that idleness and iniquity are twin evils made stronger and stronger appeal even to some of the humanitarians and uplifters. *Niles' Weekly Register*, for nearly half a century the organ of the manufacturers, calculated the wealth that could be added in the United States if all children were put to work in the factories and mills. Even the pen of Horace Mann quivered a bit when he wrote in his third annual report to the state board of education of Massachusetts that child labor in factories, if supplemented by some schooling, could be "converted from a servitude into a useful habit of diligence." With such support from the past it is not amazing to hear even now the plea that school terms cannot be lengthened in the cotton and tobacco belts of the South. There as elsewhere politics and property often resist efforts to discover and improve the conditions surrounding children and women in industry.

Reforms gained slowly. Although all the reforms which the labor movement advocated were not promptly achieved, some were gained in the thirties and forties and others followed later. The ten-hour working day was recognized by the national government in 1840, when it was introduced into the navy yard at Washington, and shortly afterwards the practice was adopted for artisans and in factories in many parts of the country. Laws for the protection of the life and health of the factory hands were enacted, imprisonment for debt disappeared, and the effort to establish schools supported by public taxes and controlled by the public will finally succeeded. The early labor forces helped to over-

come some of the inertia and indifference and selfishness of
the time and to stir up active interest in public schools.
They also had influence upon movements for general social
reform. However large or small was its influence on these
matters, this awakening of a class consciousness appeared
as the first clear demand that human rights be placed above
property rights or at least on an equal footing with them,
that education be considered a proper activity of a properly
constituted government, that the laborer is worthy of his
hire and that his wages should have first lien among the claims
of other creditors, and that neither a man's person nor his
means of livelihood should be seized for debt.

The element of charity in education. Indignant were the
protests of workingmen against the pauper school and the
element of charity in education. Labor demanded general
and equal systems of education not as charity but as the
right of every child. Then, as earlier and as later, the classes
assumed an air of condescending rebuke to the call for education for the masses. The underprivileged were often reminded that their lot was so much better than that of the
underprivileged classes in other parts of the world, that
education was the concern and care of the individual, and
that free education for all by public support was tantamount
to an arbitrary division of private property among the poor.
Many of the stock arguments heard today against public
education were shopworn even in the thirties and forties.

Imprisonment for debt. Indignant also were the protests
of the workingmen against the barbarism of imprisonment
for debt — a law which in theory applied equally to all, but
pressed most heavily upon the poor. No matter how small
the sum he owed, the debtor could be sentenced to jail until
it was paid, and deprived meanwhile of any opportunity
to work off the debt. When, in the same year that Jackson
first became president, a large meeting of workingmen declared, "One principle that we contend for is the abolition

of imprisonment for debt," there were seventy-five thousand persons in the debtors' prisons in the United States, many for trifling sums, half of them for amounts less than twenty dollars. A year later it was said that three thousand persons were annually sent to prison in Massachusetts. In the city of Boston fourteen hundred victims were imprisoned (a hundred of them women), and the only charges against them were the crimes of owing small amounts: a blind man, with a dependent family, owed six dollars; a widow, sixty-eight cents; a veteran of the Revolutionary War, sixty-six years old, only a few dollars. Some of the prisons were "veritable chambers of horrors." With no provision made for separating the unfortunate on any basis of sex or age or character, often all were thrown into one room, sometimes with little more shelter from the elements from the outside than from the vices of the depraved on the inside.

Already the American mania for organizations was appearing. There were societies to send missionaries to the heathen, to promote the sales and circulation of the Bible and religious tracts, to educate men for the Gospel ministry, to promote temperance, the observance of the Sabbath, and the comfort of convicts, to ransom the black slave, and to colonize the free negro. Benevolent and numerous were the energies of Christian America engaged in an effort to remedy, to patch up, and to repair. But while charitable societies were formed in behalf of persons imprisoned for debt, their purpose was not to abolish the barbarous practice nor to pay the debts and thus secure the liberty of prisoners, "but to furnish sufficient food, clothing, and fuel to prolong the agony of the suffering prisoners." Until reform could come at this point and at many others the rights of "life, liberty, and the pursuit of happiness," so freely promised for half a dozen decades, were to remain mere mummeries without practical meaning.

The frontier; Jacksonian democracy. The pioneers, who depended for their subsistence chiefly "upon the natural growth of vegetation and the proceeds of hunting"; the emigrant purchasers of lands, who added field to field, cleared the way for roads, put up log houses for homes, built bridges, schoolhouses, courthouses, and mills, and exhibited "the picture and forms of plain, frugal, civilized life"; and the men of capital, through whose enterprise villages were made into towns and then cities, edifices of brick were erected, and extensive fields, gardens, and orchards, schools, colleges, and churches were developed, — these three classes followed one after the other, as waves of the ocean, in that significant movement known as westward expansion.

The earliest migration took place into what is now Kentucky and Tennessee. This was before the American Revolution and after the fear of French aggression had been removed by the outcome of the French and Indian War. By 1790 there was a population of two hundred thousand in the territory west of the Appalachian Mountains; two decades later it numbered a million. Movement after movement received new stimulus as free or very cheap land and the opportunity of independence beckoned to the restless, to the unsuccessful, to the poor and the oppressed, to the brave and the adventuresome, and to all others who craved a chance to hew out their own careers under conditions of freedom from the restrictions of the older settlements. In facing fresh problems these pioneers broke off the restraints of custom and readily developed inventiveness and resourcefulness and new institutions. There was freedom beyond the Alleghenies, "the most American part of America," declared James Bryce. There the traits commonly considered the most characteristically American developed and flourished. The democracy of the West was not the dream of the theorist: in it the worth of the common man received recognition, and through it emphasis was placed upon "the right of every man to rise to the full measure of his own nature."

The democratic spirit of the frontier appeared not only in the manner of everyday life there, but was revealed especially in the constitutions framed when state governments were being established. All the Western states entering the Union after 1812, except Mississippi, accepted manhood suffrage and the doctrine of majority rule instead of the rule of property, although some of the older states in the East were still resisting attempts to remove the ancient property restrictions on the ballot and on office-holding. Even men like Daniel Webster in Massachusetts and Chancellor Kent in New York viewed with alarm the wave of democracy that threatened to overrun their respective states in the constitutional conventions of 1821 — the former stoutly maintaining that to give all men the right to vote would mean the surrender of "the wealth of individuals to the rapaciousness of a merciless gang," and the latter protesting against, and predicting dire results from, manhood suffrage, which he likened unto a mighty engine that would destroy property, laws, and liberties. But in time the influence of the West reacted on the older states, and the old property and religious qualifications for voting and for holding political offices were finally abandoned, Rhode Island and Virginia delaying the reform until near the middle of the century, and North Carolina until 1856. Opportunities of extending public educational advantages to those classes who formerly had been deprived of them widened as the franchise was extended to all white adult males. And the agitation for free schools for all, at public expense and under public control, was now to increase.

Meantime the election of Andrew Jackson as president of the United States marked the end of a political period which is not without social significance. It marked the beginning of new manifestations of more vital and growing social life. Changes now appeared which broke through traditions and precedents of the past. Jackson himself typified the changes — that democratic revolution which finally was to advance the cause of education as far as it was possible to advance it in a country countenancing human slavery.

But the elevation of this man — a "son of the soil" — to be the chief of a nation of twelve million souls served to end the old order and to begin a new. Some significance has been read into Jackson's obscure origin and his lack of formal education. Each of the seven presidents before him had come from and represented the propertied, privileged, and cultured classes, and all except Washington had attended college. Not one had ever made his living by the work of his hands. But Jackson had come from the underprivileged classes. Born in poverty, he had made his own way by his own wits and the strong common sense with which he was richly endowed. His schooling must have been of the merest rudiments, and it is not known just how, when, or where these were secured. Up to the time that he became candidate for president in 1824, when he was fifty-seven years old, most of his time had been spent on the frontier or in communities characterized by the frontier spirit. He had had wide experience in politics and in war; and though he was quick and erratic in judgment and impulsive and temperamental rather than judicial and reflective in habit of mind, he revealed wide sympathy with the views and opinions of the underprivileged and unusual capacity for leadership. As candidate for president his military reputation exceeded that of any American living at the time and assured him wide popularity. Sincere, honest, and direct in public life and singularly above reproach in private life, his courage and strength commended him to the people, whose desires he seemed to embody. "I have confidence," he declared, "in the virtue and good sense of the people."

Jackson personified their cause, and his election was an emphatic popular approval of the new political and social order with which he was identified.

New conceptions of democracy. Thus new and more vital conceptions of democracy began slowly to arise. The change appeared in the revisions of old constitutions and the adoption of new ones which revealed a growing interest in wider political equality and responsibility, the tendency to distrust large executive power, and the movement to grant more authority to the people. Confidence in the people was expanding. Property and religious qualifications for voting and for holding office were removed or reduced in the older states, where they had so long resisted the growing forces of democracy. Representation in state legislatures began to change from the basis of wealth to the more nearly proper basis of population. There was also an increase in the number of offices to be filled by popular vote and a decrease in the number of appointments formerly made by governors or legislatures.

© Detroit Publishing Co.

ANDREW JACKSON

The humanitarian movement. Other movements of social significance were appearing also during the first and second quarters of the nineteenth century. The humanitarian movement was slowly gaining strength. The number of crimes for which the death penalty had been exacted was decreased, and the abolition of that penalty was actually advocated. There were movements to abolish negro slavery, to give support to the cause of world peace, and to improve the position of women. The American Peace Society was founded in 1828. A convention of temperance advocates met in Philadelphia in 1833 with four hundred delegates from twenty-one states, and the American Temperance Union was formed. Timothy Shay Arthur's "Ten Nights in a Barroom" appeared in 1854, was dramatized, and had a wide vogue and influence. Religion shared with Jacksonian democracy the eagerness to carry light to dark places. Missionary societies were organized, and soon there was a wide extension of missionary activity, and the rivalry of the various religious denominations became keen. It was a time of frequent religious revivals and numerous camp meetings, of itinerant preachers, and of colporteurs with Bibles and religious tracts.

Education as a function of government. Along with the growing tendency to use public funds or credit to promote banks, canals, roads, and railroads, and the movement that considered government a means of promoting public welfare, was soon to go a tendency — one that was to grow stronger and stronger — to view education as an activity in which properly constituted governments could participate and properly encourage and support. Manners were still crude among the masses, and culture was still remote from all but a few. Knowledge and learning, which Jefferson half a century earlier had sought by legislative action to diffuse more generally among the people of his state, were still strange to most of the people of the United States when Andrew Jackson was president. But the children of the new nation (now fairly free from dire poverty and excess of crime), absorbed in subduing a continent and in mastering the material forces about them, and with little opportunity for leisure must wait a while longer before the new democracy was to express itself in a school system universal and free to all.

The way for education as a concern of government was clearer, however, than it had ever been, though the blight of slavery had to be removed before democracy could fully flower. But politicians were able to read the signs of the times. Governor Clinton, in a message to the legislature of New York in 1826, said that the encouragement of education was the first duty of government; and the following year he said that the right to vote could not be exercised safely "without intelligence," meaning, perhaps, that the voters should have the chance of schooling. Executives and public men in other states were expressing similar platitudes. Abraham Lincoln, in offering himself in 1832 to the people of an Illinois county as a candidate "for the honorable office of one of your representatives in the next General Assembly of this State," viewed education as "the most important subject which we as a people can be engaged in." He thought that it was of vital importance that "every man may receive at least a moderate education" in order to read history so that he may "duly appreciate the value of our free institutions ... to say nothing of the advantages and satisfaction to be derived from all being able to read the Scriptures and other works, both of a religious and moral nature, for themselves." He desired the opportunity to do what he could to advance any measure that may hasten the period when "education and, by its means, morality, sobriety, enterprise, and industry, shall become much more general than at present."

And sixteen years after he had opposed the removal of property qualifications on suffrage in Massachusetts, Daniel Webster declared, in an address in democratic Indiana, that "education, to accomplish the ends of good government, should be universally diffused. Open the doors of the schoolhouses to all the children of the land. ... On the diffusion of education among the people rests the preservation and perpetuation of our free institutions." But the story of public education is not in large part the biographies of the men who gave utterance to such fair and promising statements. Few were the politicians then or later, and few are they now, who stump their districts or states in behalf of educational questions on which voters divide. Not often have they entered into the kingdom in such manner as this. Deliverance of the masses from ignorance was to arise from other places and through other agencies.

This chapter shows some of the more potent forces which helped during the early nineteenth century to awaken among the people of this country a consciousness of the need for public education and served to strengthen the idea of schools as a function of government. These forces were economic and industrial, political, religious, and humanitarian. Through their influences the way of public education became somewhat clearer, but it was to brighten also through the influence of other agencies and of some fervid educational leaders whose work will be described in Chapter VIII.

REFERENCES AND READINGS

ADAMS, JAMES TRUSLOW. New England in the Republic, 1776–1850. Boston, 1926.

> Chapter XV deals with humanitarianism, literature, education, and the conditions of physical, moral, and mental defectives and dependents. Contains excellent references.

BASSETT, JOHN S. Life of Andrew Jackson. 2 vols. New York, 1911.

> The best work on Jackson.

BEARD, CHARLES A. Economic Origins of Jeffersonian Democracy. New York, 1915.

> Very helpful and suggestive supplementary material for this chapter.

BOGART, ERNEST L. The Economic History of the United States. New York, 1923.

> Part III (chaps. xi–xiv) deals with topics discussed in this chapter.

BOWERS, CLAUDE G. The Party Battles of the Jackson Period. Boston, 1922.

> Deals minutely "with the brilliant, dramatic, and epochal party battles and the fascinating personalities" of Jackson's administrations. Chapter II deals with "the rising of the masses." Useful bibliography.

BYRN, E. W. The Progress of Invention in the Nineteenth Century. New York, 1900.

> A historical account dealing with the period covered by this chapter.

CARLTON, FRANK TRACY. Economic Influences on Educational Progress in the United States, 1820–1850, *Bulletin No. 221*, University of Wisconsin, Madison, 1908.

> An attempt to trace the relation between educational advancement and industrial progress. Chapter III considers the growth of population and manufacture, the suffrage reforms, and the humanitarian and labor movements. A suggestive bibliography.

COMMONS, J. R. (Editor). A Documentary History of American Industrial Society. 10 vols. Cleveland, 1909–1911.

> A valuable collection of source materials. Volumes V–VIII cover the period from 1820 to 1860.

CUBBERLEY, E. P. Public Education in the United States. Boston, 1919.

> Chapter IV deals with the Sunday-school movement, school societies, Lancasterian schools, infant-school societies, and certain other influences discussed in this chapter. Contains useful references.

CUROE, PHILIP R. V. Educational Attitudes and Policies of Organized Labor in the United States. New York, 1926.

> A very careful study. Chapters II and III deal with the subject from the beginning of the American labor movement to the Civil War. The author concludes, contrary to the views of earlier writers, that "in the two decades preceding the Civil War the points of contact between our educational development and organized labor were neither many nor important." Contains a useful bibliography.

DODD, WILLIAM E. Expansion and Conflict. Boston, 1915.

> Pictures the background of certain conflicts during the period from Jackson to Lincoln and seeks to show "why things happened as they did, as well as how they happened." Chapters I and V deal with Jackson and his triumph.

FAULKNER, H. U. American Economic History. New York, 1924.

> A brief but valuable manual on economic development, with material bearing on the subject of this chapter.

FISH, CARL R. The Rise of the Common Man. New York, 1927.

> A discriminating treatment of American life in the process of re-
> making itself in the thirties and forties, presented in a delightful
> manner and showing that the "creation of a general American cul-
> ture was lagging, though it was in process of formation." The
> critical essay on authorities is full of valuable suggestions for the
> student of social history.

JOHNSON, ALLEN. Union and Democracy. Boston, 1915.

> Considers the new democracy which emerged out of the West
> and "transformed the face of society in the old states." Chapters
> XIV and XVI bear especially on this chapter.

KNIGHT, EDGAR W. Public Education in the South. Boston, 1922.

> Chapter VII describes the awakening in the states which formed
> the Confederacy.

KNIGHT, EDGAR W. Public School Education in North Carolina. Boston,
1916.

> Chapter VII traces the growth of public educational sentiment in
> that state.

MACGILL, C. E. History of Transportation in the United States before
1860. (Carnegie Institution Contributions to American Economic
History.) Washington, 1917.

> Full of information and contains also a good bibliography.

PARTON, JAMES. Life of Andrew Jackson. 3 vols. New York, 1860.

> The best documentary account of Jackson.

SIMONS, A. M. Social Forces in American History. New York, 1911.

> Chapters on the frontier, the westward migration, the early fac-
> tory system, the changing interests of the people, the labor move-
> ment, the condition of the workers, and the beginnings of capitalism
> supplement the material of this chapter.

QUESTIONS FOR STUDY AND DISCUSSION

1. Show how public opinion was slowly influenced in favor of
education as a function of the state by means of (1) public-school
societies, (2) the infant-school movement, (3) the Lancasterian
schools, (4) the secular Sunday school.

2. Criticize the methods used in the Lancasterian schools. Why
did these schools fall into disuse?

3. Show how the movement for improved means of transportation and communication developed a social consciousness. Consider the social influences of recent road-building programs in the various states.

4. List the reforms which the laboring classes advocated in the thirties and forties.

5. What contribution is made to the subject of the labor movement by Curoe's study?

6. Show how the factory system brought new social problems. List some of the problems.

7. Trace the development of the movement to abolish imprisonment for debt in your state. Point out any present-day survivals of the old practice.

8. Compare the conditions surrounding labor in the twenties and thirties with conditions surrounding farm tenancy in the cotton and tobacco belts of the South and the corn belt of the West.

9. Consider the educational significance of the decrease in the hours of the working day as a result of the wide applications of science.

10. Why did the workingmen protest against the pauper school and the element of charity in education?

11. Show how the democratic spirit of the frontier appeared in education.

12. Trace the constitutional and legal changes in regard to education which were made in your state between 1820 and 1860.

13. Indicate the social significance of the election of Andrew Jackson as president of the United States.

14. Trace the growth of the humanitarian movement in your state during the first half of the nineteenth century.

CHAPTER VIII

THE AWAKENING

Outline of the chapter. 1. The way for the educational awakening of the second quarter of the nineteenth century was prepared in part by educational publicity and propaganda.

2. This took the form of educational journals, of which Henry Barnard's was the most distinguished.

3. Reports of educational leaders were also influential. Those of Murphey, Cousin, Stowe, Barnard, and Mann were the most significant.

4. Educational conventions, memorials, and surveys were also important in the awakening.

5. The lyceum movement was likewise an effective agency of publicity.

6. But the most important forces of all were the labors of such educational leaders as Carter, Mann, Barnard, Wiley, Mills, Lewis, Galloway, Breckinridge, and Edwards.

7. The work of Horace Mann in Massachusetts was perhaps the most far-reaching in influence — his problems, policies, and achievements, and his contest with the Boston schoolmasters.

8. The educational services of Henry Barnard in Connecticut and Rhode Island were very influential, as was also his later career.

9. The work of Calvin H. Wiley in North Carolina was of a high order also.

10. Caleb Mills, through his "Addresses to the Legislature" of Indiana led the way for reform in that state.

11. These and other leaders of the period occupy a high place in the educational history of this country.

The public school, just as some other institutions and practices of the United States, was created largely by conflicts which have grown out of contending economic interests. Underlying these conflicts — conflicts which led to the removal of religious and property restrictions on the ballot, to an increase in elective offices, to the abolition of imprisonment for debt, to the improvement of the conditions of labor, and to other humanitarian and social reforms, all of which were discussed in the preceding chapter as evidences of the democratic awakening in the second quarter of the nineteenth century — were certain social forces of equal if not greater importance than the individuals who came into prominence in the struggles. These reforms were results of vital forces that helped to prepare the way for education as a major concern of government. Other agencies and influences which aided the cause of education and led gradually to an awakening in the last two decades of the ante-bellum period included educational journalism, influences from Europe, educational conventions, the lyceum movement, and such a fervid educational leadership as the country had never before witnessed. Through these forces the way of public education was finally cleared of almost all obstructions except one, and that was to be removed by the sword.

Educational publicity and propaganda. Newspapers were used slightly in the early days (as they are increasingly used today) to advance the cause of education, and then as now the leaders laid hold on the press to good purpose. Before the close of the third decade of the century many educational journals began to appear in large numbers. The list of those known to have been published by 1861 runs to one hundred and twenty one, of general, local, and specialized educational interests. Since that time the number has increased until of making many educational journals there is now no end.

Beginnings of educational magazines. One of the first attempts in American educational journalism was made by Albert Picket and his son, John Picket, proprietors of a school in New York and authors of textbooks. This was *The Academician*, a semiweekly of sixteen octavo pages, published in New York from February, 1818, to January, 1820. In it appeared articles dealing with Fellenberg's school at Hofwyl, Switzerland, the work and methods of

Pestalozzi, and a comparison of the latter's work with that of <u>Bell and Lancaster.</u> Many of the articles, sprinkled with Latin quotations and otherwise revealing the pedantry of the period, also dealt with methods and other practical school matters. *The Teacher's Guide and Parent's Assistant,* published in Portland, Maine, from 1826 to 1827, drew public attention through its articles to such subjects as the infant school, the secular Sunday school, Pestalozzian methods, schoolbooks, the training of teachers, physical education, and other topics and needed reforms. Between 1826 and 1830 William Russell published in Boston the *American Journal of Education,* which carried articles and notes on education in this country and Europe, on elementary education, on moral, physical, and personal education, and on "female education," which was described as "unspeakably important." There were discussions of pedagogical questions and of methods by which schools and schoolbooks could be improved, and articles translated from foreign educational writers. Russell was succeeded as editor by William C. Woodbridge, who continued the publication until 1836 as the *American Annals of Education*; it contained a notable series of articles upon many educational subjects. Woodbridge was followed by William A. Alcott, who was succeeded as editor by M. G. Hubbard. *The American Quarterly Register and Journal of the American Education Society,* which seems to have appeared at Andover, Massachusetts, as early as 1829 and to have continued, if not regularly, until 1843, was concerned largely with higher and theological education. *The Common School Assistant,* as its name suggests, was especially concerned with the stimulation of interest in the movement for common, or public, schools. It was published at Albany, New York, and was one of several magazines which flourished in that state for varying periods for three decades beginning with the eighteen-thirties. Horace Mann's *Common School Journal* in Massachusetts, Calvin H. Wiley's *North Carolina Journal of Education*, and Henry Barnard's *Connecticut Common School Journal* were among the more important state educational magazines of the ante-bellum period.

Barnard's *Journal of Education*. At its meeting in Washington in the winter of 1854 Barnard suggested to the American Association for the Advancement of Education the publication of a national journal of education. That organization was unable to finance the project, and Barnard undertook it on his own account in the following May. The result was the *American Journal of Education*, which was issued in thirty-two large volumes of about eight hundred pages each. It was the most encyclopedic of all the educational journals of the century and perhaps the best work on educational progress and educational material in this country or Europe. Many of the most important educational writings from Plato to Herbert Spencer, accounts of school systems everywhere, sketches of educational reformers, and many other educational subjects were published and discussed in it. Out of this work came the Report of the United States Commissioner of Education.

European influence upon educational journals. In all these pioneer educational journals there was much Pestalozzian material and many articles on the importance and necessity of free education. In most if not all of them there was evidence also of European influence upon the establishment of such journals, and in them appeared influential reports, such as those of Cousin and of Stowe, dealing with education in parts of Europe. Of the twenty or more educational periodicals established in this country before 1840 many refer to the use of such journals in Germany, and Cousin's report, which was printed in part by nearly all the twenty, mentions the fact that the Prussian government sent such publications to its teachers. *The Illinois Common School Advocate* in 1837 stated that weekly or monthly

papers "are sent to all the schools in Prussia and France at
public expense," and in 1838 *The Educator* of Pennsylvania
proposed the use of translations and quotations from the
"fifteen or twenty school journals" which were then issued
in Germany. Moreover, the educational journals were to
some extent imitations, in the field of education, of similar
publications in other fields — literature, science, art, and
medicine. "It seems strange that almost every art, science,
and profession has its peculiar vehicle of information," said
the prospectus of the *Academical Herald and Journal of
Education* (which was projected in 1812 but was never published), "while the science of education is without its advocate. Law, medicine, and divinity, commerce, agriculture,
and even the fashions and follies of the age have their 'journals,' while the art of improving the human mind, the source
whence all the others derive their consequence, is abandoned
to chance or neglect." The prospectus urged as necessary
a journal "in which proper plans and modes for the treatment and instruction of children could be published."
Whether the explanation of the origin of educational journalism in this country is found in imitation of European
practices or in rivalry to journalism in other fields, it is clear
that these early periodicals had definite and positive influence in the awakening that came during the last two decades
of the ante-bellum period.

Report on European conditions. Murphey's report.
Observations and impressions of travelers in Europe and
official reports on conditions there had served also to give
educational leaders and the public generally an acquaintance with better educational plans elsewhere. One of the
earliest of these reports, local in effect but showing European
influence, was made to the legislature of North Carolina in
1817 by a committee of which Archibald D. Murphey,
known as "the father of the common schools" of that state,
was chairman. This report (which Murphey himself wrote)

outlined in rather full detail a complete public-school plan, including "a gradation of schools regularly supporting each other, from the one in which the first rudiments of education are taught to that in which the highest branches of the sciences are cultivated." The report was presented after a general study of education in the United States and a careful study of conditions and needs in North Carolina. It revealed some acquaintance with conditions in Europe, especially "the plan which was drawn up and adopted by the national convention of France," it showed some familiarity also with the methods of Lancaster and of Pestalozzi, and it recommended as a sound basis of instruction "the excitement of the curiosity of children."

The plan included a state board of education to manage the school fund and supervise the schools,

ARCHIBALD D. MURPHEY

"Father of the Common Schools of North Carolina"

provision for elementary schools and secondary schools, respectable support for the university (which had been chartered in 1789 and had opened in 1795), and provision for an asylum for deaf-mutes. Although somewhat advanced for the time and somewhat resembling Jefferson's proposed plan for Virginia in 1779 and Condorcet's proposed plan for France in 1792, the report failed to accept fully the democratic principles of education. Murphey, like Jefferson, would give preference to poor children, who were to be educated for three years in the elementary schools free of any charges for tuition, "books, stationery, and other implements for learning"; and, like Jefferson, he would advance to the secondary schools such of the poor children "as are most distinguished for genius and give the best assurance of future usefulness." He proposed also that "during the whole course of their future education" these were to be "clothed, fed, and taught at public expense." On this point the plan was not so definite as Jefferson's. The number of these *Élèves de la patrie* (as Condorcet called them) was left by Murphey's plan to the state board of education, which was also to provide for "some just and particular mode" of advancing the children from the elementary schools to the secondary schools and on to the university. The proposal was too Utopian for the time and the state; and the bill based on it disappeared from the records after passing its first readings in both Houses. But with the impracticable features and the charity element eliminated, it later became the basis on which North Carolina built a fairly creditable ante-bellum school system.

Victor Cousin's report. A report on education in Prussia, which Victor Cousin officially made in 1831 to the French government, was reprinted in England three years later and in New York City in 1834, and had considerable influence in the United States. During these years there was wide interest in political and social reforms in this country, and efforts were made to learn what Germany had done and what France was trying to do to improve education in those countries. When Cousin's report appeared the district system of school support and control had been strong here for many years and the strength of localism was gradually increasing. His account of education in Prussia showed the authority of the state in the support and administration of education, emphasis on the training and certification of teachers, and the effectiveness of compulsory school attendance — practices which had not yet developed in the United

States. Here each little community was a law unto itself in school matters, few parents felt it their duty to send their children to school, and there was no legislation to compel them to do so. The contrast with the Prussian practice was striking. The duty of parents to send their children to school "is so national," says Cousin, "so rooted in all the legal and moral habits of the country, that it is expressed by a single word, *Schulpflichtigkeit*" (school duty, or school obligation), which corresponded "to another word, similarly formed and similarly sanctioned by public opinion, *Dienstpflichtigkeit*" (service obligation, or military service). Cousin believed that these "completely characteristic" words of Prussia contained the secret of the originality of the people, its strength as a state, "and the germ of its future condition."

Parts of this report were printed in nearly all the score of educational periodicals which were established in the United States before 1840, and the advanced educational ideas which it contained served to strengthen the position of the advocates of public education in this country. Its influence seems to have been definitely felt in Massachusetts, where it gave support to the work of Horace Mann, Charles Brooks, and James G. Carter, and in Michigan, where John D. Pierce and Isaac E. Crary, in the constitutional convention of 1835, worked to make education a distinct branch of the new state government, to create a chief state school office, and to establish schools upon the basis of state support and control rather than upon a local basis.

Calvin Stowe's report. Another official report on European schools which had influence in this country was made in 1837 to the legislature of Ohio by Calvin E. Stowe, who had been sent the previous year to Europe to purchase a library for the Lane Theological Seminary, where he was a professor. The legislature had requested him to take a look at the schools and to report his findings, and the result was his "Elementary Education in Europe," in which he contrasted conditions in Prussia and Württemberg with those in Ohio. He discussed especially the direction and thoroughness of instruction, the training of teachers, and the elementary course of study which had been enriched through the influence of Pestalozzian reforms. He recommended all

CALVIN E. STOWE

these improvements for the schools in Ohio and elsewhere in this country. He anticipated the argument that the Prussian plan was "visionary and can never be realized," and answered it by declaring that "it is no theory that I have been exhibiting, but a matter of fact, a copy of actual practice. . . . It can be done; for it has been done — it is now done: and it ought to be done. If it can be done in Europe, I believe it can be done in the United States: if it can be done in Prussia, I know it can be done in Ohio," declared Stowe.

If Stowe's theme failed to stir the emotions of multitudes as did his wife's drama of the abolitionist creed, the report was less narrow in range and more permanent in appeal than "Uncle Tom's Cabin," the sensation which a dozen years later ran into millions of copies. The report aroused the interest of legislators as well as of educators, and much of the educational advancement of the remainder of the ante-bellum period can be traced to its influence. The legislature of Ohio ordered ten thousand copies printed and distributed to every school district in the state, and later it was ordered reprinted by the legislatures of Massachusetts, Michigan, North Carolina, Pennsylvania, and Virginia.

Reports by Bache and Barnard. Other reports on European schools reached this country during the next few years. In 1836 A. D. Bache, president of Girard College for Orphans (founded in Philadelphia under the will of the famous merchant Stephen Girard for the education of orphans), was instructed by the trustees of the institution to visit similar institutions in Europe. The result was Bache's "Education in Europe," which was published three years later and which contained valuable material on Pestalozzian methods and other practices in Holland and Germany. A few years earlier Charles Brooks, who labored so earnestly for an educational awakening in Massachusetts, learned about the Prussian school system from Dr. H. Julius of Hamburg, who was a fellow passenger with Brooks from Europe to the United States. Julius later addressed the committee on education of the Massachusetts legislature; and although his address led to no action by that body, it was printed by that state and later by New York. During the years 1835–1837 Henry Barnard visited Europe and, through his journals, later discussed the educational practices which had impressed him. Moreover, in 1854 he collected and published, under the title "National Education in Europe," the most important parts of earlier reports on the subject, together with results of his own researches and studies.

Horace Mann's report. Perhaps the most distinguished and influential of all these reports was the one made by Horace Mann in 1843 to the State Board of Education in Massachusetts, of which he was secretary. In this report (known as his seventh), which followed his visit to Europe in that year, he described and appraised educational conditions in England, Scotland, France, Germany, Belgium, and Holland, with reference particularly to the materials and methods of teaching, the classification of pupils, discipline, and the training of teachers. It was filled with copious facts and ideas, and reflected the open-mindedness of Mann, who showed few prejudices to things foreign to his own country and sought to report conditions exactly as he found them. One of the most delightfully written official reports ever made in the United States, this work by Mann is well-nigh famous, not because it is readable nor yet because it aroused a protest from the conservatives and led to a controversy with the Boston schoolmasters which made in large part Mann's high place in the educational history of this country; it is important chiefly because it led to the improvement of the educational conditions in his own land, which, contrasted with the best that he had seen in Europe, he deeply deplored and sharply criticized. He suggested that Americans could learn from Europe much about the management of schools: "It seems to me that it would be most strange if ... many beneficial hints for our warning or our imitation could not be derived." He did not hesitate to say that "there are many things abroad which we, at home, should do well to imitate. ... If the Prussian schoolmaster has better methods of teaching reading, writing, grammar, geography, arithmetic, etc., so that, in half the time, he produces greater and better results, surely we may copy his modes of teaching these elements, without adopting his notions of passive obedience to government, or of blind adherence to the articles of church."

Educational conventions and memorials. Progressive educational sentiment was reflected in conventions, in official state surveys, and in reports and memorials to legislatures. Conventions of one kind or another in the interest of education were held in almost every state. In New York, New Jersey, and Pennsylvania organizations of teachers and other friends of schools held meetings and prepared addresses to the public and memorials to lawmaking bodies.

The Western Academic Institute and Board of Education, formed in 1829, sent advocates of better schools up and down Ohio, made Cincinnati the center of educational publicity for that part of the country, and urged the legislature to commission Calvin E. Stowe to study and report on European schools; the Illinois Educational Convention, with delegates from more than half the counties of the state, met at Vandalia in 1834 and a decade later at Peoria, with practical results; the Pennsylvania Society for the Promotion of Public Schools, with a membership of two hundred and fifty, began a movement in 1827, and issued addresses to the public which resulted in practical educational legislation in that state seven years later; the North Carolina Institute of Education, to promote the general education of the people of that state, was organized at Chapel Hill in 1831.

Conventions in Virginia. Although the slaveholding states did not accept the democratic doctrines of education so fully as some of the free states because of slavery, the aristocratic conception of education, sectarian interests, the rural character of the South, and poor means of communication, which retarded the revival spirit, yet a new consciousness on the subject of education was being aroused in that section of the country also. The agitation for better schools was particularly strong in the western counties of Virginia, where slavery was less extensive and where the influence of the middle class was making itself felt. In the autumn of 1841 an educational convention was held at Clarksburg (now in West Virginia), which was attended by more than a hundred delegates, many of whom were very prominent. About the same time another convention was held at Lexington and was presided over by Dr. Henry Ruffner, president of Washington College (now Washington and Lee University) and father of William H. Ruffner, Virginia's educational leader from 1870 to 1882. Ruffner prepared and had presented to the legislature a report which pointed out the defects of Virginia's school system and recommended state taxation, a state board of education, a state superintendent, normal schools, and public libraries. The chief weakness of the plan appeared in the proposal that, although the schools were to be supported by taxation, the local school officers were to designate the families most worthy of aid.

A convention held in Richmond about the same time was attended by many members of the legislature. A memorial to the legislature and an address to the people were prepared, and a bill based on the plan proposed by the meeting later passed the House but was rejected by the Senate. In 1845 another convention met in Richmond, presented a memorial to the legislature, and proposed a plan for a state superintendent, state support for schools, and provisions for training teachers. Some improved legislation resulted, but the weakening element of charity persisted to the close of the ante-bellum period. In the late eighteen-fifties, however, two sessions of the Virginia Educational Convention were held in Richmond, when the state's educational arrangements were severely criticized, particularly by Governor Henry A. Wise. As a result, attention turned definitely toward questions of reform : the complete abolition of the element of charity, the establishment of state supervision and control, the coördination of the elementary schools and the higher schools, and provision for the training of teachers. The plan proposed was to supersede the system then in operation and to correlate all educational agencies in the state. Resolutions passed by these conventions deplored "the feature of charity to paupers" as odious and degrading, recommended the organization of a teachers' association, and discussed the "ignorance and hopeless degradation of infant operatives employed in cotton and woolen factories." Despite these manifestations of interest, however, practically nothing was achieved for substantial educational improvement in Virginia during the closing years of the ante-bellum period.

Survey reports in South Carolina. Awakened interest was expressed in South Carolina also. As early as 1838 Governor Patrick Noble requested the legislative appointment of a commission to examine the school system of the state and to recommend needful alterations in it. The reports of the commissioners were placed the next year in the hands of a special commission composed of Professors Stephen Elliott and James H. Thornwell of South Carolina College, who reported to the legislature. In 1846 the State Agricultural Society appointed a committee to study and report on the "defects of the present school system." The result was a report by R. E. W. Allston the following year. About the same time a committee was appointed by the legislature for the same purpose and made its report through the chairman, Henry Sumner. All three reports recommended state support and state control and provisions for the training of teachers, but no practical results followed, and the state held back from establishing an adequate school system before 1860.

The agitation in Tennessee. An educational convention was held in Knoxville in 1847, and a memorial was sent to the legislature recommending state support, state supervision, the examination and certification of teachers, and the publication of a monthly educational journal; but nothing came of the proposed legislation. In 1853 Governor Andrew Johnson declared that the school system fell short of the "imperative commands of the constitution" and urged the legislature and the people to "lay hold of this important subject with a strong and unfaltering hand." Three years later a bill to establish a normal school failed on the third reading in the legislature on account of sectional jealousies in the state.

In Georgia and Alabama. Efforts were made in Georgia in 1845 and again in 1858 to improve the public schools of the state. At the latter date an enthusiastic educational convention attended by delegates from sixty counties was held at Marietta, an address to the people of the state was prepared, and a state board of education, a state superintendent, state support for schools, and the preparation of teachers were recommended. Near the close of the antebellum period a meeting of the advocates of public education was held in Atlanta during the exhibition of the Southern Central Agricultural Society, and the legislature was memorialized for schools "to which the children of the poorest parents shall be sent, without submitting parent or child to the jeer of pauperism. . . . Schoolhouses which shall awaken a feeling of pride in every neighborhood, and cause the richest to feel that no private teaching can afford equal advantages to the common school. . . . We must have *free public schools* in every school district in Georgia." In 1858 Governor Joseph E. Brown urged the legislature to establish an adequate school system for the state, but it failed to do so before 1860. The Alabama Educational Association, formed in 1856, held several meetings before the war, numerous local educational associations were also organized, and the *Alabama Educational Journal*, established by Superintendent William F. Perry in 1857, aided in the development of progressive educational sentiment. Educational conventions were held in the other Southern states also, but few of them before the outbreak of the war established school systems on the principles of public support and control. Perhaps the nearest approach to this ideal was made after 1852 in North Carolina under the superintendency of Calvin H. Wiley.

The lyceum movement. Perhaps the most effective educational agency which touched the lives of adults during the second quarter of the nineteenth century developed through the lyceums, those popular and voluntary societies of citizens who sought to coöperate in "the great and dignified cause of universal education." The movement sprang from democratic and spontaneous influences, and attempted to realize that patriotic injunction of George Washington's in his "Farewell Address" to "increase the institutions for the diffusion of knowledge among men." Originating in Millbury, Massachusetts, in 1826 through the work of Josiah Holbrook, it became nationally organized into the American Lyceum, which held its first meeting in New York in 1831. Its principal objects were the "advancement of education, especially the common schools, . . . the general diffusion of knowledge," and the promotion of other projects for social betterment. In the support of lecture courses (its main activity, into which were sent "some of the ablest and some of the most specious men of the times") it probably helped to make the way for the Chautauqua, so closely linked with the names of John H. Vincent and Lewis Miller, and the university-extension movements of more recent development; its effort to establish "itinerating county libraries" was an early anticipation of one of the best ideas in the modern library movement. The lyceum appeared in almost every state; as early as 1835 there were, in addition to the national organization, fifteen or sixteen state organizations, more than a hundred county organizations, and three thousand town and village organizations throughout the country. According to the *American Annals of Education* for July of that year, "The most general interest prevailed in some of the Southern states, especially Georgia and South Carolina, where the lyceum had been taken up with spirit." Flourishing in the North and East before 1860, the lyceum as an institution later became conspicuous in the West and the South, where the lecturing movement has remained popular. Among the names early conspicuous in the lyceum were Edward Everett and William C.

Woodbridge of Boston, Denison Olmsted of Yale College, Thomas H. Gallaudet of Hartford; John Grissom of New York, Thomas S. Grimké of South Carolina, B. O. Pears of Kentucky, Philip Lindsley of Tennessee, and Alva Woods of Alabama. Lyceum orators included Henry Ward Beecher, Wendell Phillips, Ralph Waldo Emerson, Oliver Wendell Holmes, Horace Greeley, George William Curtis, and Abraham Lincoln.

Educational leaders. In addition to educational journalism, reports on what was being done elsewhere, conventions and memorials to legislatures, and the lyceum movement, other influences were at work during the second quarter of the nineteenth century in behalf of better schools for the masses. But the most important forces in the awakening were the labors of a few documentary characters who were intelligent in leadership, apostolic in fervor, tireless in industry, and marked by a quiet willingness to be forgotten. True, the awakening was the result of the combined efforts of many forces, for then as now reformers could do nothing alone; but the history of education in the United States during the first half of the nineteenth century is in large part the biography of a few leaders and dreamers, at whom much fun was sometimes poked in their day and on whom bitter attacks were frequently made. For then as now the conservatives and the so-called practical man of affairs had a humorous contempt for frontier thinkers, to whom, however, civilization owes its every advance despite the perpetual belief of the practical man that he is the atlas on whose shoulders lie all the problems of society.

Some of these early educational leaders — Horace Mann and Henry Barnard in the East, Calvin Wiley in the South, and Caleb Mills in the West — stand out among the most prominent, but because of the measure of his actual achievements and the extent of his influence Mann is recognized chief among them all. The educational awakening in which he had such a conspicuous part in Massachusetts was not sudden. For two decades before he became secretary of the state board of education there, definite preparation was being made for the movement of which he is known as the leader. Perhaps the one man who did most to prepare the way for him was James G. Carter, whose place in American

educational history is no less important because the leadership of the man for whom he really prepared the way was more spectacular.

James G. Carter. A short time after his graduation from Harvard in 1820, at the age of twenty-five, Carter began to teach and to write on educational subjects. His pamphlet called "Letters on the Free Schools of New England," which described the glaring defects of education in that section and pointed out

JAMES G. CARTER

many of the weaknesses of the district system, drew public attention to the need for improvement and for the training of teachers. Bad teachers and bad texts were pointed to as the chief causes of backwardness. Carter maintained the suggestive point of view that the incompetency of teaching was due more to business and professional competition than to the negligence and indifference of the public. He classified the men teachers into those who looked upon teaching as easier and a trifle more remunerative than common labor, those who used it as a stepping-stone to some other employment, and those who, knowing their weakness, despaired of distinction in any other occupation. Later his "Essays upon Popular Education" in which he outlined a plan for the training of teachers, and his unsuccessful effort to have the legislature establish an institution for that purpose in 1827, gave him the title of "Father of Normal Schools." Largely through his influence also Massachusetts enacted in that year the first public high-school law. Ten years later, while a member of the legislature, he secured, through remarkable parliamentary skill, the passage of legislation creating the State Board of Education. To the secretaryship of this board Horace Mann, who had had a decade of experience in the lower house and in the senate of Massachusetts, was appointed.

Horace Mann and his educational philosophy. Mann was a year younger than Carter, came of a family of straitened rural circumstances and rigid Calvinism, and had received only a meager schooling in youth; but at the age of twenty he was prepared in six months, by private instruction, for the sophomore class at Brown, where he made a brilliant record. He was graduated at the head of his class in 1819. The subject of his graduating oration was "The Gradual Advancement of the Human Species in Dignity and Happiness," a theme which reflects a characteristic belief of the man throughout his life — the improvability of the race through education.

Mann now turned from a career in the law, for which he had prepared and which he had practiced successfully. He abandoned opportunity in politics, in which, through legislative experience, he had labored for humanitarian and social reforms and had used his influence to advance the best movements of the time. As president of the Massachusetts senate he had signed the act that created the position for which he was selected and in which he served for twelve years with effectiveness and distinction. As soon as he had accepted the post he offered his law books for sale and his office for rent. "The bar is no longer my forum. I have abandoned jurisprudence and betaken myself to the larger sphere of mind and morals." The next generation was to be his client. "Men are cast iron, but children are wax," he said. "I devote myself to the supremest welfare of mankind upon earth. I have faith in the improvability of the race — in their accelerating improvability."

Conditions in Massachusetts. The need for reform of the public schools was urgent in Massachusetts as elsewhere at that time. In all the states there was a lack of financial support, the term was short, the equipment was poor, and the teachers were inadequately trained. There was no supervision, committees did not visit the schools, and in two thirds

HORACE MANN

of the towns teachers were allowed to begin their schools without being certificated as required by law. There was a confusion of textbooks, and one third of the children were absent from school in winter and two fifths of them in summer. Conditions were no better even in New England. As late as 1847 the average length of term for all the schools in Maine was "eight weeks and five days to thirteen weeks and four days, for all counties." In the same year less than one tenth of all the children of school age in Vermont had as much as seventy days' schooling a year, and 6500 attended from twenty to thirty days a year, 5600 from ten to twenty days, 4300 for less than ten days, and 1800 had no schooling at all. The report was similar in Rhode Island, where more than one third of the children "attended no school for any part of the year." And in 1840 two sevenths of the 70,000 children of Connecticut "never went to school at all, with the exception of a moderate deduction to be made for those rich enough to attend private schools and academies."

Mann's effort at reform. Mann met similar conditions in Massachusetts when he began his work as secretary of the Board of Education. He turned at once to the tasks of reform. He secured and published reports on the deplorable conditions of the district schools in an effort to improve public sentiment and to make the people face the facts. He traveled up and down the state organizing and addressing public meetings and conventions, and he issued annual reports which revealed the defects of the schools and contained recommendations for correction — reports which as official documents from state departments of education have remained in a class by themselves for readableness, directness, and simplicity. These, as well as his educational addresses, revealed Mann as a master of effective language, often even eloquent and generally shot through with imagination and feeling. In addition to these two methods for arousing the public from indifference on educational matters, he edited the *Common School Journal*, through which he appealed to teachers and citizens generally in behalf of better schools. Particularly significant are these methods when it is recalled that Mann began with a meager salary and with no allowance for office or clerical assistance, and that throughout his service as secretary means of transportation and communication were slow, and the fountain pen and typewriter had not come into common use. Added to the sad plight of the schools themselves were other obstacles which stood in the way of this tireless worker. He was opposed by

all conservatives and those of pronounced prejudices —
"sordid politicians, unprogressive schoolmen, and sectarian
preachers," many of whom did not hesitate to attack him
in Sunday sermons and, through a hostile religious press, to
tear regularly into him.

Sectarianism in Massachusetts. Denominational feelings
and sectarian bias ran strong in Massachusetts as in other
states at that time. The long and strong monopoly of schools
by the church made the battle to eliminate sectarianism
from education no less fierce than the struggles which waged
over public support, public control, and the contest to remove the taint of charity from public schools. The change
from religious to secular control was very slowly made in
the old states and only after bitter struggles. In many cities
church and private schools had shared in public-school
funds; in Pennsylvania they had been aided from public
sources until 1834. The coalition of church and private-
school interest had worked the repeal of New Jersey's first
general school law of 1829 and later had forced to themselves
a share of the public appropriation for schools. In New
York the sectarian fight had been taken to the legislature
in an attempt to divide the public-school funds among en-
vious and contentious religious denominations; but out of
this conflict rose the New York City Board of Education
and state legislation that public funds could not be used in
any school which taught, inculcated, or practiced "any
religious sectarian doctrine or tenet."

The sectarian fight was particularly bitter in Massachusetts, and the question which Mann had labored years before
to settle was not finally settled until 1855. While a member
of the legislature Mann had made a speech against religious
intolerance, and the narrow religionists, whose number was
considerable, had neither forgiven nor forgotten him for
his liberal views. When he became secretary of the Board
of Education they attacked him and it and assailed the

public schools as Godless. They urged that local communities had the right to have religious instruction in their schools if they desired it, and insisted that if they were deprived of that right they were justified in withdrawing their public support of education. The issue was drawn clearly, but Mann met it squarely in public letters and through his reports, answering the criticisms and pointing out errors in arguments. He believed that the Bible was highly valuable as an aid to the building of character, but that it should be read without comment in the schools and not taught in them. Deeply religious but no narrow sectarian, he warned against any attempts to teach creeds and dogmas which he believed would destroy public education. So bitter was the controversy that an effort was made in the legislature in 1840 to abolish the State Board of Education and the normal schools. The fight continued to wage until the adoption, fifteen years later, of a constitutional amendment which the people had rejected in 1853.

The struggle on the question was intense in other states. It was finally settled generally by statutes or constitutional amendments, though echoes of the ancient fight have occasionally resounded in some states in connection with the public support of higher education. In laws and constitutional provisions after 1850 the monopoly of the Church in education — especially in the elementary schools — gave way to the increasing power of the State. The aims of the school, which had been religious during the colonial period and the early years of the national period, gradually became civic. The subject matter of instruction came slowly to be purged of sectarian and denominational elements, control of education shifted from the Church to the State, and prohibitions were set up against the diversion of public-school funds to contending religious sects who had sought public aid for the propagation of their own peculiar beliefs. The principle of nonsectarianism which was established through such bitter struggles was just as essential to the development of the American school system as was agreement upon the principles of public taxation and public supervision. Any other arrangement would have meant confusion and ultimate disaster to education.

Mann's famous controversy. Mann's skill as a fighter for causes in which he believed is exhibited best perhaps in his contest with the Boston schoolmasters, which arose out of his seventh report (1843), in which his praise of the Prussian schoolmasters caused those of Boston to suffer in contrast. The first reception of the report was very enthusiastic, but thirty-one school principals of Boston resented such expressions of Mann as "ignorance of teachers" and "sleepy supervision" and issued a keen reply, called "Remarks upon the Seventh Report of Mr. Mann." It ran to one hundred and forty-four pages. Two months later Mann replied with much severity to the extent of one hundred and seventy-five pages. Some of the principals published a "Rejoinder," to which Mann replied in "Answer to the Rejoinder to the Reply to the Remarks on the Seventh Report," which closed what is probably the most celebrated controversy in all American educational history. Private criticism naturally annoyed him, but in defense of the report he wrote: "There are owls who, to adapt the world to their own eyes, would always keep the sun from rising. Most teachers amongst us have been animated to greater exertions by the account of the best schools abroad. Others are offended at being driven out of the paradise which their own self-esteem had erected for them." But in this as in his other less spectacular fights Mann triumphed. Public opinion had been won to his side, and men like Josiah Quincy, Charles Sumner, Edward Everett, John G. Whittier, and others — merchants, bankers, and professional men — flocked to his support and raised $5000 among themselves and appealed to the legislature for a like amount to be used for the improvement of the normal schools. The outcome of the controversy strengthened public confidence in Mann and helped greatly to give him eminent place among educational statesmen.

Mann's achievements. Mann's achievements were significant during the dozen years of educational leadership in Massachusetts, which was itself the educational leader of the country. The financial support of public schools doubled, two millions were expended for improved school buildings, salaries of teachers greatly increased, a month was added to the annual school term, supervision improved and respect for skilled superintendence arose, three state normal schools were established, numerous high schools were developed, and public-school libraries were popularized. Mann undertook to improve methods of teaching and textbooks, to develop a professional consciousness among the teachers, and to place school discipline on a more nearly rational basis. These achievements were important not only in themselves but as indications also of a better educational outlook.

Mann's wide influence. Mann's influence extended not only to neighboring states, which copied the school plans of Massachusetts, but penetrated also to states in the West and elsewhere. Through the work of Domingo Faustino Sarmiento, the distinguished educator and publicist of South America, Mann's influence reached that continent also. Sarmiento visited the United States from August to November of 1847, saw much of Mann, whom he described as "a noble promoter of education," and on his return submitted to the secretary of public instruction in Chile a report of his trip which revealed the visitor as an apostle of education in the United States. In an important book, "De la Educación," which he published in 1849, he printed sections of the school laws of Massachusetts (directing especial attention to the fact that elementary education was there supported in part by general tax), described the normal schools and the training of teachers, and, in treating the subject of state control, gave considerable attention to the system in the state of New York. His summary of the educational doctrine then being slowly accepted in the United States was this: "Primary education is a branch of public administration. The State presides over education, directs and inspects it." The book influenced the secretary of public instruction to draft an organic school law for Chile, but it was so bitterly fought that a less progressive bill was enacted in 1849. However, from Sarmiento's work, inspired largely through Mann, dates the pervasive influence of the United States on educational affairs in Chile and also in Argentina, where Sarmiento served for two years as governor of the province of San Juan. In 1863 Sarmiento was sent as the representative of the Argentine Republic to the United States, where he continued his study of education. A treatise (the result of his investigations), which he sent two years later to the Argentine secretary of public instruction, contained a translation of the life of Mann. "If I could give any advice to the South American governments," Sarmiento said, "it would be that they procure the greatest possible number of copies of the writings of Horace Mann and scatter them freely in every city and village."

As president of Argentina for a term of six years, beginning in 1868, Sarmiento was in a position to put into practice some of the educational reforms which he had for many years advocated. He signed a law granting a subsidy for the establishment of a normal school of agriculture, established two national normal schools, brought university professors from foreign countries, and approved appropriations to purchase school furniture in the United States and to bring women teachers from this country to Argentina. Legislation was enacted also to promote the public translation of certain North American works on education and on the constitutional history of the United States. In 1873 Sarmiento issued a decree reorganizing the curricula of the secondary schools of the Argentine Republic according to a plan patterned closely on the work of secondary schools in the United States. One of his most influential books was called "Schools, Basis of the Prosperity and of the Republic in the United States." Mrs. Mann wrote an introduction to the translation of Sarmiento's "Life in the Argentine Republic," in which she acknowledged that her interest in the subject had arisen "both from a personal one that grew out of his peculiar relations with my husband . . . and from a deep interest in the nation whose highest aspirations rather than whose actual conditions he represents."

Mann's later career. Mann continued his work as secretary of the State Board of Education until 1848, when he was selected from Daniel Webster's congressional district to take the seat in Congress made vacant by the death of John Quincy Adams. He served out the unexpired term (he had lost the regular renomination by a very small margin through the opposition of Webster and the party machine of the state), was elected as an independent candidate by a large vote, and served in Washington until 1853, when he was made a candidate for governor. But he was not elected, and he soon cast his lot with the fortunes of Antioch College, a new denominational, coeducational, and coracial institution at Yellow Springs, Ohio, where he went as president and where he died in 1859. In his last public utterance he sounded the keynote to his useful life, "Be ashamed to die until you have won some victory for humanity."

Henry Barnard. Henry Barnard, the peer of Horace Mann in most respects, if not all, was born in Hartford, Connecticut, in 1811, attended the common schools and later an academy, entered Yale at the age of fifteen, and was graduated four years later. Like Mann, he prepared for the practice of the law but turned aside to teach, then spent from 1835 to 1837 in Europe studying schools (especially those in which Pestalozzian methods were used), became on his return a member of the Connecticut legislature from Hartford, and promptly proposed and secured in 1838 the passage of a bill to create a state board of education after the manner of Massachusetts. Barnard became its first secretary at wages of three dollars a day and traveling expenses, arranged educational conventions in every county, visited schools, carried on correspondence with more than two thirds of the teachers of the state, wrote on school architecture, and spoke at numerous meetings in behalf of the common schools, which he found in no better condition in Connecticut than Mann was finding them in Massachusetts. Through the *Connecticut Common School Journal*, which he established and edited, through his annual reports (the first one of which the famous James Kent, in his

HENRY BARNARD

"Commentaries," called a bold and startling document which "contains a minute, accurate, comprehensive, and instructive exhibition of the condition and operation of the common-school system"), and by other means he aroused the people of the state on the subject of schools. The awakening seems to have been too sudden, however, for in 1842 the politicians followed the way New York had taken in 1821, when Gideon Hawley, too active as the first superintendent of schools in that state, was removed and his office abolished.

Barnard's resourcefulness and achievements. But Barnard was more resourceful than Hawley had been. He went over to Rhode Island and addressed the legislature in joint session on the subject of education — an effort which is said to have been one of the greatest of his life. The result was the enactment of a law similar to that which Connecticut had passed and later repealed. Barnard became the first commissioner of education in Rhode Island, where he served effectively and with distinction until ill health forced him to leave. Meantime he had greatly improved the educational conditions of the state. He secured taxation for schools, distributed more than sixteen thousand educational pamphlets, established libraries of at least five hundred volumes in nearly all the towns of the state, encouraged the development of teachers' institutes for the training of teachers, promoted a traveling model school to demonstrate the best methods of teaching, and, after five years, left with a testimonial of regret from the teachers and a legislative vote of thanks for the able, faithful, and judicious manner in which he had performed his tasks — doubtless to the humiliation of Connecticut, which had legislated this eminent man out of office. But that state must have repented, for Barnard returned and served with marked success as principal of the normal school of Connecticut and ex-officio secretary of the State Board of Education from 1851 to 1855, when ill health again drove him from official life. In the latter year he helped to establish the American Association for the Advancement of Education, became its first president, and began the editing and publication of the *American Journal of Education*, which ran to thirty-two stout volumes and sucked up his fortune. Three years later he published his "Pestalozzi and Pestalozzianism," which in its revised form has remained perhaps the best source of information in English on the subject. He directed as president the University of Wisconsin from 1858 to 1860 and served as president of St. John's College in Maryland for a year before his appointment in 1867 as the first United States Commissioner of Education, a position which he filled with credit until 1870. This "scholar" of the awakening, as he has so aptly been called, died at the ripe age of eighty-nine, full of honors and of great achievements.

Calvin H. Wiley. In their fitness for educational leadership, in the problems which they faced, in the policies which they pursued, and, to a considerable degree, in the reforms which they achieved as chief state school officers, there are striking similarities between Horace Mann in Massachusetts and Calvin H. Wiley in North Carolina. Wiley was born on a farm in Guilford County in 1819, the year of Mann's graduation from college, and was prepared for college by David Caldwell, one of those effective teachers who found their way from Princeton and established academies in the Southern states in the late eighteenth century. Caldwell's "log college," located near Greensboro in 1767, soon became one of the most important institutions of learning in the South. From it Wiley entered the University of North Carolina, where he was graduated with high honors in 1840. Later he studied law and located at Oxford for the practice of his profession, edited the *Oxford Mercury* from 1841 to 1843, and still later became associate editor of the *Southern Weekly Post*, published at Raleigh and devoted to civic, educational, and industrial improvement.

As a member of the legislature in 1850 he introduced and worked for a bill which provided for the office of state superintendent of schools. The proposed legislation was unsuccessful; but two years later it was enacted, largely through the influence of Wiley, who was again a member of the legislature. Although a Whig in politics, he was appointed to the new position by a large majority of the legislature, which was Democratic. He took office in January, 1853, and served continuously as superintendent of schools until 1866, when he retired to private life. In 1872 and again two years later he was proposed as the Conservative candidate for the superintendency, which had now become an elective office, but he declined to offer himself for the post because the public schools had been brought into partisan politics. But he continued active in local educational matters, helped to establish the graded-school system in Winston, and served as chairman of the school board of that city until his death in 1887.

The way prepared for Wiley; the work of Caldwell. The way for Wiley had also been prepared. The report of Murphey in 1817 (pp. 196–198) had led to the establishment of a permanent public-school endowment in 1825 which grew so rapidly that a school system, supported by the income from it and by local county taxation, had been established in 1839. Meantime other forces were at work to widen and strengthen sentiment for public schools. Perhaps one of the strongest of these influences appeared in the work of Joseph Caldwell, another educational apostle from Princeton. Caldwell was the first president of the University of North Carolina, and served in that position from 1804 to 1812 and again from 1817 to 1835. In an address before an internal-improvements convention at Raleigh in 1829 he had declared that the state was backward in education because of the fatal delusion that taxation was contrary to democratic government. Three years later he published a series of eleven letters on education which he addressed to the people of the state. These letters were similar in purpose and tone to six letters which the Yankee schoolmaster Caleb Mills addressed to the people of Indiana between 1846 and 1852 on the same subject. Both series of letters are significant for the direct and doubtless accurate descriptions they gave of educational weaknesses in the two states and the appeal they made for improvement. No less remarkable is the fact that these voices cried out the truth without being hushed by the wildernesses whose educational shortcomings they so grimly reported and so severely criticized.

Caldwell, among other things, said that the people of North Carolina had long resisted any change in their routine legislation, and that they resisted any taxation beyond such as was required for the bare necessities of the government; compared conditions in North Carolina with those in the states which had made most improvement; pointed to the plight of the thousands of the people of the state who could not read; and declared that many of the people were indifferent to education, and that some of them boasted of their illiteracy. He discussed the economic and material conditions which resulted from inadequate education, pointed out the obstacles in the way of provision for schools, and showed how they could be removed. One of these obstacles was "the aversion with which we recoil from laws that exercise constraint upon our actions. We are people whose habits and wishes revolt at everything that infringes upon an entire freedom of choice upon almost every subject." He believed that provision for the general instruction of the people could scarcely be made "without some compulsory measures regulating the actions of individuals into particular channels directed upon the object." He proposed plans for improvement and appealed to the legislature to lead the way. "And how shall the confidence and the affections of the people be regained?" he asked. "It is by stripping off the offensive and contemptible disguise, and presenting Education in all the beauty and excellence of her proper character. No sooner shall this be done than all will fall in love with her. Her presence will be courted as the privilege and ornament of every vicinage, and under her patronage the clouds and mists that lower upon us will be dissipated." Wide discussion of conditions followed Caldwell's criticisms. The first school law of the state was enacted in 1839; and by 1853, when Wiley began his work as the chief school officer of the state, a fairly creditable educational plan was in operation in North Carolina.

Conditions in North Carolina. This defect made Wiley's task very difficult. County school officials were notoriously negligent of their duties as prescribed by law, localism was strongly intrenched, teachers were poor in preparation and migratory in habits, schoolhouses were primitive, textbooks were nondescript, and there was much misinformation and prejudice concerning public education. Sectional, sectarian, and partisan critics launched attacks both upon the schools and upon Wiley, who was trying to purge the public schools of the fatal taint of charity, which had so long attached to them, and to elevate them "from the position of a beneficence to a class to that of a fundamental interest of all the state." He attacked these and many other problems with admirable patience, intelligence, resourcefulness, and energy. He was reappointed in 1854 without any opposition, although there were wild rumors that the office would be abolished, and was continuously reappointed to it by a legislature of political opponents. In a few years the danger to the public schools, which had been threatened by sectarianism, by the private-school interests, and by partisan politics, was decreasing, and Wiley and the cause for which he worked continued to gain in public esteem.

Wiley's methods and achievements. Wiley conducted campaigns for better schools in every part of the large state, the trips being made usually by private conveyance and at his own personal expense. With no allowance for office or for travel during his early years as superintendent, the cost of these efforts to arouse public interest in favor of improved educational facilities often required half his salary. But the task never discouraged him. He collected facts about school systems in other states and made comparisons with his own. Through reports to the legislature, through the state educational journal, which he founded and edited, through the state teachers' association, which he organized and led, through newspaper articles, speeches, and conferences, —

through all these he created and directed an increasingly wholesome public opinion in behalf of common schools, which he viewed as a "vast and sublime moral organization" for the state. He encouraged and coöperated with Braxton Craven in the work of Normal College, and urged improved provisions for the training and certification of teachers.

He had published "The North Carolina Reader," at his own expense before he became superintendent, but he disposed of his interest in it immediately afterwards; it became and remained a standard in the schools, and helped to create and foster a wholesome spirit among the masses. Other texts prepared under his direction, from which he took no financial revenue, were also widely used. Wiley believed fully in the principles of free and

CALVIN H. WILEY

universal education by public support and under public control, and was decided in his advocacy of education for the negroes when they became citizens after the war. He shared with Mann the strong belief that the public schools could be made so superior to private schools that they would be universally recognized, and that the aristocratic conception of education would pass away. It was not only in the state that his leadership was recognized and his services were in demand; calls frequently came to him from other states for lectures, addresses, and educational advice. Virginia, South Carolina, and Georgia sought to copy the educational example of North Carolina. Wiley was invited to appear before the legislature of Georgia to aid that state in improving its schools. He tried to bring into harmony with the democratic principles of education every feature of the schools which his close observation found clashing with them, he "touched with a most cautious hand" every irregularity, and he used every effort "to make the schools grow in efficiency and usefulness as well as in public affection." He found it easy, just as chief state school officers have since found it and now find it, "to give opiates and tonics: but how was the glow of permanent health to be infused into a system, not mortally sick, but wasted and emaciated with obstinate, complicated chronic disorders?"

Wiley's annual report of the work of the schools for 1860, which appeared a little more than two months before North Carolina joined the Confederacy, showed that 150,000 of the 221,000 school children were enrolled in more than 3000 schools, that 2700 teachers had been licensed during the year, that more than $100,000 had been collected in local school taxes, that the average annual school term was four months, and that the average monthly salary paid teachers was about $26. He pointed to the growing tendency to build new and better schoolhouses and to improve the qualifications of teachers. At the meetings of the State Teachers' Association in the closing years of the ante-bellum period the principal subjects discussed were teacher-training and the better grading of the schools; according to Wiley the chief defect of the schools was their horizontal character, "furnishing one kind of education for children of all ages, and of every degree of advancement." A very wholesome educational sentiment continued during the war. Shortly after hostilities began the press of the state had urged renewed efforts to prevent the suspension of the schools. "In the name of the good people, and especially the children of the State, let none of the schools be abandoned," advised the

Raleigh Standard; and the *Charlotte Democrat* declared that "the children of the State must be taught to read and write, war or no war." In his message to the legislature in November, 1864, Governor Zebulon B. Vance begged that body not to forget the schools amid the great concerns of war. "Our great system of common schools is, after all, our only true and solid foundation for public education and demands your constant and fostering care." When Johnston surrendered in April, 1865, Wiley was receiving official reports from the school officers of the various counties; but during the dark days that followed, while efforts were being made to reëstablish the relations of the state with the national government, political matters absorbed public interest and the schools received little attention.

Caleb Mills. Caleb Mills was born in New Hampshire in 1806. He was graduated from Dartmouth College in the class of 1828, which numbered forty members, ten of whom, according to Barnard's *American Journal of Education*, became effective educational workers; he traveled for two years in Kentucky and Indiana in the interests of the Sunday-school movement; he then returned and entered Andover Theological Seminary, from which he was graduated in 1833. He had been greatly impressed with the educational needs of the West, and while a student at Andover he had read in the *Home Missionary* an article by James Thomason, a minister of Crawfordsville, Indiana, stating that a school was soon to be begun in that community "where a competent number of teachers may be trained to be spread over the country to teach the children of this rapidly populating district."

Conditions in Indiana. Mills wrote Thomason a letter practically outlining the plan of a campaign, which he later led, to arouse a more lively interest in the need for education, to change public sentiment, to overcome prejudice, and to awaken the public mind "to the importance of carrying the means of education to every door" — achievements which he knew would require "the work of years." Confident in the regenerative power of wisely directed general education and moved by the need of the Wabash country, this apostle of enlightenment "cast his lot with the pioneers of learning in this wilderness of illiteracy." "They are the most ignorant people in the world," General Arthur St. Clair, governor

CALEB MILLS

of the Northwest Territory, had said in 1790. "There is not a fiftieth man that can read or write." In 1840, seven years after Mills had begun work in the school that became Wabash College, one seventh of the entire adult population was illiterate, and Indiana stood lowest in literacy of all the free states. A decade later the number of illiterates had increased "to one in every five, and Indiana had fallen below

many slave states." It was to improve these backward educational and cultural conditions that Mills gave, directly or indirectly, more than forty years of his life. During most of this time he served Wabash College, took an active interest in religious and educational affairs in the state, and easily became familiar with the conditions and needs of frontier life. Many of the educational reforms between 1846, the date of the first of his six messages to the legislature, and 1879, when he died, can be traced to his influence.

In 1816 the constitution of Indiana had declared it to be the duty of the legislature, "as soon as circumstances will permit," to provide for a general system of education, from township schools to a state university, "wherein tuition shall be gratis and equally open to all." A school law had been enacted eight years later which permitted a district tax or rate bills for school support. There was little educational progress and no additional school legislation, however, until 1836, when an act — a gesture toward state taxation — was passed; but, bitterly opposed, it soon became a heated political issue and was repealed in 1837. An act of 1841, like earlier laws, did little more than legalize the practice of using public-school funds to aid private schools. Nothing more of educational importance was done by the legislature until Mills began to publish in the *State Journal* a remarkable series of "addresses to the Legislature," which appeared on the opening day of the sessions of that body in 1846 and the succeeding years, and of the constitutional convention which followed. The documents were signed "One of the People" and came to be known as the "Read, Circulate, and Discuss" pamphlets.

Addresses to the legislature. Mills expected it to be thought that he had gone out of his place in calling the attention of the governing authorities of the state to their educational duty. He did not hesitate to say that education had not received from the governors and legislators such care as the needs of the people demanded. In his appeals, marked by tact and courtesy, there was little if any reproach or bitterness; but although the tone of the addresses was kindly and their style logical and clear, they sparkled occasionally with an irony which bit without apology into "the appointed guardians of the commonwealth." The only apology he offered for his presumption was the importance of the subject. He believed that proper and efficient action in it would "awaken no sectional jealousies, alarm no religious prejudices, and subserve the interests of no political party," but would benefit every part of the state, improve all classes of the people, give permanency to their civil and religious institutions, "increase the social, literary, and intellectual capital of our citizens, and add materially to the real and substantial happiness of everyone." The dividends from public education would be paid, he said, "at the fireside of every freeman in the commonwealth" to the children of those who make the investment, in a currency that would never depreciate as long as knowledge and virtue were valued and appreciated.

Mills boldly pointed to the large number of children who were deprived of the means of an education which "should be the birthright of all, without distinction of rank or color." He appealed to the governor and the legislators to face the "whole truth, know the worst, and provide for it." In the legislature were members from rich and populous counties who perhaps did not know that "a sixth, fourth, or third of their constituents could not read the record of their legislative wisdom, nor peruse the eloquent speeches delivered in these halls and spread over the state at the expense of the commonwealth." The representatives from Jackson, Martin, Clay, and Dubois counties, where only a little more than half the people could read and write, "must feel themselves very much relieved from the burden of sending newspapers and legislative documents." He pointed out that the states with the best schools were those whose people were "willing to pay for their support from year to year." He believed that a permanent public-school endowment which relieved the state of taxation was less a blessing than a curse (a fact that Connecticut had learned to its sorrow many years earlier), and criticized severely the management of Indiana's school lands. He noted that the state had borrowed millions for physical improvements, but had not "raised a dollar by ad valorem taxation to cultivate the minds of our children. No wonder we have had logrolling legislation and practical repudiation! No marvel that

Indiana faith has been synonymous with Punic faith and her credit for years a byword in the commercial world." He used arguments which are now axiomatic in this country to show that education increases economic prosperity.

The succeeding messages followed the theme of the first, with emphasis now on one feature of an adequate public-school system and now on another. He urged legislation that was simple and plain in its meaning, wise and effective in its provisions, "and practical and energetic in its operation," and showed how such a law could be passed. His arguments for supervision have not been greatly improved upon even by the most enthusiastic advocates of the present. He noted that banks, roads, and courts required supervision and inspection. He preferred to lose his "bank stock (if I had any) through the dishonesty of a cashier, break my wagon through the negligence of an indolent road supervisor, or be defrauded of my property through the incompetence or corruption of a court, than to expose my children to the influence of ignorant and unprincipled, profane, and intemperate teachers." It would be vain, he said, to provide public funds for schools without adequate provision for competent supervision.

Mills's advanced views. Mills saw only one way to secure good schools, and that was to pay for them, and only one way to make children desire to attend schools, and that was "to make them what they ought to be." In his plea for safe and comfortable physical equipment there is rebuke for the guardians of the scores of thousands of miserable school buildings which still remain in the United States, especially in the rural areas. Then as now bright and promising children passed for blockheads in school when their dullness could be charged in part to the unwholesome conditions to which they were exposed. His reports while he was state superintendent of public instruction from 1854 to 1856 reflect advanced views of public-school administration, and his effort in 1857 to have the high office divorced from partisan politics and viewed as a professional post revealed a perspective which many of the states have not yet gained. "The father of the common schools of Indiana" did not believe, with the enemies of educational reform, that teachers should be chosen by precincts and superintendents of schools be chosen within established geographical boundaries.

SAMUEL LEWIS

Enlistment of the help of others. Mills did not work alone. His first message had appeared in the same year that a state common-school convention was held; his second, in 1847, coincided with the recommendations of that organization for a secular school system open to all and free from the taint of charity and pauperism, for funds by taxation for schools, for standard qualifications and salaries for teachers, for a state superintendent and efficient supervision, and for improved schoolhouses and more suitable schoolbooks — reforms which Mills himself was urging. As a result of these efforts the legislature ordered a referendum in 1848 on the subject of tax-supported free schools. About 78,500 people voted in favor of the proposal and 61,887 voted against it. The following year the legislature enacted a school law authorizing the counties to levy taxes on property and insurance premiums and poll taxes for school purposes, only after the counties had voted in favor of these means of school support. Another defect was the provision that private schools could, in the discretion of the township trustees, participate in the public-school funds. The vote in 1849 showed about 79,000 in favor of the plan and 63,312 opposed to it, but fifty-nine of the ninety counties voted to accept the law, which, even with its defects, was a more substantial educational foundation than the state had ever before pro-

SAMUEL GALLOWAY

vided. Two years later the constitutional provision for public education was strengthened, and in 1852 a greatly improved school law was enacted, with mandatory taxation one of its important provisions.

Leaders in other states. Educational pioneers appeared in other states during the period of the awakening and worked for the same causes, if not always so effectively and conspicuously, as those for which Mann, Barnard, Wiley, and Mills had worked. There were John D. Pierce and Isaac E. Crary, who were influenced by the report of Victor Cousin, and worked together in Michigan to have education made a branch of the state government with proper supervision. Pierce became the first superintendent of public instruction in that state. There were Samuel Lewis and Samuel Galloway in Ohio; Robert J. Breckinridge in Kentucky; John Swett in California; Ninian Edwards, who in 1854 became the first state superintendent of schools in Illinois and who worked to make the schools free; Alexander

Dimitry, who in 1847 became the first state superintendent in Louisiana; William F. Perry, who served as the first state superintendent in Alabama; and Robert McEwen, who served as the first state superintendent in Tennessee from 1836 to 1840, but lost his educational usefulness in a cloud of scandal through the mismanagement of the school funds.

These educational leaders and the other forces with which they worked had helped to remove some of the obstructions out of the way of the public school. Much progress had been made by the close of the ante-bellum period to make the schools free and nonsectarian, to place them under public support and control, and to improve their organization. Some progress had been made also in a few of the states in the training and licensing of teachers, and here and there efforts were made to provide better schoolhouses. Slowly the school term, which at best was shamefully short, was being extended. Massachusetts in 1852 had made little more than a gesture toward compulsory-attendance legislation, the only state to do so before 1860. Public high schools were slowly appearing. By 1860 there were approximately 321 such schools, with 167 reported in Massachusetts, New York, and Ohio, and about 246 colleges and universities, only about a score of which, however, were wholly or in part state institutions. For the most part they were denominational in control and supported by tuition fees, subscriptions, and driblet gifts of religious sects. In general, educational opportunity was being widened. But the district system was strong, localism was stubborn, expert supervision was almost unknown, the schools, even of elementary grade, were nowhere fully free, and the principle of public control had not yet been completely accepted when the war of 1861 to 1865 broke out over the issue of slavery. That conflict exceeded in bitterness any struggles that had yet been waged over the democratic theory of education; but with legalized slavery removed the way of public education was to become clearer.

By their warfare against ignorance, illiteracy, and indifference and for a diffusion of knowledge among the masses the dreamers and humanists of the ante-bellum period occupy places in the American awakening no less worthy than those whose names are well known in military matters, politics, letters, or science. All of them labored for unpopular causes; but they were brave enough to tell the people the truth, even though it hurt, and to make them face the facts in efforts to shock them out of their deadly complacency and into appreciation of learning and active interest in its cause.

The place of the leaders in the awakening. These leaders sought to enlighten the public mind on the benefits of public schools when the private schools were the only respectable educational agencies, when the idea of education at public expense was scorned as communistic, and when the need for universal education was not generally felt. They urged concern for the underprivileged and looked with compassion upon physical, mental, and moral delinquents at a time when feeble-mindedness, insanity, or other deformities were viewed as practical jokes played upon puny human beings by a capricious God. They advocated gentleness and kindness in the schools when discipline within and without the schoolroom was severe; when most people believed themselves conceived in the sin and born in the iniquity of the old Adam, which must be removed by a rod of iron. They urged that the school should be a happy place, when enjoyment of any kind was generally frowned upon as wicked and unregenerate. They recommended enriched and vital courses of study — music, physiology, hygiene — when few urbanities were allowed to flourish in education, when sanitation was practically unknown, and when disease was viewed as a vengeful visitation of Providence and bathtubs as undemocratic and un-American. They urged the training of teachers, state support and state control of education, child-labor and compulsory-attendance legislation, and free schools for all at a time when the people thought of democracy as the privilege to do as they pleased, and when equality was in reality only skin-deep. Most of these ante-bellum educational leaders while laboring for such unpopular reforms turned neither to the right nor to the left. They closed their careers as frontier thinkers and workers in the "larger sphere of mind and morals" with many enduring monuments about them. In the light of their problems and their achievements they were true to conscience and the common weal, and bade defiance to ignorance always and everywhere.

Other struggles. But the American principles of education were not yet fully established, notwithstanding the new forces at work during the first half of the nineteenth century and the work of the educational leaders of the ante-bellum period. The principles of public support, public control, and free, universal, and compulsory education, and the idea of training teachers and of extending public educational effort beyond the elementary school, had not been accepted in general practice anywhere in the United States by 1860. Before these principles could be practically and widely applied other struggles had to be waged.

This chapter has covered in a general way the work of educational publicity and propaganda, of official reports on conditions in Europe, of conventions, memorials, surveys, and of the lyceum movement in preparing the way for the educational awakening of the second quarter of the nineteenth century. It has also described the important work of certain educational leaders whose influences were widely felt in the struggles to establish the American principles of education. But not all these struggles were decisively won by the close of the ante-bellum period; some continue to be waged now. The contest over the principle of public-school support is the subject of the next chapter.

REFERENCES AND READINGS

ADAMS, JAMES TRUSLOW. New England in the Republic, 1776–1850. Boston, 1926.

> Pages 363 and following deal with education and contain valuable information.

BOONE, R. G. Education in the United States. New York, 1889.

> Contains useful material on Caleb Mills.

BROWN, S. W. The Secularization of American Education. New York, 1912.

> Chapters IX and X are useful supplementary material for this chapter.

COON, C. L. The Beginnings of Public Education in North Carolina: A Documentary History, 1790–1840. 2 vols. Raleigh, 1908.

> Volume I (pp. 123–145) contains the report of Archibald D. Murphey and Volume II (pp. 545–613) the letters of Joseph Caldwell.

CUBBERLEY, E. P. Public Education in the United States. Boston, 1919.

> Chapter VI deals, among other subjects, with the awakening and the work of ante-bellum educational reformers. Contains a useful bibliography.

FISH, CARL R. The Rise of the Common Man. New York, 1927.

> Chapter X deals with education for the people during the period covered by this chapter.

GRAVES, F. P. Great Educators of Three Centuries. New York, 1912.

> Chapter XIII is on Mann's work.

HARRIS, WILLIAM T. "Horace Mann," Proceedings of the National Education Association for 1896, pp. 52–63; Educational Review, Vol. XII, pp. 105–119; Report of the United States Commissioner of Education for 1895–1896, Vol. II, pp. 887–897.

> An address before the National Education Association which tells briefly of the work of Horace Mann as an educational reformer. The first reference contains other addresses on Mann. The third reference (pp. 897–927) also contains a full bibliography of Mann.

HINSDALE, B. A. Horace Mann and the Common School Revival in the United States. New York, 1898.

> Chapters IV–VIII, XII, and XIII are useful supplementary material for this chapter.

HINSDALE, B. A. "Notes on the History of Foreign Influence upon Education in the United States," Report of the United States Commissioner of Education for 1897–1898, Vol. I, pp. 591–629.

> Discusses some English, French, and German influences and the channels through which they came.

JONES, ARTHUR J. "Are our Schools Prussian in Origin?" in *Educational Review*, Vol. LVI, No. 4 (November, 1918), pp. 271–293.

> Concludes that Prussian educational ideas exerted "a tremendous influence upon American education" after 1830, resulting in the improvement of school work and the promotion of "the democratic ideals of our own country."

JUDD, CHARLES H. "Prussia and our Schools," *New Republic*, Vol. XIV, No. 181 (April 20, 1918), pp. 347–349.

> "The elementary schools of the United States borrowed their plan of organization and the general definition of their course of study from Prussia."

JUDD, CHARLES H. "Shall we continue to imitate Prussia?" *School and Society*, Vol. VIII, No. 183 (June 29, 1918), pp. 751–753.

> An attempt to answer Monroe's article in *School and Society* for June 15, 1918, referred to below. This controversy, a trifle clouded by partisanship, contrasts strikingly with the controversy between Draper and Martin, cited in References and Readings, in Chapter V.

KNIGHT, EDGAR W. Public Education in the South. Boston, 1922.

> Chapter VII describes, among other factors in the awakening in the Southern states, the conventions in Virginia, the surveys in South Carolina before 1860, and Wiley's work in North Carolina.

KNIGHT, EDGAR W. Public School Education in North Carolina. Boston, 1916.

> Chapter V deals in part with Murphey's report; Chapter VII, with Caldwell's letters; and Chapter IX, with the work of Wiley.

MONROE, PAUL. "Further Consideration of Prussia and our Schools," *School and Society*, Vol. VII, No. 181 (June 15, 1918), pp. 691–694.

MONROE, PAUL. "Shall we continue to advocate Reforms by False Arguments," *School and Society*, Vol. VIII, No. 193 (September 7, 1918), pp. 290–294.

> These two articles by Monroe are answers to the articles by Judd in the *New Republic* and in *School and Society*, referred to above, denying that the American school system is an importation from Prussia and undertaking "to vindicate the claims of early American

democracy to one of its finest products, a universal public-school system." In contrast to the Draper-Martin controversy, cited in the References and Readings in Chapter V, this controversy is marked by partisanship and the absence of engaging humor.

ROBERTSON, WILLIAM S. Hispanic-American Relations with the United States. Oxford University Press, 1923.

Chapter VIII describes the educational contacts between the United States and Hispanic-American nations and tells of the work of Domingo F. Sarmiento as an apostle of educational reform in Chile and Argentina. Contains a bibliography.

STODDARD, PAUL W. The Place of the Lyceum in American Life. Unpublished thesis for the degree of Master of Arts in Teachers College, Columbia University, 1928.

A good brief treatise, with useful bibliographical notes.

TUTTLE, J. F. "Caleb Mills and the Indiana Common Schools," Barnard's *American Journal of Education*, Vol. XXXI, pp. 135–144.

An interesting and useful account of the work of Mills.

Proceedings of the National Education Association, 1901.

Pages 390–439 contain memorial addresses on Barnard: on his work in Connecticut and Rhode Island, as United States Commissioner of Education, and on his influence in general.

Publications of the Indiana Historical Society, Vol. III. Indianapolis, 1905.

Contains Mills's letters addressed to the legislature of Indiana from 1846 to 1852 and to the constitutional convention of 1852, a memorial address on Mills by J. F. Tuttle, and an article by Charles W. Moores on "Caleb Mills and the Indiana School System."

QUESTIONS FOR STUDY AND DISCUSSION

1. Contrast the problems which faced the ante-bellum educational leaders with those facing present-day educational leaders.

2. What means of effective educational publicity are available to chief state school officers now which were not available to Mann, Barnard, Wiley, or Mills?

3. Study and evaluate the arguments offered by Monroe and Judd (References and Readings) in support of their respective positions concerning the origin of the elementary school of the United States.

4. In what way or ways were the examinations and reports on schools in South Carolina "educational surveys"? Compare those examinations and reports with a modern school survey.

5. Consider the letters of Caldwell in North Carolina and those of Mills in Indiana. Each of these men was an "outsider," but there is little or no evidence to show that either was criticized for pointing out the educational and cultural shortcomings of his adopted state. What would probably be the public response to such criticism today?

6. Compare the subjects discussed in the early educational journals with those treated in current educational magazines.

7. Compare the school plan prepared by Jefferson for Virginia in 1779 with Murphey's plan for North Carolina in 1817, and point out similarities. Was Murphey's plan entirely democratic? Was Jefferson's?

8. Read Mann's seventh report and note the parts to which the conservative Boston schoolmasters would be likely to object.

9. Make a study of the lyceum movement in your state. Compare the lyceum with the present-day Chautauqua.

10. Consider the battle which waged over sectarianism, taking Massachusetts or New York as an example, and point out any troublesome survivals of the question now.

11. Make a study of Mann's influence on Sarmiento and, through him, on education in South America.

CHAPTER IX

SECURING PUBLIC SUPPORT

Outline of the chapter. 1. A greater proportion of public funds derived principally from taxation is now absorbed by education than by any other function of the state government.

2. Although the principle of school support by this means is now accepted, the struggle over it has been long and stubborn, objection to taxation and the dread of taxation being the main obstacles to the principle.

3. Before taxation was secured many methods of school support were used. Teachers were often paid in kind and in part by "boarding round." Tuition fees, rate bills, and indirect taxes of many kinds were in wide use.

4. In the early days lotteries were popular means of raising funds for schools and for other enterprises. Permanent public-school funds, or "literary" funds, were also established as means of public-school support. In some states these funds encouraged local taxation.

5. In time it became evident that taxation was the only safe and just means of public-school support. But even permissive taxation, the first step, was resisted, lawmaking bodies moving cautiously in authorizing taxes for schools.

6. The element of charity in education and the rate bill were features of school support that were difficult to remove. Both these features were generally found in the early educational arrangements, and survivals of them may be seen today.

7. In the struggle to secure taxation the work of Thaddeus Stevens in Pennsylvania is conspicuous, his speech on the subject being very effective.

8. The story of public-school support emphasizes the importance of state taxation and the need for increased state funds, but local taxation remains today the chief source of public-school support in most of the states, increased educational burdens being assumed and borne by this means.

9. Notwithstanding increased school funds, devotion of the people to localism in school support results in gross inequalities in educational opportunities. Although the American people are rich enough to spend upon education all that they will spend, the principle of complete public-school support has not yet been fully and practically applied in every American community.

When John D. Rockefeller was earning his first money and learning to swim and to catch perch with a bent pin in the neighborhood of Owasco Lake in the eighteen-forties, his father was working in the interests of the district school there. He found the center of the school district by driving from the north to the south boundary and counting the number of times the wheel of the buggy turned. Then he drove back for half as many revolutions, stopped, and there located the plain frame schoolhouse, in which a Sunday school was also conducted. Such a chore in early public-school control, as Chapter X shows, was simple, but no simpler than public-school support, which, like school control, had its simple beginnings in the small local community or district.

Large sums expended. As pointed out in Chapter I, education now absorbs a greater proportion of public funds than does any other governmental function. More than one fourth of the net total of all public expenditures goes for public elementary and secondary schools and higher education, with the figures running to almost three billion dollars a year. Significant is the comparison of the cost of public education with that of the combined outlays for the military, for police and fire protection, and for the enforcement of prohibition. The revenues for school support come principally from public taxation — the means by which the people of a local community or a state secure the benefits of those things which they need but cannot have except by collective purchase. The public pays taxes to itself, and has slowly learned that when they are fairly levied and properly applied they become investments in its own well-being.

Long and stubborn objection to taxation for schools. School support by public taxation is today so widely accepted in this country that it is somewhat difficult to believe that this principle of American education was forced to develop through violent opposition and struggle. But, as in the case of each of the other principles of public education in the United States, sentiment in favor of this means of school support grew slowly. Even after the beginning of the national period the attitude of the public was indifferent and often hostile to the principle of taxation for schools for all the people, and direct taxation for the support of education was difficult to levy. Effective state supervision and control came slowly also, laws which were intended to encourage public schools were at first permissive and difficult to enforce, the income from permanent public-school endowments was not always used exclusively for educational purposes, and the endowments themselves were not infrequently mismanaged and exploited for private ends. During the long period through which public education struggled for recognition it was confronted at almost every turn with indifference or contempt or open hostility. These obstacles stood definitely in the way of the support of schools by public taxation. Although the American people now accept the principle that the state has the right and the power to raise sufficient funds for the support of schools for all its members by taxation on the property of all its members, they came to accept it after much argument and delay and after numerous other means had been tried and found to be unsatisfactory.

Objection to taxation. Objection to taxation remained one of the most stubborn of all the obstacles to school support. "Money is very scarce, and the times are unusually hard" observed the writer of an open letter published in a Raleigh newspaper in 1829 and addressed to the members of the legislature of North Carolina. He asked why the matter of taxation for common-school support was "never broached in better and more prosperous days." He believed that the old-field tuition schools, in which so many people had jogged along uncomplainingly, were ample for all educational necessities, and stated that those then in operation were not all filled. "Would it not redound as much to the advantage of young persons and to the honor of the state," he asked, "if they should pass their days in the cotton patch, or at the plow, or in the cornfield, instead of being mewed up in a schoolhouse, where they are earning nothing?" He thought that too much ado was being made about education, that it was not necessary "that everybody should be able to read, write, and cipher. If one is to keep a store or a school, or to be a lawyer or physician, such branches may perhaps be taught him; though I do not look upon them as by any means indispensable; but if he is to be a plain farmer, or a mechanic, they are of no manner of use, but rather a detriment." Common schools called for additional taxes, he pointed out, and he asked "any prudent, sane, saving man" if he desired his taxes to be higher. Answering the argument "that our state is far behind her sisters in things of this sort," he said the fact proved only that the other states "are before us," which was their affair. "We shall always have reason enough to crow over them, while we have power to say, as I hope we may ever have, that our taxes are lighter than theirs."

"The savage pays no tax." Shortly after the adoption of the Constitution of the United States, Benjamin Franklin wrote that everything appeared to promise that it would last, though he promptly added, "But in this world nothing is certain but death and taxes." Thirty years later Sydney Smith, the English essayist and wit, wrote about the beardless youth managing his taxed horse, which wore a taxed bridle, on a taxed road; and the dying man pouring out his medicine, on which he had paid a tax of 7 per cent, into a spoon taxed 15 per cent, flinging himself back upon his chintz bed, on which he had paid a tax of 22 per cent, and expiring in the arms of an apothecary, who had paid a license tax of a hundred pounds for the privilege of putting him to death. Both Franklin and Smith, as well as the writer of that letter to the legislature of North Carolina a century ago, expressed the ancient belief that taxation is evil, as calamitous as death, and to be evaded and avoided if possible. On the other hand, Charles D. McIver, a North Carolina educational reformer of recent years, expressed the view that taxation justly levied and properly applied is a mark of civilization. He noted that the savage pays no tax. But he could well have pointed out how difficult it had always been, and still was, to persuade or force the people of this country to pay taxes for the support of schools.

The dread of taxation. If it was unfortunate that the beginnings of education in this country should have been made and nurtured by philanthropy, it was equally unfortunate for the cause of public schools that the quarrel with King George should have turned on a matter of taxation. The use of philanthropy in the support of schools accustomed the people to the view that education was not a responsibility of the state, to be maintained by it through taxation, but a charity for the poor when given by the state at all. The quarrel with England helped to instill into the people a terrifying dread of taxation in any form or for any purpose. True, philanthropy, although mindful most often of the poor and neglected, rendered useful educational service; but through the means which it often employed the vicious element of charity became attached to practically all forms of education not directly provided by parents or guardians. The struggle to gain school support for all has been bitter throughout the history of America because of the hatred of taxation, and it is often resumed even now when legitimate extensions of educational effort are proposed. The way of public-school support has been hard in the United States.

Many methods of early school support. While taxation for education was slowly making its way many other means of school support were being used. The expenses of students at Harvard during its early life were often paid in produce.

The account book of the institution revealed such items as "a sheep weighing sixty-seven pounds; two bushels of wheat; thirty-five pounds of sugar; eight bushels of malt; a bushel of parsnips; thirty pounds of butter; three bushels and three pecks of apples; four quarters of a wether; three quarters of a lamb; a quarter of beef; a fat cow; eighteen yards of satin; five yards of kersey; three yards of yellow cotton; two thousand nails," and Governor Joseph Dudley of Massachusetts satisfied the college accounts of his son largely in Indian corn.

Salaries of teachers in grammar schools were often paid in such commodities, the agreements generally specifying "provisions," "half in wheat and half in other corn," a certain part "in corn pay" and a certain part in money, or "one half in silver money, and the other half in good merchantable boards, at the current and merchantable price," and peas, rye, oats, and barley. A teacher in Portland for fifteen years just before the American Revolution received much of his pay in cordwood and produce. One New England town, on being incorporated in 1725, ordered through town meeting that a teacher be engaged to instruct in reading and writing. No action was taken for more than a year, and then it was proposed in town meeting that the teacher's salary be the same as that of the minister. The motion was lost, as were also other motions made successively to make the salary "forty pounds, thirty pounds, twenty pounds, and five pounds." Finally the sum of three pounds was voted as the salary for the teacher, who should keep the school "at his own house and to find himself diet."

However, poorly paid teachers were not always without other reward, as the American public has been taught to believe. The town of Malden, Massachusetts, hiring Ezekiel Jenkins for three pounds a year and the benefit of certain fees from his scholars, gave him a tombstone on which appeared these words: "Malden's late schoolmaster from a painful life is gone to take his rest. His Lord hath called him home." There is the inference here that the poor teacher was to receive reward in another world for his many discomforts in this. Records of many New England towns ordering the selectmen or commissioners to engage teachers "as cheap as they can" or "on the best terms" reflect a popular practice which prevails in some places even now. Historically, the typical American community has not required encouragement to economize in paying its teachers.

Part pay in board. In the early days school support was borne in part by adding to the teacher's small wages the cost of his board, which was to be had at the cheapest place in the neighborhood. Records of the boarding experiences of the early teachers are numerous. The following experience of a New England teacher in the closing decade of the eighteenth century differs little from conditions in some communities today, especially in those remotely rural places where the teachers must put up with discomforts and even deprivations in their living arrangements:

Having been informed where I was to board, I set out for my new home on foot, carrying the greater part of my wardrobe on my back, and the remainder tied up in a bandanna handkerchief. On arriving at the place of my destination I found my host and hostess, Mr. and Mrs. Fairbanks, ready and apparently glad to see me. They were to receive for my board, lodging, and washing, 67¢ per week. Their house was made of logs with only one room in it, which served for parlor, kitchen, and bedroom. I slept on a trundle-bed, which during the day was wheeled under the large bed, where the master and mistress of the house reposed during the night.

Boarding the teacher around with the pupils (an arrangement which was used to reduce the cost of direct school support) was a popular practice in all the states from the early days and even far into the nineteenth century. In some states it prevailed until after the Civil War. Some teachers fared better, of course, than others. Among those who were fortunate for a time was that "huge feeder" Ichabod Crane, who showed partiality for the homes of his pupils who had pretty sisters or mothers famed for the "comforts of the cupboard." But not all teachers have been so favored by the female circles of rural neighborhoods. A

ICHABOD CRANE'S SCHOOL

After a drawing by F. O. Darley, by permission of G. P. Putnam's Sons

teacher in the Hartford district as late as 1825, hearing that boarding around had been voted for him, seemed resigned to his fate "to live on *squn* all winter"— a dish of the hog-killing season, when it was customary to fry for the family dinner certain portions "consisting of the liver, pancreas, and perhaps the kidneys, possibly some of the thoracic viscera also." The hogs were killed as the master went the rounds of boarding, "so that there would be fresh meat for him."

Taxation for schools difficult to secure. Nowhere in the early days were provisions for education readily and cheerfully made by governing authorities, and under special stringency they were not made at all. Many were the devices resorted to in an effort to provide for school support without the use of direct taxation. The records reveal tuition fees, rate bills, taxes on banks, licenses on occupations and commodities, the use of lotteries, gifts, and bequests, and the income from permanent public-school endowments, fines, forfeitures, and penalties, as sources of school support. Among other sources (before the community acknowledged the right to tax the property of all its members for educational purposes) appeared taxes on natural and artificial curiosities, on traders in negroes, on the sales of runaway slaves, on billiard tables, on marriage licenses, and on liquors, innkeepers, hawkers, tenpin alleys, dogs, peddlers, and auctioneers. Funds were occasionally derived from fines on officers convicted of neglecting to execute the law respecting the swine of the town, on sales or rentals of church pews, on revenue from bank and canal stocks, on income from saline lands, and even on any income that could be extracted from the sterile pine barrens "subject to the periodical inundations of the Tombeckbee River." It is a long cry, however, from these uncertain means to the certain plan of general and direct taxation on property which every state finally came to recognize as the safest and most sensible plan for school support.

Every step contested. Progress to this final stage of school support was slow, and every step was bitterly contested. Henry Barnard reported that a member of the legislature of Rhode Island in the eighteen-forties declared that a bill which Barnard was supporting to provide a small state tax for schools could not be enforced in that state, even at the point of the bayonet, if it should be enacted into law. A farmer of the same state threatened violence if the educator were ever caught on the property of this Cincinnatus preaching such a horrible "heresy as the partial confiscation of one man's property to educate another man's child." About the same time a member of the legislature of Indiana expressed the desire to leave posterity in no doubt as to his position on the subject of state support for schools by having engraved on his tombstone "Here lies an enemy of free schools." Proposals for the extensions of education are even now resisted in many places.

The use of lotteries. The lottery, believed by some people to be evil, fought by the early labor groups as a pernicious form of taxation, and now prohibited in every state and hunted down in every hole by Federal agents, was for many years a popular source of support for public schools of all grades as well as for religious and benevolent purposes. Much money was raised by this means. The state itself conducted the lottery or sold the privilege to individuals or organizations, or it collected a part of the receipts from the sale of lottery tickets. When the ethical sensitiveness of the public sharpened to the point of taking offense at the state's serving as gambler, even for good purposes, then the state generally came to use this source of income without seeming officially to place the stamp of approval upon the evil.

At Columbia. The *New York Mercury* for May 31, 1754, carried an announcement signed by Samuel Johnson, who was in charge of the newly established King's College (now Columbia University), stating: "The chief thing that is aimed at in this college, is, to teach and engage the children to know God in Jesus Christ, and to love and serve him in all Sobriety, Godliness, and Richness of life, . . . and to train them up in Virtuous Habits." One declared purpose of the college was to provide for the students "a serious, virtuous, and industrious course of life." The same issue of the newspaper carried an advertisement of a public lottery of five thousand tickets at thirty shillings each, "832 of which are to be fortunate," for the benefit of the college. Rhode Island used lotteries for the support of the common schools and also to increase the principal of its permanent public-school endowment. Between 1812 and 1838 Congress passed more than a dozen joint resolutions to authorize lotteries for educational purposes in the District of Columbia, which used this means of support for its first public schools.

In North Carolina. The public conscience of North Carolina in 1801 saw no evil in using the lottery for promoting religion and education, and the president of the university of that state today advises youth on those and other worthy subjects from a room in a building erected in part by the smiles of the goddess Fortuna. The trustees, in the infancy of this first American state university to open its doors, were expected to use their personal influence to procure purchases of the lottery tickets, the immediate sale of which involved "the interests of the University of North Carolina, and of Learning and Science generally throughout our State." Perhaps it should be said for the moral attitude of the time that the pleasures of lotteries were seldom indulged in only for the sake of gambling, but to aid some worthy cause at a time when to use property taxes for schools was viewed by many people as a public immorality.

In New York. In 1801 New York authorized four lotteries for the purpose of raising $100,000, one eighth of the revenue to be used to encourage academies and seven-eighths for the aid of the common schools. The Public School Society of New York received some of its funds from licenses to dealers in lottery tickets. The practice enjoyed official sanction until the constitution of 1821 frowned upon it as a public activity. In 1810 Delaware authorized a lottery for $10,000 for an academy. The president of Delaware College resigned in 1835 because he believed that money received from lottery licenses and accepted by the trustees for use in the institution was tainted. The trustees, a trifle pricked in conscience, hit upon the plan of refusing to accept the fund from the hands of the evil managers of the lottery, but received it from the treasurer of the state, to whom it was turned over, and after the legislature had by special action properly appropriated it to the institution. Funds for the support of an ambitious educational plan in Louisiana in 1805 were to be raised by lotteries, and two were used in that state in 1820 for the support of the school system.

Lotteries widely used. Schools, colleges, academies, and other enterprises were aided by lotteries. A dozen or more academies were aided by more than $110,000 in Mississippi after that state was admitted to the Union. A lively discussion on the morality of lotteries followed the introduction of a bill in the legislature of North Carolina in 1827 to permit this means of support for an academy which was in danger of closing its doors. Members voted against it either because they could not "reconcile lotteries to their principles, or because they did not believe the school in danger," but more voted for it. One advocate, in defending it, pointed to the practice in "the great state of New York." Another declared that he could vote for a lottery intended for a good purpose, "to prop up a declining school, for instance," with as much cheerfulness and as little reproach of conscience as he could speculate in cotton "where there was a chance of involving his family in ruin." Another, observing the tendency of men "to venture," believed that it was good policy to provide the opportunity "to keep our money at home." He pointed out that the legislature had authorized lotteries since "the first establishment of our government," and that the practice had been sanctioned "by every member of the Union." The same session that legalized this lottery declined to appropriate twenty-five cents to buy books for many poor children who were then being taught by Sunday schools to read and write.

Permanent public-school funds. Change in sentiment on the subject of taxation for school purposes began to appear in the second quarter of the nineteenth century as the ideal of democracy grew clearer. There is a noticeable change in the thirties and forties as Jeffersonian democracy more fully flowered. Meantime the change in sentiment was being influenced also by the establishment of permanent public-school endowments, popularly known as literary funds or school funds, the income from which was designed for public-school support. This form of educational support assisted in fostering and encouraging the growth of the present conception of education as a public concern and duty, and in nearly every state in the Union the public-school system was begun and set in motion by this method of financial support. These permanent public-school funds served to destroy opposition to taxation for schools by developing a wholesome educational sentiment and by stimulating local initiative and community enterprise, but these were not the purposes of such funds when they were established.

Notwithstanding the conditions which early opposed free schools, public sentiment was never unanimous against them. In most communities there were always a few public-spirited citizens who looked with favor on proposals for public schools and believed that public education was a necessity as well as an opportunity to promote an intelligent and happy citizenship. These leaders believed that the state had an obligation to make provisions for public schools; but the discharge of such a duty called for funds, and there was almost everywhere a dominating sentiment against taxation for anything except the necessary expenses of government. Schools were not yet generally considered a state obligation, and permanent endowments showed promise of furnishing greatly needed assistance.

Interest stimulated by land grants. The national land grants also stimulated an interest in schools. When Ohio was admitted to the Union in 1802 the grants of lands for purposes of education (see Chapter VI) were confirmed to that state and given state-wide application. Each state afterwards admitted received the sixteenth section for school support and two or more sections for the support of higher education. In 1803 this policy of land endowment for schools was extended by Congress to those states to be formed out of the Mississippi Territory, and in 1826 this same principle was extended to the area acquired through the Louisiana purchase. But the older states, not sharing in these congressional land grants, turned to the establishment of permanent public-school funds on their own account: Connecticut and Delaware before 1800, New York in 1805, Tennessee in 1806, Virginia in 1810, Maryland in 1812, New Jersey in 1816, Georgia in 1817, Maine, New Hampshire, Kentucky, and Louisiana by 1821, and Vermont, North Carolina, Pennsylvania, and Massachusetts by 1834. South Carolina seems to be the only old state that did not establish some kind of permanent public-school fund before 1860. In some of the states the funds accumulated before any use was made of them for school purposes; in others they were used chiefly to provide schooling for poor children.

Purposes of permanent funds. The oldest aim or incentive for establishing a permanent public-school fund is illustrated by the act of 1795, which established such an endowment in Connecticut. But the result was unexpected and unwholesome: the fund failed to make the schools free, the increase in its income gradually checked the tendency to raise local school taxes, and from 1821 to 1854 practically the only sources of school support in Connecticut were the income from the school fund, from gifts, and from rate bills, which were not abolished until 1868.

Stimulation of local taxation. Other states profited by Connecticut's costly lesson. It was clearly demonstrated that an endowment should not entirely relieve a state or a community from local school burdens, but should stimulate and encourage local effort for school support. Any other principle would not only be a moral injury to the community and to the cause for which the fund was provided, but would mean death to the cause of schools if the people were entirely relieved of all responsibility for their support. Therefore another aim in establishing school funds was to encourage local taxation. The earliest example of this principle is found in the case of New York, where it was never contemplated that the fund, established in 1805, should yield sufficient revenue to support the schools entirely. The principle adopted here was that of local taxation, and before a community could participate in a distribution of the revenue of the fund an amount equal to its share had to be raised by local levy. This principle has been generally accepted as the soundest and most stimulating to the cause of school support and, with certain modifications, soon came to be widely adopted in the United States. North Carolina seems to have been the first of the Southern states to adopt it in the distribution of income from its ante-bellum educational endowment.

In spite of their importance as stimuli to the growth of education the record of carelessness and indifference with which public-school endowments have been managed is one of the lamentable and melancholy chapters in American educational history. This record was practically universal in the early days, before education had won its proper place in public interest. Educational funds were then rarely guarded with the jealous care that their importance and sanctity demanded. Moreover, the careless manner in which they were handled showed the indifference that confronted the early movement for public schools.

Mismanagement of permanent funds. Few of the states, if any, entirely escaped from the evils of mismanagement and the exploitation of public-school funds. The tendency toward careless management appeared early and continued for many years, more rigid control by additional legislation proving but little insurance against loss. Among the recorded causes of loss may be seen almost every species of violation of public trust. In some cases the school funds were grossly and shamefully diverted from their original purposes; in other cases their management was indifferently intrusted to incompetent officials, and the result was unwise investments; in still others loans were insufficiently secured and interest was often defaulted. Dishonest management and embezzlement by officers intrusted with the care of school funds caused other losses. Happily, however, there are but few gross examples of this form of loss. The most flagrant case perhaps is found in Tennessee, where in the late thirties Robert H. McEwen, the first superintendent of public schools in that state, succeeded in using a large part of the school fund for private purposes. Failures of banks in which school funds were invested, the use of the school funds for meeting the current expenses of the state government, and the repudiation by the state of debts due to the school funds were other forms of wrongs committed against public education. It has been pointed out that if the Federal grants applied by Arkansas to its permanent school fund had been properly managed, that state would now have a permanent endowment of about $92,000,000, which would yield an annual revenue of $4,600,000, "more than a third of the total amount Arkansas expended for public schools in 1920." Instead of such a sum, Arkansas has "a nonproductive fund whose paltry income of $74,000 is, from the standpoint of a productive endowment, a pure fiction." Considering the enormous losses which have resulted from the careless management of permanent public-school funds throughout their history, the question arises whether such funds should any longer be established or those now in existence should be held by the states in perpetuity.

State	Amount	How Used
Alabama	$669,086.78	Education
Arkansas	286,751.48	General purposes
Connecticut	764,670.61	One half to education and one half to general purposes
Delaware	286,751.48	Education
Georgia	1,051,422.09	One third to education and two thirds to general purposes
Illinois	477,919.13	Education and internal improvements
Indiana	860,254.44	One half to education and one half to general purposes
Kentucky	1,443,757.40	Education
Louisiana	477,919.13	General purposes
Maine	955,838.27	General purposes
Massachusetts	1,338,173.57	General purposes
Maryland	955,838.27	Education and general purposes
Mississippi	382,335.31	General purposes
Missouri	382,335.31	Education
Michigan	286,751.48	Internal improvements
New Hampshire	669,086.78	General purposes
New Jersey	764,670.61	General purposes
New York	4,014,520.71	Education
North Carolina	1,433,757.40	Education and internal improvements
Ohio	2,007,260.36	Education
Pennsylvania	2,867,514.80	Partly for education
Rhode Island	382,235.31	Education
South Carolina	1,051,422.09	One third to education and two thirds to general purposes
Tennessee	1,433,757.40	General purposes
Vermont	669,086.78	Education
Virginia	2,198,428.04	General purposes

NOTE. This table shows the distribution of the surplus revenue in 1837 which served as a stimulus to education in many of the states. The amount each state received and the purpose for which it was used are given according to F. W. Blackmar's "History of Federal and State Aid to Higher Education," p. 46.

The surplus revenue. Notwithstanding mismanagement and exploitation these permanent public-school funds served to increase the means of school support greatly during the ante-bellum period. In many states they were largely increased by the distribution of the surplus revenue in 1837 (see table above). In some states, as already noted, the

income from the funds was used for the education of the
poor, a policy followed in large part by Virginia, New Jersey, Pennsylvania, Delaware, Maryland, and Georgia; in
others it was used to stimulate local taxation for school
purposes, North Carolina furnishing a good example of this
plan. The permanent fund was created in that state in 1825,
but it was not used until 1839, when the first public-school
law was enacted. Under that legislation the counties received from the income of the literary fund two dollars for
every dollar which the counties raised by taxation for school
purposes. In 1860 more than $200,000 was disbursed from
the state's permanent fund for the support of schools.

Decline of permanent funds. By 1890 the importance of
permanent endowments as a means of public-school support
was gradually declining. In that year less than 6 per cent
of the total revenue for public-school support was derived
from such funds; thirty years later this source of school
support was less than 3 per cent of the total. Since that
time the percentage of public-school support derived from
permanent public endowments has shown further decrease.
Professor Fletcher Harper Swift, perhaps the most competent authority on the subject, believes that the percentage
of total public-school funds derived from permanent funds
is much less than the official state and Federal reports indicate. He has pointed out that in a third of the states
which every year report revenue for school support from
this source, these so-called permanent funds exist totally
or largely on paper or as debts of the states to their schools.
A part of the permanent school fund of Nevada, of California, and of Wisconsin exists only as a state debt. All the
surplus revenue fund of Louisiana and more than half its
school fund are recognized as permanent state debts, and
practically all the so-called permanent funds in Arkansas,
Illinois, Maine, Michigan, Mississippi, New Hampshire,
Ohio, and Tennessee are debts of these states to their schools.

PERCENTAGE DISTRIBUTION OF RECEIPTS FOR SCHOOL PURPOSES FROM VARIOUS SOURCES FOR EACH STATE, AND PER CENT OF THE TOTAL RECEIPTS DERIVED FROM THE PERMANENT SCHOOL FUND AND LEASES OF SCHOOL LAND, 1925-1926 [1]

STATES	FROM STATE	FROM COUNTY	FROM LOCAL DISTRICT	FROM PERMANENT SCHOOL FUND AND LEASES OF SCHOOL LAND [2]
Continental United States	15.0	11.1	73.9	1.4
Alabama	37.5	36.3	26.2	1.1
Arizona	20.0	35.3	44.7	3.2
Arkansas	37.5	2.8	59.7	0.6
California	20.9	34.3	44.8	0.5
Colorado	0.8	26.1	73.2	3.8
Connecticut	7.6	—	92.4	0.8
Delaware	81.5	—	18.5	1.5
District of Columbia	34.6	—	65.4	—
Florida	4.9	43.5	51.6	0.9
Georgia	33.5	28.3	38.2	—
Idaho	—	33.6	66.4	8.5
Illinois	6.8	0.2	93.0	1.0
Indiana	7.4	0.9	91.7	1.7
Iowa	4.4	—	95.6	0.9
Kansas	0.2	0.5	99.3	1.2
Kentucky	27.4	28.7	43.9	0.9
Louisiana	23.0	60.8	16.2	1.0
Maine	28.4	—	71.6	0.7
Maryland	21.2	32.3	46.5	—
Massachusetts	7.8	—	92.2	0.3
Michigan	20.9	—	79.1	0.4
Minnesota	17.4	4.6	78.0	3.9
Mississippi	33.3	37.3	29.4	2.5
Missouri	9.6	0.6	89.8	1.6
Montana	3.3	40.5	56.2	8.1
Nebraska	1.4	—	98.6	3.4
Nevada	14.6	68.5	16.9	7.3
New Hampshire	10.7	—	89.3	0.6
New Jersey	20.8	0.1	79.1	0.7
New Mexico	14.0	69.6	16.4	17.7
New York	21.4	—	78.6	—
North Carolina	6.5	65.1	28.4	0.2
North Dakota	36.7	5.0	58.3	6.6
Ohio	2.3	32.6	65.1	0.4
Oklahoma	1.4	8.9	89.7	6.0
Oregon	15.4	19.4	65.2	2.0
Pennsylvania	15.1	—	84.9	0.1
Rhode Island	3.9	—	96.1	0.3
South Carolina	29.2	28.0	42.8	—
South Dakota	1.8	1.5	96.7	8.0
Tennessee	23.9	60.2	15.9	0.9
Texas	39.1	—	60.9	6.6
Utah	34.2	—	65.8	2.9
Vermont	21.9	—	78.1	1.7
Virginia	31.0	53.4	15.6	1.0
Washington	24.9	15.1	60.0	3.8
West Virginia	3.6	—	96.4	0.2
Wisconsin	10.5	8.3	81.2	0.3
Wyoming	32.6	19.1	48.3	14.2

[1] Taken from *United States Bureau of Education Bulletin No. 39*, 1927, p. 27.
[2] Included in first column.

Taxation for schools necessary. It was early discovered that the income from so-called permanent funds, land grants, gifts, license fees, and the like was too uncertain as means of support for an adequate school plan. Although direct taxation was unpopular in the early period and continued to be objectionable for a long time, this has seemed to the thoughtful leaders the only sure and safe means by which public schools could be established and maintained. Jefferson had recognized the principle as sound as early as 1779, when he proposed to the legislature of Virginia a bill "for the more general diffusion of knowledge" and endeavored to have it enacted. Other early national leaders had also advocated public support of schools.

Jefferson's view. Jefferson accepted more clearly than any other of these men the principles of free and universal education, and yet he was aware that the parents of some intellectually capable children were "too poor to give them farther education." However, he recognized individual differences. At the common schools to be established throughout the state by his proposed plan "all the free children, male and female," were to receive their schooling free for three years; but to the secondary schools, which were to be established "convenient to the youth in every part of the commonwealth," should go from each of the common schools the boy of "best and most promising genius and disposition," selected "after the most diligent and impartial examination and inquiry ... without favor or affection" by the superintendent or overseer of the common school, but with an eye to the worthy poor. Boys so selected were to receive schooling and board free in the grammar or secondary schools: those "best in genius and disposition" for four years, those of "the least promising genius and disposition" being eliminated after a year or more in the grammar school, upon the same diligent examination and inquiry as were used to select them "as public foundationers." From those who were retained through the four years in each secondary school was to be selected in the same manner one "of the best learning and most hopeful genius and disposition" to be educated, boarded, and clothed at public expense for three years at the College of William and Mary. Under this plan the education of girls was not contemplated beyond the common schools. If the element of charity seems to appear in the arrangements for boys beyond these schools, it should be noted that Jefferson sought to recognize and encourage only the capable poor, those of promising "genius and disposition." Virginia did not have his perspective of public education, and delayed for many years the establishment of schools for all. When public taxation for schools appeared, it took permissive form there as in all the states in the early period.

Permissive taxation the first step. Legislation permitting taxation for schools was obtained first, however, in the urban communities, which always learn more readily than the rural sections the value of collective action in education as in other interests. In some states the cities began schools under permissive legislation many years before general state laws on the subject were enacted. This practice appeared in Rhode Island, New York, Pennsylvania, Alabama, Maryland, and other states. Typical cases of early state legislation permitting local communities to provide schools by public taxation include the Maryland law in 1816 which allowed the people of Caroline County to vote on the subject; the New Jersey law in 1820 which permitted any county in the state to raise funds by taxation for the education of poor children; the Missouri law in 1824 which allowed districts to levy taxes for schools on petition of two thirds of the voters of the district; the Illinois law in 1825 which provided an optional district-school tax that was rendered ineffective two years later, however, by a provision that a man's property could not be taxed for school purposes without his written consent; the Rhode Island law in 1828 which permitted its towns to levy school taxes if they saw the necessity and wisdom of such action. Other permissive state laws for school taxes were enacted in Kentucky in 1830, in Pennsylvania in 1834, in Iowa in 1840, in Virginia in 1829, and in Mississippi in 1846. Legislation permitting counties to levy school taxes was common throughout the country by 1860. This was an important principle of the initial school law of North Carolina in 1839, of Tennessee in 1854, and of Indiana in 1848.

Permissive taxation unpopular. The effort to secure even permissive legislation for school taxation was resisted long and bitterly in every state. This step toward public support of schools, though feeble and halting, was taken in almost every case after long agitation and energetic campaigns in behalf of public education. The enactment of laws providing for school support by public taxation had to wait on the development of sentiment in favor of public schools. Moreover, only the expense of the teacher's salary or wages was at first considered a legitimate charge against the public; schoolhouses and equipment were not considered proper public burdens. Under the Virginia law of 1829 the inhabitants of the district were required to raise by voluntary contributions three fifths of the amount necessary to erect a schoolhouse. The local authorities could appropriate the remaining two fifths for that purpose out of the usual county appropriation (which came from the income of the permanent public-school fund), provided it did not exceed 10 per cent of that appropriation. In 1825 Ohio permitted the building of schoolhouses in local communities, but required that the sites upon which they were to be built should be donated. Two years later the repairs to buildings were limited by law in that state, and expenditures for repairs within the limit prescribed had to be authorized by a two thirds vote of the people. In 1834 the state required each parent who sent a child to school to provide his quota of the firewood. Four years later the law of the state permitted the purchase of a site for a schoolhouse and slightly relaxed the requirement concerning the authorization of repairs by a vote of the people. The story of school support in other states is similar.

In some states school desks, blackboards, chalk, window shades, stoves, and other equipment are not regarded as necessary public expenses. In many rural communities some of this equipment is even now furnished by private subscription, by funds raised by parents-teachers' organizations, and by proceeds from school or neighborhood circuses and pie parties. In 1870 the supreme court of North Carolina held that funds for the support of public schools were not necessary expenses, although funds for bridges, courthouses, and jails were necessary. A similar decision was given by the same court fifteen years later and was not reversed until 1907.

Taxation authorized slowly. Lawmaking bodies moved cautiously in authorizing taxes for the support of schools. Although 66 per cent of the counties in Indiana and 56 per cent of the people by a vote in 1848 favored provision for public taxation for schools, the legislature of that state hesitated to enact such a law and did not do so until provision was made that the law should not apply to any county until it had been accepted by a vote of the people. It required three more years before the first general state school tax was levied on all the property of that state for school purposes. Similar struggles appeared in most of the other states during the second quarter of the nineteenth century. By 1860, however, the principle of public support of schools had been generally accepted in all except the slaveholding states, and in some of these (notably North Carolina) it was accepted and partly applied.

Meantime, the steps from permissive public support to mandatory taxation for schools were timidly taken. Local communities or districts were allowed to levy school taxes at their discretion, but generally only on those who gave their consent; then permission was granted to tax all the property in the district; then assistance was promised by the state, through the income from permanent public-school funds or from the proceeds of a state tax for schools, when local communities or districts met the minimum requirements of the state; finally, district or county taxation became mandatory by state-wide legislation. In quite similar manner are these steps taken today when proposals are made for extensions of public educational effort. In local elections such proposals are frequently defeated. In 1927 the legislature of one state tabled a bill proposing a vote of the people on the question of increasing the minimum legal school term from six months a year to eight months, and in 1928 the people of another state voted down a similar proposal. The arguments preceding the action in each state closely resembled those used in the contest in Pennsylvania in 1835, when the question of public-school support was settled (at least in principle) in that state, and in the fight on the question of free schools in New York fifteen years later.

Charity and the rate bill. The classes of people who opposed education at public expense in the early period differed only slightly from those who now oppose extensions of public educational effort. The arguments used then are the arguments often used now. Free education in the early days meant education only for the poor. Numerous were the charity schools established by benevolent individuals who meant well but who helped to fasten upon free education an odium which it has been difficult to remove; the pauper-school conception, which came directly from England during the colonial period, persisted far into the nineteenth century. As late as 1867 (according to a statement of a member of the board of education of Connecticut at that time) "some able men" in Connecticut declared that "the state has no right to educate any but paupers. All others should be excluded from the public schools."

In that same year the Hartford Ministerial Association petitioned the legislature of Connecticut concerning the schools, which were suffering from "public neglect," and asked, among other things, "that all taxation for the support of common schools be henceforth on the uniform basis of property, and that the schools be made free." There as elsewhere the fight to remove the rate bill and the element of charity which inhered in it was long and bitter. The rate bill was a charge upon the parents to supplement school revenues for the purpose of paying the salaries of teachers or of lengthening the school term. It was levied upon each parent according to the number of children he sent to school.

"Shall the distinctions of rich and poor be kept up in the schoolroom?" asked the secretary of the state board of education in his report in 1868. "Shall the sons of penury be sent to a poorer seat in the schoolhouse, with the hard and humiliating taunt 'your father does not pay anything for you'?" It was in that year that Connecticut abolished this objectionable feature of school support. Pennsylvania seems to have abolished the rate bill in 1834, Indiana, Ohio, and Illinois in the fifties, Vermont in 1864, and New York in 1867. Rhode Island abolished it in 1868, Michigan in 1869, and New Jersey in 1871. Rates or subscriptions to supplement school revenues were collected in most of the Southern states for many years after the Civil War, when that section of the country was in such economic distress. In time all the states abandoned the practice. In this respect, as in so many others, the cities were more progressive than other communities, and early rid themselves of the rate bills by securing legislative authority to organize, support, and control their own school systems.

Survivals of charity. But the shadow of the rate bill may even now be seen in some of the states. Costs other than those for teachers' pay were for a long time assessed pro rata among the parents. Survivals of the old element of charity may be seen today in those states which permit the public purchase of schoolbooks and supplies only for the poor, or of shoes and clothing to enable poor children to comply with the requirements of compulsory-attendance laws. Even pensions to widows to enable their children to go to school bear in some places the taint of charity. In some states the child who accepts from the public a warm lunch at school without money and without price must first declare himself in poverty or be so declared, and receive the lunch as a charity which points its scornful finger at his indigence. He must admit the stigma of baser birth. Thus the state by permitting charity in any such form is forced first to degrade those of its members whom it seeks to lift up. It is difficult to see how schools can be considered entirely free so long as any element of charity is allowed to survive in them in any form.

The fight for taxation bitter. In the struggle to make education free are found many examples of courage displayed by the friends of the cause, which was sometimes lost for a time and sometimes won, but won always after bitter fights. It required courage for the president of the University of North Carolina to tell that state in the early thirties (see Chapter VIII) that it was indifferent to its educational needs, that "we correspond in public improvements and in popular education, not with the nineteenth century, but with three centuries ago." It is to the credit of that commonwealth that he was not dismissed from his post. It required courage for Horace Mann in the thirties and forties, and for Caleb Mills in the forties to force the people of Massachusetts and of Indiana to face the facts of their educational and cultural conditions. It required courage for Governor Henry A. Wise of Virginia in the fifties to criticize the weaknesses of the school plan of that state, which was using the proceeds of its permanent public-school fund largely as a charity for the poor, and to urge the abolition of the principle of charity and the organization of an effective educational system including elementary and high schools, teacher-training schools, an agricultural college, and a university. Ignorance of agriculture, he said, had ruined more men in Virginia than "any other cause known to me, except brandy, foxhounds, and horse-racing." About the same time the report of a state educational convention in Richmond pointed out that Virginia's failure to make the schools free involved a moral question, in that the permanent public-school fund, which was the property of all the people, was used to furnish schooling only for the poor.

"Is it right," the report asked, "to take the property of the many and bestow it exclusively on the few? . . . They are the privileged class, the aristocracy of poverty. Now is it right to exclude from all the benefits of the literary fund all the children of this glorious old commonwealth, except those who put in the plea of rags and dirt? . . . Can this injustice and partiality benefit the poor children? Is it a law of humanity, that to lift up, you must first degrade, that to elevate the soul and spirit of a child, you must first make him a public pauper? . . . Has the pauper system of education diminished the number of your intellectual paupers? Or is it, like every other system of legally supported pauperism, a fire that feeds itself?"

The work of Thaddeus Stevens. Probably no more conspicuous example of courage is found in all American educational history, however, than that displayed by Thaddeus Stevens in the legislature of Pennsylvania in 1835. The long agitation for free schools in that state had resulted in the enactment in 1834 of a school law which recognized the principle of public-school support, although the law was optional with the school districts, which then numbered 987. Of this number 502 voted to accept the law, 264 voted to reject it, and 221 declined to take any action. Many members of the legislature who had supported the law were defeated in the next election; others prevented their defeat by declining to offer themselves for reëlection. So strong were the protests against the law and so numerous were the petitions for its repeal that the senate made short work of the matter immediately after it met in 1835 by voting nearly two to one in favor of a bill entitled "An act making provision for the education of the poor gratis," which repealed the essential features of the act of 1834.

His effective speech. Stevens, a member of the House, was absent from Harrisburg much of the time while the contest waged. Many members of the legislature of 1834 had lost their places to pronounced opponents of the act of that year; a committee favoring the law reported that 32,000 people had petitioned for repeal, 2500 had remonstrated against it; the Democratic members of the legislature had held a caucus and requested the Democratic governor, who was friendly to the law of 1834, not to oppose the repeal of the act, and had reminded him that his opposition would defeat him for reëlection. When Stevens returned to Harrisburg he was informed by his colleague from Adams County, who was also a warm supporter of the act of 1834, that the senate had passed the repeal with only eight dissenting votes, that a count of votes in the House showed a majority of thirty in favor of the senate's action, and that the friends of the law had consulted and had decided it was useless to oppose its repeal. Stevens was also informed that three fourths of his constituents had petitioned for repeal. But Stevens followed his convictions; and when the fight in the House was at its fiercest he moved to substitute for the senate bill another which greatly strengthened the law of 1834, and upon the motion he made the speech which he himself regarded, even after he had won wide fame in political life, as his greatest single achievement. Probably few speeches ever uttered in a legislative body in this country produced greater effect. "The House was electrified," wrote a member of the legislature, and the "school system was saved from ignominious defeat." The governor was politically opposed to Stevens, but immediately upon the latter's triumph in the House the executive sent for him, threw his arms about his neck, and thanked him for the service he had "rendered to our common humanity." Enthusiastic friends of the school system which had been saved "had portions of the speech beautifully printed on silk and presented to Stevens."

THADDEUS STEVENS

"Sir," said Stevens, the Vermonter, addressing the speaker of the House, "hereditary distinctions of rank are sufficiently odious; but that which is founded on poverty is infinitely more so. Such a law should be entitled 'An act for branding and marking the poor, so that they may be known from the rich and proud.' Many complain of this tax, not so much on account of its amount, as because it is for the benefit of others and not themselves. This is a mistake; it is for their own benefit, inasmuch as it perpetuates the Government and insures the due administration of the laws under which they live, and by which their lives and property are protected. Why do they not urge the same objection against all other taxes? The industrious, thrifty, rich farmer pays a heavy county tax to support criminal courts, build jails, and pay sheriffs and jail keepers, and yet probably he never has, and never will have, any direct personal use of either. He never gets the worth of his money by being tried for a crime before the court, by being allowed the privilege of the jail on conviction, or receiving an equivalent from the sheriff or his hangman officers! He cheerfully pays the tax which is necessary to support and punish convicts, but loudly complains of that which goes to prevent his fellow-being from becoming a criminal, and to obviate the necessity of those humiliating institutions. . . .

"This law is often objected to, because its benefits are shared by the children of the profligate spendthrift equally with those of the most industrious and economical habits. It ought to be remembered that the benefit is bestowed, not upon the erring parents, but the innocent children. Carry out this objection and you punish children for the crimes or misfortunes of their parents. You virtually establish cases and grades founded on no merit of the particular generation, but on the demerits of their ancestors ; an aristocracy of the most odious and insolent kind — the aristocracy of wealth and pride. . . .

"It is said that some gentlemen here owe their election to their hostility to general education — that it was placed distinctly on that ground, and that others lost their election by being in favor of it ; and that they consented to supersede the regularly nominated candidates of their own party, who had voted for this law. May be so. I believe that two highly respectable members of the last legislature, from Union County, who voted for the school law, did fail of reëlection on that ground only. They were summoned before a county meeting, and requested to pledge themselves to vote for its repeal as the price of their reëlection. But they were too high minded and honorable men to consent to such degradation. The people, incapable for the moment of appreciating their worth, dismissed them from their service. But I venture to predict that they have passed them by only for the moment. Those gentlemen have earned the approbation of all good and intelligent men more effectually by their retirement than they could ever have done by retaining popular favor at the expense of self-humiliation. They fell, it is true, in this great struggle between the powers of light and darkness; but they fell, as every Roman mother wished her sons to fall, facing the enemy with all their wounds in front. . . .

"I trust that when we come to act on this question we shall all take lofty ground — look beyond the narrow space which now circumscribes our visions — beyond the passing, fleeting point of time on which we stand; and so cast our votes that the blessing of education shall be conferred on every son of Pennsylvania — shall be carried home to the poorest child of the poorest inhabitant of the meanest hut of your mountains, so that even he may be prepared to act well his part in this land of freemen, and lay on earth a broad and a solid foundation for that enduring knowledge which goes cn increasing through increasing eternity."

Lessons from the past. The story of the struggle to secure school support shows many principles which are full of meaning for public educational administration today. It shows that in a democratic community a tuition system for school support is unsound, that it is not necessary to require tuition in order to stimulate and sustain interest in schools, and that taxation for schools is evidence of interest in education rather than a means of promoting interest in it. It shows that a state cannot support its schools by the income from permanent funds, that taxation is the most important means of school support, and that local taxation should be used in part for this purpose because it enables progressive communities to make educational advance more rapidly than would otherwise be possible. This principle is especially conspicuous in the history of public education in the progressive cities of this country.

The need for increased support. The story of school support also demonstrates the importance of state taxation and the need today for increased support from state sources. Nothing is clearer than that a comprehensive free-school policy does not pauperize the people, although throughout the history of school support it has been freely predicted that this would be the result. This ancient sentiment often reappears today when proposals are made for the extension of the free-school principle to forms of educational effort not now common. If the free-school policy is in full accord with the most vital principles of democracy, all schooling should be free. Furthermore, it is to be noted that, just as low standards of the public schools in the early period were pointed to as excuses for establishing private-tuition schools, so the maintenance of high standards in public schools, the employment only of well-trained teachers, the use of courses of study adapted to modern needs, and the application of the democratic spirit in administration and in instruction will more and more increase public esteem and respect for the free-school policy. It is increasingly clear also that public schools must exemplify the principles of democracy, else the public will distrust them and withdraw support from them. Finally, the history of school support reveals, perhaps more clearly than any other feature of educational history, the importance of enlightened leadership in education. Conspicuous were the services of such men as Mann, Barnard, Pierce, Mills, Murphey, Wiley, and Wise, and of hosts of leaders of more recent times who have worked for the cause of public education.

Present conditions and tendencies. Every state now derives public-school support from local units such as districts, towns, and townships, from the state, and from the Federal government; some states use the county (in the case of Louisiana the parish) also as a unit of support. School support from local units is generally derived principally from taxes on real and personal property. Support from the state is generally derived from a general mill tax on real and personal property, from permanent public-school funds, from taxes on incomes, inheritances, corporations, stocks and bonds, licenses, certain occupations, and from poll taxes. With the demand for increased revenues for other public enterprises as well as schools, there is an increasing protest against adding to the burden of taxation on land, and the states are more and more seeking new sources of public revenue. The Smith-Lever Act passed by Congress in 1914 provided Federal aid for extension work in agriculture and home economics. Although none of this aid reaches the public schools, it does bring educational benefits to children of school age by encouraging club work among them. Since 1917, when the Smith-Hughes vocational educational law was enacted, the Federal government has been following a new policy in the aid of schools. Every state now receives aid from this source for the teaching of trade and industrial subjects and for the training of teachers in these fields. In 1918 the question arose anew whether the Federal government should not aid the states in general education, and the Smith-Towner bill was introduced in Congress for the purpose of extending such aid. The bill failed of passage, however, and has since been succeeded by other bills of the same general purpose. The latest of these proposals, the Curtis-Reed bill, is now before Congress. Important contributions to educational support are also made by numerous private foundations.

Local taxation. The simple plan of local district taxation served well the needs of the time in which it arose. Although the conditions of that period have now changed, local taxation still remains the chief source of public-school support and is defended by arguments similar to those used in the defense of this form of taxation in its beginning. Increased educational burdens are assumed and borne largely by this means. Approximately three fourths of the states receive less than one third of their public educational revenues from state sources, and only two or three derive more than half their school funds from such sources. The results of continued dependence on local school support are seen in economic and educational inequalities which are found in practically all the forty-eight states. These inequalities seem all the more strange in the face of increasing insistence — often implied in constitutional provisions for schools, hinted at in decisions of the courts, written on and spoken about by peripatetic professors at large, expressed even by legislation and often by reforms in educational organization — that the public schools are not local but state institutions and, as such, can be controlled by the state.

Increasing cost. The cost of public education increased more than 440 per cent between 1890 and 1918, and if a longer period be considered, the increased cost is even more conspicuous. This increase has been due to the increase in the educable population, to the lengthening of the legal school term, to the enactment and improvement of school-attendance legislation, to the shifting upon the school of functions once performed by the home and the community, to the enlargement of educational facilities, to the improvement in educational standards, and, in recent years, to the change in the purchasing power of the dollar. In spite of this rapid increase the demand for wider and richer educational opportunities has been even more rapid, and in spite of the vast enlargement of public educational facilities in recent years, reports come from almost every state that thousands of its youth are not provided with educational opportunities adequate for their needs.

Localism and inequalities. After more than a century of laborious effort these opportunities are not yet fully democratic or entirely free, nor are they universal. Few are the states which do not consider taxation their most stubborn educational problem, and fewer still are those which have sensible and equitable plans of taxation. And yet there is probably no state which cannot provide universal, democratic, free, and adequate educational facilities for all its members if it would formulate and follow a scientific and sound taxation system. The glaring educational inequalities in almost every state today are due for the most part to the inequities and iniquities of taxation makeshifts. Few problems of statecraft so quickly transform statesmen into pettifoggers (as the history of school taxation shows) as the problems that inhere in this ancient dread. It remains after many years one of the most puzzling of all the problems of educational administration. Failure of governing authority to grapple intelligently with it has made for much educational muddle-mindedness and public injustice, often for court delays and nebulous court decisions, for bitterness and bickerings, and, not infrequently, for grotesque expedients which result in wide differences between the theory of public support and actual practices. These differences may be found in most of the states. Most curious is the case of North Carolina, where the entire school budget of each county may annually be, and not infrequently is, adopted and approved not by the county school authorities, who are charged with the responsibility of maintaining the schools and who know their needs, but by a judge and a jury of twelve good men and true. This is an example of localism gone to seed. The educational inequalities now existing there and in every state, largely because of dependence of the schools on local revenues, are as glaring now as at any time in the nation's history. So long as this practice continues these inequalities must remain. Devotion to the ancient fetish of localism in education has made, and continues to make, such conditions inevitable in the richest nation in the world.

Ability to provide schools. The American people are rich enough to spend annually nearly as much money for tobacco, if not more, than they spend for the maintenance of their schools. In 1920 the expenditures for luxuries — tobacco, snuff, cosmetics, perfumes, face powder, chewing gum, soft drinks, and amusements — were twenty-two times greater than the expenditures for all forms of education in 1918 and 30 per cent greater than the total amount expended for public education in the entire history of the country. According to estimates prepared by the United States Treasury Department, in 1924 the people of the United States expended on luxuries $5,522,000,000, — perfumes and cosmetics costing $261,000,000, candy $639,000,000, and chewing gum $87,000,000. Strange is it that a people who expend so heavily on such indulgences shall plead poverty when increased funds are needed for schools and cry out against the mounting costs of education. Strange also are these evidences of immense economic prosperity among a people who permit such iniquitous educational conditions — multitudes of their children in "dismal and insanitary hovels" called schoolhouses, in charge of "wretchedly underpaid and proportionately ignorant, untrained, and negative teachers."

In this chapter it has been pointed out that objection to and fear of taxation stood long and stubbornly in the way of the principle of public support of schools. It has also been pointed out that before taxation for education was authorized many methods of school support were used, and that the element of charity and the rate bill were difficult to remove. Although state taxation for schools is of utmost importance, local taxation remains the chief source of public-school support in most of the states, and notwithstanding the immense economic wealth of the American people the principle of complete public-school support has not yet been fully and practically applied in every community. The result is that there are now many inequalities in educational opportunities in the United States. The battle continues to be waged over the principle when extensions of public educational support are proposed, just as it continues to be waged over the extensions of public educational control, the subject of the next chapter.

REFERENCES AND READINGS

BURGESS, W. R. Trends of School Costs. New York, 1920.

> A study of increasing school costs between 1840 and 1920.

CUBBERLEY, E. P. Public Education in the United States. Boston, 1919.

> Chapter V describes the battle for free state schools, and lists some of the arguments used for and against public support of education. It also lists the classes of people who generally favored public schools and those who generally opposed them.

CUBBERLEY, E. P. State School Administration. Boston, 1927.

> Chapter XVI (on funds and taxation), Chapter XVII (on apportionments and subsidies), and Chapter XVIII (on the subject of Federal aid) are useful as supplementary reading for this chapter. Contains very valuable bibliographies.

CUBBERLEY, E. P. School Funds and their Apportionments. New York, 1901.

> An early study of the sources of school revenue and methods of distribution.

JACKSON, G. L. Development of School Support in Colonial Massachusetts. New York, 1909.

> A historical account of the development of school support in that colony.

KNIGHT, EDGAR W. Public School Education in North Carolina. Boston, 1916.

> Chapter VIII describes the beginnings of public education in North Carolina and the operation of the first public-school law.

KNIGHT, EDGAR W. Public Education in the South. Boston, 1922.

> Chapter VI describes the establishment and operation of permanent public-school funds, and Chapter VII describes public educational arrangements in the ante-bellum South.

MADDOX, W. A. The Free School Idea in Virginia before 1860. New York, 1918.

> Tells of the battle in Virginia.

McCALL, SAMUEL W. Thaddeus Stevens. Boston, 1899.

> Contains an account of Stevens's speech in the legislature of Pennsylvania in 1835 in opposition to the repeal of the free-school law of 1834.

MORT, PAUL R. State Support for Public Schools. New York, 1926.

> Discusses the equalization of opportunity, the cost of a minimum state educational program, and the division of support between the state and smaller administrative units.

STEVENS, THADDEUS. "A Plea for Public Schools," Report of the United States Commissioner of Education 1898–1899, Vol. I, pp. 518–524.

> A famous speech made in the Pennsylvania House of Representatives in April, 1835, opposing the effort to repeal the school law of 1834, and the part which Stevens took in the memorable struggle. A useful historical note appears on pages 516–518 of the same report.

STRAYER, GEORGE D. "Financing Education on a Scientific Basis," School and Society, Vol. XVI, No. 531 (February 28, 1925), pp. 243–247.

> An article on costs and bases for estimating costs.

SWIFT, FLETCHER HARPER. History of Permanent Common School Funds in the United States. New York, 1910.

> The best authority on the history of permanent public-school funds in the United States. Contains a voluminous bibliography.

SWIFT, FLETCHER HARPER. State Policies in Public-School Finance, Bulletin No. 6, United States Bureau of Education, Washington, 1922.

> An excellent study which shows the decreasing services of permanent funds and the diminishing state support of public education.

WICKERSHAM, J. P. History of Education in Pennsylvania. Lancaster, 1886.

> Chapters XIII, XV, and XVI describe the struggle to establish free schools in Pennsylvania. One of the best accounts of public-education development in a state.

QUESTIONS FOR STUDY AND DISCUSSION

✓ 1. Account for the fact that public taxation for school purposes was so long resisted in this country.

2. Make a study of the development of taxation for schools in your state, with the constitutional and legal provisions as sources of information.

3. Contrast the views of Franklin and Smith (pp. 244–245) on the subject of taxation with McIver's view.

4. In what way was it unfortunate for the cause of public schools that the beginnings of education in this country were made and

nurtured by philanthropy? Consider the place of philanthropy in education in this country now.

5. Point out any present-day survivals of the theory that rewards other than economic made up for the poor pay which teachers have received and even now receive for their services.

6. Trace the development of any permanent public-school endowment established by your state. For what purposes is such a fund now used in your state?

7. Account for the fact that permanent public-school funds were often mismanaged.

8. Trace the uses made by your state of its share in the surplus revenue of 1837.

9. Make a study of the use of lotteries for educational or other purposes in your state. Why were lotteries finally prohibited?

10. Why were the lawmaking bodies so cautious in authorizing taxes for school support?

11. What is the significance of the speech made by Thaddeus Stevens in the legislature of Pennsylvania?

12. Study the rate bill as it has been used in your state, and point out any survivals of the element of charity in education in your state today.

13. What lessons for public educational administration may be learned from the long struggle to secure school support?

14. Why does local taxation remain the chief source of public-school support?

15. Discuss the educational inequalities in your state which arise from localism in public-school support.

16. It is often said that the American people are rich enough to do for education all that they will do. Discuss the statement.

17. Study the arguments against public schools listed by Cubberley in "Public Education in the United States" (see References and Readings). How many of these arguments are now used against proposals for the extension of public educational effort?

CHAPTER X

SECURING PUBLIC CONTROL

Outline of the chapter. 1. Each of the American states has established at one time or another some form of central administrative control of schools in order to achieve the essential educational purpose of the state, which is to protect, instruct, and train all its people.

2. The development of state control and direction of public education has been somewhat haphazard, with the result that uniformity in state school administration is unknown in the United States.

3. The beginnings of state control of education were made when the state began to give financial aid to local schools. New York was the first state to create (1812) an office to exercise central educational supervision, and Gideon Hawley was the first state superintendent of schools.

✓ 4. Maryland followed the lead of New York in 1826, and later many other states established the office. By 1850 thirty-one states and three territories had provided for it. Today the office is permanently established in each of the forty-eight states.

5. In length of term, salary, title of the office, legal qualifications and duties of the officer, and method of selection, the state superintendency of schools shows much variety. About three fourths of the states use the political method of <u>popular election</u>, which authorities on public-school administration do not look upon as sound.

6. The duties of the chief state school officer are larger and more specific now than they were during the early development of state control.

7. The state board of education is an important feature of American state school control. There are several different kinds of state boards of education, the least effective of them being the ex-officio board.

8. Professional county and city superintendencies developed slowly because of the old district system and the strength of localism, but in recent years city school administration has developed rapidly.

The essential educational purpose of the modern democratic state is to formulate and follow intelligent and progressive plans for the protection, the instruction, and the training of all its people. The state should be more than an educational tax-collector or tax-distributor or lawmaker or policeman: it should be an active and energetic social agency constantly employing its resources for the physical, moral, intellectual, social, and industrial betterment of all its members without regard to their economic or social status or any other accidental conditions or circumstances. It should undertake to safeguard the rights of all in all legitimate activities and to use its agencies for the improvement of all the people and the enlargement of their opportunities for personal and social development. Such a purpose as this, however, involves a great many more activities of an educational nature than those of establishing, supporting, and directing schools, though the educational purpose may best be seen in the arrangement which the state makes for schools.

Central state control of education. To achieve this educational purpose the American states have established at one time or another some form of central administrative control of schools. Steps toward such control were first taken in the early part of the nineteenth century, when provision was made for a state board of education and a chief state school officer. The general growth of these features of public educational administration has appeared in more recent years, however, and is clearly in process of further development even now. Today some form of state board of education and the office of state superintendent, or commissioner of schools, are established in each of the forty-eight states; but there is much variety in the provisions made for this important office, in the names by which it is officially designated, in the qualifications required of those who occupy it, in the methods of selecting them, in their tenure, in the compensation they receive, and in the scope of their jurisdiction and the kind and extent of their powers. Uniformity in state school administration is unknown in the United States.

Haphazard development. This absence of uniformity in central state control and direction of public education in this country has been due to its haphazard development. This has been in large part a result of rather definite influences. One of these was the theory of individual and local community rights, which so long prevailed because it met with such wide popular approval. This theory was in close harmony with the democratic theory of government, which included local self-government by small units, where interests were narrow and provincial. Moreover, it was natural that the people should remember the troubles with England and the war which they waged for independence. They learned to distrust centralization of power in any form or for any purpose, because it denoted autocracy and tyranny, which they taught themselves and their children to despise and resist.

A state obligation. Another influence caused slow and haphazard development of state educational control. The Constitution of the United States, by implication in the Tenth Amendment, had delegated the obligation of education to the various states; but this obligation was not directly placed upon the states, and they moved slowly to assume it. The public utterances of the leading statesmen of the early national period and the messages of governors (who urged often in very general and sometimes pious terms that legislatures provide for schools) did not move the states promptly to set up the means of education at public expense. Even Jefferson's significant bill in the legislature of Virginia in 1779 "for the more general diffusion of knowledge" failed to pass that body or to influence public opinion widely in that state. Then and for many years afterwards education was viewed in all parts of the United States not as a duty and function of government but as a church, a parental, or a family obligation. In the early national period it was not even accepted as a function of small local units of government, not to mention the central state government. The states were not required to make provision for it. As early as May, 1776, the Continental Congress had recommended to the various states the adoption of "such government as shall, in the opinion of the representatives of the people, best conduce to the happiness and safety of their constituents in particular and America in general." Following this recommendation, all the states except Connecticut and Rhode Island (which regarded their colonial charters as adequate to the changed conditions) framed and adopted constitutions. But not all of them, as noted in Chapter VI, made constitutional provision for schools, and in many of the states which did so the lawmaking bodies did not immediately or strictly observe the mandates. The states did not provide for public education until the people themselves began to feel and make vocal the need for schools and until they also developed a willingness, which at first appeared quite half-hearted, to pay for them.

Other influences. Another influence which delayed the growth of centralization in education and made for decentralization was the long traditional and historical association of schools with the church or other religious and philanthropic organizations or with other forms of private educational effort. Elementary schools were established primarily for religious purposes. It was natural, therefore, that the idea of public control of education should be slow to appear and develop in a community not accustomed to public support of schools. Devotion to the democratic doctrine of localism, the influence of the theory that the support or the control of education was not properly a function of government, and the silence of the Federal Constitution on the subject of schools made for decentralization in educational work and delayed the beginnings of state control of local schools.

Moreover, there was no American model for the office of state superintendent of schools, nor were serious suggestions for such an office made during the early national period.

City and county superintendencies were not known until the creation of the state superintendency, and the office of the United States Commissioner of Education was not established until after the Civil War. The chief state school office could not come into being until the need appeared for oversight of state funds for schools.

Beginnings of state control. The initial step in the movement to secure such oversight was taken when the state began to give financial aid to local schools. Funds were the whip hand, then as now, in compelling local communities to submit to state supervision. It was this force that guided or drove communities along the slow and toilsome road from excessive faith in localism and false standards in education to toleration for centralization in the state department of education. It was this same force that directed public opinion to the view, now generally accepted in the United States, that education is a function for the state to perform and that schools and other means of instruction and training should be maintained and directed under its supervision. This has come to be a fundamental principle of education in a democracy. The principle began to take form when the state first offered to give aid to local schools on condition that they conform to certain state requirements. This arrangement between the state and smaller administrative units marks also the origin of local distrust and resentment and often of open hostility to the power of central state control.

The need for funds. After the need for schools came to be generally recognized but before there had developed a willingness to pay for them by public taxation, the most perplexing educational problem in this country was to secure funds for their support. As noted in Chapter IX, permanent public-school funds or endowments seemed to be the solution. It was believed that such funds would make the schools free and available to all and, what was an even more attractive promise, relieve the people of direct taxation for education. Arrangements for indirect school support were likely to be popular at a time when schools were not generally considered an obligation of the state and when taxes were not looked upon with high favor even for the pressing necessities of government, such as the administration of justice, poor relief, the maintenance of jails, court-houses, and defense. Schools were not considered necessary expenses of government.

Permanent public-school funds disappointing. The inability of a permanent public-school fund to provide educational facilities without taxation or other means of support was promptly demonstrated in the case of Connecticut, which established such a fund in 1795. The experiment was costly and disappointing, and the result probably retarded education for many years and increased the necessity for rate bills, which were not eliminated in Connecticut until 1868. New York was able to profit by the mistake of Connecticut and to view the fund established in 1805 as a means not of relieving the people of local school burdens, but of encouraging local taxation for education. This principle of state aid for those communities which would help themselves has come to be accepted throughout the country as sound and stimulating.

New York in the lead. New York was the first state to create an office to exercise central educational supervision. As early as 1784 the legislature established the Board of Regents of the University of the State of New York for the purpose of creating, endowing, and controlling secondary and higher education. Specific needs for some degree of control in elementary education appeared in that state when it became necessary to distribute safely to local community schools the income from the permanent school endowment established in 1805. Between 1795 and 1800, under experimental school legislation, annual state grants had been made for schools. The funds were distributed to such localities as raised by taxation half the amounts given by the state. The absence of general direction by some central authority and the lack of cohesive power in the plan led to its failure. There was waste of money intended for educational purposes. The schools failed to command respect, because they exerted no influence, and in 1800 the legislature refused to renew the appropriation. The plan collapsed and was not revived until 1812.

State supervision of state funds. By 1812 it had become evident that whatever aid the state gives to schools must be supervised in some manner by the state to prevent a waste of funds and moral injury to the communities which had shown tendencies to escape their educational responsibilities. Central supervision in some form was necessary, and it was believed that this could best be exercised by some officer who represented the state. This officer could also collect such information as the legislature, in view of the slowly increasing recognition of the place of the state in providing education, was beginning to require. A knowledge of conditions among the people of the state and of their educational desires was necessary if intelligent and progressive school laws were to be enacted. This officer could furnish such knowledge (in part at least), and he could also stimulate educational interest among the people. To control the funds, to gather information, and to encourage educational interest were the purposes of the first state superintendency in the United States, but the greatest of these probably was to control the funds.

A new office in the United States. The office was a new one for this country. It was native in origin and was apparently influenced little, if at all, by practices in other countries. The statute enacted by the New York legislature of 1812 designated the officer as "the superintendent of common schools," who was to be appointed by the "council of appointment," which consisted of four senators, one from each district, to be chosen by the legislature. His salary was to be $300 a year, but he was "not to be under pay until he shall give notice of the first distribution of school money." His duty was to digest and prepare plans for the improvement and management of the common-school fund and for the better organization of the common schools, to prepare and report estimates and expenditures of the school moneys and to superintend the collection thereof, to direct the sale of the public lands which had been or would be appropriated as a permanent public-school fund, to prepare and provide the legislature with information concerning education, and to "perform all such services relative to the welfare of the schools as he shall be directed to perform." As evidence of good faith he was required to take an oath or affirmation to execute his trust diligently and faithfully.

The act of 1812. The act of 1812 followed a report of a legislative committee on a system for the "organization and establishment of common schools," and is one of the important educational documents in the history of New York. The committee evidently had given some rather careful study to the plans followed in other countries. In addition to the recognition of the principle of state control and provision for school-district organization, the act contains other interesting educational principles. It established the principle that all teachers should possess moral character and certain scholastic qualifications which were to be determined by local school officers. The principle of permissive taxation in local communities was established for the purpose of providing a schoolhouse (including site) and for furnishing and repairing the building. Local school officers were authorized to employ teachers and fix their compensation. The act accepted in part the principle that public education is a function of the state and should be provided and maintained under state supervision, and that to meet the state's educational obligation a system of publicly supported schools should be established and local officers should execute the educational policy of the state. The act also reflects the principle that state supervision naturally follows state support of education.

The first state superintendent of schools. Gideon Hawley was the first appointee to the office, in January, 1813. His vigorous activity in behalf of public schools later offended the politicians, however, whose behavior resembled that of offended politicians today. In 1821 they removed Hawley. They also abolished the position, designating the secretary of state to act ex officio as superintendent of the common schools, and this continued to be the status of the office in New York until 1854. In that year the office was re-created as a separate one, this time, however, under the official designation "superintendent of public instruction," a title which by that time had become more or less general in the United States. In 1904 the title was again changed to "commissioner of education," and this is today the official designation of the chief state school officer in New York.

The office in other states. The next state to establish the office of superintendent, or commissioner of education, acted fourteen years after New York had taken the initial step in 1812. Maryland created the office in 1826. Provision was made by legislation enacted in that year that a superintendent of public instruction was to be appointed by the governor and council. The language of the law was in many parts identical with that of the New York statute of 1812, and the duties of the Maryland officer were similar to those prescribed by New York. No term or salary was prescribed by the Maryland law, however, though two years later the legislature granted Littleton Dennis Teackle the sum of $500 "in full compensation for his services and expenditures as superintendent of public instruction." It seems that the office was abolished in 1828 and was not reëstablished until 1864, when the new constitution provided for a state superintendent of public instruction. The office was continued only four years, however, when it was again abolished and its duties transferred to the principal of the state normal school. It was reëstablished in 1902 as a separate office under the designation "superintendent of education," which is the present title.

Michigan was the third state and the first of the Western states to establish the office. An act of 1829 of the Territory of Michigan provided for a superintendent of common schools. That state holds the record of having had the office as a separate and continuous one longer than any of the other states. It was also the first state to make constitutional provision (1835) for the office. The title "superintendent of public instruction," prescribed in that year, has continued until the present.

GIDEON HAWLEY

The first state superintendent of schools in the United States. (From a painting owned by the New York State Education Department.)

Louisiana provided in 1833 that the secretary of state should serve ex officio as superintendent of public education, and this arrangement continued until 1847, when the office was created as a separate one. Pennsylvania specified in 1834 that the secretary of the commonwealth should serve ex officio as chief state school officer. The separate office was not established in that state until 1857.

Tennessee provided in 1836 for a state superintendent of public instruction to be elected for a term of two years by a joint vote of the two Houses of the legislature. Robert H. McEwen was selected for the position, but the law gave him no authority to enforce the educational legislation of the state or to stimulate educational interest. He was to serve merely as financial agent, or treasurer, of the permanent public-school fund, which had been established earlier. The legislature of 1837–1838 reëlected him, but became somewhat suspicious of his management of the fund and ordered him to make a report. This led to a legislative investigation. A majority of the investigating committee reported that by mismanagement and a variety of questionable schemes the superintendent had robbed the fund of more than $121,000. Suit was instituted against him and his securities when his term expired in 1840, but the litigation, which dragged over ten years and wore the color of politics, was finally compromised, the defendants paying about $10,000 in full settlement of all claims. Andrew Johnson was chairman of the committee from the House. A minority report charged that the investigation was based upon "private malice and political prejudice spurred into activity . . . by hungry expectants and party hangers-on." McEwen's defalcation gave public education a decided setback in Tennessee, and the poorly organized school system of the state was little more than a name until 1854.

The office in Tennessee was held by two other men between 1840 and 1844, when, under a wave of economy and retrenchment, it was abolished and the duties transferred to the office of the state treasurer. It was not reëstablished as a separate office until 1867. This arrangement continued until 1870, and for three years thereafter the treasurer of the state again acted ex officio as superintendent of public instruction, under which title the office has been a continuous and separate one since 1873.

Ohio provided in 1837 for the annual election, by the two Houses of the legislature, of a superintendent of common schools. Three years later the duties of this office were transferred to the office of the secretary of state, who acted ex officio until 1853. The office was again made a separate one under the title "commissioner of common schools." In 1913 the official designation of the chief state school officer of Ohio was changed to "superintendent of public instruction."

Massachusetts provided in 1837 for a state board of education, to be appointed by the governor with the advice and consent of the council of state. This board was authorized to appoint a secretary. The office in that state continued under the title "secretary of the state board of education" until 1909, when it was changed to "commissioner of education." Horace Mann was the first to hold the office in Massachusetts, and through it he rendered wide and conspicuous service to the cause of education in this country.

Kentucky established the office of superintendent of public instruction in 1838, and since that date it has continued as a separate office under the same title. Connecticut provided for the office in the same year under a law similar to the Massachusetts law of 1837. This arrangement continued until 1842, when the act of 1838 was repealed, and there was no further state supervision in Connecticut until 1845. From 1845 to 1849 the commissioner of the school funds acted ex officio as superintendent of common schools, and from the latter date to 1865 the principal of the state normal school served ex officio as superintendent of common schools. From 1865 to 1921 the office was a separate one under the title "secretary of the state board of education"; since 1921 the title has been "commissioner of education."

Now a separate office in all states. Gradually the other states created the office. By 1850 thirty-one states and three territories had provided for it. Twenty-five years later there were thirty-seven states in the Union, and all these and ten territories had established the office. Oklahoma, which was a territory until 1907, created the office in 1890. Thirty-five of the states originally created the office as a separate one, and thirteen provided that its duties should be performed by some other state officer, often the secretary of state. The office often had to struggle for recognition and for life. Frequent attempts were made to abolish it. Of the thirty-five states which in establishing the office made it a separate one, seventeen later abolished it or transferred its duties to some other state officer. Only nine of the twenty-four states and territories which by 1850 had established the office have kept it separate and continuous since that date. By 1875, however, the office had become generally accepted, and today it is permanently established in each of the forty-eight states. Since 1913, when Delaware reëstablished it, the office has been a separate and continuous one in all the states.

Terms and salaries. The term of the chief state school officer varies from one year to six years, but the four-year term is found in twenty-four states, and the two-year term in fourteen. Generally the term is fixed by constitution or by statute. The tendency today is toward a longer term than formerly. It is believed that a long and fixed term has the advantage of protection from political interference. During such a term a superintendent of strength and professional fitness has the opportunity of formulating and executing constructive educational policies. On the other hand, it is difficult to remove a weak and professionally unfit superintendent before the expiration of his term. The absence of legal means to dispose of such an official might become a real obstacle to educational progress. In New York, New Hampshire, and Vermont the chief state school officer serves during the pleasure of the state board of education, which regularly appoints him for an indefinite term.

The salary of the chief state school officer is a measure of the state's conception of the importance of the office and, perhaps, a measure also of the strength and leadership of those who occupy the office. Low salaries were generally the rule in the early history of the state superintendency, and this rule prevailed until comparatively recent years. In 1896, for example, the largest salary paid to this office was $5000 in New York. Massachusetts paid $4500; Michigan, only $1000. The average salary paid in that year to the chief state school officers of the United States was less than $2500. In 1909 the average salary had been increased to about $2700, with many of the states paying, however, only about $2000. Today the salaries range from $2000 to $12,000, with the average a little better than $4000.

Although the chief state school officer is the nominal head of the state school system, in many states his salary is less than that of many other educational workers. Presidents of state universities and colleges and of state normal schools often receive larger salaries than the superintendent, or commissioner of education, and nearly all the states have one or more city superintendents whose salaries are greater. Moreover, it was recently pointed out that in some states the salary of this official is less than that paid to school principals and to teachers in elementary and high schools. It is significant that the lowest salaries paid to the chief state school officer are generally found in those states where he is elected by popular vote, and the highest in those states where he is appointed. In the states where he is elected the average salary is a little more than half that which is paid to him in states where the method of selection is by appointment.

Many titles to the office. It is perhaps significant that nearly a score of titles have been used to designate the chief state school officer in the United States since the office was first established more than a century ago. In the early days there was indifference toward the value of the office; later enlarged public conceptions of its importance developed. Today the office is designated by about half a dozen titles. The West and the South seem to prefer "superintendent of public instruction"; "commissioner of education" is widely used in the North and the East, and in recent years the tendency has been to adopt this title whenever changes are made. Massachusetts adopted it in 1909, New Jersey in 1911, Vermont in 1915, New Hampshire and Minnesota in 1919, Rhode Island in 1920, Connecticut in 1921, and Maine and Tennessee in 1923. About two thirds of the states make constitutional provisions for the office, and the remainder provide for it by statutes.

Legal qualifications. Seventeen of the states prescribe no qualifications whatever for those who hold the office of state superintendent, or commissioner of education. In such states the office is open (in theory, at any rate) to any respectable citizen irrespective of educational qualifications. Some of the states specify such requirements as to age and residence as would generally have to be met by state officers who are elected by popular vote. Rather general educational qualifications are required in some of the states, such as graduation from a standard college or experience in teaching and school administration. In most of the states the office has been held by men. Recently, however, it has been held by women, especially in some of the Western states where interest in woman suffrage appeared early and perhaps received its greatest support. In no Eastern or Southeastern state has a woman served as the chief state school officer.

Duties of the state superintendent. During the early history of the chief state school officer his duties were not numerous. For the most part they were statistical, clerical, exhortatory, and advisory. He was expected to look after the state school funds and see that they were properly apportioned to those local communities which met the requirements for state aid, to make statistical reports to the legislature or the state board of education, and to visit various parts of the state and, by public speeches or conferences with the people, encourage interest in schools. Today, however, his duties are numerous and his powers are generally broad. In the selection of textbooks; in the organization of courses of study; in the formulation of policies of public-school finance, of the training and certification of teachers, and of accrediting high schools and colleges; in the initiation of school legislation and even in the interpretation of school laws; in the determination of standards for school buildings, child-welfare work, school-library extensions, and adult and vocational education, — in these and a host of other matters vital in a modern school system he may, and often does, have large powers and influence. The increased duties of this office indicate the change from localism to centralization in public education.

This change indicates also the enlarged conception of the importance of public education, and the emphasis which more and more is being placed on public educational leadership and expert direction. Theoretically, an improved type of intelligent and professional direction is required as much in public education as in modern highway engineering, health and sanitation work, agriculture, and other activities of modern state governments. The state superintendent, or commissioner of schools, must be a professional leader. The need is no longer for a clerk, a politician, or a professor and lecturer at large. The public educational needs of a modern state require that the chief school officer be equipped with a high order of business and executive ability, professional consciousness, a keen sense of public educational duty, generous scholarship, a broad vision of the social needs of the state he is serving, apostolic fervor and unselfishness, and even a quiet willingness to be forgotten. No other state officer occupies so important and strategic a place for moral and social leadership as the superintendent of public schools.

Methods of selection. The best theories of the importance of the chief state school officer, however, are not practically applied. This fact is revealed especially in the method most commonly used for selecting him. Since the creation of the office in New York in 1812 at least half a dozen methods of filling it have been used. Today three methods are in common use : appointment by the governor, appointment by the state board of education, and election by popular vote. Although the method recognized as best by authorities on public-school administration is that of appointment by a properly constituted board of educational control, about three fourths of the states use the political method of popular election, which is prescribed by the constitution of those states or by their statutes.

Viewed in the light of the best educational experience and the soundest principle of educational administration, this method of selecting the chief state school officer limits his effectiveness and influence. Election by this method is generally on the basis of partisan nomination, and hence it binds the officer to party pledges and often identifies him with active party politics. His duties require such training and fitness and professional qualities as are rarely at home with those qualities which generally commend men to the political leaders and bosses. Moreover, election by popular vote limits the choice to citizens of the state. This method has been discarded as vicious in the selection of all the newer experts. Chairmen of highway commissions, highway engineers, and heads of state boards of health are not chosen by popular vote. No city would select its superintendent of schools by such means. No state would select the president of its university or the head of one of its colleges by popular vote. The argument that many states still select their chief state school officers by this method is not sound ;

neither is the argument that the method keeps the schools close to the people sound. The important thing is to keep the people close to the schools, which is a very different matter.

Enlarged powers of control. The initial statute creating the first state superintendency in the United States prescribed the duties of that office. The superintendent was required "to digest and prepare plans for the improvement and management of the common-school fund, and for the better organization of common schools; to prepare and report estimates and expenditures of the school monies, to superintend the collection thereof, to execute such services relative to the sale of the lands, which now are or hereafter may be appropriated, as a permanent fund for the support of common schools, as may be by law required of him; to give information to the legislature respecting all matters referred to him by either branch thereof, or which shall appertain to his office: and generally to perform all such services relative to the welfare of schools, as he shall be directed to perform, and shall, prior to his entering upon the duties of his office, take an oath or affirmation for the diligent and faithful execution of his trust."

An important court decision. These general and somewhat vague duties stand out in rather sharp contrast to those found in the legislation covering the duties of the state superintendent in New York and perhaps other American states today. The absence of specific powers is in even greater contrast to the large and definite powers with which the office is now clothed in many states. This increase in centralized authority in education represents the gradual change from localism and other extreme educational applications of democracy to centralization. The following example serves to illustrate this:

Judge Chester B. McLaughlin of the Court of Appeals of New York State, in an opinion handed down in July, 1926, held that State Commissioner of Education Frank P. Graves was within his official rights when he directed the board of education of Union School District Number Two, Town of Brookhaven, Suffolk County, to raise by tax sufficient funds to provide for the transportation of children of school age who lived so far from the school that they could not otherwise attend. The order of Commissioner Graves was given in March, 1924, after he had made an investigation of parents, but instead of obeying the order the local school board referred the case to the people of the school district, who voted against the tax.

The opinion of Judge McLaughlin is significant in the educational history not only of New York State but of the United States, in that it shows both the increased powers of the chief state school officer and the increased public respect for the educational interests and rights of children. The opinion noted that the law permitted the formation of small schools into a larger district, called a "union free-school district," and that when such a district was formed, its board of education was given sufficient power to provide equal educational advantages for all the children of the district. If the board should neglect to make such provision or should neglect or refuse "to carry out the object for which the district has been formed," the chief state school officer has by the school law of the state sufficient authority to compel action. The decision is an illustration of localism yielding to centralization; of alleged local rights surrendering to central power, not in the interest of tyranny and despotism, however, but in behalf of the rights of the children and in the interest of general public welfare. It is an illustration also of the changed conception of the democratic state, whose preëminent concern should be for the protection and improvement of all its citizens.

The state board of education. Closely connected with the chief state school officer is the state board of education, now found in all the states. The board first appeared in New York in 1784. It has continued to the present and, with the office of commissioner of education of New York, represents perhaps the largest state educational control to be found in any American state. In the same year Georgia chartered the first American state university; and a year later it passed an act under which all forms of public education in the state were to become a part of the university, whose Senatus Academicus was to act in an advisory capacity toward all schools established or supported by public funds. This plan of state educational control, remarkable for its centralization, was impracticable, however, and proved to be a failure. In 1817 the territory of Michigan created a university which was to have control over all the public schools to be established within the state, but this part of its purpose was never realized.

In the boards created to manage the "literary funds" or permanent public-school endowments may also be seen the genesis of state boards of education. The funds set up in Virginia in 1810 and in North Carolina in 1825 are examples. The beginnings of a state board of control appear also in legislative committees to whom reports of school funds were regularly made. However, it was in 1837, in Massachusetts, that the first real state board of education, with a secretary or a state superintendent of schools, was established. Connecticut created a state board of commissioners for common schools and provided for a secretary in 1839. Kentucky, Arkansas, Ohio, Indiana, and North Carolina provided for some central state control through a board of education or superintendent of schools by 1852. Since that date some form of state board has been established in all the states as enlightened public sentiment for the proper direction of schools increased.

Types of boards. There are four different kinds of state boards of education in the United States at the present time: (1) the board whose members are all appointed, (2) the board whose appointed members predominate, (3) the board whose members are all ex officio, and (4) the board whose ex-officio members predominate.

The ex-officio state board of education, whose members are generally state officers, is regarded by authorities in school administration as unsafe and as the most rudimentary of all. Generally the powers of such a board are not clearly defined. Moreover, the members are generally elected for other purposes than those of educational supervision and direction, which should be the primary purpose of a real state board of education. They are generally elected upon a party platform, and are therefore committed to party programs and are subject to the fortunes and misfortunes of party politics. In the interest of the harmony of the party they must jealously guard its every policy, whether it promotes education or not. The unstable character of such a board also counts heavily against it. To secure continuity of policy the membership of a state board of education should be subject only to gradual changes. In the ex-officio board the danger is always present that the membership may change completely and suddenly at the end of a political administration.

The type of state educational control now generally approved by authorities in public-school administration consists of a small number of representative citizens appointed by the governor for long terms. The principal functions of the board should be legislative and supervisory, and the actual direction of the schools should be in the hands of the executive officer of the board; namely, the superintendent, or commissioner of education. The selection of this officer is one of the most important duties of the board.

The properly constituted state board of education is able to systematize and supervise all the public educational forces of the state. This makes for economy and the elimination of waste, which is inevitable when there is division of responsibility. Such a board also makes for orderly progress, a process so necessary in the conduct of a state school system, with its tens of thousands of teachers, its multitudes of children to be instructed, and the immense expenditures that must come from public taxation. Public education is today one of the big interests of the American people, and it demands a high order of competent counsel and executive direction. The state board of education should correspond somewhat closely to the board of directors in a business organization. Just as system increases the effectiveness of an industrial corporation, so does it increase the effectiveness of public schools.

The history of public education in the United States shows that movements in the direction of a general and uniform public-school organization often meet with opposition from local communities. They have resisted centralization of power. But the objection to competent state oversight of local educational effort often arises from a misunderstanding of the true nature of education and of the relation of schools to the general well-being of the commonwealth. State boards of education whose duties are properly and clearly defined make for educational progress. This is particularly true when such boards decline to become political bodies with selfish or partisan ends to serve and when the general welfare of the state becomes and remains their preëminent concern. Such boards are able to respond to new conditions and needs as they arise, to devise wise educational policies, and to protect the schools from indifferent or hostile legislation.

The increasing importance of state boards of education will become more thoroughly appreciated as public opinion becomes more and more enlightened. Numerous surveys of state school systems in recent years point to the same conclusion. Most of them have been made by organizations of national prominence, such as the Carnegie Foundation, the General Education Board, and the United States Bureau of Education. The general tendency of the states to accept the recommendations of the survey commissions and remove the administrative handicaps of the state boards of education is one of the hopeful signs in American education.

Local supervision and control. Professional county and city superintendencies were also slow to develop. As education came to be considered a function of the state, however, the need arose for some form of control in administrative units below the state to oversee state funds or school lands in the counties or other units, to supervise local school officers and teachers, and to enforce the general school law of the state. The county school officer, known as county superintendent of schools or county superintendent of education or county superintendent of public instruction or county superintendent of common schools, slowly evolved through constitutional provision or the general school law of the state. Often he served in ex-officio capacity, just as did the state superintendents. Sometimes the office developed out of the chairmanship or presidency of the county board of education or other county offices. The early duties of the chief county school officer were generally clerical and fiscal, although he often had authority to visit the schools and sometimes he was expected to examine and certificate teachers. Beginning in the fourth and fifth decades of the nineteenth century, the county superintendency was established in ten or a dozen states by the time of the Civil War, and a few years later it was provided in most of the states. Election by popular vote early came to be the favorite means of selection; and this practice (still followed by many of the states) helps to prevent the requirement of professional fitness of county superintendents of schools, which remains one of the weak spots in public educational administration in many of the states. Educational progress has been considerably slower in county and rural sections than in the cities, which now generally demand professionally trained superintendents for their schools.

But this demand was not made very early even by the cities, because of the district system and the strength of localism which so long prevailed in them. Before the Civil War professional superintendents were very few, one may almost say practically unknown. For example, in 1832 Buffalo, New York, had several small school districts, each having a schoolhouse and one teacher. Five years later, when the legislature of the state incorporated the city and provided for an appointment of the superintendent of common schools, who was to "possess all the powers and authority and be subject to the duties and obligations of the inspectors of common schools of the different towns of this state," the city had seven districts and seven teachers. In 1839 the number of districts was increased to fifteen, each with one school. The first superintendent was appointed in the summer of 1837 to coördinate and oversee the schools of the city, but he was not a professional officer in the present-day meaning of the word "superintendent." His functions were identical with those of town school-inspectors in New York and so-called school-visitors in New England, who were not professional schoolmen. He was a layman and served without pay. He resigned in a few months and was succeeded by another man, who received a salary of $75 for the first year. During the next decade five or six men served as superintendent of the schools of Buffalo, but no one of them for more than two years consecutively. In 1844 one of them recommended that the time of the superintendent be devoted exclusively to the schools, and two years later the superintendent stated that his private business made it impossible for him to continue his educational work, which was not his principal interest. Elsewhere the practice was similar to that followed in Buffalo.

First city superintendency. Providence, Rhode Island, probably furnishes the earliest example of a full-time professional superintendent of city schools in the United States. In 1836 Cambridge, Massachusetts, engaged at a salary of $250 a year a man who bore the title of superintendent, but his functions were probably similar to those of the usual New England school-visitors, who also have been known locally as superintendents. Buffalo, as already noted, appointed a superintendent in 1837. Louisville, Lexington, and Maysville in Kentucky each had an "agent of the public schools" in 1838 under a law enacted in that year to establish a system of common schools in that state. An agent seems to have been appointed in Louisville as early as 1834, with a salary of $400, to visit the schools and to establish night schools for the benefit of apprentices. At that time the principal of the grammar school of that city received a salary of $700; six years later he received a salary of $900, and that of the agent was $800. The agents of these Kentucky cities may have performed some of the duties of the superintendency, although that office did not fully develop even in Louisville until much later. In 1839 St. Louis, with two schools, — one with two teachers and the other with only one, — engaged a superintendent but paid him no salary. The real beginning of the superintendency in that city seems not to have been made until 1851, when James H. Tice began the work at a salary of $1500 a year. It is probable that the experiences of these and other places, which depended upon laymen for part time, led Providence in 1838 to adopt a school ordinance providing for a superintendent of schools. Nathan Bishop, a tutor in Brown University, was chosen by the school committee for the position, upon which he entered on August 1, 1839, and to which he gave his entire time until 1851, when he resigned to become superintendent of schools in Boston. Samuel S. Green, who has been called the second professional superintendent in the United States, went from the principalship of an academy at Worcester to the superintendency of schools in Springfield, Massachusetts, in 1840, and succeeded Bishop at Providence in 1851.

Recent development in cities. In most of the cities school administration was a very simple matter, the local district trustees and the people of the districts exercising almost complete control. As late as 1870 only twenty-seven city superintendents of schools were employed in the entire country, and in only thirteen of the thirty-seven states. Buffalo, Louisville, and Providence had appointed superintendents before 1840, and Springfield, New Orleans, Rochester, Columbus, Syracuse, Baltimore, and Cincinnati, by 1850. During the next decade the office was established in Boston, Gloucester (Massachusetts), Worcester (Massachusetts), New York, Brooklyn, San Francisco, Jersey City, Newark, Cleveland, Chicago, St. Louis, St. Joseph, Indianapolis, and Milwaukee. Albany seems to have created the office in 1866, Kansas City in 1867, and Washington in 1869. Although the Civil War checked the development of city school supervision, one hundred and forty-two of the one hundred and seventy-five cities which had as many as eight thousand people had city superintendents of schools by 1876. Since that time city school administration has developed rapidly throughout the country. The progress which the United States has made in education in recent years has been due in large part to the cities, where the best experience in educational administration and supervision has been evolved.

This chapter has described the slow and haphazard growth of the principle of state control in education, which has resulted in a lack of uniformity. The beginnings of state control were made when the state gave financial aid to local schools; but since 1812 each of the states has established some form of central administrative control of schools, although practices vary widely among the states. County and city administrative agencies have also been established. Some of the conditions and problems of public educational administration and supervision have been described in the chapter, which also points out that because of the strength of localism the principles of expert control and professional supervision have not been fully applied in practice in all American communities. Localism also stands in the way of the training of teachers, as will be shown in Chapter XI.

REFERENCES AND READINGS

BLAIR, F. G. Centennial Celebration of the Enactment of the First Free School Law in Illinois. Springfield, 1925.

> Contains an interesting introductory statement, comments on the first school law in that state, a facsimile of the law, and other useful information.

CUBBERLEY, E. P. Public Education in the United States. Boston, 1919.

> Chapter VI, entitled "The Battle to Control the System," is useful supplementary material for this chapter.

CUBBERLEY, E. P. State and County Educational Reorganization. New York, 1914.

> The constitutional and legal provisions for education in the hypothetical state of Osceola.

CUBBERLEY, E. P. State School Administration. Boston, 1927.

> Chapters VI–XI are excellent. Very useful bibliographies.

DUTTON, S. T., and SNEDDEN, DAVID. The Administration of Public Education in the United States. New York, 1913.

> Chapters IV–VII deal with topics treated in this chapter.

JUDD, CHARLES H. "General Summary and Conclusions on State Educational Organization in New York," Rural School Survey of New York State, volume entitled "Administration and Supervision." Ithaca, 1923.

> A good criticism of conditions and needs in New York.

KNIGHT, EDGAR W. Public School Education in North Carolina. Boston, 1916.

> Chapters VIII–X describe the early development of state control in North Carolina.

MARTIN, GEORGE H. The Evolution of the Massachusetts Public School System. New York, 1894.

> A good account of the struggle to gain state control and supervision in Massachusetts.

McCRACKEN, THOMAS C. "The State Board of Education," *Journal of the National Education Association*. Vol. XII, No. 5 (May, 1923).

> A helpful discussion of the subject.

REEDER, W. G. The Chief State School Officer, *Bulletin No. 5*, United States Bureau of Education. Washington, 1924.

> An excellent study.

WEBSTER, W. C. Recent Centralizing Tendencies in Education. New York, 1897.

> Shows the tendencies of the period.

Reports of the State Educational Survey Commissions.

> Made by the United States Bureau of Education, the General Education Board, and other agencies, and published at different places and times, these studies are very valuable for students interested in the subject of this chapter. The more important are listed in Cubberley's "State School Administration," pp. 304–305.

QUESTIONS FOR STUDY AND DISCUSSION

1. Point out any survivals in your state of the traditional objection to centralized control in education.

2. Why does the district system of school control continue so popular in some states?

3. Why do so many of the states continue to elect their chief school officers by popular vote, although their chief highway engineers, secretaries of boards of health, and university presidents are not elected by such means?

4. Point out the arguments against the popular election of state or county superintendents. Why are city superintendents not elected by popular vote?

5. Why do cities generally have better schools than the rural sections?

6. What is meant by the "county unit of school organization and administration"? What are the advantages of such a plan as you understand it?

7. What are the weaknesses of the district system of public educational control?

8. In states which elect their county or state superintendents of schools by popular vote what educational qualifications are usually required? What qualifications do you consider desirable for these educational officers?

9. Trace the evolution of the county superintendency in your state; of the state superintendency.

10. What is the best type of state board of education? What are the weaknesses of the ex-officio type?

CHAPTER XI

THE TRAINING OF TEACHERS

Outline of the chapter. 1. Interest in the proper training of teachers was slow to develop in the United States, although the idea was early advocated.

2. The plan of Thomas H. Gallaudet (1825) was among the earliest proposals to receive attention and to be discussed, and reports in this country of practices in Europe served to stimulate interest.

3. Perhaps the earliest attempt to train teachers in the United States was made by Samuel McCorkle in his academy, Zion Parnassus, in North Carolina as early as 1785. In 1823 Samuel R. Hall had a school in Vermont in which teachers were trained.

4. The first efforts in New York were made in connection with academies. Massachusetts, influenced by Carter, Mann, and Brooks, was the first state to establish state normal schools.

5. Schools for the training of teachers were gradually established in other states, though the development in the South was slow before 1860.

6. By 1870 the theory of schools for the professional training of teachers had been generally accepted, and in many states such institutions had been established, but organized materials of instruction were meager.

7. With Pestalozzianism came materials for the professional training of teachers, and normal schools had increased rapidly by 1900.

8. In recent years the work of training teachers has been reorganized and standards have been improved.

9. In addition to normal schools and teachers' colleges, the training of teachers is undertaken in teachers' institutes, in colleges and universities, in summer sessions, in high schools, and through correspondence courses and extension courses.

10. With all these agencies, however, there is not yet an adequate supply of trained and excellent teachers in any state.

"Educate men for the business of teaching, employ them, and pay them when educated," urged Samuel R. Hall, who in 1823 opened in Vermont one of the earliest seminaries for teachers in the United States, and who a few years later published "Lectures on Schoolkeeping," the first American textbook on education. He and other educational leaders of that period viewed the proper training of teachers as an important public matter, but it was many years later before wide interest in the subject was developed. The problem was long neglected. Even now it is one of the persistent educational problems in the United States. It remains difficult largely as a result of the conditions which have so long delayed the development of intelligent public educational support and control (see Chapters IX and X). The purpose of this chapter is to point out the slow growth of the movement and the conditions that now surround the training of teachers.

A perpetual public duty. Each of the states has ordered that schools be established for the education of all its children. Under the democratic theory of education each of these children, no matter where he may live or how poor or humble his condition, is entitled to as good a teacher as his state can afford. Moreover, the teachers with whom a public-school system begins each year should be stronger and of higher rank in training, in teaching skill, and in personal culture than the average of the teachers in the service of that system any previous year. The duty of training, of rewarding, and of retaining in the schools a wholesome supply of adequately equipped teachers has become and remains a perpetual duty binding upon every American state.

The idea that prospective teachers should have special preparation for their work arose out of the influence of the Protestant revolt. Along with free, secular, and universal education Luther and other leaders in that movement advocated the training of teachers. But the idea of teacher-training appeared late and was slow to develop in the United States. It was nearly two centuries after Massachusetts had ordered the establishment of schools before the state provided for the training of teachers for those schools. After Connecticut had provided for schools it was nearly one hundred and seventy-five years before there was even a suggestion that the state establish an institution exclusively for training teachers, and it was several decades later before such a school was provided. The idea of education as a function of government was slow in developing, and it was natural that the idea of training teachers should not arouse much public interest. Successful teacher-training practices in Europe were among the influences that finally aroused interest and led to discussions of the subject.

Early advocates. Even before the close of the eighteenth century men advanced the theory that teachers should be trained for their work. It is often stated that the first reference to the subject by an American writer appeared in the plan for Benjamin Franklin's academy about the middle of the century. One of the purposes of this school was that "others of the lesser sort might be trained as teachers." In the *Massachusetts Magazine* for June, 1789, appeared an article on "The Importance of Studying the English Language Grammatically," in which it was suggested that "young gentlemen designed for schoolmasters" should be examined annually in reading, writing, arithmetic, and English grammar and be indorsed by competent authority; and that no "man ought to be suffered to superintend ever so small a school except he has been first examined . . . and authorized for this purpose." The article insisted upon the proper training, selection, and some form of certification of teachers.

The first definite proposal in the United States for a school designed exclusively for the training of teachers appears to have been made by Denison Olmsted in an address at Yale College in 1816 on "The State of Education in Connecticut." (Olmsted later was a professor at the University of North Carolina, and still later a professor at Yale.) In the address he recommended a school in which prospective teachers could "study and recite whatever they themselves were afterwards to teach," in order to gain a better knowledge of the subjects and of the "principles and the art of teaching." In this proposed school attention was to be given to the organization and management of schools.

About a decade later James L. Kingsley, another Yale professor, in an article in the *North American Review*, made suggestions for the training of teachers to give "new vigor to the whole system of education." He thought the prevailing method of ascertaining the qualifications of teachers "a very imperfect check on the intrusion of ignorance. The teachers, it is understood, have now very seldom any other preparation than they receive in the very school where they afterwards instruct, or in the school of some neighboring district, where the advantages for improvement are no better." The condition which Kingsley deplored was to remain a stubborn educational problem for many decades, and to a certain extent it may be found in parts of the United States today.

William Russell, a teacher in an academy in New Haven, published in 1823 a pamphlet entitled "Suggestions on Education." In this and in the *American Journal of Education* (one of the earliest professional magazines in the United States, of which Russell became editor in 1826), he attributed the weakness of the common schools to the lack of trained teachers. He believed that this weakness could be removed by teacher-training schools. In "Suggestions on Education" he said, among other things, that "the common schools for children are in not a few instances conducted by individuals who do not possess one of the qualifications of an instructor, and in very many cases there is barely knowledge enough to keep the teacher at a decent distance from his scholars. ... The effects of such an improvement [schools for training teachers] in education seem almost incalculable. The information, the intelligence, and the refinement which might thus be diffused among the body of the people would increase the prosperity, elevate the character, and promote the happiness of the nation to a degree perhaps unequaled in the world."

In 1829 appeared Henry E. Dwight's "Travels in the North of Germany, 1825–1826," which contained an account of the successful practice of seminaries for the education of schoolmasters in that country. It also pointed out that "to understand a subject will not of itself enable one to impart a clear view of the best mode of communicating knowledge to the minds of children," a capacity which Dwight said could be acquired only by previous preparation or by long experience. He urged the proper preparation of school-teachers for Connecticut, and said that with such teachers "the intellectual character of the mass of inhabitants would in one generation not only become superior to that of every other people, but it would become the wonder and admiration of our country."

In a lecture in 1833 on the necessity of educating teachers, Samuel R. Hall declared that there was not in the entire country at that time "one seminary where the educator of children can be thoroughly qualified for his important work." In comparison, he pointed to thirty seminaries in Prussia for the purpose of training teachers. It is probable that examples and practices in Europe influenced thought on the subject in this country. In 1825, for example, Walter R. Johnson of Germantown, Pennsylvania, suggested in an article or pamphlet that schools for training teachers be established similar to those in Prussia; and in the same year Philip Lindsley, the acting president of the College of New Jersey, urged in an address at Princeton the necessity of teacher-training institutions. "We have our theological seminaries, our medical and law schools, which receive the graduates of our college and fit them for their prospective professions, and whenever the profession of teaching shall be duly honored and appreciated, it is not doubted but that it will receive similar attention and be favored with equal advantages." Shortly afterwards Lindsley became president of Cumberland College in Tennessee (later the University of Nashville). In an address there he emphasized the necessity for properly prepared teachers, and said that until "schoolkeeping be made an honorable and lucrative profession suitable teachers will never be forthcoming in this free country."

Gallaudet's plan. These earlier discussions do not seem to have attracted so much general attention to the subject as did an article by the Reverend Thomas H. Gallaudet on "A Plan of a Seminary for the Education and Instruction of Youth." This article appeared in the *Connecticut Observer*, published in Hartford, on January 4, 1825. Gallaudet is also well known for his early interest in teaching deaf-mutes. Selections from the article were printed in newspapers, and the plan was later discussed in educational conventions in Hartford. It proposed a school for training teachers, to be supported by the "liberality of the public" and equipped with a library containing "all the works, theoretical and practical, in all languages, which could be obtained upon the subject of education," and a practice school of "indigent children and youths." The training, which should be given to those young men who expected to devote their lives to teaching, was to consist of lectures on the subject of education, reading and studying the best books on the subject, and practice teaching in the experimental school. Those who finished the course of study were to receive a certificate or diploma recommending them "to the confidence of the public." In this plan appeared the essential features found today in schools for the training of elementary teachers. In recognition of Gallaudet's influence the students of the first state normal school, established in New Britain, Connecticut, in 1850, formed a Gallaudet society.

European influence. Educational leaders in this country derived some inspiration on the subject of normal schools through contact with the reports of European practices. In 1819 John Griscom of New York published his "Year in Europe"; William C. Woodbridge of New England published in Russell's *American Journal of Education* valuable letters on European conditions, and especially the work of Pestalozzi and Fellenberg; a part of Victor Cousin's "Report on the Condition of Public Instruction in Germany, and particularly Prussia," made to the French government in 1831, was also printed in the United States and aroused some interest in normal schools, especially in Massachusetts and Michigan; in 1837 Calvin E. Stowe of Ohio made his influential report on "Elementary Education in Europe," which was reprinted and distributed by legislative authority in Pennsylvania, Massachusetts, Michigan, North Carolina, and Virginia; in 1835–1837 Henry Barnard visited schools in Europe and made interesting reports in educational journals; in 1839 A. D. Bache of Pennsylvania published his "Education in Europe"; and in 1839 *The Connecticut Common School Journal* published a number of articles on normal schools, giving their history in certain European countries. It is evident that teacher-training practices in Europe had influence in this country.

The first attempts. Probably the first attempt to train teachers in the United States was privately made by Samuel McCorkle, a graduate of Princeton of the class of 1772, near Salisbury, North Carolina, in 1785. His academy, known as Zion Parnassus, which maintained a high order of scholarship and had an extensive influence, was well known for its teacher-training department from its founding to 1811. The school also gave free tuition and books to worthy students. McCorkle declined a professorship at the University of North Carolina in 1795, preferring to continue the work of his academy, in which he prepared scores of students for their higher education. Six of the first seven graduates of the University of North Carolina were prepared at Zion Parnassus.

In the school which Samuel R. Hall opened in Vermont in 1823 for the training of teachers, a three years' course was offered in which the subjects taught in the common schools were reviewed and some training in the art of teaching was also furnished. The students in this school gained practice by teaching in the rural schools during the winter. Hall's experiment was similar to McCorkle's in North Carolina, in that the feature of training teachers was added to the regular work of an academy. In 1829 Hall published his "Lectures on Schoolkeeping," said to have been the first American textbook on education. This book became popular and probably stimulated interest in teacher-training. It was officially used in the districts of New York State and officially recommended for the use of every teacher in Kentucky at public expense.

SAMUEL R. HALL

Author of the first American textbook on education

Early efforts in New York. The first attempts to train teachers in New York were made in connection with the academies. Governor DeWitt Clinton, in his message to the legislature of that state in 1826, urged that a school be established for the training of teachers. However, the belief seems to have been strong there that the training of teachers was an obligation upon the colleges and academies, and the governor's recommendation was not accepted. But the following year an act was passed which had for its purpose, among other things, the promoting of "the education of teachers"; and although this purpose was not immediately attained, this was the first act in the United States for the training of teachers.

Teacher-training features were found in some of the academies of the state in 1831, and three years later the legislature assigned certain public funds to be used by the academies in the training of teachers under regulations of the Board of Regents. Eight academies were added in that year to the list of those which trained teachers, and four years later eight others. The report on this work in 1840 showed that the students preferred the academic to the professional subjects, that many of them did not remain throughout the entire course of three years, and that there was no provision for practice teaching. The report recommended schools designed expressly for the training of teachers as having some "advantages over any other method." Opposition to special training schools for teachers continued, however, and funds were given to eight more academies to provide teacher-training facilities; but in 1844 this feature of the academy work was abolished, probably as a result of a legislative report on normal schools in Massachusetts, and the state normal school at Albany was established. In 1862 state aid was given to the Oswego Normal School, which four years later was adopted as a state institution.

In New England. In the eighteen-twenties James G. Carter urged the public establishment of normal schools for Massachusetts, making his appeal chiefly through his "Essays on Popular Education," which appeared in the *Boston Patriot* in 1824–1825 and attracted wide notice. He pointed out the economic waste resulting from ill-prepared teachers, and asserted that knowledge of a subject was not a guaranty of ability to communicate it to others. He believed that schools for the proper training of teachers should be established and maintained by the state as a part of the state school system. Two years later Carter petitioned the legislature for funds to establish normal schools; but the petition was denied. He showed his faith in the idea by opening through his own efforts a private teacher-training institution at Lancaster, but this attained very little success.

THE ORIGINAL NORMAL-SCHOOL BUILDING AT BRIDGEWATER, MASSACHUSETTS

Massachusetts. But Carter did not relax his efforts to secure normal schools. The idea of the professional training of teachers was gaining in favor in Massachusetts and was receiving support from the American Institute of Instruction. Carter himself had helped to establish this organization in 1830, and a year later had lectured before it on the "necessary and most practicable means of raising the qualifications of teachers." By 1836 the establishment of normal schools had become a practical issue in Massachusetts. At that time Carter was in the legislature and a member of the committee on education, and a year later he drafted and sponsored the legislation which set up the first board of education in that state. He became one of the first members of this board, and Horace Mann became its first secretary.

They united their efforts with those of the Reverend
Charles Brooks, whose lectures before the legislature and
throughout the state on the need for trained teachers were
impressive and effective. His theme everywhere was "as
is the teacher so is the school." Brooks traveled more
than two thousand miles in his own buggy and at his personal expense to present to the people the need for normal
schools. Meantime Carter
and Mann were working
with the legislature, which
finally appropriated the
sum of $10,000 to match
a like amount offered by
Edward Dwight, a citi-
zen of Boston, for the
purpose of establishing a
state school for training
teachers. As a result the
first state normal school
in the United States was
opened on July 3, 1839,
at Lexington, Massachu-
setts. Two months later

REVEREND CHARLES BROOKS

the second school opened at Barre, and in September, 1840,
the third was opened at Bridgewater. Five years later the
board of education changed the name of these institutions
from "normal schools" to "state normal schools."

To these schools boys were admitted at the age of seventeen and girls at the age of sixteen, upon declaration of
intention to teach and by a successful examination in reading, writing, arithmetic, orthography, English grammar,
and geography. The course of study was one year in length
and included, in addition to the subjects enumerated above,
composition, rhetoric, logic, drawing, algebra, geometry, bookkeeping, navigation, surveying, statistics, the constitution

and history of Massachusetts and of the United States, physiology and hygiene, mental philosophy, music, natural philosophy, "the principles of piety and morality common to all sects of Christians," and the "science and art of teaching with reference to all the above-named subjects." Connected with each normal school was an experimental, or

CYRUS PIERCE

Principal of the first state normal school, at Lexington, Massachusetts

practice, school in which the students practiced under the direction of the principal and the observation of their fellows. In the practice school the "knowledge which they acquired in the science of teaching is practically applied. The art is made to grow out of the science, instead of being empirical."

Connecticut. Connecticut in 1838 created a state board of education with a secretaryship, to which Henry Barnard, who had been chairman of the legislative committee that drafted the bill, was appointed. He began at once to urge the legislature to establish "at least one seminary for teachers," and he informed the public of actual conditions through official reports, the press, and public addresses. Though he strongly favored normal schools he showed a willingness to accept training departments in academies for a time, and even organized at Hartford a voluntary course of training for teachers. Many arguments were offered against normal schools, but Barnard had a ready answer for them all. In 1849, after a committee had visited Massachusetts and New

York and studied the teacher-training plans in those states, provision was made for a normal school, which was opened in 1850 at New Britain.

Maine and Rhode Island. In the early eighteen-sixties Maine established two normal schools "to be thoroughly devoted to the work of training teachers," to take the place of the academy system, which had been established in 1846 and had been declared a failure. The state superintendent, the Reverend Edward Ballard, questioned the ability of a high school or academy to "qualify teachers as well for their work as the institutions especially established for this purpose." He believed that the work could not be equal to that of normal schools. Rhode Island established its first state normal school in 1852.

In other states. Schools such as were set up in New England, the sole purpose of which was to train teachers, came to be generally favored over the academy plan which New York had tried. Superintendent John D. Pierce, in his first report in 1836, had recommended for Michigan either the New England plan or the New York plan; but in 1843 Superintendent Ira Mayhew, in his report for that state, showed preference for normal schools, which he believed to be "indispensable to the perfection" of a public-school system. Six years later a normal school act was passed, and in 1853 the Ypsilanti Normal School was opened.

Wisconsin undertook to maintain normal classes in colleges and academies after 1857, but the experiment was not successful. Superintendent J. L. Pickard in his report in 1863 said that the normal classes were "almost always subordinate departments" and were inadequate to the educational needs of the state. He urged the founding of normal schools, which were established in that state a few years later. Iowa and New Jersey established their first state normal schools in 1855, Illinois in 1857, Minnesota in 1858, and Pennsylvania in 1859.

In the South. The rise of public normal schools in the South before 1860 was naturally tardy. Sentiment in favor of public schools was slow to develop in that section, largely because of class distinctions which had grown up around and as a part of negro slavery. It was but natural, therefore, that interest in normal schools, which were intended

JOSEPH CALDWELL

The first president of the University of North Carolina, and a strong advocate of teacher-training

as one of the best means of elevating the common schools, should not be so strong as in New England or in some of the other states. But even in the South the obvious value of teacher-training institutions was recognized. In one way or another educational leaders as well as other leaders in all these states advocated the establishment of normal schools at public expense.

North Carolina. In 1832 President Joseph Caldwell of the University of North Carolina, in a pamphlet (see Chapter VIII) entitled "Letters on Popular Education addressed to the People of North Carolina," strongly advocated "an institution for preparing schoolmasters for their profession, upon the most improved methods of instruction." The principal of the school which he proposed was to "be selected, with time and opportunity for inquiry, from the whole field of the United States." He maintained that the business of an instructor in common schools was itself "an art not to be comprehended and established in the habits of an

individual without much time, education, and discipline."
He recommended a seminary with a two years' course of
study and an observation and practice school. Those who
finished the course were to be certificated as prepared to
teach. He urged the necessity of training "to prepare men
for the schoolmaster's profession, as the lawyer, the physician, the mariner, the cabinetmaker, and men of other
professions are trained with much application to their several
employments." He deplored the educational conditions in
his state, saying that the "evil which is the greatest of all
is the want of qualified masters."

In 1838 the directors of the North Carolina literary fund
(the state's permanent public-school endowment) urged the
legislature to establish "normal schools." At that time the
state had not provided for public schools ; and the recommendation of these directors, who formed something of a
state board of education, included normal schools as an
essential part of a state-wide public-school system. The
plan proposed was made after a study of educational plans
in Massachusetts, New York, Pennsylvania, Ohio, and even
in Europe. In these American states normal schools developed after public elementary schools had been established.
In North Carolina, which did not establish common schools
until 1839, the establishment of normal schools was proposed
as an essential part of a public-school system. "We must
establish normal schools for the education of our own
teachers, and we need entertain no hope of accomplishing
the favorite object of the state in any other way," declared
the report, which also urged the creation of a superintendency of common schools.

Nothing immediate came out of this report ; but in 1852
provision was made for the state superintendency, which
was continued until 1866 under the direction of the same
officer, Calvin H. Wiley. In 1853 the state began its first
public effort at training teachers at Union Institute, from

which Trinity College, now Duke University, later developed. Union Institute was under the direction of Braxton Craven, who published in 1850 a rather comprehensive plan for training teachers. The pamphlet had wide circulation and some influence. As a result the legislature the same year gave authority to the institution to issue certificates to its graduates as sufficient evidence of ability to teach in any of the common schools of the state, without further examination by the county school boards. Two years later a new charter was granted to the institution, and its name was changed to Normal College. The governor of the state was made ex-officio president, and the state superintendent ex-officio secretary of the trustees. From that time until 1859, when the name was changed to Trinity College and all public relations severed, Normal College continued its work of training teachers in a course that comprised the work of three years. The state made no other attempt at the public training of teachers, however, until 1876.

Virginia. As a result of educational conventions in Virginia (see Chapter VIII) in the eighteen-forties definite recommendations were made for the establishment of normal schools in that state. One of the most valuable of these was prepared by Henry Ruffner, who was president of Washington College (now Washington and Lee University) and father of William H. Ruffner, Virginia's superintendent of public schools from 1870 to 1882. Henry Ruffner presided over a convention in Lexington in 1841, and he presented to the legislature a state school plan which included, among other modern features, schools designed especially for the training of teachers. Later a convention held in Richmond made the same recommendations to the legislature, but it was not until 1884 that the Old Dominion established a normal school.

South Carolina. The story is much the same in South Carolina, which also delayed action, although a school system principally for poor children had been established by the state in 1811. As early as 1839, however, Professors Stephen Elliott and James H. Thornwell of South Carolina College were requested by the governor to make a study of conditions in the state and report an improved school plan. The report pointed out the need for normal schools and urged that they be established. In 1847, as a result of action by the State Agricultural Society the preceding year, appeared another report, prepared under the direction of R. E. W. Allston, urging state supervision and a normal school with a "model school attached." Later a legislative committee of five members, with Henry Sumner as chairman, made similar recommendations, which were substantially indorsed by an educational convention in Columbia still later. Charleston, which by legislative permission inaugurated a school system in 1856, two years later established a girls' high school with a normal department. The value of normal schools was recognized, and their establishment by the state was urged; but nothing came of the recommendations, and it was not until 1895 that South Carolina established a state normal school.

Florida. In 1851 the legislature of Florida established the East Florida Seminary and the West Florida Seminary, the first purpose of these institutions being "the instruction of persons, both male and female, in the art of teaching all the various branches that pertain to a good common school education; and next, to give instruction in the mechanic arts, in husbandry and agricultural chemistry, in the fundamental laws, and in what regards the rights and duties of citizens." But the teacher-training departments seem not to have been very strong, and it was not until 1887 that Florida established a state normal school.

Louisiana. In 1858 the legislature of Louisiana established a normal-school department in the public high school in New Orleans, and the following year an appropriation of

$5000 was made for its support. In 1860 the sum of $10,000 was appropriated for buildings on condition that the city would appropriate a similar sum, and forty-eight pupils, to be selected by the governor, were to be admitted free of tuition charge. A legislative appropriation of $3000 was made to this school in 1862. The first state normal school was established in 1884.

Other states in the South. In 1848 the legislature of Mississippi considered the question of establishing a state institution for the training of teachers, and the trustees of Mississippi College at Clinton made an effort to have that institution transformed into a normal school; but the legislative committee on normal schools made an adverse report on the subject. In the same year a special legislative committee on normal schools was appointed. It made a report and offered a bill to establish a state normal school, but both the report and the bill were laid on the table and given no further consideration. Two years later the general school commissioner, in bringing the matter to the attention of the legislature, said that the state was forced to look to other sections of the nation and to other countries for teachers and "to overlook their foreign accent and stupid vulgarity, or be entirely deprived of school privileges." But it was not until 1910 that Mississippi established its first state normal school. The institution appeared in Arkansas in 1872, in Texas in 1879, in Georgia in 1889, in Maryland in 1896, and in Kentucky, Alabama, and Tennessee after 1900.

Conditions about 1870. By 1870 the idea of separate and distinct schools for the professional or special preparation of teachers had been generally accepted (in theory at least) in the United States, and provision for such schools had been made by twenty-two states. During this early and somewhat experimental period there was no common agreement in theory or practice on the length of teacher-training courses, which varied from one to three years. In his report to the legislature in 1866 the superintendent of common schools in Ohio stated that the course in most of the schools of the United States was two years in length, "with a one-year's course in a few of them." The primary purpose of the schools was to increase the teaching power of the prospective teachers through such exercises as should impart to the students "a thorough teaching knowledge of all the branches ordinarily taught in common schools. This includes not only a mastery of the subjects as knowledge, which is the first requisite for successful teaching, but also a mastery of them as subjects to be taught to others. This is the one distinctive idea which runs through every lesson and exercise."

Another purpose was to furnish "the prospective teacher a practical knowledge of the guiding principles of his art, and to enable him to reduce such principles to something like a philosophical system. In other words, the second aim is to teach the science of education. This is usually sought to be accomplished by lectures." A third purpose was to acquaint the prospective teacher with the "best methods of instruction and government, including the methods especially applicable to each stage of the child's progress and to each branch of knowledge." Each recitation was "conducted with a view of unfolding the true method of teaching the topic." Finally, and not least important of the aims of the school, the student was enabled to acquire "skill in the art of teaching by an application of his knowledge of principles and methods in actual practice" in the model school and under the supervision and criticism of skilled teachers. Thus by the close of this early period or down to about 1870 the normal school was emphasizing the academic or subject-matter courses found in the common schools, somewhat old methods of teaching, and the demonstration of the conventional teaching technique.

Improved methods and materials of teaching awaited a new attitude toward child life, and this did not develop until Pestalozzianism, Herbartianism, Froebelianism, the new psychology, and other forces began to make themselves felt.

Meager materials of instruction. Before the appearance of these new forces and influences the materials of professional instruction for teachers were rather meager. Few books on the subject of teaching were available. Educational theory was passed on indifferently to teachers and prospective teachers by the published lectures of the practitioner, by teachers' manuals and guides, and by elementary treatises on educational principles and practices as viewed by the more active and successful schoolmasters of the period. But even this kind of material was scarce before 1860. The books most widely used in the early teacher-training institutions were Hall's "Lectures on School-keeping," which appeared in 1829, Jacob Abbott's "The Teacher: or Moral Influences employed in the Instruction and Government of the Young," which was published in 1833, and "Theory and Practice of Teaching," by David Page (the first principal of New York's first state normal school), which appeared in 1847 and went through twenty-five editions by 1860. Educational journalism had a modest beginning in the eighteen-twenties, but did not gain particular strength until much later. Methods of teaching had not undergone much change since colonial days. The child had not yet been recognized as the center of the teaching process, emphasis in the classroom was still on deadly memorization and the hearing of lessons, and relics of the cruelty of Calvinism still lingered in the severe discipline of the time.

Later development. Beginning with Pestalozzianism, however, which came in chiefly through the Oswego movement after 1860 (see Chapter XVI), materials of a professional nature slowly became available for the work of the agencies set up to train teachers. Later Herbartian and Froebelian ideas added to the professional subject matter which could be used in the teacher-training schools, and these institutions, both private and public, showed rapid growth after 1870. In addition to the publicly supported normal schools found in twenty-two states in 1870, a few cities were maintaining this type of institution to train and improve their own teachers, and there were many private normal schools also.

After 1870 the normal-school idea grew somewhat rapidly. By 1900 the number of public schools engaged in the training of teachers had increased to 170, and the private normal schools numbered 118. The public normal schools had over 43,000 students and graduated 8700 in that year; the students in the private schools numbered 20,000 and there were 1600 graduates. The leading subjects taught in the normal schools of the period included the history of education, the theory of education, school organization and supervision, school management and discipline, school hygiene, psychology and child study, ethics, school laws, and practical pedagogy.

As late as 1900 the typical normal school provided only two years of work beyond the high school. For a long time it was essentially a high school with some professional work added. Generally the normal school admitted its students from the elementary school; its primary purpose was to train teachers for the common schools. In some states even now, particularly in the South, normal schools with high-school departments are to be found.

Reorganization in recent years. Since 1900 the normal schools have gradually tended to increase their requirements. With the growth of public high schools it has been less and less necessary for the normal schools to provide high-school instruction, and they have more and more been able to require high-school graduation for admission. As early as 1918 nearly half the states had fixed this as the standard of admission. Today the commonly accepted standard of professional training for teachers in the elementary schools is two years of work beyond graduation from a standard high school. This standard is generally met by fulfilling the requirements for a diploma from most of the normal schools. Graduation from a standard college, following the completion of a standard high-school course, is today generally regarded as the minimum academic preparation necessary for teachers in high schools.

Present tendencies. Historically, however, the certificate that was accepted for teaching in the elementary schools was also accepted for teaching in the high schools. This practice was followed generally before high schools were standardized. With high-school standardization, it seemed desirable that high-school teachers should have a broader scholarship and longer training than the normal schools furnished through their curriculum, and the tendency developed to require college graduation of high-school teachers. The normal schools thus found themselves in their original position of training teachers only for the "common schools," which was the purpose of the normal schools in the days before public high schools developed.

In this way arose the theory that one type of teacher-training differs from another in dignity. The work of preparing teachers for the high schools came to be considered a less humble service than that of preparing them for the elementary schools. Moreover, the chief officers of normal schools, which trained elementary teachers, were generally called "principals," and the heads of colleges, which gained a monopoly upon the training of teachers for standard high schools, "presidents." And one educator should not differ from another educator in a democracy. Graduates were ambitious to have a "big" institution for their alma mater. These conditions led to a movement in recent years to change the name of teacher-training institutions from "normal schools" or "normal colleges," which formerly conferred no degrees, to "teachers' colleges," with the power to confer degrees. Colorado, Illinois, Kansas, and Missouri were among the first states to permit their normal schools to become teachers' colleges with the privilege of granting degrees.

The present tendency is toward four-year colleges, to be developed and maintained as a part of the public-school system for the professional preparation of teachers for all kinds of elementary and secondary public schools. In 1927 there were about a hundred normal schools or teachers' colleges which offered four years' work above standard secondary schools, and granted degrees. Nearly 90 per cent of these were state teacher-training schools, the remainder being municipal or private.

Standards of teacher-training have greatly improved in the last quarter of a century; but many of the agencies for the professional preparation of teachers are clearly below the level of effectiveness which modern educational ideas demand. One of the criticisms often heard is that the work of training teachers which is essentially of collegiate grade, whether it is given in normal schools, teachers' colleges, or schools of education in colleges and universities, is too often below the level of work done in colleges of liberal arts. Surveys of teacher-training work in such states as Pennsylvania, Massachusetts, and Louisiana indicate other weaknesses. It appears from such surveys that students preparing to teach are, in general, of a lower economic status than students in other departments; that the teachers as a class are relatively inferior in scholarship, and that their salaries are less; that teacher-training institutions are relatively deficient in physical equipment; that many of them are not adequately equipped with model or demonstration schools; and that public funds for teacher-training institutions are proportionally less than those appropriated to liberal-arts colleges and agricultural colleges.

The latest official reports show 382 normal schools and teachers colleges, which are the principal agencies for the preparation of teachers in the United States. In these institutions more than 245,000 students are enrolled. City normal schools and colleges, schools or departments of education in universities and colleges, and teacher-training departments in high schools have more than 172,000 students who are preparing to teach.

Teachers' institutes. While the normal school was yet in its infancy itinerant, or moving, normal schools, generally known as teachers' institutes, appeared as an attempt to meet the need for trained teachers. The institute was probably distinctly American in origin. For a time it did the work of the normal school in many states by offering to teachers an opportunity to review the subjects taught in the common schools and to study methods of teaching and school management. Often the institute was inspirational and entertaining. General sessions, open to the public, served to create interest in public education. Through the institute also new school subjects were often introduced. The work at best was doubtless fragmentary and haphazard, and the effort to make the lectures entertaining was sometimes ridiculous. Barnard cautioned the teachers in his institutes in Rhode Island against considering them as substitutes for thorough study and practical training. The term varied in length from a few days to six weeks. Attendance was at first voluntary, and fees were charged those who enrolled. Later, however, attendance came to be more or less compulsory, and the cost of the institute came to be borne by the public.

Beginning in Connecticut in 1839 under the leadership of Henry Barnard, the institute soon found its way into other states. They were developed in many parts of New York by 1844, and in 1847 the legislature gave aid to provide them in the various counties. As early as 1844 Rhode Island made it the legal duty of the state commissioner of public schools to establish teachers' institutes "where teachers and such as propose to teach may become acquainted with the most improved and successful methods of arranging the studies and conducting the discipline of public schools." A "model school" was established in connection with the early institute in Rhode Island.

The institute appeared in Massachusetts and Ohio in 1845, in Vermont, New Hampshire, Michigan, and Illinois in 1846, in Maine and New Jersey in 1847, and in Pennsylvania in 1848. By 1860 it was found in a dozen or more states. North Carolina seems to be the only Southern state to have had institutes before the Civil War. These were established by W. H. Doherty, who came to the state from Antioch College, Ohio, where he had been associated with Horace Mann. After 1867 the Peabody Fund greatly stimulated the development of the institute in the South.

In the early institutes instruction was given by well-known teachers, including Charles Davies, the author of mathematical textbooks, Thomas H. Gallaudet, Henry Barnard, Horace Mann, James P. Wickersham, William Russell, Louis Agassiz, and Arnold Guyot. A Providence newspaper commenting upon the work of the institute in Rhode Island said, "No teacher can have witnessed the courteous manners, and the thorough instruction, even for a day, of such gentlemen (as have favored this institute by their presence and services) without having a better standard of teacher in his mind." When state school systems became better organized after 1860 the teachers' institute became a somewhat regular feature of public school work. It is still conducted in some states, but its place is rapidly being taken by summer schools, which have become numerous and popular. The need for it has been decreased also by the increase in normal schools, teachers' colleges, and schools of education in colleges and universities. As professional standards for teachers are raised, as teachers' meetings and conventions for the discussion of educational topics of current interest, and as other means of improving teachers in service are developed, the teachers' institute will probably disappear entirely.

In colleges and universities. Probably the first effort made to train teachers in the higher academic institutions began in 1832 in the University of the City of New York, now New York University. A chair of the philosophy of education was established for training teachers of the common schools, and from 1832 to 1834 Thomas H. Gallaudet served as professor. About 1850 Brown University established a course in didactics, or the science of teaching, but four years later it was abolished for lack of funds. Horace Mann introduced the subject at Antioch College in 1853. In 1873 the University of Iowa introduced a professional course for teachers, and four years later the University of Missouri made an unsuccessful attempt at such work. Lectures on education were given at Hiram College in Ohio between 1870 and 1882 by President Hinsdale, following a practice which began there in 1856. As early as 1860 State Superintendent of Public Instruction John M. Gregory volunteered to give pedagogical lectures at the University of Michigan, which established a chair of pedagogy in 1879. In the early eighties President F. A. P. Barnard of Columbia University recommended in his reports that special courses for teachers be set up, and a course in the philosophy of education was the result. From this modest beginning has developed Teachers College, the most influential institution in the United States for the training of school-teachers and administrators. By 1897 more than half of four hundred and thirty-two colleges and universities reported by the United States Bureau of Education were giving courses for the special training of teachers. Courses, departments, schools, or colleges of education are now found in most of the colleges and universities of the country.

Opportunities for the serious and advanced study of education in these institutions are, however, of somewhat recent origin. Education as a field worthy of study came to be accepted by them very slowly. Their graduates had entered the work of teaching without special preparation. It was not unnatural, therefore, that they, or the colleges which they attended, or the communities in which they taught, or the public generally should look upon teaching as requiring no special preparation and should come to believe that the arts course in colleges and universities was the best training for teaching. The prevalent theory was that, if there must be special preparation for teaching, the normal school was the place to provide it and not the college or the university.

Pedagogy reluctantly admitted. When courses in pedagogy or education finally found their way to the door of the colleges and universities, they were generally reluctantly admitted, assigned subordinate places, and kept in humility as long as possible. Some of the conditions which made them unwelcome in the colleges and universities also helped to keep them subordinate. The pioneer professors of pedagogy in these institutions were doubtless often effective and were generally picturesque, but they were not always standardized and orthodox products of the colleges and universities. Many of them had not bowed the knee to the gods of the graduate schools. They were innocent of the idolatry of doctoral dissertations and the methods of scientific research. Their methods were anecdotic and reminiscent of their experience in teaching and managing schools. Organized materials for pedagogical instruction were scarce until after 1900, and the practical experience of the early professors of pedagogy formed a large part of the materials of their courses. The standards of their work, which was limited to a few fields, were not always high, — probably little if any higher than the normal school standards, — and its claim to scientific character could not always be supported.

Still under prejudice. These and other conditions caused courses in pedagogy or education early to fall under the heavy prejudice of other departments. They still suffer from this affliction. Even today college and university faculties often view courses in education as vague and the professors who give them as visionary and perhaps deficient in disciplined learning. However, such courses meet the practical school needs of teachers, and the professors giving them are often sought for advice on practical school problems. Thus the departments and schools of education have helped to give the college and the university a new meaning. They are helping to demonstrate to a doubting public that the work of higher educational institutions does have a direct relation to everyday affairs. Interest of schools of education in such affairs naturally draws criticism from other university departments, because academic jealousy, arising out of peculiar fears and mistrusts, works in numerous ways its blunders to perform. In the most neighborly university it is not uncommon for committees on graduate instruction to give unusual scrutiny to courses submitted for graduate credit by their colleagues in education, even though these colleagues are for the most part quite different from the pioneer professors in the subject. Not all of them are the vapid and spiritless lecturers at large that tradition makes them; many have a store of disciplined information and of generous scholarship which they endeavor to use for the improvement of educational conditions about them.

Recent years have witnessed much improvement in the work of schools or departments of education in the colleges and universities, where the scientific study of the subject has received most attention (see Chapter XVII). Work of graduate as well as undergraduate grade has developed, and specialization in many branches of education has resulted. Today, in spite of indifference and hostility from other departments, education has become one of the most useful subjects offered in these higher institutions of learning. On them many states depend in large part for the preparation of many of their teachers, school administrators, and educational specialists of various kinds. For the most part normal schools and teachers' colleges still have a monopoly of the training of teachers for the elementary schools; but schools or departments of education in private institutions as well as in state-supported colleges and universities are rendering wide public service in the preparation of teachers and supervisors for high schools, normal schools, and colleges, and of other educational workers.

The summer session. The summer session, which has become a regular period of instruction in most of the colleges and universities of the United States, is now a very active agency in furnishing courses in pedagogy and education, and is widely used by prospective teachers and those already in teaching service. The somewhat rapid development of summer schools in recent years has been stimulated by the growing need to provide opportunities for further study for teachers and other professional people who cannot leave their work in regular term times. It has been stimulated also by the need to make fuller and more continuous use of the rather expensive educational plants and the numerous college and university faculties.

The work of Agassiz. The summer school had its origin in the organization of field work in some of the sciences taught at the universities. As early as 1869 Harvard conducted a seaside laboratory at Buzzards Bay, Massachusetts, under the direction of Professor Louis Agassiz, the famous naturalist, who three years later issued from the

Museum of Comparative Zoölogy at Cambridge a circular describing "a course of instruction in natural history to be delivered by the seaside in Nantucket during the summer months, chiefly designed for teachers who propose to introduce the study into their schools, and for students preparing to become teachers." Eminent scientists were on the list of the instructors in this first summer school in the United States. Emphasis was chiefly upon research for the benefit of university teachers and students and of teachers of science in secondary schools. The evident value of this early summer work in natural history led Harvard almost immediately to provide opportunity for summer study in other sciences, and later in other subjects. Other efforts more permanent than Agassiz's experiment followed under scholarly guidance at Woods Hole, Massachusetts, and Cold Spring Harbor, Long Island. Outgrowths of these beginnings are many biological schools of the present chiefly concerned with original research.

The Chautauqua. Another influence on the early development of the summer school arose out of the Chautauqua movement. The Chautauqua Assembly, which was formed at Chautauqua Lake, New York, in 1874, under the leadership of Bishop J. H. Vincent, of the Methodist Church, is said to have grown out of a religious camp meeting and a Sunday-school institute. Popular summer meetings with inspirational lectures soon came to be characteristic features of the Chautauqua, which became popular and was widely imitated in the United States. Soon most of the universities and many of the colleges caught the idea of summer courses for teachers.

Recent development. Work of this kind was begun at the University of North Carolina in 1877, but it was suspended eight years later, to be revived, however, in 1894. Summer work was provided at the University of Wisconsin in 1887 under the auspices of the teachers' association of the state, and five years later Cornell established a summer session. Other universities and colleges followed, until now the summer school is an important part of the organized facilities for higher and professional education. It is serving thousands of teachers and prospective teachers every year. Probably one third of all the teachers of the United States are found annually in summer, or vacation, schools.

In the light of the recent rapid development and the present wide popularity of the summer school it seems somewhat surprising that the practical-mindedness of the American people should have so long permitted the idleness of their educational plants. This idleness was enforced by the traditions of the old academic year, which allowed college and university buildings, libraries, laboratories, and other equipment to remain empty and unused through the summer months. The economic sense of the American people finally came to abhor the disuse of their immense educational resources, and the existence of the physical plants and teaching staffs in educational institutions appeared as an argument for their fullest use.

Aside from this very economic argument, there arose the demand for opportunity for vocational and professional study and advancement. With the increased applications of science had come increased leisure, leisure which people of intellectual interests sought to use for their own personal improvement. The summer session also appealed especially to teachers. Definite plans for certificating and paying teachers on the basis of professional study began to develop in the various states, and numberless teachers were thus encouraged to attend summer school in the interest of increased teaching effectiveness, of larger salaries for themselves, and in the interest also of the public good. Three fourths of the more than fourteen thousand students in the summer session at Columbia University in 1928 were registered in Teachers College.

Conditions and tendencies. Significant also is the increasing variety of the provision for instruction in summer sessions. Gradually some institutions are endeavoring through this means to provide courses similar to those offered in regular term time. In addition there are scientific field courses often conducted away from the institutions. Courses in languages, in government and international affairs, and in art are carried on in Europe. Vassar invites mothers to courses in euthenics. Bryn Mawr offers courses to working women. At the University of Virginia, at Williamstown in Massachusetts, at Athens in Georgia, appear summer institutes for the study of domestic policies and contemporary vital problems of local, municipal, state, and national governments. Public affairs are discussed in nontechnical language by able men of practical affairs who have influence in public life today. The ideas of Agassiz in 1869 and of Vincent in 1874 renew their strength with the coming of every summer.

Summer schools do not always resemble the early educational efforts out of which they developed. Few of them, if any, are as scientific or scholarly throughout as the summer work begun by Agassiz. That provided limited opportunity for scientific specialization and appealed to only a few students. Nor are all the summer schools of the present conducted on the Chautauqua or Sunday-school model designed by Vincent. They are generally open to all teachers or prospective teachers who think they can profit by the program, and in many the popularization of the program is encouraged. Moreover, the state certification requirements for teachers have helped greatly to swell the enrollments in summer schools, and some of the larger ones number their students by the thousands. The criticism that American education has become in part a matter for mass production applies with considerable force to the training of teachers in the typical American summer session.

Inadequate provision for training teachers. Teacher-training arrangements in high schools are probably temporary expedients. The plan has been tried in more than half the states and abandoned in some of them. It is likely to be discontinued as soon as state normal schools are prepared to meet the need for better-prepared teachers. Fully 78 per cent of all students who are in teacher-training institutions are found in institutions under public control and support. Thousands of teachers are enrolled also in extension and correspondence courses in normal schools, colleges, and universities.

Despite all these agencies for the training and improvement of teachers, statistics show that fully half a million of the school children of this country are still taught by teachers who have not advanced beyond the elementary school, and three million by teachers who have never completed the work of the high school.

In the work of training teachers, as in other parts of the public-school system, increasingly more funds are needed. These funds must be provided by taxes, and taxes must be authorized by legislatures, which are often composed of politicians whose habit generally is to tell their constituencies that a free people flourish on reduced tax rates. But even legislators under proper guidance can catch sight of the truth that better teachers are essential to the progress and the safety of a community or a state. When this truth is learned, provision is likely to be made for a wholesome supply of adequately trained teachers for all the children.

Present problems. The story of the movement to train teachers in the United States shows that the preparation of a sufficient number of properly trained teachers is a persistent public educational problem which faces every state. It shows also that equality of educational opportunity can never be attained until this problem is solved. From this story it may be learned that good teachers arise only among a people who themselves discriminate between the mediocre and the excellent, between that which is superficial and that which is genuine; and that the responsibility for leading a people to a proper appreciation of good teachers rests ultimately upon the governing educational authorities of the state.

Improvement in the preparation of teachers can be assured only when the educational leaders are themselves satisfied with nothing less than a body of teachers possessing adequate training and enjoying a professional recognition that will attract and satisfy any high aspirations and economic needs of the ablest men and women. Governing authority can open the doors to finer preparation for the lives of those who teach, in the interest of those who are taught. Educational inequalities, now obvious in most of the states, must continue to exist so long as teachers are inadequately trained and indifferently rewarded.

This chapter has indicated some of the causes of the slow growth of interest in the training of teachers in the United States. Only a little progress had been made by 1860; but since that time the theory that teachers should have professional training has been accepted, and schools for this purpose have been established in all the states. In recent years the work has been reorganized, standards have been raised, and facilities for the professional training of teachers have increased; but with all the agencies now available for this work, there is not yet an adequate supply of properly trained teachers in any American state. Moreover, the conditions surrounding teachers and teaching are still unwholesome and unattractive in many American communities, notwithstanding the progress made in recent years. Some of these conditions are discussed in Chapter XII.

REFERENCES AND READINGS

BENSON, C. E.   The Output of Professional Schools for Teachers. Baltimore, 1922.

> A careful study of more than eight thousand graduates of twenty-two institutions.

BUCKINGHAM, B. R. Supply and Demand in Teacher-Training. Columbus, Ohio, 1926.

> A careful study of the conditions and needs in Ohio, with suggestive recommendations.

CUBBERLEY, E. P.   State School Administration. Boston, 1927.

> Chapters XXII–XXV, each with a useful bibliography, bear directly on many of the topics discussed in this chapter.

DEARBORN, N. H.   The Oswego Movement in American Education. New York, 1925.

> A recent study of this important movement.

GORDY, J. P.   Rise and Growth of the Normal School Idea in the United States, *Circular of Information No. 8*, United States Bureau of Education, Washington, 1891.

> An excellent historical account of the subject.

GREENWOOD, E.   "The Little Read School Marm," *World's Work*, December, 1924.

> Contains amazing facts of the inadequate preparation and fitness of teachers.

HIGHSMITH, E. M.   American State Normal School Curricula. Chapel Hill, 1922.

> An unpublished doctoral dissertation at the University of North Carolina. Contains, among other useful matter, a concise account of the history of the normal school and a bibliography.

KNIGHT, EDGAR W.   Public School Education in North Carolina. Boston, 1916.

> Chapter VII discusses Caldwell's letters, and Chapter IX has a brief account of North Carolina's first state normal school.

MANGUN, VERNON LAMAR. The American Normal School. Baltimore, 1928.

> A very excellent study of the rise and development of the normal school in Massachusetts. Contains valuable information hitherto inaccessible.

MEADER, J. L. Normal School Education in Connecticut. New York, 1928.

> A doctoral dissertation at Teachers College, Columbia University, which traces the origin and development of normal schools in Connecticut and the reorganization of the teacher-training program in 1923–1924.

MONROE, WILL S. History of the Pestalozzian Movement in the United States. Syracuse, 1907.

> An important account of the Oswego movement and the spread of Pestalozzian principles and methods, with a bibliography.

NOBLE, STUART G. "From 'Lectures on Schoolkeeping' (1829) to 'Introduction to Education' (1925)," *School and Society*, Volume XXIII, No. 600 (June 26, 1926).

> An interesting discussion of the development of materials for the training of teachers.

NORTON, ARTHUR O. (Editor). The First State Normal School in America. Cambridge, Massachusetts, 1926.

> The journals of Cyrus Peirce, the first principal of the normal school at Lexington, Massachusetts, and of Mary Swift, a member of the first class there.

Proceedings of the National Education Association, 1922.

> The report of the committee of teachers' colleges made to the Department of Superintendence. Very valuable.

The Professional Preparation of Teachers for American Public Schools, *Bulletin No. 14*, Carnegie Foundation for the Advancement of Teaching, New York, 1920.

> A study of the normal schools in Missouri by a staff of experts under the direction of W. C. Bagley and W. S. Learned. Contains a brief historical account of the rise of normal schools written by I. L. Kandel.

Reports of the State Educational Survey Commissions. See References and Readings for Chapter XVII.

> Each of these reports has one or more chapters that deal with the training of teachers.

QUESTIONS FOR STUDY AND DISCUSSION

1. Account for the slow development of public agencies for the training of teachers.

2. Trace the development of European influences on the training of teachers in the United States during the nineteenth century.

3. Why have the colleges and universities held an attitude of hostility or indifference to departments or schools of education in their organization?

4. Why did New York abandon the plan of training teachers in connection with the academies?

5. Make a study of the development and present conditions of teacher-training agencies in your state.

6. Note the perspective which Caldwell had for the training of teachers in North Carolina in 1832.

7. Compare the purpose of the normal schools in 1870 with their purpose now.

8. Why is the work of preparing teachers for the high schools looked upon as less humble than that of preparing them for the elementary schools?

9. Study the findings of surveys of teacher-training work in the United States as given on page 331, that students preparing to teach are of lower economic status than other students and relatively inferior in scholarship. How can these conditions be improved?

10. Trace the development of summer sessions in the United States.

11. Outline a plan for the adequate training of an adequate supply of teachers for your state, and see how such a plan differs from what the state is now doing for the training of teachers.

CHAPTER XII

TEACHERS AND TEACHING

Outline of the chapter. 1. The problem of providing a sufficient supply of excellent school-teachers and managers is not yet solved.

2. Historically the typical American teacher is unattractive, made so both by tradition and the fact of his actual unattractiveness, and also by localism and the influence of the church in the early days.

3. The inferior scholarship of the early teachers was the subject of remark by such observers as Coram, Jefferson, Caldwell, Olmsted.

4. For a long time teaching was not a regular occupation; certification requirements were nominal and locally administered, and the economic reward of teachers was small. Some of these conditions have continued to prevail.

5. In the early days the private lives of the people were under the close scrutiny of the minister-teacher; today the private lives of teachers are under the eye of the people. In some places queer demands are made upon teachers.

6. Instability is a distinct characteristic of teaching in the United States, resulting in economic and educational waste. The decreasing proportion of men as teachers during the last half-century is also a serious problem in American education.

7. Many obstacles have prevented the development of a teaching profession, but in spite of them teaching is increasing in dignity, and public confidence in it is gradually enlarging.

Early in the nineteenth century the more prosperous tradesmen of a certain community, dissatisfied with the small progress which their boys were making under the teacher, clubbed together and got a schoolmaster of their own. He seemed to be a clever young man, but he proved an unsteady one, who was regular only in his irregularities, and "got diurnally drunk."

They got rid of him and hired a licentiate of the church, who promised well for a time. He seemed to be a steady and thoughtful young man and, withal, a painstaking

346

teacher; but he came in contact with some zealous sectarians, who succeeded in conjuring up such a cloud of doubt
around him regarding the propriety of infant baptism that
both his bodily and mental health became affected by his
perplexities, and he had to resign his charge. The prosperous
tradesmen then hired still another teacher, a person of a
high if not very consistent religious profession, who was
always getting into "pecuniary difficulties, and always
courting, though with but little success, wealthy ladies."
And this teacher also, "losing health and heart in a labyrinth
of perplexity," soon resigned. The experience of this community was not altogether unlike that of many others.

A difficult problem. The problem of securing and retaining good teachers in the United States, as the preceding
chapter shows, has always been difficult. It was not an
easy problem in the seventeenth century. It was troublesome in the eighteenth and even in the nineteenth, and it
is often vexatious even now. Although numerous agencies
are maintained for the professional training of teachers, and
although every year probably sees improvement in those
who manage and teach schools, the problem of providing a
sufficient supply of good school managers and teachers is not
yet solved. The vocation of teaching is still unstable in the
United States. There is also a rather discouraging lack of
selective methods in recruiting the teaching ranks in the
schools.

Characteristics of early teachers. One does not have to
exercise any freedom that belongs to the story-teller to
furnish a rather faithful account or picture of American
school-teachers. The records themselves tell the story.
Although he has greatly improved and is becoming more
and more reputable, the American school-teacher as a type
has a shady past. He has not always been an inspiring
figure or even a person of good repute. Ugly things have
been said about him, often because he was ugly. Often he

was ignorant, sometimes almost illiterate, and knew little
more than his pupils, if any more. Occasionally he was a
man of doubtful probity in his private life, unapproved for
moral excellence. He was shiftless, migratory, and itinerant, poorly paid and as poorly esteemed by the public, and
lacked in professional standards largely because no such
standards had been established. Now and then, if the records
are to be believed, he was given to loose living and was
generally unwilling to assume social responsibilities. He
was always poor in this world's goods, and his nominal
wages were often paid in part by the practice of "boarding
around." He was generally poor in spirit except when he
was in a state of inebriety, a not uncommon condition of the
teacher in the early days. The typical American school-
teacher has also been a timid person; aggressiveness is not
a mark of all school-teachers today. Ichabod Crane, the
timorous Yankee who was chased at night by his Dutch
rival in love masquerading as a headless horseman and
frightening Ichabod out of his job and away from the
neighborhood, is not altogether a fiction of literature. As
a type of the early American teacher he is probably not an
exaggeration.

Historically unattractive. The teacher is historically an
unattractive person not only because tradition and his actual
unattractiveness made him so, but because he and his profession have suffered severely from the evils of localism, the
local-rights theory of the small community. The school
district, no matter how small, was early taught to exercise
its right to select and to license its own teachers, and it was
encouraged by an attractive and popular political philosophy to resent any interference from a larger administrative
unit. It was slow to give up any of its early rights, the jealous exercise of which discouraged standards by which good
teachers and good teaching could have been had and known.
The need for better teachers was not likely to be keenly felt

by the local community. Home-grown teachers — favored daughters or other relatives of district-school officials — were employed to teach in schools in which they had received their only formal education. These teachers were good enough for the families of the neighborhood and were acceptable to all, except those whose sons or daughters were unsuccessful candidates for the local teaching positions. School-teaching could not be considered professional under these conditions, which prevail in many communities today.

The influence of the church. The church, especially during colonial times, also served to prevent teaching from acquiring a professional character. In New England, where education was so long in the hands of the church, teaching was looked upon as a function of the clergy. The teachers were often ministers, and those candidates who were not ministers were generally examined by them. In the middle colonies education was for the most part parochial, the clergymen serving as teachers, and in the Southern colonies the church was not without authority in the control of those who taught. The fitness of candidates to teach school was determined in large part not in a professional manner or on the basis of educational preparation, but by the religious condition of the candidates, and for this a certificate or testimonial was required. Perhaps in these practices may be found partial explanation of the belief (still prevalent in some communities) that the superintendent, principal, or teacher of the school should be able at any time and even upon short notice to perform certain functions ordinarily performed by the minister.

Inferior scholarship. Scholastic requirements of the early schoolmaster were not high. In New Hampshire, for example, as late as 1719 the ability to teach children to read and write was the only educational requirement, and seventy years elapsed before arithmetic was added as a subject which the master was expected to teach. This was doubtless the practice elsewhere as well. In a commencement speech at Yale as late as 1816 Denison Olmsted said that the ignorance and incompetency of schoolmasters were the chief defects of the schools at that time : "teachers whose geography scarcely transcends the mountains that bound their horizon; whose science is the multiplication table ; and whose language, history, and belle-lettres are all comprised in the American Preceptor and Webster's Spelling Book."

The religion and moral character of the candidate must bear appropriate certificate, of course, but this was generally the signature of a minister or ministers, representing him to be a sober man and not of vicious conversation. If one may judge from the behavior of some who were thus certificated, however, this very narrow way to the schoolroom was not always as straight as the certificates indicated. Moreover, it is evident that the ability to maintain in the school the discipline which prevailed in the roughest kitchen, and the skill to mend quill pens, kept some teachers in their posts longer than their religious or educational qualifications could justify. There are records in New England, however, of the dismissal of teachers by vote of the town meeting, and occasionally there as elsewhere a teacher was engaged "for a time of trial."

Early teachers deficient. The rector at Annapolis, Maryland, reported in the late seventeenth century that the occupation of school-teaching was in a very low state. He noted that upon the arrival of every ship "with either redemptioners or convicts" schoolmasters were "regularly advertised for sale," just as were weavers, tailors, or those who followed other trades. He noted little difference except that schoolmasters "do not usually fetch so good a price as the latter." It should be remembered, however, that at that time convicts were easily made by imprisonment for very slight offenses.

Observations of Coram. Robert Coram, writing in 1791 on a plan for the general establishment of schools, devoted one chapter to the "wretched" state of the country schools in the United States and "the absolute necessity of a reformation." The teachers were described as "generally foreigners, shamefully deficient in every qualification necessary to convey instruction to youth, and not seldom addicted to gross vices. Absolute in his own opinion, and proud of introducing what he calls his European method, one calls the first letter of the alphabet *aw*. The school is modified upon this plan, and the children who are advanced are beat and cuffed to forget the former mode they have been taught, which irritates their minds and retards their progress. The quarter being finished, the children lie idle until another master offers, few remaining in one place more than a quarter. When the next schoolmaster is introduced, he calls the first letter *a*, as in *mat*; the school undergoes another reform, and is equally vexed and retarded. At his removal a third is introduced, who calls the first letter *hay*. All these blockheads are equally absolute in their own notions, and will by no means suffer the children to pronounce the letter as they were first taught; but every three months the school goes through a reform — error succeeds error, and dunce the second reigns like dunce the first."

On the eve of the American Revolution it was said that most of the school-teaching in Maryland was done by "instructors who are either indentured servants or transported felons." Private schools in Delaware in the early eighteenth century were often in charge of men "brought into the country and sold for servants. Some schoolmasters are hired by the year, by a knot of families who, in their turn entertain him monthly, and the poor man lives in their houses like one that begged an alms, more than like a person in credit and authority. When a ship arrives in the river it is a common expression with those who stand in need of an instructor for their children, *let us go and buy a schoolmaster*. The truth is, the office and character of such a person is generally very mean and contemptible here, and it cannot be other ways until the public takes the education of children into their mature consideration."

Jefferson's criticism. Thomas Jefferson, commenting in 1820 upon the failure of Virginia to provide adequately for its educational needs, said that the little education the state then had was "imported, like beggars, from other states, or we import their beggars to bestow on us their miserable crumbs." There as elsewhere in the United States, then and for many years afterwards, teachers of scholarship, ability, and proper fitness for the work of teaching were not often found in the common schools. The occupation of the teacher was in low repute, and those who were qualified for teaching would not engage in it. Many reasons were given in the second quarter of the nineteenth century in explanation of the fact that teaching held the unfit and excluded the fit. Those who were capable of teaching regarded the occupation as disreputable. The work was considered too laborious, and it paid too little. It attracted those who could do nothing else, those who had some physical misfortune, and those who could outbid capable teachers.

"In the schoolhouse," wrote a correspondent in a Virginia newspaper in 1843, "there is often installed a man with a heart of stone and hands of iron; too lazy to work, too ignorant to live by his wits in any other way, whose chief recommendation is his cheapness, and whose chief capacity to instruct is predicated by his incapacity for other employment." He saw little opportunity for children "in these temples of indolence." Many of the teachers were "invalids, some were slaves to drunkenness, some too lazy to work, most of them entirely ignorant of the art of teaching, and a terror to their pupils. There were a few ... who possessed culture, intelligence, morality, ability."

Caldwell's description. President Joseph Caldwell of the University of North Carolina noted in the early eighteen-thirties that the occupation of schoolmaster was regarded with contempt. "Is a man constitutionally and habitually indolent, a burden upon all from whom he can extract a support? Then there is one way of shaking him off; let us make him a schoolmaster." Those who had wasted their property and had ended in debt through indiscretion or misconduct; those who had ruined themselves and corrupted others "by dissipation, drinking, seduction, and a course of irregularities"; those who had returned from prison, the destitute of character, the untrustworthy, — these and others as vulgar and ignorant conducted schools, he asserted. "In our present mode of popular education," he said, "we act upon the principle that schoolkeeping is a business to which scarcely anyone but an idiot is incompetent, if he only knows reading, writing, and arithmetic, . . . and our primary schools are kept sunk down to the lowest point of degradation, and education is disgraced by our own misconceptions and mismanagements." Public contempt for teaching was one natural result.

In South Carolina. In his message to the legislature of South Carolina near the middle of the nineteenth century the governor of that state asked: "Who are the teachers of our free schools? Are they men to whom the legislature can commit, with confidence, the great business of education? What is the amount of their literary qualifications, and what is the tone of their morality?"

Answering his own questions the governor said that as a class the teachers were "grossly incompetent to discharge their high and sacred functions. . . . With but few exceptions, they are very ignorant and possess a very easy morality. With the poor pay allowed them, we cannot reasonably calculate upon a better state of things. The men who take charge of our public schools, and accept so miserable a pittance as the reward of their labors, are they who cannot get employment on any other terms. . . . It is now in South Carolina a reproach to be a teacher of a free school, as it is regarded as prima-facie evidence of a want of qualification. . . . You cannot command superior talent and attainment, without adequate compensation." The governor thought it social injustice to expect one to work in the "most useful of all professions, at a rate that will not supply the wants of nature."

During the first quarter of the nineteenth century there swarmed into some of the Southern states "a class of stiff, formal pedagogues, despised by our boys, because they represented so little that appealed to the human side of the normally healthy boy, be he North or South." They were described as "the type of pedagogue that caused our boys to guffaw over their weary platitudes and formal manners." School-teachers were nondescript in these and in other states until comparatively recent times. In addition to ministers, who were not always effective and estimable, there were adventurers, and in the colonial period indentured servants who kept school only to keep from starving.

Teachers not all inferior. The social position held by the early teachers differed quite as much as they themselves differed in personal character or scholarship. The number of those who were unfit by nature or training for creditable teaching service must have been large, and they were largely responsible, as are incompetent teachers today, for the low public esteem in which teaching in general was too often held. All early teachers were not so ignoble and so incompetent, however, nor as lax in morality as tradition has made many of them. But not all the early teachers were so unattractive or deficient. A few were men of scholarship who made teaching the principal work of their lives. These constituted a group who kept alive the nobler traditions of the schoolmaster and strengthened public confidence in his occupation.

Teaching not a regular occupation. Numerous were the duties of early teachers. Among the religious and civic chores demanded of one schoolmaster, in addition to duties directly connected with the school, were those that required him to act as court messenger, to serve summons, to conduct certain ceremonials of the church, to ring the bell for church services, to lead the church choir, to dig graves, and "to perform other occasional duties." The strong tradition of minister as schoolmaster has remained in the United States. The ghost of the old demand for a teacher who could preach (an arrangement taking rank next to that of having a preacher who would teach) still stalks occasionally in many American communities. Even in recent years some rural communities have been willing to employ the combination preacher-teacher who gives to the conventional tasks of the school whatever time remains after he has officiated at the neighborhood baptisms, weddings, and funerals and has met any other demands of the church, which he believes is his best-beloved.

Physicians often served as teachers in the early schools, the time which they lost from their teaching duties through the emergencies of their medical practice being made up later. Toward the end of the colonial period one Aaron Hutch, an ordained pastor of a church in a New England community, followed the work of schoolmaster along "with his clerical and agricultural pursuits." Tradition has him teaching Latin and Greek to students who were forced to follow him at the plow. But his resourcefulness as minister, farmer, and teacher enabled him to meet many different kinds of engagements. Such conditions served, however, to prevent teaching from acquiring a professional character. Only in comparatively recent years has the teacher begun to adopt his work as a regular occupation instead of using it as a stepping-stone to something else or to supplement his earnings from other sources.

Early certification practices. The old theory that almost anyone could teach almost any school subject has also served to retard the growth of uniform certification practices. The licensing of teachers early became a local function, the distinctly local character of the early schools making this custom both natural and popular. The arrangement was simple, and it seemed democratic. The fitness of candidates for teaching positions was generally determined in a somewhat informal and often haphazard fashion. When the public-school idea developed and it seemed necessary and desirable to take the educational task of certification from the local communities and transfer it to a larger unit of control, such as the county or the state, stubborn resistance on the part of the local authorities generally followed. The struggle which accompanied attempted changes from localism to centralization in public education was often intense at every point. Especially did attempts to centralize the certification, or licensing, of teachers meet with bitter opposition. However, the contest was finally won by the state, and today practically all the states exercise some form of centralized control in the matter. Generally public funds cannot be paid to teachers who do not hold certificates authorized by the state, if not actually issued by it. This development, which has naturally been very slow, marks the growth of state control of education in this country very clearly.

The effect of this early method of licensing teachers may even now be seen. Private teachers were usually required to have no license except the approval of the minister, but those who had charge of community or public schools had to exhibit some evidence of their fitness and receive approval from some properly constituted authority. In New England the local minister generally examined the candidate, primarily, however, to make certain that he was sound in religious faith. In schools under the direction of the Established Church license to teach came from the Bishop of London, sometimes, perhaps, from the colonial governors. The applicant had to be in good standing with and strictly in conformity to the Anglican faith. In the parochial schools in New Netherland and some of the middle colonies teachers were generally permitted to conduct schools by the authority of the church. In this ecclesiastical authority, which in most cases was generally rigidly exercised, appears further evidence that the religious motive was dominant in school instruction in colonial days.

Even Ezekiel Cheever, who heads the list of eminent colonial schoolmasters and whose memory is still revered in New Haven, Ipswich, Charlestown, and Boston, where he served so well, had the censure of the church passed upon him because of "his contradicting, stiff, and proud frame of spirit"; and Henry Dunster, the first president of Harvard, could not escape public admonition and the necessity of resigning his post when he expressed himself as opposed to the baptism of infants. Nathaniel Eaton, the first professor in Harvard and acting president until the appointment of Dunster, was fined and dismissed from his position for flogging one of his assistants.

Early requirements. Religious and not educational qualifications, and the capacity to maintain discipline, were required of all teachers, who were generally expected to be persons of good moral character. The act of 1812, which established common schools in New York, required the local school authorities to examine all applicants to teach. Every teacher was required to hold a certificate signed by at least two of the local authorities, showing "that he is duly qualified to teach a common school, and is of good moral character." Other states enacted similar requirements, and these have remained a part of the school laws of all the states.

Before legislation was enacted on this subject, however, teachers were expected to possess evidence of a good char-

acter. Some of them must have found such evidence difficult to secure, if certain records of the early period are to be
accepted as accurate. In North Carolina, as late as the
middle of the nineteenth century, a man applied for the
position of teacher in a common school. It was necessary
then, as it had been earlier and is now, for the teacher to
give evidence of good moral character. But this man, who
was notorious for his bad habits, had difficulty until he found
a friend who gave him a "certificate of good moral character
during school hours." This satisfied the local requirements,
and the man was employed.

Effect of poor pay. The pittance which the teacher has
received has also helped to keep him in an unattractive light;
his professional status has been kept low through his low
wages. Small salaries have been the result of the inability
or the unwillingness of the public to pay for good teachers
and provide working and living conditions attractive enough
to get them and hold them. The influence of localism, already noted, was often so stubborn also that until recently
state departments of education remained powerless to require creditable educational standards or minimum-salary
scales for teachers. Thousands of children, especially in rural
communities, are still unprotected from the indifference and
penury of small localities and the negligence of the state in
the matter of providing an adequate and equitable plan of
public-school support. This negligence, obvious also in the
adequate provision for the training of a sufficient supply of
properly prepared teachers (see Chapter XI), prevents the
development of superior teachers and encourages an unde-
sirable attitude toward teaching both on the part of the
public and on that of promising young men and women who
might be induced to seek training for it.

**Private lives of teachers formerly under close public
scrutiny.** In the early days the private lives of the people
were generally under the close scrutiny of the minister-

teacher, especially in New England. There were such exceptional cases, of course, as that of an early teacher in Northampton, Massachusetts, who, although his title of "Mister" indicated some standing in the community, fell upon evil days through his tendency to use profane language and was fined by the court for cursing. Now, however, the private life of the teacher is often under the careful eye of the people or their representatives. It is not unusual to find communities which in undertaking to regulate the private lives of their teachers often deny them that personal freedom normally allowed to others. It would be difficult to find a community that desires to have a questionable mayor or chief of police or minister or tax-collector or librarian, any more than it desires a questionable teacher, but these public servants are not always so restricted in their manner of living. An effort may be made by neighborhood sentiment to regulate the dress of the teacher, but not of the mothers of the children she teaches. The grocer's boy may ride unnoticed with his best girl, but in some communities the teacher or the principal does so at the cost of unpleasant comment or the reports of scandal mongers. The news passes from tongue to tongue through members of the ladies' aid society on to Kiwanians and Civitans and perhaps even to members of the school board, who have been known even in recent years to take official notice of the harmless personal and intimate indulgences of the community's hired man or woman.

Some queer requirements now. Occasionally one reads that colleges and normal schools demand of teachers a declaration of Fundamentalist faith in matters of religion and of science, and professors looking for jobs are expected to sign on the dotted line. "By the way," writes the president of one of these higher levels of learning to a prospective teacher, "while we cannot be accused of narrowness or undue sectarianism, we do not think we are unreasonable in requiring that all members of our faculty belong to the Baptist Church and help disseminate its doctrines among our young people. You are, I presume, a Baptist, of course." This young professor was not a Baptist, though he was a well-trained teacher of successful experience, held the highest earned degree from America's most eminent university, had made distinct contributions in his field of study, had given up an influential position in teaching to help make the world safe for democracy, and, after the armistice, sought to reënter his profession. But he could not qualify in the effort to make young people safe for the Baptist Church. "By the way," wrote the president of another institution which was ready to sign the same young man in its employ, "do you use tobacco? While I think there are greater evils than smoking, I would not knowingly appoint to my faculty a man who uses tobacco in any form." The young man could not qualify for this post, because the war had driven him to smoke.

Now and then one discovers ridiculous requirements exacted of teachers in public neighborhood schools. In one set of these regulations which were found in use in a Southern state and reported by a correspondent to a distinguished national weekly, the teachers were expected to make and keep the following promises in regard to their conduct:

I promise to take a vital interest in all phases of Sunday-school work, donating of my time, service, and money without stint for the uplift and benefit of the community. I promise to abstain from all dancing, immodest dressing, and any other conduct unbecoming a teacher and a lady. I promise not to go out with any young men except in so far as it may be necessary to stimulate Sunday-school work. I promise not to fall in love, to become engaged or secretly married. I promise to remain in the dormitory or on the school grounds when not actively engaged in school or church work elsewhere. I promise not to encourage or tolerate the least familiarity on the part of any of my boy pupils. I promise to sleep at least eight hours a night, to eat carefully, and to take every precaution to keep in the best of health and spirits in order that I may be better able to render efficient service to my pupils.

Waste and damage from instability. The educational wastefulness and actual damage that are inevitable in unstable and constantly changing teaching groups defy calculation. The injury to helpless children thoughtlessly placed under the charge of young and inexperienced instructors who replace, and are likely to be replaced by, others similarly young and inexperienced is often tragic. The economic waste, more readily measured, is enormous. The annual expense of training teachers runs into large figures, and the return to the public in the length of service by those who receive training is small. From the standpoint of public well-being teacher-training is probably one of the most extravagant forms of education in the United States, and extravagance and waste will continue until teaching becomes stabilized.

Whatever the merits of the arguments for and against partial or complete security of tenure for teachers, remedial measures can be found to improve the conditions. Rigid standards of selection can be set up for prospective teachers; a more rational and sensible training can be given the fit, and the unfit can be eliminated; economic rewards more nearly commensurate with the economic needs and social aspirations of the ablest men and women can be provided. Too long has the teacher been supposed to subsist upon the nebulous satisfactions of his labor. Too long has public suspicion that the teacher is careless, unbusinesslike, and unfit for manly matters been deepened by his inability to pay promptly the butcher, the baker, and the candlestick-maker. In addition to provision for his material needs, safeguards from personal grudges and political exploitation must be thrown around the teacher's work, not primarily in his interest, but for the protection of the children and the school. Pensions and retirement allowances, today fully developed in only a few of the states, would have influence in stabilizing and improving the work of teaching.

Including administrative officers, nearly a million men and women are now engaged in school work in the United States, more than three fourths of them in public elementary and high schools. Whatever the minimum age set by law for these educational workers, the tenure of positions is short. According to a recent careful study the annual replacement of teachers ranges in the various states from 4 per cent to nearly 50 per cent, with 16 per cent as the average for the country as a whole. Replacement in the rural schools of some states reaches 68 per cent. The teaching service of the average teacher in the United States is only four years; in rural schools, only three years. The average tenure of superintendents is only three years. These facts support the statement made at the beginning of this chapter that the vocation of teaching is still very unstable in this country.

 Some of the conditions which underlie the instability of teaching have already been noted: tradition, the lack of social status and dignity, low professional standards, and inadequate standards of economic reward. Among the women teachers, who are more numerous than the men teachers, marriage is probably the chief cause of the instability in teaching. Thousands of girls annually leave high school and enter the normal school to get a veneer of specialized training so that they may drift into teaching (which they consider a trifle higher in the social scale than clerical occupations) as an economic stop-gap until they marry. Unless this event remains only the substance of things hoped for, they plan to teach as few years as possible, meantime avoiding the cultivation of any professional features which may mark them as schoolma'ams.

Many teachers are still ashamed of their work because of its traditions, and often they wear an air of apology for it. They are still an unselected group, largely because conscious efforts are rarely made to recruit the teaching ranks by selective methods. Normal schools, teachers' colleges, and schools of education in colleges and universities neither exert themselves to attract promising and superior young people to the work of teaching, nor are they always zealous in excluding the unfit. Administrative officers in such institutions have caught the mania for numbers which now afflicts American education so direly. Moreover, the wide practice of exempting from tuition charges those who agree to teach in the schools of the state for a specified minimum period does not promote the profession of teaching, but it does encourage those of lower economic status and sometimes those who are relatively inferior in scholarship to seek refuge for a time in what seems to them a sheltered occupation protected from the aggressive competitions of other activities. There is still irritating truth in the Shavian indictment that "those who can, do; those who can't, teach; and those who can't teach, teach how to teach." While this indictment stands, teaching must remain to thousands of those who enter it merely a job. They will continue to drift from place to place; they can develop no professional consciousness, no definite professional aim, no useful community relationships.

The hire-and-fire policy. Add to this condition another cause of the instability of teaching, the practice of the annual election or appointment by those who employ teachers and their hire-and-fire policy — the one-year-contract plan. This is the source of much hardship and discontent. The story, not altogether a lovely one, contains many discouraging chapters. In one month sixty-eight teachers, all of satisfactory rating and recommended by the superintendent for reëngagement, were dismissed without notice in one city. In another city seventy-six teachers and principals were dismissed without notice or reasons at a special meeting after the schools had closed in June. In still another twenty-one teachers were dismissed because they were loyal to the superintendent, whom political influences were seeking to dismiss. There is the story also of Superintendents Finegan of Pennsylvania, Chadsey of Chicago, Withers of St. Louis, Ettinger of New York, who were dismissed for political reasons, and of McAndrew of Chicago, so recently persecuted by politics of the lowest order.

Ezekiel Cheever, perhaps the most distinguished teacher in the American colonies, died in 1708 in the ninety-fourth year of his age, with a record of seventy years as a skillful and faithful schoolmaster. Thirty-eight of them were spent in one community after Cheever had reached the age of fifty-six. Today half the American states require that candidates for teaching positions in the public schools shall have reached the ripe old age of eighteen. Five states set seventeen as the minimum, one state fixes sixteen, a few require that the candidates shall be twenty years old, one state demands that its centers of light and leading shall be directed by teachers of that rich experience which comes only to those who wait until they are twenty-four, and a few do not specify any age requirements.

The passing of the schoolmaster. The earliest schoolteachers in the country were schoolmasters and not schoolmistresses, and schoolmasters they remained for many years. Before the Civil War few women engaged in teaching except in the academies and private schools, although such educational leaders as Mann of Massachusetts and Wiley of North Carolina believed that women were especially adapted for teaching small children and recommended them for the work. In the early days, however, women were not educated. Moreover, they were not given freedom to indulge in activities outside the home, nor were they considered capable of maintaining the discipline which the times required. Immediately after the Civil War, however, they began to enter the work of teaching, and in recent years the number has greatly increased.

The constantly decreasing proportion of men as teachers during the fifty years from 1870 to 1920 presents an important problem in American education, a problem which has been only slightly noticed. Although the absolute number of men engaged in teaching in the public schools of the United States increased about 41 per cent during that period, the absolute number of women engaged in teaching in such schools increased nearly 385 per cent. The percentage of women teachers increased from 61 to 86, and the percentage of men teachers decreased from 39 to 14. This phenomenon has led an English observer to make the cynical comment that the American male teacher will soon be as extinct as the buffalo. Since 1920, however, the percentage of men serving in elementary and secondary schools has shown a slight increase.

The lack of a high and definite professional status for teachers, administrative machinery which often is more or less political in nature and which often cramps teachers of professional aspiration and outlook, the low esteem in which teaching is even now generally held in the United States, and the inadequate salaries paid for teaching, are given as some of the causes which have driven men from the schoolroom. But as the occupation of school-teaching acquires a higher character through increased professional requirements, public respect for it will increase; and as the administration of education improves and the economic reward for teaching increases, men of ability will increasingly prepare for the work, enter it, and remain in it.

Increase in dignity of teaching. Although teaching has probably not yet reached the professional level that is demanded in medicine or perhaps even in law in most American states, the tendency is ever toward a higher and more dignified professional status. Teaching now ranks favorably in professional requirements with the ministry, and it does not always suffer by comparison with engineering and other specialized professions. The increased and increasing public confidence in the power of the school and other means of instruction, and the recognized dependence of civilization upon education, give to the teacher a more important position than he has ever known in this country. His social position is higher today than it has ever been, and in general he is better trained, is more nearly adequately rewarded, and occupies a larger place in public confidence. "Let the soldier be abroad if he will, he can do nothing in this age. There is another personage, — a personage less imposing in the eyes of some, perhaps insignificant. The schoolmaster is abroad, and I trust him, armed with his primer, against the soldier in full military array." For many years before it was expressed by Lord Brougham a century ago, few leaders even shared this view of the teacher. Too long had he been an object of contempt and often even reproach, but he is now increasing in dignity and enlarging his sphere of influence. More adequately equipped than ever before, he is now trusted more confidently as a light to guide, although not every American community has gained Brougham's perspective.

But the people are slowly getting this view and demand better teachers than formerly. The public is coming to ask that those to whom children are intrusted for instruction shall be men and women of stalwart moral constitution, that they shall possess the thing called character. It is coming to know that teachers are not teachers merely of subject matter, but of youth and of men and women, and that personal and business integrity should be to them matters of inner principles rather than of legalistic requirements externally imposed — that they should be men and women of conscience as well as of science. The public knows that no teacher can climb beyond the limitations of his own character. It asks that the teacher possess not only good educational and professional training, but also those qualities which make him a person and not a thing; that he be human, with initiative and resourcefulness, industry, tact, intellectual and moral honesty, and perhaps some sense of humor — a great help to the teacher in time of trouble. But although the public applauds a sane sense of humor, history is full of warning to the teacher who becomes a buffoon through the indulgence of levity. The history of American education reveals that few humorists have been elevated to superintendencies, college presidencies, deanships, headships of departments, or similar posts of educational responsibility. These places are usually filled by solemn men, some of whom, however, have been known to become comical afterwards.

The influence of good teachers. The American public is also coming more and more to require that its teachers shall know their special subjects well and thoroughly and as many other subjects as possible, that their information shall be accurate and well disciplined, and that their learning shall be liberal. The public is developing respect for scholarship and distrust for pedantry, and the teacher is coming to view scholarship not only as sound learning but as a means of improving man's estate. He is becoming loyal to serviceable truth and is seeking to humanize learning and to emancipate it from the suspicions with which it has so often been beset. He is coming to know that the real test of teaching is in the product, that the effect of good teaching endures. The public and the teachers are coming to accept as sound the appraisal of teaching made a few years ago by Rhodes scholars who had previously studied at twenty-three private colleges and universities and at fourteen state universities. The most significant characteristic of the teacher described by these men as best was, "There was more of an inspiration for clean, honest living in his teaching." The American teacher is coming to recognize that learning has larger responsibilities than those it owes to itself; that the most overt breach of duty of which he can be guilty is willful blindness to the needs of his time and place or cynical indifference to the practical bearing of learning upon such needs. As the American public increases its respect for the service of learning and heightens its desire for excellence in teaching, the teachers themselves will then be more often cheered by the true dignity of their work and less ridden by the routine of their craft, to which the souls of so many are still subject. Then both public and teachers will know that the influence of great teachers outlives that of kings, potentates, military leaders, presidents, or governors of their age; that immortality for the teacher is gained only when he blossoms in the lives and works of others, than which there is no higher immortality.

In this chapter effort has been made to point out briefly some of the important conditions that have surrounded American teachers from the colonial times to the present and to show the influence of such factors as tradition, localism, and the church. Some of the problems involved in securing, training, rewarding, and retaining an adequate supply of effective teachers and the causes of instability in the teaching profession have been noted. Although many obstacles have delayed the development of the profession, teaching has recently increased greatly in dignity, and public confidence in it is gradually enlarging.

This enlarged confidence is evidence that the respect of the American people for the service of education continues to increase and that their confidence in the American principles of education continues to widen. The principles of public support and public control of education, of free and universal education, and of the training of teachers are accepted, even though not one of them is fully applied in actual practice; but every year sees a wider and fuller practical application of each of these principles. And there is no better example of the purpose of the American people to put into practice the educational doctrines they profess than the effort they have made, and continue to make, to extend and widen educational opportunity for all. The story of that effort is related in Chapter XIII.

REFERENCES AND READINGS

ALMACK, J. C., and LANG, A. R. Problems of the Teaching Profession. Boston, 1925.

> Chapters XII–XIV deal with questions of the tenure, salaries, and pensions of teachers.

BARNARD, HENRY (Editor). *American Journal of Education.* 32 vols.

> The student should consult the analytical index of this work to find materials bearing upon the subject of this chapter. See especially Vol. XIII, pp. 123 ff., and 748 ff.

COOK, K. M. State Laws and Regulations governing Teachers' Certificates, *Bulletin No. 22*, United States Bureau of Education, Washington, 1921.

> A careful account of practices, with references to periodical literature.

COON, C. L. The Beginnings of Public Education in North Carolina: A Documentary History, 1790–1840. 2 vols. Raleigh, 1908.

> Volume II (pp. 559 ff.) tells of the lack of fit teachers in that state.

CUBBERLEY, E. P. "The Certification of Teachers," Fifth Yearbook of the National Society for the Study of Education, Part II, 1906.

> A discussion of conditions at that time and suggestions for reform.

CUBBERLEY, E. P. Public Education in the United States. Boston, 1919.

> Chapter VIII (pp. 241 ff.) has some material on the character of early teachers.

CUBBERLEY, E. P. State School Administration. Boston, 1927.

> Chapter XXIV deals with appointment, tenure, pay, and pensions. Contains a good bibliography.

FURST, CLYDE, and KANDEL, I. L. Pensions for Public-School Teachers, *Bulletin No. 12*, Carnegie Foundation for the Advancement of Teaching, New York, 1918.

> A very useful study of the subject, showing conditions and setting up principles on which a pension system should be established.

HANSEN, ALLEN OSCAR. Liberalism and American Education in the Eighteenth Century. New York, 1926.

> Contains descriptions of conditions in that period by Coram and others.

KNIGHT, EDGAR W. Public Education in the South. Boston, 1922.

> Chapter VIII (pp. 294 ff.) shows conditions in the ante-bellum South.

MADDOX, W. A. The Free-School Idea in Virginia before the Civil War. New York, 1918.

> Chapter VIII tells of the indifferent qualifications of teachers in that state in the ante-bellum period. Contains an excellent bibliography.

Reports of the State Educational Survey Commissions. See References and Readings for Chapters XI and XVII.

> Throw light upon conditions surrounding teachers in the states in which surveys have been made.

QUESTIONS FOR STUDY AND DISCUSSION

1. Account for the present instability of the teaching personnel in the United States. How can teaching be professionalized and stabilized?

2. Criticize the plan or arrangement for certificating teachers in your states, pointing out its weaknesses.

3. In the early days the teachers were men, but since 1870 women have entered teaching in larger numbers. Account for the passing of the schoolmaster.

4. What is the relation between low-salary schedules for teachers and the inferior scholarship of those who enter teaching? What effect can adequate salaries have upon the professionalization of teachers?

5. Study the freakish requirements for teachers quoted on page 360. Point out any such requirements with which you are acquainted.

6. Account for the persistent belief among many people that the teacher can live in large part upon the nebulous satisfaction of his service to mankind.

7. Why do so few young men and women of superior ability and high promise enter teaching as a life work? How can they be induced to prepare for and enter teaching?

8. List any arguments you can think of in favor of pensions for teachers; list any arguments against pensions.

9. Some states require that their teachers shall be at least seventeen years old, and in half the states the minimum age required is eighteen. Discuss the effect of such age requirements upon the attitude of the public toward teaching.

10. Criticize the hire-and-fire policy.

CHAPTER XIII

EXTENDING THE SCHOOLS UPWARD

Outline of the chapter. 1. After the Latin grammar schools of the colonial period came the academies, which were private secondary schools.

2. The academies extended widely and had wide influence, though many of them were humble in origin and unpretentious.

3. The manual-labor schools and the military schools were variants of the academy.

4. The public high school, slow in growth in the early period, has recently had phenomenal development. Although it has greatly improved in recent years, it still presents many problems.

5. Although Benjamin Franklin's perspective for higher education was not gained early, the rise of private higher educational institutions was rapid after the Dartmouth College decision. Public institutions of higher education were slow to develop.

6. Technical and professional schools, with Rensselaer Polytechnic Institute leading the way, slowly developed in the early period, but interest in scientific research later had influence upon the schools.

7. The struggle to gain for women educational opportunities equal to those provided for men has been long and bitter, but in recent years interest in the subject has widened.

8. Recent development in higher education has been very rapid, and with the large increases in the enrollment of students new problems have arisen.

Attempts to extend public educational effort upward were often resisted as stubbornly as were the attempts to establish elementary schools at public expense. The old aristocratic conception of education — the belief that support of schools was not a legitimate responsibility of the state, and the age-old notion that the masses neither deserved nor needed education beyond the merest rudiments — stood in the way of public secondary and higher education far into the nineteenth century. These obstacles have not yet been entirely removed in all parts of the United States.

The Academies. After the Latin grammar school of the colonial period appeared the academy, the second type of secondary school to be established in the United States. It began about the middle of the eighteenth century and held high place for nearly a hundred years, until it was displaced by the public high school, which soon gained the monopoly in the field of secondary education, a monopoly it has continued to hold. The academy was a highly respectable means of education. It flourished in all parts of the country and was particularly strong in the Southern states, where the public high school was slow to develop. The most phenomenal period of growth of the academy, which was the product of the frontier period of national development and the laissez-faire theory of government, covered the first half of the nineteenth century.

The word "academy" had been used often in educational essays to describe a school of one kind and another. Milton, in his "Tractate on Education" in 1644, had used it to describe a school that would furnish "a complete and generous culture." Defoe had used it in "Essay on Projects" (first published near the close of the seventeenth century) in a similar way, but also to designate a society of learned men who desired to promote the arts, sciences, and literature. Benjamin Franklin, who claimed to have been influenced by "Essay on Projects," formulated, near the middle of the eighteenth century, a plan for the public education of the youth of Pennsylvania which showed the influence of the celebrated English author. The pamphlet which contained Franklin's plan had an extensive circulation and was widely read, and by 1800 numerous schools appeared in the United States which in organization, management and courses and methods of instruction followed Franklin's suggestions.

Characteristics of the academies. The earlier academies were often largely denominational in control, the motives back of their establishment having root in sectarian interest and pride. As denominations increased, however, impatience with sectarian strife was aroused and protests were made against using the school for the purpose of teaching blind obedience to religious dogma and formalism. Meantime, there was also prevalent the belief that broad aspects of religion had a place in education, and the academy slowly grew into a school which, although colored by a religious spirit, was largely nonsectarian. It was also less exclusive than the Latin grammar school had been, and reflected a growing democratic spirit. Some of the academies were small, modest in their claims, and local in their patronage, and some of them were called old-field schools. Others were more pretentious, were better equipped, and had a wider patronage.

In general the academies were private institutions. They owed their origin to private enterprise and benefaction, and were often under the control of self-perpetuating boards of trustees and therefore subject to no outside supervision. Generally they were laws unto themselves. At the hands of the legislatures they sought corporate powers through grants of charters — the right to own and control property, to receive legacies and endowments, and to employ and dismiss teachers. Sometimes authority was given them to grant degrees or to confer diplomas and distinctions, and some of them were given the privilege of raising funds by lotteries. Generally the property of academies was exempt from taxation, and not infrequently their teachers and students were exempt from military and road duties. Going under a variety of names, — academy, institute, seminary, collegiate institute, and sometimes college, — some of these secondary schools were open to girls only, some were coeducational, and others were open only to boys and young men. Tuition charges were generally made, although not infrequently the legislatures required that poor children should be taught free in return for the privilege of lottery or an occasional subsidy or grant from the state. Some of the academies prepared students for college; in others the courses of study were designed to meet the needs of those who did not seek admission to college or into the learned professions. This type of secondary school, which appeared when a large educational domain was unoccupied, belonged to no conscious educational system, but was singularly independent.

Many of the academies became educational centers. They lent a broadening influence to those who could not go to college, and performed in other ways some of the functions now performed by the modern high school and often some of the work done in college. Taking over from the Latin grammar school such traditional subjects as Latin, Greek, and mathematics, which had been favorite college-preparatory subjects and which remained until about 1800 the required subjects for admission to college, the academies gradually expanded their courses of study. During the first half of the nineteenth century only a few subjects were added to the old college-admission requirements: geography about 1807, English grammar about 1819, algebra about 1820, geometry about 1844, and ancient history about 1847. To these conventional subjects many of the academies added English literature, certain branches of natural science, modern foreign languages, natural and moral philosophy, ethics, surveying and navigation, English composition, oral reading and declamation, bookkeeping and other commercial subjects, as well as the fundamental subjects of reading, writing, and arithmetic. Dresden work, tambour work, embroidery, painting, and drawing were offered in schools to which girls were admitted. The principal in one academy in 1805 advertised to teach, with the aid of one assistant, belles-lettres, rhetoric, ethics, metaphysics, Hebrew, French, Italian, algebra, geometry, trigonometry, navigation, mensuration, altimetry, longimetry, Latin, and Greek, in addition to reading, writing, arithmetic, geography, and English grammar. Another promised in 1818 to give in her "female academy" instruction in orthography, reading, writing, arithmetic, English grammar, needlework, drawing, painting, embroidery, geography, the use of maps, and the scanning of poetry. Practice in oral reading and in the declamation of patriotic pieces of prose and poetry was very common as an effort to develop an enthusiastic and devoted American spirit. The physical equipment of the academies was not above the standards of the time; and the teachers, generally rigid disciplinarians and often thorough in instruction, were often no better trained professionally than were teachers in other types of schools.

Rapid extension of academies. Many academies followed the institution which Franklin established in Philadelphia. One of the most distinguished of those in Massachusetts was Phillips at Andover, founded in 1778, the object of which was not only to instruct youth in the languages and sciences, "but more especially to learn them the great end and real business of living." The academy was so rapidly established that by 1830 there were nearly a thousand such schools in the United States. Twenty years later nearly that many were in New England alone, more than 1600 in the Middle Atlantic states, nearly 2700 in the Southern states, about 750 in the upper Mississippi Valley — more than 6000 in the entire United States, with 260,000 pupils and more than 12,000 teachers. The largest number had been incorporated and established in New York, Pennsylvania, Massachusetts, Kentucky, Virginia, North Carolina, and Tennessee. In some states attempts were made to provide for systems of county academies; in others some form of financial support or other substantial encouragement was occasionally given.

Influence of the movement. The influence of the academies was wide. They stimulated interest in the training of teachers and became the forerunners of normal schools;

they became the nuclei from which many colleges grew, and they served to encourage the education of women. As the principles of public support and control of education strengthened and gained in popular favor, the place of the private secondary school came to be questioned, the demand for the extension of public educational effort to include the secondary school made itself felt, and slowly the idea gained that education above that furnished in the elementary school was properly a function of the state. But the academies, flexible in curriculum and largely free from the entrance requirements of the colleges, were able to reach, before the rise of the public high school, the youth of the growing middle classes who had not yet knocked at the doors of the higher places of learning where the classics and theology still held sway. These new secondary schools, although charged in the late ante-bellum period with opposition to public education, nevertheless served to break the hold that traditional curricula and methods had upon education above the elementary school.

Humble origins of some academies. Evidence of the humble origins of some of the early academies appears in the reported experiences of that class of teachers whose migratory habits took them from place to place in the latter part of the eighteenth century and the early part of the nineteenth. Significant is the testimony of John Davis, an Englishman of more than ordinary education, who, in "Travels of Four Years and a Half in the United States" (published in London in 1803) tells of his teaching experiences in New York, Virginia, and South Carolina about the turn of the century. Armed with letters of introduction from Jefferson and other men of prominence, Davis opened in a log hut on a Virginia plantation "what some call an academy, but others an old-field school," to which on the opening day came all the farmers in the neighborhood who had any children to be educated. "Each man brought his son, or his daughter, and rejoiced that the day was arriving when their little ones could light their tapers at the torch of knowledge." Davis "was confounded at the encomiums they heaped upon a man they had never seen before," as they eagerly sought to exchange "perishable coin for lasting knowledge." If he would continue with them for seven years they would erect for him "a brick seminary." For the present, however, he was to occupy "a log house, which, however homely, would soon vie with the sublime college of William and Mary and consign to oblivion the renowned academy in the vicinity of Fauquier Court House." Davis proceeded at once to instruct his pupils, not "only truant boys, but some of the fairest damsels of the country," exhorting them to diligence of study. Those common books which "were only designed for common minds" he threw aside or allowed to gather the dust of the shelf — the unconnected lessons of this writer, the tasteless selections of that, the "florid harangues" and "somniferous compilations" of others — and substituted the "charming essays of Goldsmith and his not less delectable novel," the impressive works of Defoe, and the mild productions of Addison, which "conspired to enchant the fancy, and kindle a love for reading," in an effort to engraft on the minds and language of his pupils the thoughts and diction of these writers.

Judge A. B. Longstreet, in "Georgia Scenes," describes an academy in Georgia in 1790 as "a simple log pen, about twenty feet square, with a doorway cut out of the logs, to which was fitted a rude door made of clapboards, and swung on wooden hinges." The roof was also of clapboards, held in place by heavy logs placed on them, and the chimney was built of logs. A large plank "wrought from the half of a tree's trunk entirely with the axe, attached to logs by means of wooden pins," served the entire school as a writing desk. Barnas Sears, who left the presidency of Brown University to become in 1867 the first general agent of the Peabody

Fund, said that "intelligent persons, belonging to different states," had assured him that they were educated in such schools as Davis and Longstreet described as academies.

Denominational pride. Although the management of most of the academies of the later period was free from sectarianism, yet many of the earlier ones, as has been indicated, had their origin in denominational pride. Some of them grew out of the influence of the Germans, the Quakers, the Baptists, the Methodists, and the Scotch-Irish Presbyterians. The educational work of these last was more significant, perhaps, than that of any of the other dissenters. Their faith in the value of education and their high esteem for an educated ministry led them to encourage schools of secondary and collegiate grade. Their influence was especially strong in the South, where many of the graduates of Princeton spread and promoted the "log college" movement. Among the most effective of these educational and religious leaders who found their way into the Southern states was David Caldwell, a graduate of Princeton in 1761, whose log college near Greensboro, North Carolina, was known for the excellence of its work. Another was Moses Waddell, a North Carolinian, who conducted schools in Georgia and South Carolina. Students came from many adjacent states, and under Waddell's tuition many of them were prepared for Princeton, Harvard, and Yale. There is a tradition that in his school at Willington, South Carolina, dull boys were made to prepare a hundred lines of Virgil, and that some of the brightest boys prepared as many as a thousand lines for a single recitation. Another effective teacher was James Hall, a graduate of Princeton in 1774, who established Clio's Nursery and Science Hall in Iredell County, North Carolina, about the beginning of the Revolutionary War. Still another was Samuel McCorkle, who was graduated from Princeton in 1772. McCorkle later opened near Salisbury, North Carolina, a school called Zion

Parnassus, in which was made one of the earliest attempts at teacher-training in the United States, if not the earliest.

John Chavis, negro. One of the most remarkable of all these Presbyterian teachers was John Chavis, a full-blooded, free-born negro whose ability attracted the attention of his white friends in North Carolina, where he was born about 1763. He was sent to Princeton to show whether "a negro would take a collegiate education." The experiment seems to have been successful. After leaving college Chavis went to Virginia, but returned to his native state in 1805 and continued his religious and educational work under the auspices of the Presbyterian Church. He opened a classical school which was attended by the best white people of the community, and some of the students boarded in his family. Chavis had an unusual knowledge of Greek and Latin and the Scriptures and was a man of impressive manner. His English was said to be remarkable for its purity and for its freedom from "negroisms." Powerful as a preacher and teacher, he continued his formal work until the state legislature in 1831 forbade negroes to preach. The late John Spencer Bassett said that he learned "from a source of the greatest respectability" that Chavis "was received as an equal socially and asked to table by the most respectable people in the neighborhood." Race prejudices had not yet been aroused.

Variants of the academy. The manual-labor schools and the military schools were two interesting variants of the academy. The former received an impetus through the industrial work of the Pestalozzian-Fellenberg movement, which attracted attention in the first quarter of the nineteenth century. In 1806 Fellenberg, a companion and colaborer of Pestalozzi, established at Hofwyl, Switzerland, an institution in which he combined literary instruction and manual labor. The students pursued their school work in the mornings and farmed in the afternoons. Henry Barnard believed that this institution, which continued for forty years and attracted wide educational attention, had a larger influence than any other institution in Europe or America in the nineteenth century. Through its work physical exercises began to claim attention in the United States, and through discussion the public mind came to be more or less educated to an appreciation of their value. Physical training and gymnastics slowly came to ask places in the schools, but this agitation proved somewhat disappointing, although it served to draw attention to the physical needs of students. Confidence in the power of formal physical exercises later weakened, however, and the so-called gymnastic movement finally collapsed. Later, attention was gradually called to physiology and hygiene as aids in the preservation of health, and campaigns began for introducing these subjects into the schools. With the failure of the formal-gymnastics movement, Fellenberg's idea of combining manual labor and intellectual pursuits was eagerly seized upon as the solution of the problem of health in schools. Advocates of agricultural and mechanical work in educational institutions appeared early, but the movement did not gain much force until near the close of the first quarter of the nineteenth century. Interest in the experiment slowly increased, however, and for two decades or more manual-labor schools sprang up in numerous places.

The beginnings of manual-labor schools. The earliest school of this character in the United States seems to have been established at Lethe, South Carolina, under the will of Dr. John de la Howe in 1786. It had a useful career from 1805 until the Civil War, when the loss of endowment forced its suspension. The manual-labor feature was introduced widely in theological institutions, colleges, and academies, and by 1830 most of the states had one or more institutions in which manual labor was used. The preservation and invigoration of health were no doubt powerful motives in the introduction of manual labor in many literary institutions, but the supposed hygienic value probably had no more weight in promoting its adoption than the promising pecuniary advantage of the scheme or its value as an agency for recruiting sectarian ranks during a period of intense denominational controversy. Wherever practicable, farms and shops were provided for such schools, the time being divided between manual labor and study.

The work of Theodore D. Weld. The theoretical side of the experiment culminated in the early thirties, by which time the movement had also attained considerable practical proportions. Elias Cornelius, editor of the *American Quarterly Register* and secretary of the American Education Society, lectured and wrote on the subject, and the Fellenberg system continued to be advocated by numerous educational leaders. In June, 1831, an enthusiastic meeting of manual-labor advocates was held in New York, with the result that the Society for Promoting Manual Labor in Literary Institutions was formed, and Theodore D. Weld was appointed as its general agent. Weld had been connected with the Oneida Manual Labor Institute at Whitesboro, New York, one of the institutions made conspicuous by its manual-labor feature from 1827 to 1834. Enthusiastic in advocating the new system, Weld made a tour of many states in the interest of the plan, and in 1832 he made a report which contained the most elaborate presentation of the movement ever published, setting forth the claims of manual labor as a necessary part of a sound educational system.

Arguments for manual-labor schools. The report advanced many ingenious and plausible arguments in favor of manual labor in schools. It claimed that the system of education in practice at that time jeopardized the health of the students, tended to effeminate the mind, was perilous to morals, failed to stimulate effort, destroyed habits of industry, and was so expensive that its practical results were noticeably antidemocratic. Moreover, Weld argued in the report that the manual-labor feature furnished the kind of exercise best suited to students, and that military exercises, quite proper in strictly military schools, were not adapted to any other and would not be until fighting became the appropriate vocation of man and "human butchery the ordinary business of life." Ordinary gymnastic exercises were not suitable because they were not productive of material resources. Manual labor would correct all these and numerous other educational defects. It would furnish exercises "natural to man" and adapted to intellectual interests, it would produce happy moral effects, and it would equip the students with valuable practical acquisitions. In addition to these advantages it was further claimed that the plan would promote habits of industry, independence of character, and originality, and would render "permanent all the manlier features of character." It would also afford opportunity and facilities for "acquiring a knowledge of human nature." It promised to reduce the expense of education, to increase wealth, and to make all forms of honest labor democratic and honorable by destroying any absurd distinctions in society which made one's occupation the standard of one's worth. Finally, manual labor would preserve republican institutions.

Collapse of the movement. This organization, which Weld served as secretary for only one year, had a short life, and his successor was never appointed. Practically all the institutions that tested the new plan soon abandoned it as unsatisfactory, and the movement finally collapsed. Practical difficulties rather than weaknesses inherent in the plan cooled enthusiasm for it, and the introduction of athletics in schools and colleges later proved a substitute for the physical features of the scheme. However, the manual-labor idea was not lost. It reappeared (in part at least) in

the Morrill Act of 1862, which has greatly influenced industrial education in the United States, and in the manual-
training movement of recent years. Through these means
have been achieved some of the purposes which the earlier
movement sought to attain.

Military schools. With the establishment of the United
States Military Academy in 1802 the military type of school
began to develop. It was highly favored, especially in the
Southern states. In 1819 Captain Alden Partridge, for some
time superintendent of the academy at West Point, founded
at Norwich, Vermont, the American Literary, Scientific, and
Military Academy, and twenty years later he founded a
similar institution at Portsmouth. In the latter year the
Virginia Military Institute was established at Lexington
upon a plan which followed closely the plan of the school at
West Point. Schools with military features were established
elsewhere and had grown to a considerable number by the
middle of the nineteenth century.

The public high school. With the gradual improvement
of the elementary schools there developed from the so-called
middle classes, which were slowly increasing in political
strength, a demand for wider educational opportunity in
secondary schooling for their children. Generally only
those who were able to pay the tuition charges could attend
the private academies, and the rising democratic feeling
voiced a demand for high schools supported by taxation and
open to the poor as well as to the rich. A few high schools
had been early established in New England : perhaps the
first in Boston in 1821, one in Portland, Maine, in the same
year, a few others in Massachusetts a few years later, and
one in New York City in 1825. But the Massachusetts
law of 1827, which was passed largely through the work of
James G. Carter, marks the beginning of the public high-
school movement. This act, which provided for elementary
schools and required a tax-supported high school in every

town of five hundred families or more, was soon copied by
New Hampshire, Maine, and Vermont. This new type of
school, which arose to provide at public expense an educational opportunity not offered by the elementary schools,
one that had hitherto been provided only at private expense,
and to prepare youth for such pursuits in life as they were
likely to follow, is one of the earliest examples of a purely
American educational institution. In origin it shows little if
any foreign influence, and
appears to have been es-
tablished to meet the
needs of the masses.

By 1840 about a dozen
of these new institutions
had been established in
Massachusetts, where the
public high school arose
and earliest developed.
Perhaps as many more
had been set up in other
states, including Maine,
Vermont, Pennsylvania,
and New York. By 1850

THE FIRST AMERICAN HIGH SCHOOL,
BOSTON, 1821

Louisiana, Rhode Island, Michigan, Ohio, and Connecticut
had each one or more such schools, and ten years later there
were about a hundred in the entire country. By 1880 the
number had increased to eight hundred, and two decades
later to more than six thousand. The development of this
type of school since 1900 has been one of the phenomena
of American educational history, the private secondary
schools meantime gradually declining.

Early growth slow. However, the growth of the public
school had to push its way against the obstacles of objection
to taxation, the permissive character of legislation on elementary schools, and the strength of localism. Although

these gave way more readily in some states than in others, there was almost always a contest. Often it was between an academy, supported by tuition fees or by the private generosity of the community where it was established, and the proposal for a free and public high school. But as public responsibility for elementary education became more fully acknowledged, the chance for the high school became brighter. Massachusetts and New York led the way in the movement, other Eastern states followed, and as urban centers developed in the West the high school appeared there. But in the South, where there were few cities until recent years and where the ghost of the old aristocratic theory of education stalked so long, the growth of public high schools was slow. The movement, which received its earliest stimulus from the Peabody Fund after the Civil War, was greatly encouraged and supported through the work of the General Education Board after 1903. The enormous increase in economic wealth and in legislative liberality and the continued encouragement of the General Education Board have enabled the Southern states, crippled so long by war and reconstruction, to make rapid progress in public-high-school work in recent years.

Permissive legislation. Legislation in public secondary education was permissive rather than mandatory in many of the states during the early years of the movement, as had been true of legislation on elementary education at public expense. Often the law, even when mandatory, was attacked in the courts in an effort to answer the natural question of the legal right of a state or a community to use public funds for high-school support. The issue was clearly drawn in Michigan in 1872 and as clearly settled by a decision in the Kalamazoo case, in which the court held that the high school was a proper part of the public-school system. This decision became the legal precedent for other states and greatly influenced the development of the high school at public expense, although some of the states were slower than others to acknowledge the responsibility. Today the high school is generally accepted as a part of the educational system of each state. Increasingly are public funds provided for its support, and increasingly are the facilities of public secondary education being placed within the reach of all American growth.

Recent improvement. Although many of these early schools were high schools only in name, being at best loosely

A MODERN HIGH-SCHOOL BUILDING

connected with the schools above and below, improvement has been gradually made in the nature and quality of high-school work. Some of the subjects once found in them have been placed in the upper grades of the elementary schools, and other subjects have been added to the high-school course. Although its original purpose was not to prepare students for college, the public high school has always made provision for such preparation, and probably this is even now its dominating aim. The high school is still recognized as a part of the educational ladder up which the American youth may climb or creep from elementary school into the arts college or the professional schools. Moreover, the high school has influenced college-entrance requirements, and these in turn have influenced it. As new subjects have crowded in, the high school has lengthened its course from two to three years and then to four years. It has introduced electives, and some schools have set up such parallel courses as the ancient classical, the modern classical, English, history, scientific, manual-arts, household-arts, agriculture, business and commercial, pedagogical, specialized vocational, and trade and industrial. The effort is to meet as far as possible the individual needs and capacities of the pupils and to help them to find and open doors to new and more wholesome opportunities. Once hard and fixed, the high-school courses of study are now becoming more and more varied and flexible.

More and more, also, effort is being made to connect the work of the high school with that of the elementary school and of higher education. Articulation is now closer than formerly. As early as 1893 definite recommendations were made by the Committee of Ten, and a few years later by the Committee of Five. Out of these and other suggestions the scope of secondary education is being extended downward by what is known as the junior high school and upward by the so-called junior college. The one movement seeks to afford a richer educational opportunity to provide for individual differences, to coördinate elementary and secondary education more closely, to furnish educational guidance, and to save time; the other undertakes to solve the problems arising in the increased numbers who desire and deserve educational advantages beyond those provided by the conventional high school, in the congested conditions of the colleges, and in the demand for easier access to higher educational opportunities and for the reduction of expenses involved in leaving home for such advantages. The junior-high-school movement has developed rapidly, but the junior college has not yet made wide popular appeal.

Present problems. A general view of secondary education in the United States at the present time reveals apparent disorder, with confusion in the organization of the
schools, in the courses of study and their administration, in
the variety of professional standards among the administrators and teachers, in the machinery used to promote the
pupils, and often also in the methods of financial support.
Abundant is the evidence of chaotic conditions in these and
perhaps other phases of public secondary work, not only
when the field as a whole is viewed, but often when the
high-school systems of the states themselves are viewed.
But beneath the confused and confusing standards, due
largely to growth, there is discernible a purpose that promises increasingly to harmonize with the democratic theory of
education, and that purpose is increasingly being accomplished. The rate of increase in public-high-school enrollment during the last three or four decades, nearly twenty
times as great as the rate of increase of the total population,
is convincing evidence of growing success in the effort of the
American people to universalize secondary educational opportunities. The public high-school promises to become more
and more democratic.

Colleges and universities. As was pointed out in Chapter V, all but one of the colleges established before the close
of the colonial period grew out of religious, or sectarian,
motives, the single exception being that of Franklin's
Academy, which developed into the College of Philadelphia
and later into the University of Pennsylvania. Richly
endowed with a lively imagination, an inquiring mind, and
a boundless love for learning, Benjamin Franklin, who had
himself never attended college, was far in advance of his
contemporaries as an educational statesman. He was aware
of the wide social benefits that would come from the right
kind of higher education. New members of the Junto
(a scientific and literary association formed by Franklin in

1727 and later developed into the American Philosophical Society), members organized from printers, shoemakers, and carpenters, were to have three questions put to them: Do you sincerely declare that you love mankind in general of whatsoever profession or religion? Do you think any person ought to be harmed in his body, name, or goods for mere speculative opinions or his external way of worship? Do

ELIHU YALE

From a portrait in the collection of Yale University

you love truth for truth's sake and will you endeavor impartially to find and receive it yourself and communicate it to others? On such liberal and democratic principles Franklin would erect a higher educational institution at a time when Harvard and Yale were still classifying their students according to the social prestige of their families. He would provide also a secular and scientific course of study when all the other colleges of the colonies were established upon a sectarian and theological program, and would provide for instruction in mathematics, surveying, and navigation, in mechanics, in chemistry and physics, in history, civics, and government, in trade, commerce, and accounting, in international law, in natural history, and in modern languages — an anticipation of the most enlightened program of a liberal university. This chart for higher learning came from a self-educated man whose mind had never been enslaved by educational formalism and ritual. If Franklin could have had his way a revolution would have been begun in higher education, but tradition was strong, and in "the interest of peace and endowment a compromise was made."

Throughout the colonial period and far into the national period there was no established policy for the public control of education, either elementary, secondary, or higher. The charters issued by legislatures to colleges were viewed as grants of powers and privileges to be enjoyed under the private initiative of chartered institutions. But after the Revolutionary War some of the states — among them Massachusetts, Connecticut, Pennsylvania, New York, and New Hampshire — attempted to gain larger control over the colleges which they had chartered.

DANIEL WEBSTER

Who made a celebrated argument in the Dartmouth College case

The Dartmouth College case. These efforts continued until the decision of the Dartmouth College case in 1819, when the Supreme Court of the United States held unconstitutional and void acts of the Legislature of New Hampshire which had amended the charter granted to Dartmouth by George III in 1769. The opinion of the court restated the argument of Daniel Webster, who appeared as counsel for the college, of which he was a distinguished graduate. Webster held that the charter of a private corporation was a contract which could not be impaired by legislative act. The far-reaching effect of this decision did not fully appear, however, until large and powerful corporations began to develop, and the guaranty of the inviolability which the court had thrown around a private educational corporation was later given to business corporations also. The Fourteenth Amendment, which became a part of the Constitution of the United States in 1868, after defining citizenship, prohibited any state from making or enforcing any law which abridged "the privileges and immunities of citizens of the United States," from depriving "any person of life, liberty, or property, without due process of law," and from denying "to any person within its jurisdiction the equal protection of the laws." In the slaughterhouse cases, which came up from Louisiana in 1873, [in the Southern Pacific Railway Company cases in 1882 and 1886, and in the Chicago, Milwaukee and St. Paul Railway Company case in 1889, a new meaning was given to the principle of law evolved in the Dartmouth case, the court holding that a corporation is a person within the meaning of the Fourteenth Amendment and entitled to its protection.

The significance of the decision. The decision in the celebrated Dartmouth College case, one of the most important events in American educational history, gave to private educational institutions and their endowments peculiar protection from political interference. With the way now cleared, interest in higher education quickened, and the next half-century was marked by a feverish denominational effort to establish colleges. By 1800 a dozen or more had been added to the list of nine founded during the colonial period. More than a score appeared between 1820 and 1830, nearly twice as many between 1830 and 1840, more than twoscore between 1840 and 1850, more than ninety between 1850 and 1860, seventy-three between 1860 and 1870, sixty-one between 1870 and 1880, seventy-four between 1880 and 1890, and more than fifty between 1890 and 1900, by which latter date there were nearly five hundred educational institutions of collegiate grade in the United States. But, as had been the case of the secondary school, the field of higher learning was held largely by private or denominational interests and has continued to be so held. At the close of the ante-bellum period only about a score of nearly two hundred and fifty colleges were state or public in control and support. Some were very small and weak and of doubtful reputation for standards of scholarship. But the increased number of such institutions reflects the growing appreciation which the religious leaders of the time felt for the need of education. Most of these colleges were supported by tuition fees and subscriptions from individuals with denominational interests, and generally they were administered by clergymen.

Rapid rise of private institutions. Educational foundations, then, were established early, were not numerous or large until comparatively recent years, and grew for the most part out of religious influences. Most of the colleges founded during the past century have been privately controlled and privately supported. Probably two thirds of the higher educational institutions of the United States are now directly or indirectly private in support and control. Whether or not the religious agencies desired to duplicate the educational facilities already established by the state, the colleges established by such agencies represent the offerings of the church for the training of its own leaders, and perhaps as an influence upon secular education, but also as a means of promoting public welfare generally. The policy of strict denominational control, so manifest in the power of the denomination to elect or confirm the majority of the trustees or in the requirements that a majority of the governing body be members of the controlling denomination, arose as a protective measure and has continued as such. Many of these colleges doubtless began in denominational loyalty, and some of them probably arose out of sectarian competition, but most of them have broadened their conceptions to include general public service.

Slow growth of public institutions. Parallel with the development of private and denominational colleges was the growth of higher education under public support and control, but keen competition with the former and the objection to taxation for higher education made the growth of the latter type of institution very slow. The effort to extend public education upward from the elementary school to the high school and on to the college was bitterly contested at every step. The University of Georgia was chartered in 1785 and opened in 1800. The University of North Carolina was chartered in 1789 and, under the leadership of William R. Davie, was opened in 1795; but neither was in a real sense a public institution. The University of Vermont, chartered in 1791, was rechartered in 1838 as a state university. The University of Virginia was opened in 1825, one year before the death of its illustrious founder. The University of Indiana was set up in 1820, the University of Alabama in 1831, and the University of Michigan in 1841. Most of the new states provided for universities in their initial constitutions. At first these institutions were poorly and often grudgingly supported by the states which had created them, and many of them were burdened with denominational restrictions and pestered by petty political interference — afflictions against which not all of them have yet become fully protected.

WILLIAM R. DAVIE

Founder of the University of North Carolina, the first state university

Jefferson's University of Virginia, established by the legislature of the state, to be under the management of a board of visitors, or trustees, who were to be appointed by the governor, set out free (in theory at least) from the traditional curriculum of higher education and also from sectarian influences. Courses in ancient languages, in modern

OLD EAST BUILDING, THE UNIVERSITY OF NORTH CAROLINA, BUILT IN 1793

This is the first building to be erected upon a state-university campus and is still used as a dormitory

languages, in mathematics, chemistry, medicine, law, moral philosophy, and natural philosophy, offered a wide range of electives to the students, who were to be taught by the best-trained professors available anywhere. Jefferson believed that men who acquired the habit of thinking for themselves and of following "reason as their guide" were more easily and safely governed than those who were "debased by ignorance, indigence, and oppression," against which and all other tyrannies over the minds of men he had sworn "eternal hostility." But the noble view which he had for higher education was early obscured by denominationalism, and his theory of freedom in teaching and learning did not pass promptly into fact, the eminent Thomas Cooper being one of the earliest victims of the religious bigotry of the Old Dominion.

Technical and professional education. The establishment of the Rensselaer Polytechnic Institute at Troy, New York, in 1824, marks the beginning of technical education, and interest in training for scientific work (in which there has been enlarged activity since the passage of the Morrill Act in 1862) quickly followed. In the plan which Stephen Van Rensselaer outlined for the organization and government of the school, intended for the instruction of "persons who may choose to apply themselves in the application of science to the common purposes of life," the principal object was "to qualify teachers for instructing the sons and daughters of farmers and mechanics, by lectures and otherwise, in the application of experimental chemistry, philosophy and natural history, to agriculture, domestic economy, the arts and manufactures." He would increase the total of human happiness through the use of scientific thought, he would make the school a teacher-training agency, and he would admit women as well as men. Domestic economy was included in the proposed curriculum.

Rensselaer's pioneer work. In Rensselaer Institute appeared other pioneer educational efforts: something of a summer session, of a "university afloat," and of extension work. In 1829 provision was made for the "traveling term" of ten weeks in the summer, with daily forenoon lectures and examinations in mineralogy, geology, botany, zoölogy, chemistry, philosophy, and practical mathematics, with a library and a specimen room fitted up on the ship, and with provision for the "direct inspection of the subjects under discussion." The afternoons were to be given to the collection of geological specimens and plants. "The flotilla will move slowly, so as to allow sufficient time for collecting specimens," stated the announcement, which predicted "that two boats may become extended seminaries of learning which shall literally carry useful knowledge to every part of our extended empire." The route of this floating summer school was up the Hudson, stopping at the Palisades, West Point, the Catskill Mountains, on to Albany and Troy, through the Erie Canal to Utica, and eventually to Niagara. The cost for passage, board, and instruction was fifty-four dollars. The students were promised plain and nutritious diet adapted to hardy exercise, but no provision was made for "ardent spirits." In Rensselaer's guidance of students, who were encouraged to work independently of the professors, appears an early example of the present tendency toward "honor courses" in the American college; and in the provision for "a *parlor course* of lectures, illustrating all the important principles of chemistry and philosophy in a neat, cleanly manner," is to be seen the germ of modern university-extension service.

Attention to science. After Rensselaer came other institutions with interest in science or emphasis on it. About the middle of the century Brown University began to offer a course without Greek and with emphasis upon modern subjects, leading to the degree of bachelor of philosophy. With the establishment in the late forties or the early fifties of the Lawrence Scientific School at Harvard, the Sheffield Scientific School at Yale, the Chandler School of Science at Dartmouth, and the Polytechnic Institute of Brooklyn, the degree of bachelor of science appeared. Instruction in civil engineering had been included in the work of Union College, Schenectady. Michigan organized an agricultural and industrial college in the fifties, and out of the Farmers' High School, which was set up in Pennsylvania about the same time, grew the Pennsylvania State College. In these institutions the way was prepared in part for the Morrill Act of 1862, which became the basis of the land-grant colleges. Meantime other influences were working in the same direction. In 1853 the legislature of Illinois presented to Congress a resolution which urged "a system of Industrial Universities liberally endowed, in each state in the Union, coöperative with each other, and with the Smithsonian Institution of Washington" to provide "a more liberal and practical education among the people."

Horace Greeley, in an editorial in the *New York Tribune*, praised this proposal as "a noble step forward," and said that scientific and practical education could not come too soon; and J. B. Turner, the great advocate of the principle underlying the Morrill Act, asked: "Was God mistaken when He placed man in a garden, instead of an academy? ... Or when He made His son a carpenter instead of a rabbi? Or when He made man a man instead of a monk? No; God's ways are ever ways of wisdom and truth; it is Satan who has continued to put in the world useless nerves and brains, without bodies or souls, and to call the process by which the result is reached, education." Before the land-grant colleges were set on their way the School of Mines at Columbia, the Massachusetts Institute of Technology, the Worcester Polytechnic Institute, and Lehigh University were opened, to be followed by many other technological institutions later. Slowly the sciences came to receive the attention and place in collegiate education that had formerly been allowed only to theology; to the classics, and to syllogisms.

Characteristics of early professional schools. Medicine, law, dentistry, and pharmacy developed slowly. Superstition stood in the way of science and encouraged the quack, the medicine man, and the shyster. Doctors and lawyers in the early days generally received the meager preparation which the conditions of the times permitted, largely by methods of apprenticeship; and when so-called schools of medicine and law appeared at Pennsylvania, Columbia, Harvard, Dartmouth, Maryland, Yale, and Virginia between 1765 and 1826 the instruction was very poor and the period of training ridiculously brief. Many of these early schools were private in nature — mere money-making arrangements for the proprietors, who were smart enough, however, to make use of the names of the colleges to which such schools were attached. A school of dentistry was opened at Baltimore in 1839, and a few years later another was set up at Cincinnati. One of the earliest schools of pharmacy was established at Philadelphia in 1822.

By 1870 there were perhaps half a hundred medical schools, but all of them were inadequate and, measured by present-day standards, wretched. For many years after the Civil War the teaching of medicine was a social disgrace and far below the standards of Europe. Incompetents, quacks, and malpractitioners were numerous. Even at Harvard the medical students, who were required to take only two courses of lectures in the subject, and these for only about four months, could receive degrees upon passing a very nominal examination and upon the certificate of a medical school or physician that they had read medicine three years. The head of Harvard's medical school in 1870 believed that written examinations were impossible for medical students because most of them could not write well enough. Steps toward reform were taken at that institution, however, shortly after Charles W. Eliot became its president in 1869. Dr. Eliot secured the coöperation of Dr. Oliver Wendell Holmes of the medical faculty, placed the medical school upon a standard academic basis, and set up a course of three academic years. But the overseers were reluctant to approve the proposed reform until Eliot had produced proof of deaths which had resulted from the ignorance and carelessness of a recent graduate of the school. Under Eliot's leadership Harvard also led reforms in legal education, which had had a long career of backwardness, while lawyers looked on with scorn. With the introduction of the case method the study of law was in time to be set on its way to a new interest and life.

Early advances in science. Advances in scientific research, later to increase in number and in the value of their applications, slowly came to attract the notice of Americans. James Smithson, an Englishman who died in 1829, gave to the United States government more than half a million dollars "for the increase and diffusion of knowledge among men," and thus laid the foundation for the Smithsonian Institution, chartered in 1846, which has had a wide scientific influence. In 1837 J. D. Dana of Yale published his work on mineralogy. Ormsby M. Mitchel established an observatory at Cincinnati, Asa Gray at Harvard was making important contributions in botany, John James Audubon, a native of New Orleans, had much earlier begun the work that made him the first ornithologist of the time, Louis Agassiz at Harvard was making distinguished researches in geology and zoölogy, Benjamin Silliman at Yale was collecting minerals and lecturing in chemistry and geology, and Matthew F. Maury at Virginia was "exploring the mysteries of hydrography" in an effort to find the paths of the seas. In the late forties the American Association for the Advancement of Science was formed "to promote intercourse between American scientists, to give a strong and more systematic impulse to research, and to procure for the labors of scientific men increased facilities and wider usefulness."

Effect upon schools. Science was becoming a new and strange force in the intellectual life of the United States and was later to change the work of the schools. But slavery, which had stood in the way of the applications of science in ancient Greece, served to delay their progress in America. Slavery, with its prerogative and privilege and the class distinctions which it encouraged, had to be removed before science, which is always democratic and knows no distinctions, could take the field fully against ignorance, disease, superstition, and irrational fears. Democracy could not, in the words of Tocqueville, induce many men "to cultivate science for its own sake," but it could increase "the number of those who do cultivate it" and who could profit by its uses. In time scientific investigations were widened in application to the practical needs of men. Before 1860 inventions and discoveries included the reaping machine, the cotton gin, the sewing machine, the vulcanization of rubber, the cylinder printing press, the use of anthracite, friction matches, illumination through petroleum, the steamboat, the locomotive, the telegraph, the submarine cable, and advances in medical science, including the use of anæsthetics, and since that time hundreds of other applications of science have contributed to progress and to the promotion of human betterment. More and more was the way prepared for the introduction of science into the schools.

The education of women. The struggle to gain for women educational advantages equal to those enjoyed by men has been a long and hard one. The dream of Matthew Vassar, who wished "to inaugurate a new era in the history and life of woman" and to give to her "all the advantages long monopolized" by man, was slow to come true because of prejudice, conservatism, and the dismal predictions that damage would be the result if learning should be advanced to the weaker sex. Vassar believed that woman could be educated "within the rational limits of true womanliness and without the slightest hazard to the attractiveness of her character," but the last century was closing before the dominion which men had so long held in and over education had been broken. This reform was hastened by several forces. As early as 1848 a convention was held at Seneca Falls, New York, said to be the first concerted effort ever made in behalf of woman's rights, the delegates going a step beyond Jefferson in 1776, in declaring that "all men and women are created equal." But their demands for equality with men in education, in economic opportunities, in voting, and before the law were laughed at and condemned by press and pulpit. Since that time the movement for woman's rights has grown steadily, hastened no more definitely by any force, however, than by the change in economic conditions, which have sent women increasingly into gainful occupations, particularly since the World War.

MARY LYON

Slow development. But practical educational opportunities were at first grudgingly permitted to girls and women. Except for a meager elementary education they had little or no advantage until the rise of the academy, which furnished the beginnings of higher education for women in the United States. The nineteenth century had advanced considerably before the doors of any college were opened to women. Emma Willard founded Troy Seminary in 1821, and Mary Lyon founded Mount Holyoke Seminary fifteen years later. Rockford College, Elmira College, Vassar, and Wesleyan in Georgia (said to be the first woman's college to confer degrees) were other institutions set up before 1860 for the education of women. Meantime Oberlin College on its establishment in 1833 had opened its doors to women on an equal footing with men, and at the same time had refused to shut them in the face of persons of color; and two decades later Antioch College, under the leadership of Horace Mann, also became coeducational and coracial. Genesee College (1850), which became Syracuse University in 1870, was coeducational from its beginning. The University of Utah and the University of Iowa were opened to women on their establishment near the middle of the century, and other state universities soon fell in line, Indiana, Michigan, and Wisconsin, in the sixties or early seventies, and finally all of them. Private institutions soon relaxed their requirements: Cornell in 1872, the Massachusetts Institute of Technology a decade later, and the University of Chicago in the early nineties. Columbia made peace by establishing Barnard as a coördinate college in 1889, and Harvard set up Radcliffe five years later. Yale and the University of Pennsylvania admitted women to their graduate departments in 1892, and Columbia to its nonprofessional graduate schools in 1900. In the meantime Vassar in New York, Wellesley and Smith in Massachusetts, and Bryn Mawr were founded, the last-named offering graduate courses also. "But the graduate schools of Harvard, Princeton, and the seaboard state universities of the South were almost without exception barred against women" at the turn of the century. Despite the caution which the institutions were still trying to exercise against the invasion, the rate of increase of men in colleges and universities between 1890 and 1910 was about 214 per cent as against 438 per cent for women in coeducational institutions and 348 per cent in colleges for women. On the other hand, the idea of professional training for women had less popular favor even as late as 1900, but since that time interest in it has continued to widen.

Recent development in higher education. Since the middle of the nineteenth century, when most of the colleges were still offering a single course (largely of Greek, Latin, and mathematics) leading to the degree of bachelor of arts, many changes have taken place in higher education. Even before the close of the century the most progressive and best-developed institutions were offering a variety of courses leading to different undergraduate degrees. After the opening of Johns Hopkins University in 1876, the first real graduate school to be established in the United States, several of the best-equipped institutions began to offer courses of graduate grade leading to the degrees of master of arts, master of science, doctor of philosophy; Yale had been the first institution to grant the degree of doctor of philosophy, in 1851. From a training ground for preachers — the essential characteristic of the colonial colleges — the typical American college has slowly grown, has enlarged its facilities, and has widened and liberalized the educational opportunities which it offers; and the representative American university now has from a dozen to a score of schools with separate courses, from the arts to agriculture and animal husbandry, leading to degrees. More and more do students crowd the doors of the colleges, which more and more seem to seek, if sometimes blindly, new and better ways of serving the state and of promoting public well-being generally. In the recent development of the colleges and universities, into which millions of public and private funds annually find their way, appears one of the most significant influences in all American history.

In recent years, especially since the close of the World War, public appropriations for higher education have greatly increased. As late as 1870 even the state universities had been only meagerly supported, and in general their growth was slow. In 1890 the entire public support of universities and colleges amounted to only $1,383,000, and two years later to only $2,118,000. A quarter of a century later, however, the states appropriated more than $21,000,000 for instruction and administration in their agricultural and mechanical colleges alone, nearly $4,000,000 more for their agricultural experiment stations and extension service, and more than $14,000,000 for new buildings and equipment. In 1918, the University of California received legislative support of $2,000,000, and the University of Illinois received from a state-wide tax more than $2,000,000. The total public appropriations for college and university work in that year were more than $33,000,000. In 1926 the total amount received from public sources by higher educational institutions for current expenses alone was above $81,000,000. The total income, including additions to endowments, was more than $176,000,000, and for private institutions it was more than $303,000,000.

The development of higher education in the United States has been so rapid that one person in every 212 in the entire country is now attending college or university. The Western states, with a small negro and foreign population, and some of them with few separate normal schools, surpass the other sections in relative numbers of college students. Utah, with one for every 99, leads all the states in the number of college students residing in the state as compared with the total population, and the District of Columbia comes next, with one college student for every 103 of the total population. Oregon has one for every 121 persons and Nebraska one for every 126. Nearly one fourth of the students attend college or university outside the state in which they reside, although conditions vary greatly. More than 90 per cent of the California students attend colleges and universities in that state, and the percentage is almost as large for Texas. On the other hand, students residing in New Jersey, Connecticut, Wyoming, Delaware, and New Hampshire leave their home states in large numbers for higher educational opportunities elsewhere, because of an actual dearth of college and university facilities to accommodate the large number of students, the lack of variety in curricula, or the comparative ease with which excellent institutions can be reached in neighboring states. Less than 22 per cent of the college students in New Jersey attend college in that state, and nearly 26 per cent of the students resident in Massachusetts go elsewhere to college. In several of the states the colleges and universities draw their students very largely from their own population.

Tendencies and problems. Perhaps the most prominent present-day tendency in higher education appears in the wide discussion of its purposes, the reëxamination and restatement of objectives having been provoked chiefly by the rising costs of higher educational institutions and the recent tremendous growth in attendance upon them. Thousands of youths, whose parents were not college-bred, have accepted at face value the statements of college presidents and professors that wide opportunities lie in attendance upon the college and university. Youth has responded to the appeal and is annually flocking to college by multitudes. Enrollments in higher educational institutions have increased nearly six times as fast as the general population during the last three decades. Costs have also mounted. But many of those who in the lean years of college attendance were the strongest advocates of higher education now often display a lack of faith in it as a panacea for individual and social ills. Numerous and loud are the protests that the colleges are being filled with "nitwits," and cries of alarm and of dismay come from professors and administrative officers in the face of statistics of the higher mortality of their students. The mania for numbers and the "college contagion" have provoked an academic hysteria and a feverish excitement in which presidents, professors, and deans find it difficult to preserve their patience and peace. Hope has seemed to appear, however, in studies and reports on these new problems of the colleges, in such arrangements as "freshman week," and in orientation courses, faculty counselors, and other expedients which are becoming more and more fashionable. If these opiates or tonics fail to remove the chronic disorders of higher education, then perhaps the need for better college teaching may finally come into prominence. Although instruction has probably improved in the elementary and secondary schools in recent years, scientific methods have not yet been applied appreciably in teaching in the higher institutions or in their administration. The improvement of instruction, which is still the primary purpose of the college, is probably the largest single need in higher education in the United States. On this need Emerson gave prophetic warning to higher education half a century ago. The colleges, he said, can highly serve their times only when "they set the hearts of their youth on flame." Until this need is met honestly and definitely the dean's despair must continue to deepen.

In preceding chapters an effort has been made to trace the movements to secure public support and public control of education and to train teachers and to improve them and the conditions of their work. This chapter has briefly traced the growth of the academy, the public high school, private and public higher educational institutions, technical and professional schools, and the movement for the higher education of women. Some of the problems in higher education today have been indicated also. The remainder of the book is devoted to accounts of actual educational practices, of the problems of education in the Southern states (which, largely because of the Civil War and Reconstruction, until recently have found extraordinary difficulty in providing schools), of later developments in education, and of present-day tendencies and problems. To the first of these subjects, attention is given in Chapter XIV.

REFERENCES AND READINGS

ANDERSON, L. F. "The Manual-Labor School Movement," *Educational Review* (November, 1913), Vol. XLVI, pp. 369–388.

> Deals principally with the Fellenberg movement in the United States.

BLANDIN, I. M. E. History of Higher Education of Women in the South Prior to 1860. New York, 1909.

> Brings its subject down to the date of the Civil War.

BROWN, E. E. The Making of our Middle Schools. New York, 1903.

> Has excellent chapters (iv–xii) on the academies and (xiii, xiv) on the rise and growth of high schools. Contains a useful bibliography.

COON, C. L. North Carolina Schools and Academies, 1790–1840. Raleigh, 1915.

> A documentary history of secondary education in North Carolina for half a century. Very valuable.

CUBBERLEY, E. P. Public Education in the United States. Boston, 1919.

> Chapter VII is useful supplementary reading for this chapter.

GOODSELL, WILLYSTINE. "The Education of Women," in Twenty-Five Years of American Education (I. L. Kandel, Editor). New York, 1924.

> Deals with developments for the quarter-century from 1898 and existing conditions.

GOODSELL, WILLYSTINE. The Education of Women. New York, 1923.

> Includes a useful historical account.

GRIZZELL, E. D. Origin and Development of the High School in New England before 1865. New York, 1923.

> A useful study of the subject. Contains an excellent bibliography.

INGLIS, ALEXANDER. Principles of Secondary Education. Boston, 1918.

> Chapter V deals with the development of secondary education.

INGLIS, ALEXANDER. The Rise of the High School in Massachusetts. New York, 1911.

> A good account of the high school in that state.

KLEIN, ARTHUR J. Higher Education, *Bulletin No. 34*, United States Bureau of Education. Washington, 1927.

> A biennial survey covering the years from 1924 to 1926.

KNIGHT, EDGAR W. The Academy Movement in the South. Chapel Hill, North Carolina, 1920.

> Traces the development of this type of secondary school in the states that formed the Confederacy.

KNIGHT, EDGAR W. "Manual Labor Schools in the South," *South Atlantic Quarterly*, July, 1917.

> Traces the rise, spread, and final abandonment of this experiment in education in the Southern states.

KNIGHT, EDGAR W. Public Education in the South. Boston, 1922.

> Chapter IV describes academies in the Southern states, the manual-labor schools, and the work of John Chavis.

KNIGHT, EDGAR W. Public School Education in North Carolina. Boston, 1916.

> Chapter IV gives an account of the academy in that state.

REISNER, EDWARD H. Nationalism and Education since 1789. New York, 1922.

> Chapters XV–XVIII contain material bearing upon this chapter.

TAYLOR, J. M. Before Vassar Opened. Boston, 1914.

> A useful account of the early movement for the higher education of women.

TEN BROOK, A. American State Universities and the University of Michigan. Cincinnati, 1875.

> An account of the origin and growth of state universities to 1875, with Michigan as an example.

THWING, C. F. A History of Higher Education in America. New York, 1906.

> Gives accounts of the early colleges, the state universities, courses of study, and the education of women. Separate histories of the more important colleges and universities may be found.

WINDES, EUSTACE E. Trends in the Development of Secondary Education, *Bulletin No. 26*, United States Bureau of Education. Washington, 1927.

> Very suggestive of present conditions and tendencies.

QUESTIONS FOR STUDY AND DISCUSSION

1. In what respects was the academy in the United States a native product? In what respects was it an inheritance from Europe?

2. What were the characteristics of the academy? What were the results of the academy movement? Why did the academy disappear?

3. Consider the arguments advanced in favor of manual-labor schools. Were they sound arguments? Why did the manual-labor experiment fail?

4. Consider the curriculum which John Davis used in his academy in Virginia (p. 378) and notice how he undertook to develop in his pupils the love for reading.

5. In what respects may the work of John Chavis be considered remarkable?

6. Trace the academy movement in your state. Trace the development of public high schools in your state.

7. Point out the significance of the Kalamazoo case in the history of public high-school development in the United States.

8. List some of the problems of the public high school now.

9. What was Franklin's view of higher education?

10. What is the significance of the questions which members of the Junto were asked?

11. State the principle of law evolved in the Dartmouth College decision. Point out any connection between that principle and the Fourteenth Amendment to the Constitution of the United States.

12. What effect did the Dartmouth College decision have upon higher educational development in the United States?

13. Trace the development of higher education in your state, of higher education under public support and control, and of the education of women.

14. Make a study of medical education in the United States; of legal education; of technological education, including the land-grant colleges.

15. Trace the influence of inventions and of scientific research and discovery upon education in the United States.

16. Why did education for women develop so slowly in this country?

17. Point out some of the new problems in higher education and the solutions that are being suggested for them.

18. Account for the alarming extent of failures among college students. Offer suggestions for the improvement of this condition.

CHAPTER XIV

LATER PRACTICES

Outline of the chapter. 1. The low educational standards of the first half of the nineteenth century were due in part to the low standards of life in general.

2. Buildings were crude and equipment was meager, as reports of conditions in many places show.

3. Teachers were poorly prepared, and some of them were ignorant, but generally they were as competent as the standards of the times demanded.

4. Materials of instruction were meager and of poor quality, and uniform texts were slowly provided. The spellers, primers and readers, arithmetics, grammars, histories, and geographies help to reveal the theories of the period.

5. Complaints of the slave states against the textbooks of the time finally led to the preparation and publication of books for use in Southern schools.

6. The school rules of the period show the severity of discipline of the time.

7. Schoolmasters were often turned out of their schools. The practice of boarding the teachers around among the homes of the children was common.

In Chapters VI–XIII, inclusive, attempts were made to describe the educational promise of the late colonial and early national periods, to indicate some of the more potent forces which produced the principles of the American school system, to describe the ante-bellum awakening and the work of some of the leaders in that movement, and to trace the growth of public educational support and control, the training of teachers, and the extension of public educational effort beyond the elementary school. The present chapter undertakes to give a general account of actual educational practices during a large part of the nineteenth century. But

411

the difficulties in the way of an adequate report on practices, especially for the earlier part of the century, are
numerous. An abundance of competent material is not
easily available. The poor system of bookkeeping in use,
when any was used at all, prevents an intelligible account
of the fiscal features of schools; local school officials, either
ignorantly or negligently, often failed to keep proper records,
and the reports of state educational officers were often irregular and indefinite. However, a study of the material
available affords a view, if a somewhat imperfect one, of the
physical equipment, of the teachers, of the materials and
methods of teaching, and of other practices which help to
reveal the standards of the time.

Low standards. If the modern student is shocked at the
reports of the ugly conditions which surrounded school
children in the early nineteenth century, he should consider
the conditions which also surrounded adults and life in
general. Standards of education could not be high among a
people whose standards of living were low, who knew few
comforts and many deprivations, and among many of whom
the decencies of life were so often neglected. Most of the
schoolhouses as late as 1860 were of the meanest kind, but
it should be kept in mind that at that time four fifths of the
people of the United States lived in rural areas and that
probably "half of these dwelt in log houses of one or two
rooms." Intellectual life was bottomed upon old notions,
many of them little more advanced in 1860 than at the
beginning of the century. For most Americans sin was the
same as Satan, who was active in destruction; there were
two worlds, and this was not one of them: one was high
above, and the other was correspondingly deep below. Sick-
ness was looked upon as a visitation of Providence; mos-
quitoes, flies, and other pests were regarded with complacency; many diseases which have since been controlled
took heavy tolls on life; and filth and vermin abounded.

Provisions for baths were exceedingly rare even in the cities, and when a president of the United States placed a bathtub in the White House in the early fifties the innovation aroused a storm of protest. Legislators tried to pass laws against bathtubs. Governing authority in Philadelphia failed by a few votes to enact an ordinance prohibiting bathing between November 1 and March 15, Boston required on behalf of the public health that baths should be taken only when prescribed by a physician, and even the medical fraternity assailed the practice as a menace to health and predicted epidemics of rheumatic fevers and inflammation of the lungs. It was a time when the wildest ideas of dreamers and reforming cranks included temperance, the abolition of human slavery, and the emancipation of women; when the public held a heartless or indifferent view toward physical defectives and confined the insane "in cages, closets, cellars, stalls, pens; chained, naked, beaten with rods, and lashed into obedience," as Dorothea Dix found conditions in Massachusetts in the early forties; when young and old were herded indiscriminately in unspeakably filthy jails, — the most depraved criminals and little children who were held guilty of petty offenses being thrown together. Under conditions such as these it was not strange that the public should also neglect the health, the morals, and the minds of children in school.

Buildings and equipment. The early American schoolhouses were neither charming nor comfortable, and most of them were located among surroundings inviting neither to body nor to mind. Localism operated in this as in other educational matters, each district or neighborhood having full freedom to do as it pleased without let or hindrance from a superior unit. It determined the kind of schoolhouse it would have and where it should be erected, just as it determined the kind of teacher and the length of the school term. Generally the schoolhouses in the rural districts were located in waste and wild spots which the plow had deserted to broom sedge and rabbits. The records abound in accounts of ugly and cheerless places as sites for schools. In the villages or more populous communities they were sometimes placed in some snug corner near the churchyard and the cemetery, and at recess times the boys could decorate the erect headstones or leap along the flat-laid slabs "without touch grass." A community which drove a large trade in pork had a killing place only a few feet from the door of the school where scores of pigs in a single day died for the general good of the community. The squeals of the pigs outside often rose high above the general murmurs of the noisy children inside the house, for many of the schools in the early days were known as "loud" schools, the children being required to repeat their lessons aloud while memorizing them. The superintendent of a North Carolina county, reporting to State Superintendent Wiley in 1857, "had but one thing to regret, that so few of the districts taught a *silent school*. I told the teachers that I had no power to reform; this belonged to the district committees. But I used every effort which reason and fair argument suggested, to remove the prejudice which exists on that subject. Some two thirds of the districts teach a *noisy* school."

Log houses. In remote rural communities the schoolhouses were constructed of logs, the chinks being stopped with wood and daubed with clay. One end of the typical house of the early days was almost wholly taken up with a fireplace. The chimney was constructed of billets of wood, and was only partly protected from the fire by a thick lining of clay. In the other end of the room was the only window, an opening which admitted both air and light at the same time. Toward the end of the ante-bellum period the fireplace began to yield to the unjacketed stove, which occupied the central position in the room. On one side of the house was the door, which creaked on wooden hinges, and near it there hung a forked stick which served as a pass to all whom nature or idleness had rendered uneasy. No one ever dared to leave the room, however urgent the call, when the forked stick was missing from its peg. The other side of the house was minus a log, the vacant space serving to light the general writing desk, a plank extending horizontally the entire length of the room. During the routine of the day every pupil was required at a given signal to take his copy book, place himself at this desk, and set about the task of learning to write. The rough benches on which the children were forced to sit trained them to early habits of self-denial, if not mortification of the flesh, in support of the popular disciplinary doctrines of the time. The feet of many of them never rested on the floor, and little was their relief when the forked stick was missing.

The log house which was used for school purposes in Virginia by John Davis had one room and a half and stood on blocks about two feet and a half above the ground, and under it the hogs, the dogs, and the poultry of the neighborhood came and went freely. The ceiling and walls were unlathed and unplastered and indifferently covered. Davis also used the house for sleeping quarters, and in rainy seasons was compelled to move his bed to the most comfortable corner. The house had only one window, "but no glass nor shutter. In the night, to remedy this, the mulatto wench who waited on me contrived very ingeniously to place a square board against the window with one hand, and fix the rail of a broken-down fence against it with the other. In the morning when I returned from breakfasting in the 'great big house,' (my scholars being collected), I gave the rail a forcible kick with my foot, and down tumbled the board with an awful roar. 'Is not my window,' said I to Virginia, 'of a very curious construction?' 'Indeed, indeed, sir,' replied my fair disciple, 'I think it is a mighty noisy one.'"

Typical conditions of early schoolhouses. Samuel C. Goodrich ("Peter Parley," as he called himself on the title-

pages of his numerous textbooks) gives a description of a
school he attended in New England in the early nineteenth
century which may aptly fit the schools in practically all
sections of the country at that time and in most sections
until much later. The surroundings were bleak and desolate,
loose, squat stone walls inclosed the fields close by, and
briers and pokeweed flourished in the gravelly soil. The
schoolhouse was of the rudest construction. The fireplace
was six feet wide and four feet deep, and the chimney flue
was "so ample and so perpendicular that the rain, sleet, and
snow fell directly to the hearth. In winter the battle for life
with green fizzling fuel, which was brought in lengths and cut
up by the scholars, was a stern one." Often the fuel, "gushing with sap as it was, chanced to let the fire go out, and as
there was no living without fire, the school was dismissed,"
to the joy of the scholars. The children were all seated on
benches made of slabs or "outsides," which were supported
by four straddling wooden legs set into auger holes. Somewhat earlier Robert Coram described as wretched the buildings used for schools throughout most of the United States,
"sorry hovels, neither wind-tight nor water-tight; a few
stools serving in the double capacity of bench and desk, and
the old leaves of copybooks making a miserable substitute
for glass windows." In most of the schoolhouses of the
ante-bellum period the rafters above furnished the boys
noble exercise in climbing when the teacher chanced to be
absent for a few minutes.

In New York. "The great majority of the schools" of
New York State in 1844 were officially described as naked
and deformed, in comfortless and dilapidated buildings, with
"unhung doors, broken sashes, absent panes, stilted benches,
yawning roofs, and muddy mouldering floors." . . . Only
one third of the schoolhouses were reported in good repair,
another third "in only comfortable circumstances," while
more than 3300 "were unfit for the reception of either man

or beast." About 6000 lacked convenient desks or seats, nearly 8000 lacked "any proper facilities for ventilization," and 6000 were destitute of "facilities for securing modesty and decency." Approximately 600,000 children were in "these miserable abodes of filth and dirt."

In Connecticut. In more than seven eighths of all the schoolrooms officially visited in Connecticut in 1841 "the amount of air per child was less than one half that considered necessary for the prisoners in the state prison at Wethersfield or the county jails of Hartford, New Haven, and Norwich." Other conditions of neglect were referred to as a "burning shame and a deep disgrace to the state. It is unworthy of a civilized country, and indicates a state of things that ought to exist only among savages." Only one of forty schoolhouses, found in a survey of one county in 1839, had any means of ventilation, although the average size of "these childpens was eighteen and a half feet long, seven and a half wide, and only seven feet high," and into each "was crowded an average of thirty children." *The Common School Journal* called this condition "the slave-ship stowage of children" and contrasted the schoolhouses with the pens with "promenades," which the enterprising farmers were providing for hogs.

In other New England states. New Hampshire in 1847 made little if any better showing. "Multitudes" of its schoolhouses were described as "absolutely dangerous to health and morals," in the flourishing villages as well as in the countryside. A survey in Rhode Island in 1844 revealed the fact that only 312 of the 405 schools which were supposed to exist under the law of the state could be found, and most of these were in bad condition. Massachusetts did not seriously suffer in this respect by comparison with the other Eastern states, although of twenty-nine "rich and populous towns" which failed in 1838 to maintain schools as required by law only two complied with it in 1839. The schoolhouses of Maine and Vermont seem to have resembled those in other states. As late as 1857 Vermont had 760 which were described as "bad," "miserable," or "unfit for use."

Conditions slowly changed. If it was "the destiny of New England, and eminently so of New Hampshire, to produce mind" (as the chief school officer of that state complacently claimed in his report for 1847), that privilege of the section of the United States which has always had a pardonable pride in its schools must have been surrendered or adjourned during these years. If the physical conditions which surrounded the education of children there were as bad as they were reported, they were probably no better elsewhere in the ante-bellum period. And only slowly did conditions change for the better. Improvement in school equipment appeared first in the cities, where the most wholesome conditions are now generally found, for in this as in other educational matters the urban places have always taken the lead. The physical conditions of schools improved slowly in the rural areas, and even now some of them are deplorably deficient and dangerous to the health and morals of children. The average value of rural schoolhouses in the Southern states in 1900 was only one hundred dollars. One fifth of all the schoolhouses in North Carolina and Virginia at that time were of logs, and this condition was typical of the entire South. Only 168 of more than 7000 schoolhouses in Virginia in that year had modern provisions for ventilation. In 1914 there were 165 log hovels used as school buildings in North Carolina, which probably had made at that time greater progress in providing modern school equipment than any other of these states. A recent state school survey describes many schoolhouses for white children in a prominent state as dangerous and unfit for use; the drinking water used in a great many of them was found upon examination to be contaminated. Many of the old-fashioned and primitive one-teacher schools still remain — probably

150,000 of them, in which there are more than 4,000,000 rural children. There were more than 7000 of these one-teacher schools in New York State in 1925. The conditions in many of these small schools in many of the states are probably not much better than those recently found by the survey just mentioned.

The teachers. Chapter XII describes in a general way the conditions of teachers and teaching in the early schools; and some of these conditions had not greatly improved by 1860. Moreover, many of the teachers were probably quite at home in the unlovely physical surroundings of the schools they managed, in the later as well as in the earlier period, if the records are to be believed. Most of the teachers were home-grown, with meager preparation, and with almost no professional training, and some of them were positively ignorant. The professional training of teachers was slow to develop, and few teachers were in other respects prepared to give superior instruction. The wages were extremely small. Even in Massachusetts the average wages paid to a woman teacher were "on a level with those paid to the lowest in the mills," reports James Truslow Adams, "and only about one-half those paid to skilled female labor. The average wages, exclusive of board, paid to the women was $6.49 a month and to men $23.10," figures which do not vary very much for the other states. In 1838 county school authorities in Ohio complained "of the almost utter incompetency of teachers," and one of them reported that "of 156 examined 53 were very poorly qualified and but 51 understood, 'either wholly or in part,' geography, English grammar, and history. The county was compelled to accept them, else many schools would have been left without teachers." Similar conditions were reported in other sections of the country throughout the ante-bellum period.

Teachers as competent as the times required. However, the teachers were generally as competent as the standards of the time required, for then as now the average American community had as good teachers as it desired. According to official reports in 1844, many of the "self-styled teachers" lashed and dogmatized in "miserable tenements of humanity" in New York, and were described as "low, vulgar, obscene, intemperate, and utterly incompetent to teach anything good." But this was "the dark side of the picture in that state," as Catherine Esther Beecher reminded the readers of her "Evils Suffered by American Women and Children" (published in 1846), in which the wretched school conditions were described. It was to the credit of the chief school official of that state that he should present the facts in an effort to arouse resentment and a desire for improvement. But if the condition was so bad in New York, which, as Miss Beecher believed, "excels most of the other states in her care of education," "how much worse then must it be in those states where less is attempted!" In her praise of New York for not being "ashamed to search out her defects and publish them, that they may be remedied," she warned the states afflicted with complacency with what they had done against the danger of blindness to their educational needs. Those states which were behind New York "in efforts have a still more fearful reckoning yet to come," wrote Miss Beecher, who, in the light of what has happened in that state and elsewhere, showed the gift of prophecy.

The hard road of learning. Fortunate was the child who could make encouraging progress under such conditions as surrounded most of the schools, though the enterprising children were sometimes able to achieve the alphabet in a single session, as did Samuel C. Goodrich under "Aunt Delight, a maiden lady of fifty, short and bent, of sallow complexion and solemn aspect." Seated on a low chair, she called up the children one by one and required each "to make his manners" by giving a small, sudden nod, as a preliminary to lessons. Then she placed the spelling-book before the pupil and, with a penknife, pointed to each of the letters of the alphabet, inquiring monotonously "What is that?"

Many were the trials endured by the teachers in the grievous misprints and errors in textbooks, especially the arithmetics, and in those higher schools where Latin was taught the teachers often complained of the errors in the texts. A hard sum which the teachers might tug over for hours often turned out to have the answer wrong. In one case, which is probably typical of this kind of trouble, the teacher talked earnestly about the blunders in a certain book and commended the merits of Pike's "A New and Complete System of Arithmetic," which he had studied and considered the pink of perfection in figures. A copy of the treasure was found and borne by the children in triumph to the teacher. His eyes glistened with delight over the prospect that now the course of arithmetic would run smooth. The children soon learned that they "were still the sport of mischievous printers, and that every hard sum, even in Pike, had the answer wrong." The teachers who claimed proficiency in Latin often insisted upon the use of books which carried an English translation in columns parallel to the text. But they were prudent in their advice that the pupils place their hands over the English when they undertook to translate. This the pupils did if the English were completely memorized; but fingers were slippery when memory failed.

Some typical teachers. J. Marion Sims, the famous surgeon and gynecologist, learned his letters at the age of five and learned to spell in two syllables by the end of his first term, conducted in the summer of 1818 in South Carolina. His teacher was a Scotchman who often flogged the boys very severely "and stood some of them up in the corner with a fool's cap on." His teacher the following year was an Irishman of fifty-five years, tyrannical, a rigid disciplinarian, and sometimes cruel, who "was badly pock-marked, and had lost an eye by smallpox — otherwise a handsome man." He invariably flogged every boy, whether good or bad, the first day, and with great brutality. In an advertisement of Price's "Thrashing Machine," a school in Alabama somewhat later, Price, the thrasher, in announcing to parents the date of opening, urged them to "send me your devils and incorrigibles and I will make good boys of them." If punishments could work the transformation, Price made good his promises, for he thrashed upon the slightest excuse.

"I spent the winter of 1842 in one of the counties west of the Blue Ridge, and concluded to make up a little school, which was my first attempt in that line," testifies one of the teachers of the period here considered. "In that day a man was regarded as competent to teach school if he could 'read, write, and cipher.' I met with a young man in the neighborhood who aspired to teach also, and he put me through a kind of examination, giving me some of his hard questions, his hardest being a sum in the Double Rule of Three, which I readily worked, and so my reputation was established. I commenced teaching, having scholars ranging from the little tow-headed urchin to the grown-up boy and girl. I had the old-style rules to govern the school, but exercised but little moral influence over it, for the reason that I was not moral enough to do so.

"I will not undertake to give an account of the morals prevailing there at that time, but will note a few incidents, by way of illustration. A little while after the school had gotten under way, among the day scholars there came a full-grown young woman who, after school was dismissed, wished me to go home with her, which I was too bashful to do, but promised to go the next evening, which I did, and found that her whole object in coming to school that one day was to get me to go to her home and write a love-letter for her to her sweetheart, who was a rowdy fellow, and who was in jail at that time. I wrote the letter as she dictated it, and it certainly was a most gushing affair."

Materials and methods. Immediately after the Revolutionary War many textbooks by Americans began to appear. The patriotic believed that the practice of importing books from England, which had so long and largely supplied the colonies, was very improper, because it involved the hazard of exposing the impressionable children of young democrats to the monarchical ideas and national prejudices of stubborn aristocrats. The result was an increase of books and of the subjects taught in the schools. The increase was slow at first, but by the end of the antebellum period there had been added to the curriculum of reading, writing, spelling, and arithmetic the three subjects of grammar, geography, and history, although these were by no means found in all the public schools in 1860 — only in the better urban schools. Orthography, good behavior, English language and grammar, and arithmetic had been added by Massachusetts in 1789 to the simple subjects of reading and writing, which had been named in the law in 1647; geography was added in 1826, and United States history three decades later. In 1822 a committee of the Free School Society of New York considered "the propriety of instructing some of the oldest, most orderly, and meritorious" of the children in schools under the direction of the society "in some of the higher branches of an English Education, say Grammar, Geography, History, Mathematics, etc.," and the change was made shortly afterwards. In 1831 Ohio gave cities and towns permission to add other subjects to the three R's, which had been specified in its first school law in 1825, and in 1848 geography and grammar were prescribed for all the schools. The state superintendent of schools in North Carolina recommended in the early fifties that women teachers be examined only in reading, writing, arithmetic, and spelling, but that men teachers be required, in addition, to take examinations in grammar and geography. These were considered advanced subjects, and county school officers often reported the number of "grammar and geography scholars" in each school. Reading, writing, arithmetic, spelling, grammar, geography, and history represented about all the subjects that typical public schools undertook to teach before the Civil War, and not all of them were so ambitious. Some attention, slight or otherwise, was also given to manners and morals, as the rules of the schools reveal.

Nondescript textbooks. Uniformity of texts was not common before 1860, and one of the evils which naturally resulted was the multiplicity and frequent changes of books, which caused unnecessary expense to parents and guardians. Teachers were often embarrassed by having large schools with nearly every child in a separate class. Those who had a special interest in educational advancement occasionally urged the adoption of uniform texts in an effort to drive out poor books, to prevent frequent and unwise changes, and to aid in developing a form of student classification and grading which was not otherwise possible. Although so-called uniform texts were not officially adopted generally before 1860, occasional "lists" were suggested or recommended by state school authorities.

The "Old Blue Back." The most famous of all spelling texts was Webster's, popularly known as the "Old Blue Back," which was in wide use in the schools of this country until comparatively recent years. This book and scores of other texts which appeared during the ante-bellum period were intended or used not only for the purpose of teaching spelling, but also as primers, readers, moral instructors, and guides. For two decades after its appearance Webster's book bore the high-sounding title of "The First Part of a Grammatical Institute of the English Language." Later the name was changed to "The American Spelling Book," and later still to "The Elementary Spelling Book." Each printer who

published the book varied minor parts of his issue according
to his own fancy: one issue carried a portrait of "The
Father of his Country," and another bore a woodcut of
the author which "made him look like a porcupine." When
the first edition was in preparation Webster had to give
bond to guarantee the printers against any possible losses;

but in 1817 one publisher gave the
author "three thousand dollars a
year for his term of copyright,
and another gave forty thousand
for the privilege of publishing editions for fourteen years." At the
time of the author's death, in
1842, a million copies of the book
were being distributed annually.
The book may even now be obtained from one of the prominent
American publishers.

NOAH WEBSTER. JUN. ESQ.

PORTRAIT IN AN EARLY EDITION
OF THE "OLD BLUE BACK"

The influence of this book is
difficult to estimate. Spelling became a fad almost simultaneously
with its appearance, and "spelling bees" soon came to be a very
popular school exercise. The "Old
Blue Back" was generally the
first book put into the hands of the child when he entered
school, and often it was the only book many children ever
studied. The reading lessons in it were intended "to com-
bine, with the familiarity of objects, useful truth, and practical principles." A moral catechism on humility, revenge,
industry, sobriety, pride, honesty, and other subjects, and
short stories (each with a moral appended) were some of its
other features.

Other spellers. Comly's "New Spelling Book," published at Philadelphia in 1806, was also widely used as a

reader as well as a speller. The reading matter was of a more or less serious nature, which was a characteristic of nearly all schoolbooks of the period. One of the first thoughts which the youth met in this book was "All of us, my son, are to die." Another widely used speller was Hazen's "Symbolical Speller and Definer," which appeared in 1829. The principle on which it was prepared was *Verba explicantur symbolis,* and the work seems to have been intended to supplant certain spellers in which difficult words occurred "before the pupils could acquire sufficient knowledge of letters to read them with facility." The principle of pictorial representation was also used in the book, and connected with each picture were several words which rimed with the name of the object represented. Certain advantages were claimed for this arrangement, since "in learning to spell, the sounds of the letters and the forms of the words are the chief objects of recollection."

Primers and readers. Numerous also were the primers, many of them following the pattern of their illustrious predecessor the New England Primer, which had such a long and active life. "The American Primer,"a little book of seventy-five pages, was also popular. The reading lessons which it contained consisted of short stories illustrating obedience, goodness, love, mercy, forgiveness, and fondness for school, for books, and for parents and playmates, much religious verse, and numerous moral tales. The list of reading books was even larger than that of primers. Reading, together with writing and ciphering, occupied the major portion of the curriculum during that time, and almost any printed matter which could be furnished the children served as a textbook on the subject.

The ambition of all readers was to assist young people to read with propriety and effect, to improve their language and their sentiments. "and to inculcate some of the most important principles of piety and virtue." Purity, propriety, and elegance of diction characterized many of the selections included in the readers. These included narrative selections, didactic pieces, argumentative selections, descriptive selections, pathetic pieces, dialogues, and public speeches suitable for purposes of declamation. "The New York Reader," also popular, contained selections from the Proverbs, the Psalms, Hume's article "On History," select sentences concerning "God and his attributes," the story of Cain and Abel, the story of Job, and Pope's "Universal Prayer." Some of the readers contained instructions on the principles of good reading : the "proper loudness of the voice," distinctness, the due degree of slowness, pronunciation, emphasis, tones, pauses, and the proper manner of reading verse.

Arithmetics. Because of the high esteem in which mathematics was held as a practical science, arithmetic occupied a very important place in the curriculum. In the very early period children received some instruction in the subject upon entering school, in some cases before their fourth birthday. Mental arithmetic was recognized as a separate subject, and in some schools two periods a day were often given to arithmetic from "the third or fourth grade to the eighth, inclusive." An instructor in institutes in New York and Massachusetts said in 1866 that it was the all-absorbing study in the public schools throughout the country, and "occupies more of the time of our children than all other branches united." In this, as in reading, a wide variety of texts were in use. Of these Colburn's "First Lessons in Intellectual Arithmetic," Dilworth's "Schoolmaster's Assistant," and the works of Pike and Jess were used most extensively. Colburn's book, the result of practical work which the author had done as a teacher of mathematics and tested in actual use before publication, possessed a merit not always found in the texts of the time. Barnard's *American Journal of Education* said in 1856 that the book "enjoyed a more enviable success than any other schoolbook ever published. . . . It has been said to be 'the only faultless schoolbook that we have.' It has certainly wrought a great change in the manner of teaching arithmetic." It was one of the best examples of the early adoption of Pestalozzian methods in this country. Dilworth's text appeared much earlier than Colburn's and went hurriedly through many editions. Two other arithmetics, also very popular, were "A New and Complete System of Arithmetic," by Nicholas Pike, and "The American Tutor's Assistant," by Zachariah Jess.

Pike's book. Pike's work, first published in 1788, was the first book of "its kind composed in America." It was very comprehensive and exhaustive, and although it was too difficult for use in the lower schools, it went through many editions and was very popular and widely used. In 1840 it was reported in use in half the counties of Virginia, and about the same time a book store in Raleigh advertised that a hundred copies had just been received for sale. The comprehensive character of the book appears in the large number of subjects treated in it. A partial list shows, in addition to the usual arithmetic processes, such topics as the extraction of the biquadrate root; pensions in arrears at simple interest, barter, alligation medial; pendulums; a perpetual almanac; the time of the moon's southing; how to find the year of indiction, how to find the value of gold in the currency of New England and of Virginia; a table of values of the sundry pieces in the several states; comparisons of the American foot with the foot of other countries; a table of dominical letters according to the cycle of the sun; how to find the dominical letter according to the Julian and Gregorian methods; a table by which Easter could be calculated from the year 1753 to the year 4199; plane geometry; "plane rectangular trigonometry"; "oblique angular trigonometry"; algebra; conic sections; and "the proportions and tonnage of Noah's ark."

Many of the riddle-like and puzzling exercises reveal the emphasis placed upon the disciplinary values which were then claimed for arithmetic. The following examples serve to illustrate :

How many barleycorns will reach from Newburyport to Boston, it being forty-three miles?

How many days since the commencement of the Christian Era?

How many minutes since the commencement of the American War, which happened on April 19, 1775?

How many seconds since the commencement of the war, April 19, 1775, and the independence of the United States of America, which took place July 4, 1776?

Nine gentlemen sat at an inn, and were so pleased with their host, and with each other, that, in a frolic, they agreed to tarry as long as they, together with their host, could sit every day in a different position; pray how long, had they kept their agreement, would their frolic have lasted?

A gentleman making his addresses in a lady's family, who had five daughters: She told him that their father had made a will, which imported that the first four of the girls' fortunes were together to make £50,000, the last four £66,000, the three last with the first £60,000, the three first with the last £56,000, and the two first with the two last, £64,000, which if he would unravel, and make it appear what each was to have, as he appeared to have a partiality for Harriet, her third daughter, he should be welcome to her: pray, what was Miss Harriet's fortune?

An ignorant fop wanted to purchase an elegant house; a facetious gentleman told him he had one which he would sell him on these moderate terms, viz., that he would give him a penny for the first door, 2 d. for the second, 4 d. for the third, and so on, doubling at every door, which were 36 in all: It is a bargain, cried the simpleton, and here is a guinea to bind it; pray, what would the house have cost him?

Ciphering books and slates. Probably because of the scarcity of texts in the early period the ciphering book was the common method used to teach arithmetic. This was a blank book made of a quire of paper folded and sewed together, and often crudely bound in cloth or cardboard, similar to account books of the present. Most of the ciphering books were homemade, though children of the well-to-do often had the "store bought" kind. The teacher had his own, which he had himself made when he was learning the science of ciphering, and from it he set sums for his pupils. For each sum was a rule for its solution, and with sums set and rules given, the pupils usually were left to their own initiative and effort, for they received little or no help from the teachers, most of whom had little or none to give. When the pupil had completed the work the answer was shown to the teacher, who compared it with his own. If identical, the work received the teacher's approval, and it and the rule were ordered copied in the pupil's ciphering book; but if not identical, the pupil had to do it all over again.

Before slates came into use the ciphering was done on scraps of paper, often of very coarse quality. "The old gentleman, as usual, took out his manuscript, compared the slate with it, and pronounced it wrong," so a typical record runs. The boy returned to his seat, reviewed his work, and finding no error in his computation, took it again to the teacher, who growled at the boy, compared the work with his own manuscript and finally exclaimed: "See here, you nurly [gnarly] wretch, you have got it 'If four tons of hay cost so much, what will seven tons cost?' when it should be 'If four tons of *English* hay cost so and so.' Now go and do it all over again." "His master sets him a sum in addition," says another description of the method used, "and it may be tells him he must carry one for every ten; but why, is a mystery which neither master nor scholar gives himself any trouble about; however, with a deal of pains, he at length gets his sum done, without ever being asked, or knowing how to read the sum total, or any number expressed in the statement.

"But it is ciphering, and that is sufficient. If he is taught to commit any of the rules to memory, he learns them like a parrot, without any knowledge of their reason, or application. After this manner he gropes along from rule to rule, till he ends his blind career with the rule of three; and in the end, the only and truest account he can give of the whole is, that he has been over it. But he has completed his school education, and is well qualified to teach a school himself the next winter after."

Not much knowledge or skill in the subject was expected of teachers in those days. "I shall not forget," said a teacher referring to his first experience with an examination (which the law required to be conducted by the three county commissioners instead of the township trustees) to test the fitness of candidates to teach. The only question asked him was What is the product of 25 cents by 25 cents? "We had only Pike's arithmetic, which gave the sums and the rules," but such a problem could not be found in the book. "The examiner thought it was $6\frac{1}{4}$ cents, but was not sure. I thought just as he did, but this looked too small to both of us. We discussed its merits for an hour or more, when he decided that he was sure I was qualified to teach school, and a first-class certificate was given me." The records reveal other evidence of the low standards of the time.

Grammars. Grammar was not generally required in the ante-bellum schools; the teachers were not examined on it, and the subject was therefore not widely taught. Textbooks on grammar did not, like geographies and histories, serve well as readers, and for this reason the subject was somewhat late in finding a place in the curriculum. The early texts were unduly intricate and difficult to explain or to understand, and the subject was regarded as meaningless and dreary. The prefaces of many of the early works were often apologetic and deplored the general lack of interest in the subject.

"The Father of English grammar." Lindley Murray, who is known as the "Father of English grammar," published his first book on grammar in 1795. It became popular immediately not only in England but in America, where (especially in the higher schools) it was so extensively circulated that Murray's name soon came to be a household word. Although it was a work of considerable merit for the time the book was severely criticized "for its obscurity, blunders, and deficient presentation of etymology." One of Murray's friends said to him, "Of all the contrivances invented for puzzling the brain of the young, your grammar is the worst." Later, however, Murray's "Grammar," "Exercises," and "Key" came to be regarded as standard texts, and they maintained that position for many years. The book went through fifty editions, and an abridgment of the original work had more than a hundred and twenty editions of ten thousand copies each. The primary purpose of this work was to teach the correct use of spoken and written language and to assist the more advanced pupils "to write with perspicuity and accuracy." But another purpose of the book, as of many grammars of the period, was to furnish moral instruction, which was sought through examples of principles and rules and exercises under them.

Kirkman's book. Kirkman's "English Grammar" followed Murray's very closely in plan, but avoided some of the errors which the latter work contained. Its illustrations were apt and lent themselves to clearness and comprehension of the principles illustrated. The book sought to be "of practical utility in facilitating" the mental progress of youth, but it presented no attractive graces of style to charm, no "daring flights" to astonish, and no deep researches to gratify the literary connoisseur. It undertook, on the other hand, to make interesting and delightful a study which was regarded as tedious, dry, and irksome. In "Hints to teachers and private learners" the author said that he hoped to help abolish the absurd practice of causing learners to commit and recite definitions and rules "without any simultaneous application of them to practical examples." The final instructions to the young learner were: "Become learned and virtuous, and you will be great. Love God and serve him, and you will be happy."

Methods in grammar. In the main the book sought to teach the pupils what they should not say rather than what they should say in speaking and writing. In one column appeared the "improper" words, and in another the "correct" words, thus:

aint	are not
haint	have not
taint	'tis not
baint	are not
maint	may not
waunt	was not
woodent	would not
mussent	must not
izzent	is not
wozzent	was not
hezzent	has not
doozzent	does not
tizzent	'tis not
whool	who will

Among the numerous provincialisms and vulgarisms which Kirkman said were common in the spoken language in New England and New York were the following:

I be goin. He lives to hum.	I am going. He lives at home.
Hese been to hum this two weeks.	He has been at home these two weeks.
You haddent ought to do it.	You ought not to do it.
Yes I had ought.	Certainly I ought.
Taint no better than hizzen.	'Tis no better than his.
Izzent that are line writ well?	Is not that line well written?

The following errors were reported as common in Pennsylvania:

I seen him. Have you saw him? Yest, I have saw him wunst; and that was before you seed him. I done my task. Have you did yours? No, but I be to do it. I be to be there. He know'd me. Leave me be, for Ime afear'd. I wish I haddent did it; howsumever, I don't keer; they cant skeer me. Give me them there books. He ort to go; so he ort. I diddent go to do it. Don't scrouge me. I know'd what he meant, but I never let on.

The following expressions were mentioned, with their corrections, as belonging to Maryland, Virginia, Kentucky, and Mississippi:

Tote the wood to the river. Have you focht the water? Carry the horse to water. He has run aginst a snag. Is that your plunder, stranger? I war thar, and I seen his boat was loaded too heavy. Whar you gwine? Hese in cahoot with me. Did you get shet of your tobacca? Who hoped you sell it?

Teachers deficient in grammar. "Grammar has been attended to very indifferently, in our town schools, for all past time," reported the committee of Provincetown, Massachusetts, in 1843, although the law of the state required the teaching of the subject. "There are but few scholars who study it at all, and few indeed who have made much proficiency in it." And in the same year the school officials of Westport reported that as there were some schools in which grammar had never been taught, and "few or none who wish to pursue it ... for these reasons the committee has been urged to grant certificates to teachers deficient in grammar," although over in New Hampshire a county official in 1839 believed that "a portion of the time now devoted to grammar and arithmetic ought to be spent in the proper study of mankind." Clerks of county examiners in Ohio about the same time complained of the incompetency of teachers in grammar, geography, and history. A decade later conditions had improved somewhat, although complaint was still made and continued to be made for several years.

A large number of texts in grammar were sold annually about the middle of the nineteenth century, but they were used generally in schools of the "larger and more prosperous towns, and at best only in a perfunctory way in the schools of smaller communities." During the first half-century of the national period the rote method of teaching largely dominated, attention being given to memorizing, to the correction of false syntax, and to parsing — practices transferred from those customary in the study of Latin grammar. During the next quarter of a century these traditional methods still prevailed, but efforts were made to make the children understand the subject, to use visual and oral instruction, and to give some practice in composition. A large number of the schools provided no opportunity for composition, because "not one teacher in ten can write with tolerable ease and correctness," said William B. Fowle, in an editorial in the Massachusetts *Common School Journal* in 1852. In an institute in that state two years before "we required 117 teachers to write what they could in fifteen minutes on 'happiness.' At the end of fifteen minutes, but seven teachers had done anything, and four of these had requested to be excused from writing. Three more periods of fifteen minutes were given, and only twenty teachers had been able to write anything in the end. How can such teachers give instruction in English Grammar?" he asked. Meantime, however, changes both in the conception of the purpose of grammar and in the methods of teaching it were being made slowly. The change in theory is illustrated in statements made in 1823 and in 1847. At the earlier date Goold Brown said of his text, "The book itself will make anyone a grammarian." He maintained that "the only successful method of teaching grammar is to cause the principal definitions and rules to be committed thoroughly to memory." In 1847 Samuel S. Greene, also the author of a text on the subject, held that "the only successful method of obtaining a knowledge of the art is by means of construction and analysis." But many years were to pass before grammar was to be humanized, many pedagogical wars waging in the meantime over the subject.

History. History also found a late place in the elementary school, largely because the higher institutions were tardy in recognizing its value in the course of study. Before 1850 instruction in the subject was provided in the colleges in connection with other subjects, usually philosophy and English. Its value as a means of furnishing a broad interpretation of the world was not recognized, nor was it believed that history was capable of making direct appeal to human interests, to curiosity, to the imagination, of developing enlightened patriotism, or of strengthening intellectual habits. Many of the early texts contained neither maps nor illustrations, and the methods of teaching history, the function of which was conceived as ethical and religious, were often unsound for such purposes.

Although some cities had included the subject in their courses of study earlier, history was not generally taught before the Civil War. The numerous texts on the subject before that date indicate, however, that it was used, though perhaps largely for practice in reading. One history of the United States and three of New England had appeared by 1821, and during the next decade eleven histories of the United States and three state histories had been published. Most of these and subsequent texts were often in merest outline, a plan which characterized many of the texts on the subject until near the close of the nineteenth century. Moreover, teachers were poorly prepared to give instruction in the subject, which must have been only imperfectly understood by the children.

Early texts in history. The preface to one of the earliest texts stated that "while our schools abound with a variety of reading-books for children and youth, there has never yet appeared a compendious history of the United States fitted for our common schools." In 1828 Goodrich's (Peter Parley) "History of the United States" appeared, and although this text was popular and widely circulated, it too was deficient in illustrative material and continued so until 1832, although numerous editions of the work appeared in the meantime. In that year an improvement was made in the book. In the same year Noah Webster published a "History of the United States," in which he discussed, among other things, "our English ancestry from the dispersion at Babel, to their migration to America." The work did not extend beyond the adoption of the Federal Constitution, however, because "an impartial history cannot be published during the lives of the principal persons concerned in the transactions related, without being exposed to the charge of undue flattery or censure; and unless history is impartial, it misleads the student, and frustrates its proper object."

THE FIRST AMERICAN GEOGRAPHY [1]

A chapter on "Advice to the Young," intended to "serve, in a degree, to restrain some of the common vices of our country," showed the moral purpose of the subject.

Geography. Geography slowly acquired a high position in the courses of study. It had received little attention in the public schools of New England before the second quarter of the nineteenth century, even the higher schools there and

[1] From Clifton Johnson's "Old Time Schools and School Books." (The Macmillan Company.)

elsewhere neglecting the subject until far into the century. When it first appeared in the lower schools it was not treated as a separate subject, nor was it intended to furnish a knowledge of world movements, of current events, or of the economic and commercial relations of man. The early texts were encyclopedic in character, and the dictionary type of information which they contained was used largely as memory exercises. The books also served as readers and histories rather than as means of learning about the earth as the home of man. There is evidence also that the early geography texts were intended to furnish moral instruction. If ministers seem to have been more numerous than others as authors of the early texts the explanation is probably to be found less in the fact that they were among the best-informed classes than in the fact that theology and geology must not clash. The Mosaic explanation of the origin of the world was accepted by most first-rate people.

Morse's text. The pioneer text on geography was by Jedidiah Morse. It appeared first in 1784, and a few years later appeared his "American Universal Geography," which claimed to be "a view of the present state of all the empires, kingdoms, states, and republics in the known world, and of the United States in particular." Several revised editions were issued, and by 1800 the book contained about fifteen hundred pages. In his introduction to an edition of 1793 Morse commends an English text, Guthrie's "Geographical Grammar." This book stood high in the estimation of Americans, among whom it had had a wide circulation. However, Morse thought its deficient and false descriptions of the United States and its disproportionate accounts of Great Britain were capital faults, and that the American youth should be protected from such books. "There is no science better adapted to the capacities of youth, and more apt to captivate their attention than geography," declares Morse, who deplores the neglect of this part of their education, and "the want of suitable books on the subject has been the cause." With this lament he found (as have scores of textbook-writers since his day) excuses enough for another book on the important subject, and "in the following sheets" he endeavored to bring the important "branch of knowledge home to the common schools, and to the cottage firesides," to accommodate it to school use as a reading book,

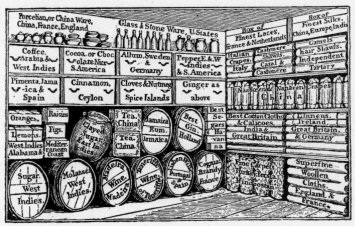

FRONTISPIECE OF WILLARD'S GEOGRAPHY FOR BEGINNERS (1826)

Exhibiting the products of various countries

"that our youth of both sexes, at the same time that they are learning to read, might imbibe an acquaintance with their country, and an attachment to its interests."

But the material in the sheets which followed was an unorganized mass of statements, many of them inaccurate and otherwise subject to some of the criticisms Morse had made of Guthrie. "These geographical treatises," said a contemporary critic, discussing the books of the time, "form a mere aggregation and index of rich materials, a lexicon rather than a true textbook. And therefore ensues, despite the undenied interest of the subject and its high claims, the mechanical and unfruitful method only too common —

the crowding of the memory without judgment, without thought." And this remained the type of geography used in the schools until the influence of the German geographer Karl Ritter (1779–1859) made its way into this country and helped to make Pestalozzian principles known. True, Jesse Olney published in 1828 his "Geography and Atlas," which passed through many editions, some of which numbered eighty thousand copies. Olney was one of the first teachers in this country to adopt Pestalozzi's principles in the teaching of geography. He helped to initiate the idea of home geography and recommended the use of maps, pictures, diagrams, and atlas, and the importance of introducing the beginner to "the town in which he lives."

Peter Parley's texts. Attempts to make geography interesting to children were made by Peter Parley (Samuel G. Goodrich), who used geographical rimes in his books. Another feature of his "Method of Telling about Geography to Children," which appeared in 1829, was its moral and religious character. "The flood, or deluge," he says, "took place about 1650 years after the world was created; that was more than 4000 years ago. The history of the Jews, which is related in the Old Testament, is continued from the time of Noah to the birth of our Saviour, which was 1829 years ago. The history is exceedingly interesting, and perfectly true. The early history of almost all other nations is a great part of it false; but the Bible tells us nothing but what is worthy of belief." Another chapter told of the birth of Christ. "Let us never, never, forget to hold in deep reverence the name of the one who has been such a benefactor to the world." And the final sentences in the concluding chapter were: "Let us fear to do wrong, because God can punish us. Let us love to do right, because God will reward us."

New and improved methods of writing and teaching geography were slowly becoming known in the United States by the close of the ante-bellum period through reports of travelers to Europe. Later these methods were made increasingly popular through the work of Arnold Guyot, the Swiss who had studied under Ritter, who came to Massachusetts in 1848 and served until 1854 as inspector and institute lecturer for the Board of Education of that state, and who in the latter year became professor of geology and physical geography at Princeton; and of Colonel F. W. Parker, whose effective educational services in Massachusetts and Illinois were very conspicuous during the last quarter of the nineteenth century.

Geographical jingles. An interesting feature of instruction in geography was the practice of singing out facts, the names of the states and their capitals, and the names of the rivers on which these were located, chanted generally "with no change in the words, but with a rising inflection at the end of the first line, and falling at the end of the second." The numerous variations improvised on this form sometimes revealed "the inventiveness of teachers or others musically or poetically endowed." There is some evidence that the alphabet and the multiplication tables were some times sung, and occasionally, "if the teacher wanted to air the room, we would all march up and down the aisles singing (to the tune of Yankee Doodle) 'five times five is twenty five and five times six is thirty'; and so on up."

This old method was used far beyond the ante-bellum period and in some states even until the nineties or perhaps later. In his "Method of Telling about Geography to Children," Peter Parley had made use of rimes which were to be repeated by the pupils. One of them began:

> The world is round, and like a ball
> Seems swinging in the air,
> A sky extends around it all,
> And stars are shining there.

And after listing many matters treated in the subject:

> And now geography doth tell,
> Of these full many a story,
> And if you learn your lesson well,
> I'll set them all before you.

A text of 1851 contained a song about the various states, somewhat different from the chants which became so popular; it gave details of climate, population, products, or any peculiar characteristics, and was to be sung to the tune of "Auld Lang Syne," according to Mark Sullivan, who has reported in "Our Times" (Vol. II, chap. iv) many examples of geography as it was chanted. The same textbook offered compilations of other geographical information, which were arranged in verse and adapted to popular tunes of the time.

Examples of the method, which the children enjoyed, and which was believed to be an aid to memory, included:

> Maine, Augusta, on the Kennebec.
> New Hampshire, Concord, on the Merrimac.
>
> Vermont, Montpelier, Montpelier, Montpelier,
> Vermont, Montpelier, the capital Montpelier.
>
> Massachusetts, so they say,
> Has Boston East upon its bay.
>
> New Jersey, with its fruits so fair,
> Has Trenton on the Delaware.
>
> New York, so they say,
> Has on the Hudson, Albany.
>
> Delaware, Dover, on Jones's Creek, Sir!
>
> North Carolina, famous for tar and turpentine and gold,
> Its capital is Raleigh, by River Neuse controlled.
>
> California, Sacramento (la-si-la-sol-la-si-do),
> And this comprises all, sir (la-si-do-si-re-do-do).

State of Maine, Augusta,
  Tol-le, rol-le, rol-le.
New Hampshire, Concord,
  Tol-le, rol-le, rol-le.

Now the peninsulas we sing,
Alaska leads the rime.
Then Melville, Nova Scotia,
A-comes, all in the Northern clime.
In Southern regions, Florida,
With Yucatan, we meet,
Then California follows next,
To make the list complete.

So round and round each bay and sound,
Each mountain, cape, and river,
So round and round the world we bound
In concert all together.

Writing. Perhaps the only fine art taught in the typical public schools in the period here considered was handwriting, and courthouses today contain interesting evidence of the success of the instruction. The superior handwriting in which deeds and wills of the period were often copied arouses admiration in this day when documents, public and now increasingly private, are done by typewriter. But in the early days school children were encouraged "in the pursuit of the useful and elegant accomplishment of writing," and the teacher who could write a copperplate hand and flourish angles and corkscrews, even while balancing himself on one leg, had standing to speak of in the neighborhood and was as much in favor as a celebrity in ciphering who knew his tare and tret.

In the days when the children wrote from copies in the teacher's handwriting, much of his time was consumed in setting copies and in making or mending quill pens, although in some city schools twelve-year-old children were expected to know how to make their own. The practice of setting

copies with pens or on slates was not uncommon in rural
schools until near the close of the nineteenth century. With
the introduction of copy slips (the first American set was
probably Caleb Bingham's, published in 1796) the teaching
of writing consumed less of the teacher's time. When blackboards came in (probably as early as 1809, although they

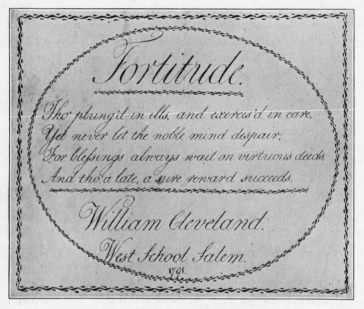

EXHIBITION PIECE OF A STUDENT'S WRITING
Courtesy of the Essex Institute

were not in common use until much later), one copy could
be set for a number of pupils, who counterfeited it as best
they could. The copies were usually statements of moral
sentiment, such as "Aim at perfection," "Honesty is the
best policy," "Waste not, want not." Old schoolbooks also
testify to an interesting by-product of the practice: by
way of relaxation from the assigned tasks in writing the
children often ornamented their books with many scribblings.

Motivation in writing. The ambition to write well seems to have been strong in the common schools as well as in the private schools, where it was especially encouraged. The orator at the first commencement of Henry Dean's Writing School in Salem, Massachusetts, in 1804, after speaking at length to the parents, praised the girls, who were permitted to attend the summer session, for the exhibit of their improvement in writing, and extolled the art as one "of remote antiquity, highly ornamental, and of the most extensive utility. By this art all others are preserved, disseminated, and perpetuated. . . . So great and manifold are the advantages derived from it, that many wise and good men have concluded that it was not of human but divine origin." This ambition to write well was sustained also by rigid discipline. The danger of slips, blunders, blotches, and mistakes in spelling and marking was increased by the manner of keeping the ink. Before the days of patent desks and inkwells the ink was kept in small bottles, which were easily upset. Often, with the stoppers lost, the children put in cotton, not infrequently enough to absorb the ink, which had to be squeezed out. A mark or a sprawl consequent upon a fragment of cotton sticking to the pen was for many children a sad experience.

The slave states and textbooks. Many years before the close of the ante-bellum period, as the agitation over slavery became heated, more and more complaints were heard in the South against books which had been prepared and published in the North. The complaints were loudest against the books used as readers. As early as January, 1844, the *Southern Educational Journal*, one of the first educational magazines published in Alabama, advertised a series of readers which "have been carefully revised and freed from all objectionable pieces." The objection to the readers then in use was that they were "made by people whose political institutions differ from ours, and thrown upon the children of the South." At a meeting of the Southern Commercial Convention, held in Savannah in December, 1856, and composed of delegates from the Southern and Southwestern states, a committee was requested to take the subject of schoolbooks under consideration and to select and prepare a suitable series of books in "every department of study, from the earliest primer to the highest grade of literature and science, as shall seem to them best qualified to elevate and purify the education of the South." In this action appeared evidence of the growing sectionalism of the period. "We can, and we must print, publish, and teach our own books; we must not permit our foes to compose our songs and prepare our nursery tales, reserving for ourselves only the privilege of framing husky statutes, and holding commercial conventions." From that time until the outbreak of the Civil War efforts were increased in the South to prepare the texts used in that section and to encourage Southern publishing enterprises.

Confederate texts. During the war the Southern states undertook to supply their own school textbook needs, and many of the books published in that section bore such sectional titles as "The Confederate Primer," "Dixie Primer," "The Confederate Ryming Primer," "The Southern Primer," "The Confederate Speller," "The Dixie Speller," "The Dixie Reader," "The Southern Confederacy Arithmetic," and "The Geographical Reader for the Dixie Children." There were also grammars, books on foreign languages, dictionaries, catechisms, and hymnbooks, and a "Confederate edition of the New Testament." Extracts from a primary geography arranged as a reading book for the common schools and published in Raleigh in 1864, illustrate the temper of the time. Under the caption "The United States" the children were taught this:

This was once the most prosperous country in the world. . . . In the meantime both English and American ships sent to Africa and brought away many of those poor heathen negroes and sold them for slaves. Some people said it was wrong and asked the King of England to stop it. He replied that "he knew it was wrong; but that slave trade brought much money into his treasury, and it should continue." But both countries afterwards did pass laws to stop this trade. In a few years the Northern States, finding their climate too cold for the negro to be profitable, sold them to the people living farther south. Then the Northern States passed laws to forbid any person owning slaves in their borders.

Then the Northern people began to preach, to lecture, and to write about the sin of slavery. The money for which they had sold their slaves was now partly spent in trying to persuade the Southern States to send their slaves back to Africa. And when the Territories were settled they were not willing for any of them to become slaveholding. . . .

In the year 1860 the Abolitionists became strong enough to elect one of their men for President. . . . So the Southern States seceded. . . .

This country possesses many ships, has fine cities and towns, many railroads, steamboats, canals, manufactures, etc. The people are ingenious and enterprising, and are noted for their tact in "driving a bargain." They are refined and intelligent on all subjects but that of negro slavery; on this they are mad."

Under the title "Southern Confederacy," the children were taught this:

This is a great country! The Yankees thought to starve us out when they sent their ships to guard our seaport towns. But we have learned to make many things; to do without others. . . . The Southern people are noted for being high-minded and courteous.

The following questions and answers were intended to serve as a review of the reading selections in the book:

Q. What kind of men should we elect to govern our country?
A. Good and wise men.
Q. Why?
A. "When the righteous are in authority, the people rejoice; but when the wicked beareth rule, the people mourn."

Q. Where do you learn this?

A. From the Bible.

Q. Will God curse a nation because of wicked rulers?

A. He says he will.

Q. Has the Confederate States any commerce?

A. A fine inland commerce, and bids fair, sometime, to have a grand commerce on the high seas.

Q. What is the present drawback to our trade?

A. An unlawful Blockade by the miserable and hellish Yankee Nation.

Discipline and rules. The rigidity of discipline, evident in the numerous rules which were considered so indispensable for even the smallest schools, reflect the prevailing theories of the period. They were established upon a theology and a penal code little less severe and brutal than men had lived and died under in earlier days. Most of these rules require no comment nor explanation, so clearly do they speak for themselves. Those in a school in one of the Southern states included the following:

The punishment shall consist of whipping, slapping in the hand with the rule, riding the ass, and expulsion, according to the gravity of the offense.

All boys and girls may laugh, without noise, when anyone is mounted on the ass, but no one shall speak to him, or make gestures or ugly mouths at him, in token of derision.

When the master tells an anecdote the students are not bound to laugh immoderately, though it will be considered respectful to give some indication of their being pleased or amused.

Whenever one enters or leaves the house, if a boy he shall bow, and if a girl courtesy, to the master, and when a stranger comes in all shall rise and do the same toward him.

When the boys meet a stranger on the road they must take off their hats and bow: they are enjoined to be, on all occasions, respectful and attentive to their seniors and not to talk in their presence except when bidden.

Every boy shall consult the comfort and convenience of the

girls before his own, and whoever is caught standing between a female and the fire shall be whipped.

If a boy is caught laughing at the homeliness of a girl or calling her ugly names, he shall ride on the ass.

Giggles are detestable, and when a girl is amused she must smile gracefully, or laugh out; and if the master catches anyone snickering he will indicate and reprimand her in the presence of the whole school.

Every offender, when called on, must fully inform on himself, remembering that by telling the truth he palliates his offense.

When the master's rule falls at the feet of anyone, he and all his guilty associates must come with it to the teacher.

The master will inflict on every common informer the punishment due to the offense of which he maliciously gives information.

As it is God who gives the mind, and as he has bestowed more on some than on others, it shall be considered a grave offense to laugh at or ridicule anyone who is by nature dull or stupid, such persons being entitled to general commiseration rather than contempt.

The girls must remember that the exemptions to which their sex entitles them are to be used as a shield, and not as a sword; and they are therefore enjoined to eschew the abominable and unlady-like habit of indulging in sarcasm and attempted wit at the expense of the boys. Whenever a girl loses the docility, gentleness, and benignity becoming her sex, she forfeits her title to the forbearance and deferential courtesy of the males.

No one shall, out of school, speak disrespectfully of the master or of a fellow student.

No one shall ridicule, laugh at, or make remarks about the dress of another; the boys are enjoined to be kind and courteous to the girls, the girls to be neat and cleanly in their dresses, and all to act as if they were brothers and sisters — the children of the same parents.

Let the words of the preacher be held in constant remembrance, "Remember thy Creator in the days of thy youth."

The punishment of riding on the ass was generally inflicted for long-continued and gross neglect of study, vulgarity of manners, and insults to girls. The culprit, wearing a large pair of leather spectacles on his nose and a paper cap on his head with the inscription "Fool's Cap" in Roman letters, was mounted astraddle one of the joists, being assisted up by a few cuts of the master's switch, which sometimes played at intervals across his legs during the hour that he held his seat. This punishment was inflicted only on the male pupils.

Another set of rules, signed by the teacher and carefully learned by the children, prescribed the punishments for each infraction. The rules are reproduced here exactly as the teacher wrote and numbered them in 1848:

No.		Lashes
1.	Boys & Girls Playing Together	4
2.	Quareling	4
3.	Fighting	5
4.	Fighting at School	5
5.	Quareling at School	3
6.	Gambleing or Beting at School	4
7.	Playing at Cards at School	10
8.	Climbing for Every foot Over three feet up a tree	1
9.	Telling Lyes	7
10.	Telling Tales Out of School	8
11.	Nick Naming Each Other	4
12.	Giving Each Other Ill Names	3
13.	Fighting Each Other in time of Books	2
14.	Swaring at School	8
15.	Blackgarding Each Other	6
16.	For Misbehaving to Girls	10
17.	For leaving School Without Leave of the Teacher	4
18.	Going Home with each other without Leave of the Teacher	4
19.	For Drinking Spirituous Liquors at School	8
20.	Making Swings & Swinging on Them	7
21.	For Misbehaving when a Stranger is in the House	6
22.	For waring Long Finger Nailes	2
23.	For Not Making a bow when a Stranger Comes in or goes out	3
24.	Misbehaving to Persons on the Road	4
25.	For Not Making a bow when you Meet a Person	4
26.	For Going to Girls Play Places	3
27.	Girles Going to Boys Play Places	2

No.	Lashes
28. Coming to School with Dirty face and Hands	2
29. For Caling Each Other Liars	4
30. For Playing Bandy	10
31. For Bloting Your Copy Book	2
32. For Not making a bow when you go home or when you come away	4
33. Wrestling at School	4
34. Scuffling at School	4
35. For Not Making a bow when going out to go home	2
36. For Weting Each other Washing at Play time	2
37. Girls Going to Boys Play Places	2
38. For Hollowing & Hooping Going Home	3
39. For Delaying Time Going home or Coming to School	4
40. For Not mak.g a bow when you Come in or go Out	2
41. For Throwing Any Thing Harder then your trab ball	4
42. For Every word you mis In your Hart Leson without good Excuse	1
43. For Not Saying yes Sir & no Sir or yes marm or no marm	2
44. For Troubleing Each others Writing affares	2
45. For Not washing at playtime when going to Books	4
46. For Going & Play.g about the Mill or Creek	6
47. For Going about the Barn or doing Any Mischief about the Place	7

The following rules of a school in an Eastern state indicate that it was under the control of the Society of Friends, and the ninth rule in the list reflects an effort to inculcate in the young a humaneness that seems not to have been common at the time:

1. The scholars are to be at school at the hour appointed with their faces and hands washed and their heads combed.

2. They are with cheerfulness and attention to observe the instructions of the Tutors, and always pay them due respect.

3. They are to study their lessons in silence, and to avoid unnecessary conversation with each other in school time.

4. They are to behave themselves at all times in a gentle obliging manner, becoming virtuous children. The boys to treat the girls with that manly respect and decency which is due to their sex; and the girls the boys with a becoming reserve and modesty.

5. If disputes at any time arise among them, they are not to use provoking words or blows, or give way to a sullen or revengeful temper, but report the matter to be decided by the Master.

6. They are carefully to observe true grammar, plainness of speech in using the singular number to a single person, and in every other respect avoid such additions in their address to others as are inconsistent with truth.

7. And in regard to their conduct when out of School, it is desired that the scholars may duly attend our religious meetings and when there behave with stillness and sobriety.

8. That they do not spend their time on first days in sports or any way that tends to disturbance.

9. That they carefully avoid speaking evil of anyone, treating aged persons with disrespect, making a mock of the lame, deformed, or those deprived of their senses.

10. That they do not throw sticks, stones, dirt, or snowballs at any person or dumb creature; but behave themselves modestly, civilly and kindly to all.

11. That they avoid such amusements as are noisy, dirty, or dangerous, and all such as arise from a covetousness of each others property.

12. That they not only shun all indecent behavior in themselves, but the pernicious conversation of others, especially the shameful and exceedingly sinful practices of lying and swearing.

Rules for the government "of the common school in District No. 47," in Stanly County, North Carolina, less than three years before that state joined the Confederacy, follow exactly as they were signed by J. F. Stone, the teacher, after they had been "read, approved and adopted."

Art. 1st Each scholar will present him or herself at school with face and hands clean, and hair combed.

Art. 2d When they arrive at school they will take their books and seats, and be studying their lessons, whether their teacher arrived or not.

Art. 3d In book time they will not laugh or talk, but mind their books, and study their lessons.

Art. 4th No scholar will be allowed to go out more than once for each lesson they recite (unless in cases of extreme necessity) the males one at a time, the females not more than two at a time.

Art. 5th At play time the males and females will not associate with each other in any play or pastime.

Art. 6th At all times and on all occasions they will avoid cursing and swearing, lying, stealing, quarelling, fighting, wrestling, climbing trees, throwing rocks at random, or using any vulgar or profane language such as liar, fool, etc.

Art. 7th Telling tales out of school without first acquainting the teacher with what may take place or happen, is out of order and should be avoided.

Art. 8th Going home with each other of evenings without the permission of parents and teacher will be a violation of the rules of school.

Art. 9th Private property is sacred to the owner; therefore any encroachment on the enclosure of any citizen will be a violation of social order and the rules of this school.

Art. 10th In going to and from school the several scholars are required to keep the strictest rules of order, and not be whooping, hallowing, and playing by the way, as bad children frequently do.

Art. 11th Should one of your parents or other persons visit the school, as they enter the door you will rise from your seats to do them honor.

Art. 12th Any grown scholar who will not submit to the above rules and refuse to be corrected for a violation of the same, will be expelled from the school.

Few evidences of gentleness. Not often does the student find evidences of gentleness in ante-bellum educational practices. Reforms in school discipline were to come much later. Apparently also little effort was made to adapt the work of the school to the varying capacities of the children. However, "the happy medium in the education of children is not to overburden them, nor leave them at liberty to be idle," suggested a writer in New Jersey before the end of the eighteenth century, in hints which were "only speculative," because he had never had "an opportunity of reducing them to practice." But he believed that something could be done to make the work of the school "less difficult" and "more agreeable" for the children. If they are overburdened "they will despair and dislike their studies," he said, and if they are left in idleness they are "apt to meditate and do mischief and disturb the school." Among other things he suggested that the children be divided into classes, "also to read according to their different abilities, that each may be a help to the others, and their equality be a stimulus to extol." Two of the eight suggestions which he made for the management of a school are suggestive in this connection :

Every regulation should be well considered and approved before it is proposed to the children and then an implicit observance should mildly be exacted, and in every part of the government of the school it is necessary for the children to obey with punctuality, which if kindly but firmly required will become habitual and easy to them, and its good aspects in the stillness and decorum of the school be manifest to all.

In order to give the master time to examine the cypherous works, mend pens, inspect the copies literally as they are wrote, for which end he should have them brought to him every two lines, attend minutely to the children's reading, and to every other part of good order, with as little interruption as possible, it will be best to have the cyphering and copy books left at the master's desk every evening, that he may set the sums, rule and set the copies for the next day or lay out the pieces for them ; this, though it will employ some time between evening and morning school, will make his task much more easy in school hours, prevent the confusion incident to the master being hurried there, and will assist him to that calmness and leisure absolutely necessary for the right oversight of a school and improvement of the pupils.

Turning out the teacher: boarding around. "Nothing but the bulldog" in resolute teachers could keep down rising storms toward the end of term time or as holidays approached, as Edward Eggleston so accurately shows in "The Hoosier Schoolmaster"; for in Indiana as elsewhere in the early days, and in some of the more pioneer places until after the Civil War, the boys "turned out" the teacher if he had not granted the customary holidays, which were generally deducted from his time. Many schools were broken up in this manner by big and burly boys, even in sedate Massachusetts and even as late as 1837. In Eggleston's classic example the struggle for the mastery in Indiana was between the teacher, who had intended to grant a holiday if he was asked to do so, and Hank Banta, "the ringleader in the disaffection," who had managed to draw into it "the surly Bud," who was in favor of making the request before resorting to the extreme measure of barring the teacher out of the schoolhouse.

As the Christmas holidays began to draw near in a North Carolina school in the forties, it was talked around that the usual custom of turning out the schoolmaster was to be observed. When the crisis came he gave in and accepted the terms decided on — a treat of half a gallon of brandy for an eggnog, for his views on the liquor question were not so decided as were those of some of his successors in that state in after years. But the eggnog was described as a failure, because the eggs could not be had; but the brandy and the milk were put into a kettle and put on the fire, "and a kind of a stew was made that couldn't exactly be named, and it was thus dealt out to the crowd."

Another case, settled in a very different manner in South Carolina a little earlier, was witnessed by J. Marion Sims and reported in "The Story of My Life":

The first quarter of Mr. Quigley's school was about to terminate, and the big boys agreed to turn him out and make him treat before the beginning of the second quarter. It was the teacher's habit, every day, to take a walk of fifteen or twenty minutes, about eleven o'clock in the morning, calling to his desk some of the larger boys to keep order during his absence. No sooner had he descended the foot of the hill leading toward the spring than the three larger boys in the school began barricading the door. There was only one door to the cabin, and by taking up the benches, which were ten or fifteen feet long, and crossing them diagonally, one to the right and another to the left, in the door, the benches projecting as much outside as inside the house, a complete barricade was formed which could easily be defended against assault from without. When the old gentleman saw what had been done he became perfectly furious. He was so violent that he easily intimidated the ringleaders. He swore that he would not give up, and would not treat, and that he was coming into the house whether or no. At last he commenced to climb on the roof of the house, and to throw a part of it off. It was covered with boards held on by poles. The ringleaders, seeing that he was sure to effect an entrance anyway, became intimidated, and agreed to remove the barricade if he would promise not to whip them. After parleying a little while, he promised that he would not flog the ringleaders. He was a man of most violent temper, and, although fifty-five years of age, he was very strong and active. The ringleader of the gang was young Bob Stafford. He was tall, slender, and very strong; but was evidently afraid of the teacher, and showed the white feather decidedly. As Mr. Quigley came in he walked up to young Stafford, who stood trembling in the middle of the room, and said: "Sir," as he drew his big fist back, "I have a great mind to run my fist through your body!" I had always thought Mr. Quigley would do whatever he said, expecting every minute to see the old gentleman's fist come out through his back.

The practice of boarding the teacher around among the homes of his pupils was noted in Chapter IX as one means used by the neighborhood to help toward paying for his services. The custom was common in the rural district schools until the Civil War, in some sections of the country until much later, and in very recent years has been followed among some of the negro schools in the South. Under the arrangement some teachers fared better than others, but there is evidence that many of them were luckless.

It can be seen from the material in this chapter that the educational standards of the first half of the nineteenth century were low in the United States, as were also the standards of life in general. These low standards appear in the requirements or the lack of requirements of the time for buildings and equipment, for teachers, and for materials and methods of instruction. In some of these features of educational work the standards continued low, even after years of agitation for improvement. In others, however, much improvement has been made recently as a result of influences which will be treated in the last two chapters. Before those influences are taken up, however, attention is drawn in Chapter XV to the peculiar conditions in education in the Southern states.

REFERENCES AND READINGS

ADAMS, JAMES TRUSLOW. New England in the Republic, 1776–1850. Boston, 1926.

> Pages 363 and following supplement this chapter and cite useful references.

ARROWOOD, C. F. "The Backwoods School in American Fiction," *School and Society*, Vol. XXVIII, No. 718, September 29, 1928.

> An interesting account, with references.

CALDWELL, OTIS W., and COURTIS, STUART A. Then and Now in Education, 1845–1923. Yonkers on Hudson, 1924.

> An interesting description of school conditions of the past. The appendix contains valuable documentary material.

COON, C. L. North Carolina Schools and Academies, 1790–1840. Raleigh, 1915.

> Documentary materials which supplement this chapter.

CUBBERLEY, E. P. Public Education in the United States. Boston, 1919.

> Chapter VIII deals largely with practices. Contains suggestive references and questions for discussion.

DODD, WILLIAM E. Expansion and Conflict. Boston, 1915.

> Chapter XI gives an interesting general account of culture in the United States in the late ante-bellum period.

EGGLESTON, EDWARD. The Hoosier Schoolmaster. New York, 1892.

> Gives what is perhaps the best and most interesting picture of the backwoods school. Contains an excellent account of the practice of turning out the teacher.

FITZPATRICK, F. A. "The Development of the Course of Study in American Schools," *Educational Review* (January, 1915), Vol. XLIX, pp. 1–19.

> Traces historically the course of study in Boston.

JOHNSON, CLIFTON. Old-Time Schools and School-Books. New York, 1904.

> A very interesting account.

KNIGHT, EDGAR W. Public Education in the South. Boston, 1922.

> Chapter VIII deals with practices in the South before 1860. Contains a bibliography and questions.

KNIGHT, EDGAR W. Public School Education in North Carolina. Boston, 1916.

> Chapter X is on ante-bellum educational practices in North Carolina. Contains references and questions.

LONGSTREET, AUGUSTUS BALDWIN. Georgia Scenes. Augusta, 1835.

> In this book, which had later editions, appeared articles previously published in magazines and newspapers which tell of life in Georgia during the first half-century of the Republic. See also reference to Wade, below.

MAGRUDER, MARY. "Writing," *Journal of the National Education Association*, Vol. XV, No. 6 (June, 1926).

> A brief but interesting historical account.

MICHAUX, R. R. Sketches of Life in North Carolina. Culler, North Carolina, 1894.

> Contains information concerning school practices in North Carolina in the forties.

MONROE, W. S. Development of Arithmetic as a School Subject, *Bulletin No. 10*, United States Bureau of Education, Washington, 1917.

NELSON, A. H. "The Little Red Schoolhouse," *Educational Review*. Vol. XXIII, No. 3 (March, 1902), pp. 304–315.

> Describes "The Up Island School" of Eastport, Maine, near the end of the ante-bellum period.

REEDER, R. R. The Historical Development of School Readers and Methods of Teaching Reading. New York, 1900.

A valuable treatment of the subject.

SIMS, J. MARION. The Story of My Life. New York, 1885.

Contains good accounts of school practices in ante-bellum South Carolina.

WADE, JOHN D. Augustus Baldwin Longstreet. New York, 1924.

A study of the development of culture in the South, made round this man of varied talents and occupations, which throws much light upon intellectual conditions in the lower South. Contains a valuable bibliography.

WEEKS, STEPHEN B. "Confederate Text-books (1861–1865)," Report of the United States Commissioner of Education, for 1898–1899, Vol. I, chap. xxii. Washington, 1900.

A bibliography of texts used in the schools of the Southern states during the war.

WILEY, CALVIN H. Alamance, or the Great and Final Experiment. New York, 1847.

Chapter III describes school practices in North Carolina in the second quarter of the nineteenth century. Chapter V is on turning out the master.

QUESTIONS FOR STUDY AND DISCUSSION

1. Account for the opposition to bathtubs when they first appeared.

2. Why were so few of the early schoolhouses built in attractive places? How did the rough houses and equipment fit in with the prevailing disciplinary doctrines of the time?

3. Inquire into the condition of any remotely rural schoolhouses in your state now. How many one-teacher schools remain in your state? Why have the physical conditions of rural schools improved so slowly?

4. Consider the teachers of the period covered by this chapter. Does a community or a state now have as good teachers as it desires?

5. Under the discouraging conditions of the early schools the way of learning was hard for the children. Is there any danger in the tendency of modern pedagogy to provide many aids for the children?

6. What are the advantages of uniform textbooks? What are the disadvantages?

7. How are the books used in the public schools in your state selected? What is the meaning of "political adoption" of school textbooks?

8. Compare the old methods of teaching spelling with the methods in use today. What method is now considered the best?

9. What was the purpose for which arithmetic was taught in the ante-bellum period? What is the principal purpose now? Point out any value in the examples given from Pike's text (p. 429).

10. Compare the purpose and methods of early geography-teaching and the purpose and methods of the present. What was the value of the jingle method?

11. How have textbooks in grammar and the methods of teaching this subject changed in recent years? Consider these changes in the case of history.

12. Why did slates go out of use in the schools? Point out the changes that have taken place in the teaching of writing. Is attention to this subject likely to increase or to decrease?

13. Explain the persistence of severe discipline in school.

CHAPTER XV

UP FROM SLAVERY

Outline of the chapter. 1. A little more than three decades after the close of the Civil War the Conference for Education in the South was organized, and numerous meetings were held throughout that section, with far-reaching results.

2. Educational conditions in the South at the close of the last century were very backward, with short school terms, meager public educational expenditures, a high percentage of illiteracy, ineffective educational administration, and other defects.

3. Walter H. Page pointed out in "The Forgotten Man" in 1897 that war, reconstruction, economic destitution, racial conflict, partisan politics, sectarian dogma, and the aristocratic theory of education were the conditions through which men had been forgotten in the South.

4. The educational conservatism of the Southern states after the war was in part a heritage of the ante-bellum South, but the public school had been scorned as one of the fruits of reconstruction. Page issued a call to a "wiser statesmanship."

5. The Conference of Education in the South, the Southern Education Board, and the General Education Board were means of educational propaganda and of substantial educational support. Educational campaigns were conducted throughout the Southern states.

6. The work of these agencies had a wide practical influence on the improvement of education in the Southern states, but, notwithstanding the progress made, those states continued to rank low when compared with national standards.

7. The tendency to improve the administrative organization of public education has been stronger in the country at large than in the Southern states, which still have short school terms, irregular attendance, low salaries of teachers, considerable illiteracy, few libraries, and few opportunities for graduate study.

8. The educational progress of the Southern states since 1900 has been remarkable, measured by their own past records; but there are evidences of complacency, although educational inequalities are still very striking.

9. The Southern states, which are no longer poor, can attain to national standards in education, although the need for better school facilities is constantly increasing.

When Fort Sumter was attacked in 1861 the institution over which armies were to clash for four bitter years had been sanctioned in America by Church and State for nearly two and a half centuries. Thirty-six years later battle lines were again formed in the South, and again the issue was slavery; but this time it was slavery in a different form, although it also was heavily sanctioned by the centuries and assented to by Church and State. In 1861 the call to arms came from the presidents of two nations, and the demand was for soldiers and sailors armed with muskets and swords to tear at each other over the bondage of black men. In 1897 the call to battle came from an editor from the South and a preacher from the North, and the demand now was for humanitarians and unofficial statesmen equipped with facts and figures. Now North and South joined hands and united to break the bonds of multitudes of enslaved whites and blacks. A war of bloodshed followed the call of 1861, and the result is well known to every schoolboy in the land; but it was a war of enlightenment that followed the call of 1897, and few people within the scenes of that crusade and fewer without know how or why it began or what results it has achieved for Southern life and education.

WALTER H. PAGE

Whose speech "The Forgotten Man," aroused the Southern states to more active educational effort in the early part of this century

"The Forgotten Man." The editor was Walter H. Page. A native of North Carolina, but then living in the North,

he knew the South as few men of his time knew it. He h
learned at first hand of its resources and its weaknesses, its
callous spots and its sensitive spots, and all its other characteristics. Perhaps his place in the campaigns carried on to
restore and rebuild old commonwealths can never be fully
appraised; but one thing is clear: he gave to the cause of
education in the South "that one thing which is worth
armies to any struggling reform." He gave it a phrase so
simple that all men could understand it, a phrase capable
of living in the popular mind and moving it to action. For
"The Forgotten Man," the title of a speech which Page
made at a woman's college in North Carolina in 1897, became the rallying cry of a crusade against poverty and suffering, against ignorance and illiteracy, and against all the
ills which stalk in their steps.

The preacher was Edwin Abbott of St. James's parish,
Cambridge, Massachusetts. When Page, in frank and vigorous language, was describing the tragedy of the forgotten
man, Abbott was seeing the sad spectacle with his own eyes.
In an extended journey through the South during the summer of 1897 he saw the region in all its wretchedness: its
backward economic life, its meager facilities for schools, and
the despair of a people broken in spirit. The conditions
startled him and also deepened his interest in a part of his
country which had been crushed by misfortune and was still
helpless in its isolation. The need and opportunity for co-
operation, for mutual counsel and sympathy, and for constructive effort at once impressed him.

Genesis of the Conference for Education in the South.
In the writing room of a hotel at Capon Springs in the Blue
Ridge Mountains, near the boundary between Virginia and
West Virginia, Abbott told the proprietor, Captain William
H. Sale, something of the need of education in the South,
and proposed a plan for a conference of the friends of
the cause. Sale viewed the matter with interest and later

approved the plan. Abbott named a provisional committee on arrangements, a list of prominent people was drawn up and Captain Sale invited these to be guests at his hotel, a program was arranged, speakers were selected for the first meeting, and the Conference for Christian Education in the South, later changed to the Conference for Education in the South, came into being in the summer of 1898. This organization, established for the purpose of recalling and restoring forgotten men in the South, was unique in American educational history, and to its banner finally flocked thousands of men and women from many walks of life and from three fourths of the American states. Its services in the South and for the good of the whole country appear significant, however, when the conditions that surrounded the South's forgotten men are considered.

Backward conditions. When Page was speaking in 1897, 26 per cent (one in four) of the white people of his own native state were illiterate, to say nothing of the sheer illiteracy and dense ignorance that enveloped the negroes. Similar conditions were found in the other Southern states. At that time there was no adequate state school system anywhere in the South. The idea of education at public expense had not yet become a conviction there. Public education was not an interest of the average citizen. The tradition of education as a luxury and privilege for the rich and the well-born still lingered.

Some of the Southern states at that time were spending less than fifty cents per capita annually for the support of schools. In some of them school-teachers were receiving for their services less than the State allowed for the hire of convicts. From one fifth to one fourth of the schoolhouses were log — miserable tenements of humanity, unfit for man or beast, destitute of any facilities required by modesty and decency. Only one hundred and sixty-eight of more than seven thousand schoolhouses in Virginia had modern

THE UNIVERSITY OF GEORGIA IN ANTE-BELLUM DAYS

provisions for ventilation, and conditions were probably no better anywhere in the South; in fact, the ideal of the "log school" was not infrequently trotted out as a reproach to any suggestions of improvement. The annual school term ranged from sixty days to ninety-three. Less than 60 per cent of the children were enrolled in school and less than 40 per cent attended daily. Teachers were deficient in training, and county superintendents, and often city superintendents too, were lacking in training and leadership — briefless lawyers, broken-down preachers, hungry country editors. State departments of education were undeveloped, and state superintendents were clerks or pitiful political appendages — politicians, soldiers, patriots, or patrioteers. There was not a public high school of standard grade in the South, and not one Southern state had enacted any compulsory-school-attendance legislation. Legislative proposals on this subject were generally opposed by the argument that the time was not ripe for such an advanced step.

Higher education. The conditions surrounding higher education were not much better. The colleges and universities of the South, some of them old and high-spirited, did not rank along with those in other sections of the country. Whether state, private, or denominational, most of them were struggling for existence. Benefactions to higher education had not yet reached that section of the country in such quantity as they poured into the colleges and universities of other regions. All such institutions in the South had only one tenth of the productive funds of the colleges and universities of the United States, one seventeenth of the scientific apparatus, one seventh of the volumes in libraries, and one seventeenth of the total physical equipment. The annual income of one private university in the East alone exceeded the annual income available for higher education in eight of the Southern states. There were no important publishing houses in the South, almost no libraries, and established habits of reading among the masses were practically unknown. As a market for books the South was almost barren. Measured by any national standards of the time, Southern education of any grade or degree was forced to the bottom of the list, a condition that had prevailed for many years. Under such conditions it was inevitable that men should have been forgotten.

How men had been forgotten. But how had these conditions arisen? By what fate had so many men been forgotten? The answers are found in war, in reconstruction, in the economic destitution which resulted from these twin calamities, in the bitterness of racial conflict, in partisan politics, in sectarian dogma, and in the aristocratic theory of education. The dead hands of the past still rested heavily upon the South, and its forgotten men were content to be forgotten. Praised by politicians for virtues which they had had no opportunity to acquire, taught by tradition to hate all forms of taxes and to view with suspicion any suggestion for economic or social betterment, these forgotten men were a dead weight to progress. They were taught, and they believed, that what was good enough for their fathers was good enough for themselves and their children. It was not uncommon for preachers to join in the chorus and to tell the forgotten man that his poverty and wretchedness were in reality blessings in disguise, means of special grace. And if he became despondent and felt the need of consolation for his hopeless condition, he could have it from stump and pulpit, from both of which he was reminded that many of his kinsmen had been killed in war for the glory and honor of his state.

The war. No accurate and fair report can be given of the progress which the South has made in public education since 1898 without taking into account the fearful odds it faced at that time. Few if any people anywhere ever had to struggle with such stubborn obstacles. For a generation

1861 - 1865

economic desolation had made it difficult for the South to meet adequately its educational and other social needs. Four years of war had worked an almost complete economic collapse. Factories, public buildings, railroads, houses, barns, farm implements, even seeds for planting had been destroyed. Banks had been ruined. The labor system had been demoralized. State treasuries had been depleted, state credit lost, and for decades public finances remained in a perilous condition. These states had quickly become and had long remained a region of poor roads, of agricultural backwardness, of millions of unused acres, and of multitudes of mortgages. The masses of the people were often actually in want.

Reconstruction. Congressional reconstruction had followed the war and, not satisfied with robbing the South of the little which the war had spared, had run its fingers deep into the pockets of posterity. Upon the future generations of North Carolina it piled up a debt of more than $35,000,000, nearly one third of the total valuation of that state's property at that time. Upon Louisiana was heaped a debt of $40,000,000, upon Alabama $18,000,000, upon Tennessee $14,000,000, and upon all the Southern states more than $300,000,000. The proceeds from these bonds were not often used to repair and restore the waste places in Southern life; instead they were squandered, for the most part by venal and ignorant officials and legislatures, through hundreds of cases of flagrant fraud and extravagance. Thus crippled, the Southern states were unable to finance their own economic recuperation.

The tyrant Cotton. Added to the desolation of the period and the broken spirit of the people were millions of helpless and ignorant negroes who but yesterday were slaves, most of them destined to lives of day labor and farm tenancy. Cotton, which had been king in ante-bellum days, was now a despot. The South came to know little else but cotton, which, even under a system of tenancy, rapidly encroached upon fields formerly used for other Southern staples. Six of the ten leading grain states in the eighteen-thirties were in the South, but in 1900 only three of these ten states which produced most of the corn of the country were Southern. Agricultural diversity as a remedy for economic adversity had not yet been learned.

The efforts of the people to restore their economic life during these years were often tragic. Living expenses for thousands of humble families, both black and white, were borrowed to make cotton. Southern banks of slender resources borrowed credit from banks in the North and East and gave the promise to use it to raise cotton, the coming crop being given as security; from these Southern banks the local merchant borrowed on the same promise that the credit would be used to grow cotton, and from the local merchant the local farmer or landlord borrowed and used the credit himself or extended it to his tenant for the sole purpose of raising cotton. The cotton crop was thus mortgaged, often before it was planted, and its value was generally spent before the crop was harvested.

Under these crop-lien arrangements neither landlord nor merchant nor banker encouraged or permitted the tenant to raise food for the family or feed for the mule. The tenant bought provisions on credit with the landlord, who had the credit with the merchant, who had it from the local banker, who had it in the North or East, with time prices for provisions much higher than cash prices. When the cotton was picked the tenant was forced to sell it, no matter what the price, to the landlord, who owed the merchant, who owed the local banker, who owed the banker in the North or East. Farming on shares, cropping, crop liens, and tenancy formed a vicious cycle of economic despotism. Merciless forces daily drove agriculture more and more toward a base servitude and sent the curve of the curse of tenancy steadily upward. The South was in economic bondage, there was no sound basis for social reform, and public education was poverty-stricken.

Racial conflict. Another heavy handicap against which public education was struggling had its roots in racial conflict. Much of the misery of the South thirty years ago had resulted from the sudden and indiscriminate gift of the ballot, three decades earlier, to men unprepared for its proper use. The immediate political results of congressional reconstruction were startling, and the spectacles that followed for many years caused sober men to question whether true democracy involved universal suffrage. The price of political vice, corruption, villainy, and outrage seemed too great to pay for it. The negro was exploited by demagogues and designing politicians, and under the domination of his ignorance and irresponsibility there followed an orgy of riot and rascality, of frenzied and dissolute political revelry. Democracy quickly became no less a mockery than it had been in the ante-bellum days.

The negro continued a barrier to education in the South as public energies became more and more absorbed in the fierce conflict to eliminate him from politics. Intimidation, open bribery, the stuffing of ballot boxes, the manipulation and falsification of election returns, had developed into fine arts. By those and other illegal means the dangers of negro domination were somewhat averted during a decade or more after the close of reconstruction; but the negro vote continued dangerous because it was uncertain, and it was uncertain because it was generally purchasable. The wits of political factions among the whites were pitted against each other in the bid for their black brother's ballot. But the devices used were crude, unpleasant, and illegal. Open and avowed suppression of the negro vote appeared safer and much more respectable than fraud and chicanery if the methods chosen could be made to wear the color of legality. Finally, by means now well known, reconstruction was undone, and the ballot was taken from the illiterate negro. In the meantime, however, public education had been subordinated and often sacrificed to less worthy if more pressing interests. The education of both whites and blacks had fallen pitiably into neglect. Public schools could not be encouraged so long as public energies were required to wrest government and political power from ignorant negroes and their unconscionable allies.

STUDENT TYPES AT THE UNIVERSITY OF GEORGIA [1]

The picture at the left is of a student of ante-bellum days, and the son of a rich planter. In the center appears a student soldier. At the right is a student of the reconstruction period

Southern conservatism. To the economic ruin and the political chaos that marked the three decades immediately after the close of the Civil War must be added another obstacle which stood stubbornly in the way of public educational development. The conservatism of the South after the war was a heritage of the ante-bellum South, with its roots running far into the past. It was a difficult obstacle to remove because it was persistent and subtle. The Southern people had not neglected to provide for the training of leaders in the ante-bellum days. In 1860 there were nearly 26,000 college students in the South (not counting the large number of Southern students who were attending col-

[1] From E. M. Coulter's "College Life in the Old South." Copyright, 1928, by The Macmillan Company. Reprinted by permission.

leges in the East) in comparison with nearly 17,000 college students in the Northwestern states and about 10,500 in the Eastern states. The University of North Carolina ranked second in enrollment of students, with Yale heading the list. The University of Virginia and the South Carolina College were likewise influential institutions. But nowhere in the South had full preparation been made for the education of the masses. The old system of class education had not helped them. If Southern opinion on education under leaders such as Wise in Virginia and Wiley in North Carolina had not been so fully aroused as had opinion in New England under Horace Mann and Henry Barnard, it was due in part to the social conservatism of the South, grown strong under the influence of slavery, upon which the old landed aristocracy was established. Relics of the aristocratic structure of opinion loitered in the ruins for decades after the war.

Attitude of the South toward schools. In such an atmosphere it was not strange that education for all at public expense should not have been looked upon as a function of government in the South in 1898. Moreover, the public school, free and open alike to all, was scorned as one of the fruits of reconstruction. It promised equal opportunities to the plain people, who before the war had been counted among the underprivileged, in other sections of the country as well as in the South. The public school was now open also to the training of a people who recently had been in a state of legal servitude. "Your free schools," wrote a professor in a Southern college to his state superintendent of schools a few years before Page pictured the forgotten man, "like not a few of the other pretensions of radicalism, are in fact exactly opposite to the name falsely assumed." He argued that the principle by which "the State intrudes into the parental obligation and function of educating all children is dangerous and agrarian." The theory that the child

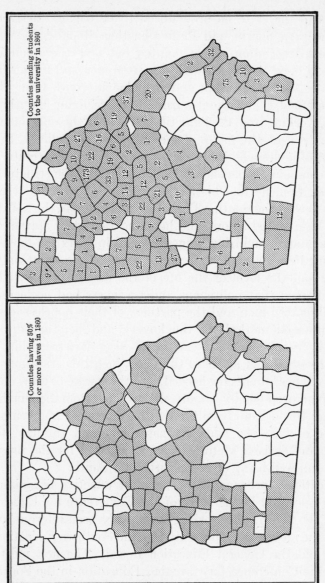

The figures on the map at the right show the number of students sent by each county in Georgia to the state university in 1860. Note that most of these were slaveholding counties, as shown by the map at the left. (From E. M. Coulter's "College Life in the Old South." Copyright, 1928, by The Macmillan Company. Reprinted by permission)

Counties sending students to the university in 1860

Counties having 50% or more slaves in 1860

belongs to the state he pronounced to be pagan, "derived from heathen Sparta and Plato's heathen Republic."

Page's description. Page pointed out how these conditions had filled the South with forgotten men and forgotten women — the latter "thin and wrinkled in youth from ill-prepared food, clad without warmth or grace, living in untidy houses, working from daylight till bedtime at the dull round of weary duties, the slaves of men of equal slovenliness, the mothers of joyless children — all uneducated if not illiterate." These common people should be considered in the structure of civilization, he told his audience, startled by a doctrine almost new in the South. True, here and there in the South it had been stated before, and here and there had appeared a quickening of civilizing influences, and in spots the movement for better schools had slowly gained force. But only a little had the level of the life of the masses been lifted. Page charged that politicians and preachers had neglected these forgotten men and the partners of their hopelessness, the dull-faced mothers of the hovel; and he, the editor from the South, issued a call to a "wiser statesmanship." Only the organized agencies through which this statesmanship could work were now needed, and these were to grow out of the plan proposed by Abbott, the preacher from the North. Through this organization the Southern people came courageously to face the odds against them, and through its work many decisive victories were to be won for the prosperity and well-being of both North and South.

Educational propaganda. The most effective organized agency appeared in the work of the Conference for Education in the South, whose origin has already been referred to, and in the movement represented by the Southern Education Board and the General Education Board. The first meeting of the Conference for Christian Education in the South (also known as the Southern Conference Movement and the Ogden Movement) was held at Capon Springs, West Virginia, and the Reverend T. U. Dudley, Bishop of Kentucky, an alumnus of the University of Virginia, and late Chancellor of the University of the South, Sewanee, Tennessee, was elected president. At the second conference, held the following year at the same place, the name was changed to the Conference for Education in the South, and Dr. J. L. M. Curry, general agent of the Peabody and Slater boards, was elected president. The third conference also met at Capon Springs, and Mr. Robert C. Ogden of New York, one of the most sympathetic friends public education in the South ever had, was elected to the presidency and served in that position for many years. To his generous enterprise, resourcefulness, and administrative wisdom much of the success of the conference was due. For several years he invited numerous people in the North who were interested in education to attend these annual meetings as his guests and provided special trains for their accommodation. In this way influential people of that section became acquainted with those of congenial spirit in the South and thus gained a safer knowledge of the perplexing problems and needs of Southern life.

Formal resolutions of the early conferences were significant. They dealt with the importance of thoroughness of elementary instruction, longer school terms, better-qualified teachers and better buildings and equipment, traveling libraries, and industrial education. Impressive also is this resolution of the second conference:

Resolved, That the education of the white race in the South is the pressing and imperative need, and the noble achievements of the Southern Commonwealths in the creation of common school systems for both races deserve not merely the sympathetic recognition of the country and of the world at large but also give the old and high-spirited colleges and universities of the South a strong claim upon a generous share of that stream of private wealth in the United States that is enriching and vitalizing the higher education of the North and West.

Succeeding meetings of the conference were held at Winston-Salem, Athens, Richmond, Birmingham, Columbia, Lexington, Pinehurst, Memphis, and other cities in the South. At the instance of the conference the Southern Education Board was organized in 1901 to aid in the development and the wise direction of educational sentiment and to help toward securing larger policies for education by appealing to the resources of taxation and local forces for self-development. The board neither held funds nor distributed them. Extensive and systematic field work was planned with Dr. J. L. M. Curry as supervising director, President Edwin A. Alderman, then of Tulane University, President Charles D. McIver of the North Carolina Normal and Industrial College, and President H. B. Frissell of Hampton Institute as district directors. President C. W. Dabney, then of the University of Tennessee, was selected as chief of the bureau of investigation, information, and publication; and the services of Dr. P. P. Claxton, then of the University of Tennessee, and Professor J. D. Eggleston, Jr., of Virginia were secured for the bureau of publicity, which was established at Knoxville.

Educational campaigns. The plans and purposes of this novel campaign for education met with the instant approval of the Southern press and with the practical support of the leading people at that time engaged in school work in that section. Able advocates of better schools came forward and enlisted their services in the movement: college and university presidents and professors, lawyers, business men, officeholders, and other builders of public opinion. The most practical school questions were discussed in the meetings which were now held throughout the South: better buildings, increased school funds, improved teaching, improved legislation for schools, and more effective educational organization and administration generally. People gathered in schoolhouses, churches, courthouses, public halls, in city and country alike, to hear discussions of the ways and means of improving education for their communities. Popular education was the theme before multitudes, and enthusiasm for it spread widely and grew warm among the people. In the meantime the General Education Board was formed (1903) for the purpose of wise and systematic coöperation with the Southern Education Board, to investigate, collect, and present actual facts concerning educational conditions in the South and to render financial assistance within the discretion of its trustees and the limits of its resources. Its services to education in the South have been large and varied and have formed a wise and effective demonstration of method.

The General Education Board. The work of the General Education Board in the South followed four main directions. Through the United States Department of Agriculture it made large contributions for the promotion of practical farming under an agreement begun in 1906. Demonstration farms were employed under supervision of demonstration agents, whose work was extensive and effective. State demonstration agents also conducted work among boys and girls under actual farming conditions through boys' and girls' clubs. The promotion of secondary education constituted another important service of the board, which appropriated to the state universities or to the state departments of education sums sufficient to pay the salaries and traveling expenses of high-school experts. Through this means hundreds of secondary schools were built and maintained. In addition to these services the board made gifts for higher education in the South, as well as in other sections of the country, to increase endowments and equipment. It also contributed largely to the support of negro schools, mainly those for the training of teachers, and appropriated funds for the expenses of rural-school supervisors, who worked under the direction of state departments of education in each of the Southern states, for the promotion of better educational, economic, and social conditions of the colored people. Other services of the board were rendered to medical education, to schools of education, and in helping to finance studies or surveys of state school systems.

The educational advance. The work of these agencies had at once a powerful and practical influence on educational development in the South. Active campaigns for better schools and for improved educational facilities generally were promoted, beginning in North Carolina in 1902, in Virginia in 1903, in Georgia and Tennessee in 1904, in South Carolina, Alabama, and Mississippi in 1905, and in Arkansas, Florida, and other states in 1908. Most of these campaigns were continued for several years with fruitful results. Improvements appeared in many ways: the educational provisions of the constitutions and laws were revised and strengthened, the school revenues were increased by 100 to 200 per cent in a decade, the improvement of schoolhouses was marked, the annual school term was lengthened to one hundred and twenty-one days by 1910, and the enrollment and average daily attendance increased. Illiteracy decreased, local taxes for schools multiplied, teachers' salaries increased considerably in comparison with those paid in 1900, progress was made in the training of teachers through state-supported normal schools and teacher-training agencies in institutions of higher learning, and the certification of teachers was put on a better basis. The revival movement also gave impetus to the development of high schools, which began to be established in rural communities as an integral part of the state school systems. Interest in the consolidation of the smaller schools into larger, better-graded, and better-equipped schools began to grow, rural libraries increased, school-improvement and parent-teacher associations were formed, child-labor and compulsory-attendance legislation appeared and was expanded, and supervision through a better type of county superintendent began to show improvement here and there in these states.

Gains made. By 1915 the average annual school term had lengthened to one hundred and thirty days. The average term for the United States in that year, however, was approximately one hundred and sixty days. The average annual salary of all teachers was $328 in the South and $543 for the country at large. The average annual expenditure per child of school age was $8.50 for the South and $22.19 for the United States, and the value of school property per capita of school population was $18 and $79 respectively. Approximately 72 per cent of the school population in the South was enrolled as against 74 per cent in the United States; nearly 69 per cent of the enrollment (50 per cent of the school population) was in average attendance in the South compared with 76 per cent of the enrollment (56 per cent of the school population) in the country as a whole. Out of 8906 public high schools reporting a four years' course of study in the United States in 1915, with an enrollment of 1,362,514 pupils (about 5 per cent of the school population), 1466 such schools with 150,607 pupils (about 2 per cent of the school population) were in the South. A study by the United States Bureau of Education in 1922 reported in the Southern states 1575 secondary schools, public and private, approved by the state departments of education and accredited by the state universities.

The low rank of the South. Notwithstanding the progress made, however, most of the Southern states continued to rank low among their sister states. Measured by attendance in elementary school and in high school, in length of term, and in expenditure (per child of school age, per child attending, and per teacher for salaries) they ranked among the forty-eight states in 1918 as follows: Texas thirty-sixth, Florida thirty-seventh, Virginia thirty-ninth, Tennessee fortieth, Louisiana forty-second, Georgia forty-third, North

Carolina forty-fourth, Alabama forty-fifth, Arkansas forty-sixth, Mississippi forty-seventh, and South Carolina forty-eighth. In that year the waste as a result of nonattendance, due to ill-prepared teachers and to lack of adequate child-labor and compulsory-attendance laws, was about 33 per cent, with 25 per cent as the corresponding figure for the United States. The percentage of the school population enrolled in high schools of all grades was 9.3 in the United States and 5.1 per cent in the South. The increase in teachers' salaries generally had been substantial, but the average annual salary paid to public elementary and secondary teachers in the South was less than four fifths of the average for the United States.

The explanation. The explanation of this low educational position is not hard to find. With limited funds the Southern states must provide two systems of education for large numbers of children scattered over wide areas. They had relatively a larger school population than the other sections of the country. For each thousand adult males in these states there were 1279 children of school age, whereas the corresponding average was 789 in the North and 600 in the West. Moreover, the estimated average true value of all property for each child of school age in the South was approximately one third that of the Northern states and one fourth of that of the Western states. In addition, there was the disadvantage of sparsity of population in the South. North Carolina, Tennessee, and Virginia were the only Southern states with more than ten white children. None had an average of ten colored children of school age to the square mile. Moreover, the policy of separate schools was accepted as permanent. In the Northern states the average density of school population was from three to ten times greater than that of the South, and in the Western states, where the school population was small, it was largely concentrated in the irrigated regions, the rich river valleys, and the mining towns and was not so widely distributed as in practically all the Southern states.

Those states were rapidly finding their duty, however, not in the measure of their resources for school support but rather in the measure of their needs for it. With less than normal power they had to bear abnormal burdens. Between 1900 and 1915 the increase in public-school expenditures for the United States was 180 per cent, in the South it was 280 per cent, and the policy of increased expenditures for the enlargement of educational facilities was rapidly coming to be accepted as permanent. The expenditures for public-school maintenance for the school year 1922–1923 for the states reporting were Arkansas $9,000,000, Florida $10,000,000, South Carolina $11,000,000, Georgia $15,000,000, North Carolina $20,000,000, Louisiana $20,000,000, and Virginia $22,000,000. Virginia had public-school property valued at nearly $33,000,000, an increase of nearly 400 per cent since 1910; and the value of schoolhouses erected in North Carolina during that school year was $25,000,000, nearly twice the total value of all school property in that state in 1918. The public schools of Alabama between 1918 and 1921 made 74 per cent as much progress as in the period from 1890 to 1918.

Reforms and tendencies. The tendency to improve administrative organization of public education had not made the same progress in the South, however, as in the country at large. Of the nine states in the Union still retaining ex-officio state boards of education, four were Southern states (Texas, Florida, Mississippi, and North Carolina), and all the Southern states except Tennessee still elected their state superintendents of schools by popular vote. In seven of those states county boards were elected by popular vote, and Texas, Florida, Mississippi, South Carolina, and Georgia continued to elect county superintendents of schools by that method. These latter officers were appointed by the county boards of education in North Carolina, Arkansas,

Louisiana, and Alabama by the county courts in Tennessee, and by the state board of education in Virginia. In theory the county was the unit of local school administration, but in practice it was the district, with many of its traditional functions, though there was a hopeful tendency toward making the county the unit for the support and direction of public schools. Of significance also was the intelligent manner in which several Southern states had approached these administrative problems through commissions to study and report on educational conditions.

With the enactment of a compulsory-attendance law in Mississippi in 1918 the last of the Southern states became committed to the policy of requiring children between certain ages to attend school for all or some part of the school term. This movement had begun in the South in 1905 with the passage of initial legislation on the subject in Tennessee. North Carolina followed in 1907, Virginia in 1908, Arkansas in 1909, Louisiana in 1910, South Carolina, Texas, Florida, and Alabama in 1915, Georgia in 1916, and Mississippi in 1918. Revisions, extensions, and improvements were made in some of these states after the introductory enactments, though such legislation was still local and optional in character and very defective, and lacked the full force of public approval needed for its complete success.

Child-labor legislation, closely related to compulsory-attendance laws, was found in all the Southern states in 1923, but reform was needed there also. Some of the states had made beginnings in legislation and practices designed to protect dependent and delinquent children. Perhaps one of the most advanced and complete plans, not only in the South but in the country at large, was that set up in North Carolina in 1919. It provided for county boards of public welfare and a juvenile court in every court in every county, with jurisdiction over all delinquent, neglected, and dependent children under sixteen years of age. Improvement had appeared also in general health regulations and the physical examinations of school children, and in renewed efforts, largely as a result of the war, to eliminate illiteracy, with which the South was still shamefully burdened. Other hopeful signs of educational progress appeared in the tendency to improve the status of the public-school teacher by raising and standardizing the qualifications to teach and by making provisions for the teachers to meet the requirements by enlarging teacher-training facilities. The tendency was toward state rather than county certification and toward accrediting approved university and college diplomas and accepting credentials of teachers from other states. The Southern states, which have had such a bitter and discouraging experience since 1861, have made much educational progress since Page in 1898 reminded them of their obligation to the "forgotten man."

The South and national standards in education. The faculty of an American university recently received from the institution's Committee on English Composition a communication deploring the general problem of illiteracy on the campus. It pointed out that most of the freshmen entered the university quite unprepared in the elements of English composition. It also reported that approximately 40 per cent of them were so noticeably deficient that they were not admitted to freshman English until they had passed a more elementary course consisting largely of review work in English grammar, a subject which should be learned before they leave high school. The communication went on to inform the professors that the average freshman in the institution exhibited a stage of progress which, measured and judged by national standards, was normal for second-year high-school students, and that some of the less well-prepared freshmen "actually write like pupils in the fourth or fifth grade." Appeal was made for collective action of the university faculty in a crusade to remove illiteracy from the students and, if possible, to give them a respectful feeling for their mother tongue.

Those who designate the Southern states as the Sahara of the Bozart or the Bible Belt, or describe them by other terms which suggest or are meant to suggest educational and cultural backwardness, will perhaps readily locate this institution in that section of the country. Colleges and universities in other parts of the United States are probably now and then afflicted with some freshmen who take liberties with the language and exhibit other evidences of illiteracy. But the Southern states are most conspicuous for this grievous condition and for the position which they occupy below national standards in other educational matters. When the actual facts are exhibited the illiterate condition of these university freshmen is not difficult to understand. Educationally the South still suffers by comparison with any other section of the United States or with the country as a whole, notwithstanding its progress during the last quarter of a century.

Short school terms. If the amount of educational opportunity which a state or a community provides for its children is one fair test of its educational effectiveness, the South must take low rank. The average annual school term of all the forty-eight states exceeds by nearly a month and a half that which is now provided by the Southern states, and some of the most backward of these fall below many of the more advanced states by nearly three months a year. In some schools for white children (the Southern states maintain in the same district one school for negro children and another for white children, and, except in the cities, the term for the negro children is not always the same as that for white children) the term is only five months or even less a year. Fully a third of the school population of a state which claims to be the most progressive of all the Southern groups are in schools with only a six-month term, which is to say that these children receive annually only two thirds as much schooling as the children in the really advanced states. Moreover, the quality of the educational opportunity of these children is inferior because the poorly trained and ineffective teachers gravitate to the short-term schools.

Irregular attendance. The evil effects of such schools and such teachers — both plentiful in the South — are reflected in the matter of attendance. A good teacher probably determines, as nearly directly as any other single factor, the attendance of children at school. The percentage of nonattendance is higher in the South than elsewhere in the entire country, though this is due in part to ineffective compulsory-school-attendance legislation. Each pupil enrolled attends school annually only 72 per cent as many days in the South as in the entire country, and the average child in the entire United States gets two years of schooling more than does the average child in the South. Stated differently, the average American child gets nearly seven years of schooling, his average Southern cousin gets a trifle less than five, and his poorer relatives in at least three Southern states get only a bit more than four years of schooling in their allotted threescore and ten. Taken as a whole the eleven strictly Southern states are a region of a little less than fifth-graders. Texas, the most advanced of them all in this respect, has not yet reached the sixth grade and is behind the most advanced of its sisters outside the South by more than three years.

Low salaries. Similar conditions appear in the matter of the salaries paid to teachers. The average annual salaries of teachers, principals, and supervisors are only 58 per cent as large in the Southern states as in the entire forty-eight. In three or four of these states the salaries are only half as large as in the entire United States, and in one of them they are only a little more than a third as large. Outside the South the states most advanced in this particular are rewarding their teachers more than four times as well as is the least advanced state in the South. The Southern states are also very deficient in intelligent and comprehensive plans for the training of teachers. Important teaching positions in some normal schools are occupied by people with only two years of college training, and the salaries of some of them are not more than $100 per month. Salaries of the professors in the colleges and universities of the Southern states are on a lower schedule than those paid in such institutions in other parts of the country.

Physical equipment. The South is also far below national standards in the physical equipment of schools, an important measure of educational effectiveness. In the average value of school property per student enrolled it does only 45 per cent as well for its children as does the country at large, and in the total expenditures per pupil in attendance on public elementary and secondary schools it does only half as well as the average of all the forty-eight states.

High-school attendance. In the percentage of children in high school all the Southern states except Texas occupy places at the bottom of the list. It is estimated that nearly half a million white children do not have access to high-school advantages of any kind — good, bad, or indifferent. Moreover, studies in one representative Southern state show that its high-school graduates are less well educated than first-year high-school students in states with advanced school systems. Out of this condition comes the problem that is now confronting the Committee on English Composition in one Southern institution.

Illiteracy. But sheer or near illiteracy in the South is not confined to the classic shades of college and university campuses : its blight is spread to wider areas, notwithstanding some effort to remove it in recent years. One tenth of the adult native white population of a Southern commonwealth which officially declares itself to be the pacemaker in industry, agriculture, and substantial progress are unable to read a single work of Darwin or the Book which crusaders would protect from his attacks. Two hundred and sixty thousand native-born white women in sheer illiteracy now inhabit the eleven Southern states, one hundred and fifteen thousand of them in the three states of Louisiana, North Carolina, and Tennessee; and there is an equal or even larger number of native Southern white men forgotten in the same suffocating loneliness.

Libraries. In public libraries the South is at the bottom of the list. The average per capita circulation of public-library books in the United States is five times greater than that in the South, which is the leanest book market, except for school texts, in the entire country. The showing in college libraries — private, denominational, and state-supported — is somewhat similar. In this power to attract scholars, to develop leadership, to invite and encourage research, and to minister to the spiritual and cultural needs of the people the South is doing only one fourth as well as other sections of the country. A distressing deficiency closely related to this fact appears in the lack of opportunities for graduate study in the South. In all the broad region between the Potomac and the Rio Grande there is not a graduate school that can be measured creditably by national standards — not one of first rank. Probably the two which show up to best advantage are in the University of Texas and in the University of North Carolina. Except for Florida, with hosts of tourists and realtors who must keep up with what goes on in the world, the Southern states rank at the bottom of the list as readers of the leading magazines. That state ranks sixteenth from the top. As readers of newspapers the country at large makes a threefold better showing than the Southern states.

Even the recent repeated efforts of Southern state legislatures to say that Adam was not a monkey have not stimulated the reading habit markedly in that section, although the commonwealth which claims Dayton as its Fundamentalist capital (one of three states with monkey laws on the statute books) heads the list of the Southern states in the per capita circulation of public-library books, or did in 1925, in primo anno Scopes. In that year it was doing in this respect nearly three times as well as three of its sisters in the South and nearly twice as well as three others. It may be noted, however, that at that time the annual school term of Tennessee fell short of the average for the entire United States by only a month or a trifle less. By these exhibits it appears that the taste of Southerners does not run to literature.

Partisan politics. To these shortcomings must be added another, which is found in many states outside the South — that of the political color of the educational arrangements. The Southern states still select their chief state school officers on a strictly political basis, and all except one still choose them by popular vote, as they do their high sheriffs, constables, and coroners. Some of them still select local and county school officers in the same way. When the head of the school system is chosen on such a basis he is constantly identified with partisan politics and bound to party pledges. Although he occupies potentially a most strategic position for moral and educational leadership, actually he is often practically helpless. The real duties of such an officer require a fitness by nature, a professional training, and other qualities which are rarely at home with such qualities as usually commend men to political bosses. The political character of the state superintendency in the South prevents the prescription of educational qualifications for those who occupy it; and the office is open, in theory at any rate, to any respectable citizen and voter without regard to professional fitness. If this officer shows professional courage he is likely to go the way of Gideon Hawley in New York State more than a century ago or of Thomas E. Finegan in Pennsylvania in 1923, or be transferred in the twinkling of an eye to a professorship in a normal school, to the presidency of the state agricultural college, or to some larger field of harmlessness. The pittance of pay that this important educational officer receives also proclaims the low public esteem in which he is still held as a professional worker.

If the South has at no time in the past attained fully to national standards the explanation is historical, at least in part. Slavery kept it from accepting completely the democratic doctrine of education during the ante-bellum period; and on account of other conditions which arose out of the war and its aftermath and which have already been noted, Southern education of all grades and degrees was forced down to the lowest rank in the nation. The late Governor Charles B. Aycock of North Carolina, in a campaign for better schools during the first decade of the present century, was in the habit of thanking God for the sister state of South Carolina, which obligingly kept his own state from the very bottom. These two states, one a traditional mountain of conceit and the other a traditional valley of humility, were then painfully propping up the educational rank of their other sisters. The eleven Southern states, as far down in the line then as they could get without leaving the Union, have remained in this humble position and are found there today, in spite of the progress they have made in the quarter of a century that has passed since Aycock gave thanks.

Recent progress. Measured by its own record, however, the educational progress of the South since 1900 has been remarkable. For example, in 1900 the value of all the public-school property in North Carolina, which since that time has probably done as well as any Southern state or better, was approximately $1,000,000, and in that year it expended a similar amount to maintain its public schools. Today its school property is valued at nearly $100,000,000 and its annual bill for public-school support is above $35,000,000. The other Southern states have made corresponding if not always as great advances. Measured by its needs and by national standards, however, the South is not yet an educationally advanced section of the country. The Southern state which has made the greatest progress should do twice as much as it now does for the maintenance of its schools in order to rank educationally even as an *average* state among the forty-eight — a place to which not a single Southern state has yet attained.

Present problems. Two questions naturally arise out of a study of present conditions in the South : First, why are these states so far behind their sisters when measured by accepted tests of educational effectiveness? Secondly, inasmuch as the other states are also advancing while the South moves ahead, can that section of the country ever attain to national standards in education?

Whatever the causes of the South's educational backwardness in the past — economic destitution and despair, the presence of the negro and the bitterness of racial conflict, partisan politics, sectarian dogma, or the specter of the aristocratic theory of education — that section cannot any longer properly point to poverty in explanation or defense. The ghost of aristocracy still walks here and there — as it does elsewhere perhaps — during the seasons for voting or levying school taxes, but its shadow grows less with the passing of each such period. The twin calamities of war and reconstruction from 1861 to 1876 helped very properly to explain and to justify the South's educational deficiencies a quarter of a century ago, when the South was poor ; but today the South is a region of such bulging bounties and powerful economic resources that the alibi of poverty cannot be established. True, the maintenance of a dual-school system (separate schools for the children of each of the two

races is a settled policy in every Southern state) increases the
burden. True also, the South has many children who are
often scattered over wide areas. But these are not insuper-
able obstacles in the way of education. The South has the
wealth to support schools adequately for all its children.

Evidences of complacency. Complacency is probably a
more nearly correct answer to the first question. This is
perhaps the South's deadliest affliction at the present time.
The Southern states are intoxicated with their own prosperity and progress. Satisfaction with what they have done
in recent years is beginning to blind them to the things they
should do now and in the years ahead. Educational inequalities in these states are in some respects as glaring now as
they were twenty-five years ago. But the fervidly patriotic
Southerner does not hesitate to describe as "conspicuous"
many educational achievements that would pass unnoticed
in really advanced states. Moreover, exaggerated claims of
progress by intelligent and influential Southern leaders can
be interpreted as actual defenses of the South's educational
and cultural deficiencies.

The Southern press reveals abundant evidences of this
affliction. An influential member of the legislature of a
prominent and proud commonwealth said upon the floor of
that body that his state is spending too much money for
education and asks for a study of the matter. Many of the
white children in that state, not to mention the negro children, have only a hundred days of schooling a year. The
most influential man in another Southern state, a state with
short school terms, said to hundreds of citizens whose bal-
lots sent him to high political position, "Although it may
have one of the shortest school terms in the United States,
the schools of this state are the best in the world." In a
speech before two thousand voters a candidate for governor
declared, "No people on earth have equaled or excelled the
educational progress of this state in recent years."

The Speaker of the House of Representatives of a Southern state, in a statement given to the press, asserted, "Although I do not have the facts I should not wonder if the amount of money spent for public schools in this state is as much per capita as any state in the Union." He had made no effort to ascertain the facts, but his statement was probably believed by most of the people who read it. The commonwealth of which he was boasting should double its funds for public schools in order to be ranked even as an average state. Another Southern citizen, who desired to serve his state in high office and was permitted the opportunity, declared to a multitude of voters, "Speaking in terms of the rate of progress made in public education in the past quarter of a century, our commonwealth has undoubtedly outstripped any state in the Union." A prominent and practiced vote-getter flattered many hundreds of his constituents by saying, "No government on earth, in the short space of twenty-five years, has written and incarnated in the life of a people more of the platform of Jesus Christ than has the Democratic party in our state." He thought it positively wrong for any citizen to suggest that there was anything wrong with the schools. "The spiritual and cultural life of this state has kept pace with its material advance," he said, "and the path of the program of progress in our commonwealth is as the dawning light that shineth more and more unto the perfect day."

The solutions. If the South would attain to national standards in education, frank admission of its educational shortcomings is the first safe step toward that achievement. It is the facts of its present educational deficiencies and not recitals of them which now defame the South. If these facts are faced honestly neither the South's need for greatly enlarged educational facilities nor its ability to meet the need can be denied. The Southern states can put within the reach of every child within their borders public educational advantages much more nearly adequate than those now provided. The standards of the best in education can be made the standards of the South, and any other goal is unworthy of its need and ability. But until this initial step is taken the Southern states are likely to remain heavily handicapped by another affliction: the South has not yet thoroughly learned that provincial prejudice is not patriotism and that acute sensitiveness to just criticism is not loyalty. These are social insanities which help to perpetuate educational backwardness. Indifference to its weaknesses or failure to admit them is more of a reproach to the South than the weaknesses themselves.

The Southern states are no longer poor. In recent years they have made such a giant stride from poverty to prosperity that they are now able to do almost anything for public schools, public roads, and public health. The World War, moreover, not only revealed the weaknesses of education there, as in other parts of the United States, but it also helped the South to find itself. Under the impetus of the call to fight, to give, and to do for others what it had not felt fully able to do for itself, the South found fresh hope and new energies. The call for food for American soldiers and those of Europe, the campaign against waste, and the drives for the Red Cross and for Liberty Bonds led the South to thoughtful consideration of new enterprises and of old ones undeveloped. More nearly complete remedies for its shortcomings were thus revealed. The measure of the South's conscience on schools and other means of intellectual progress must now be taken neither from its impatience with criticism from without nor from its ability to build schools, but rather from its constantly growing need for education. Just as the chief problem of the South twenty-five years ago was to secure complete agreement on education, so the chief need today is to educate. The task today is little less conspicuous for its magnitude and difficulty than it was then.

The task now is to build schools on a sound basis of financial support, professional direction, and supervision, so as to furnish every child equal educational rights — "the opportunity 'to burgeon out all that there is within him'" to use the words of Aycock, North Carolina's educational governor. Then, and then only, will the people of the South be enabled

CHARLES B. AYCOCK

North Carolina's educational governor

to observe fully, faithfully, and intelligently their constantly enlarging relationships and, in paraphrase of Jefferson, the earliest of the South's educational statesmen, to understand what goes on in the world and to keep their part of it going on right.

It should be seen from the foregoing discussion that the establishment and maintenance of public educational facilities have been difficult problems in the Southern states since the Civil War. But many reforms and improvements have been made there during the last quarter of a century. Measured with the past record of the Southern states, the progress made seems phenomenal. Much work still remains to be done in the Southern states, and some obstacles persist after many years of agitation to remove them. But with the enormous increase in economic wealth these states can now move forward in education if the danger of satisfaction with what they have already done can be averted.

Attention is turned in the next chapter to later educational developments in the country as a whole.

REFERENCES AND READINGS

BEARD, CHARLES A., and MARY R. The Rise of American Civilization. New York, 1927.

> Chapter XVIII (of Volume II) contains a brief discussion of the Civil War and reconstruction.

COULTER, E. MERTON. College Life in the Old South. New York, 1928.

> An excellent account of the college in the growth of civilization in the Old South, the University of Georgia taken as the type. Very useful bibliography.

DUNNING, W. A. "The Undoing of Reconstruction," *Atlantic Monthly* (October, 1901), Vol. LXXXVIII, pp. 437–449.

> A scholarly and delightfully written account of the means by which the Southern white people resumed control of affairs in their states.

FLEMING, W. L. Documentary History of Reconstruction. 2 vols. Cleveland, 1906–1907.

> A comprehensive and admirable compilation of source materials on the social as well as the political aspects of reconstruction; an indispensable work on that period.

FLEMING, W. L. The Sequel of Appomattox (The Chronicles of America). Yale University Press, 1919.

> A very interesting brief account of the reunion of the states. Contains chapters on the church and the school, carpetbag and negro rule, and the restoration of home rule. Contains very useful bibliographical notes.

HENDRICK, B. J. The Life and Letters of Walter H. Page. 2 vols. Garden City, New York, 1922.

> Chapters I and III of Volume I deal with the reconstruction period and with the "forgotten man."

HENDRICK, B. J. The Training of an American, chaps. ii, vi, xi. Boston, 1928.

> College life in the South in the seventies, the backward conditions, and the struggle for education are described through the life and letters of Walter H. Page.

KNIGHT, EDGAR W. "Education in the South," in Twenty-five Years of American Education (I. L. Kandel, Editor). New York, 1924.

> Traces the development of education in the South from 1898, with comments on the effect of the period of reconstruction.

KNIGHT, EDGAR W. The Influence of Reconstruction on Education in the South. New York, 1913.

> Points out some effects of that period upon education in the states which had formed the Confederacy.

KNIGHT, EDGAR W. Public Education in the South. Boston, 1922.

> Chapters IX–XIII, inclusive, cover the topics treated in this chapter.

KNIGHT, EDGAR W. "Reconstruction and Education in Virginia," *South Atlantic Quarterly*, January and April, 1916.

KNIGHT, EDGAR W. "Reconstruction and Education in South Carolina," *South Atlantic Quarterly*, October, 1919, and January, 1920.

> Studies of the period of reconstruction in two states.

LINGLEY, CHARLES R. Since the Civil War (Revised Edition). New York, 1926.

> Chapter I is a very good description of the period of reconstruction. Contains an excellent bibliography.

NEVINS, ALLAN. The Emergence of Modern America, 1865–1878. New York, 1927.

> Chapters I and XIII are valuable supplementary material for this chapter. An excellent bibliography appears on pages 416–418.

NOBLE, STUART G. "The Education of the Negro," in Twenty-five Years of American Education (I. L. Kandel, Editor). New York, 1924.

> Traces the development of negro education from 1898 and points out existing conditions.

NOBLE, STUART G. Forty Years of the Public Schools of Mississippi. New York, 1916.

> Discusses the subject of negro education with reference to Mississippi.

NORDHOFF, CHARLES. The Cotton States in 1875. New York, 1876.

> Gives a picture of the carpetbag misrule.

PAGE, THOMAS NELSON. "The Southern People during Reconstruction," *Atlantic Monthly* (September, 1901), Vol. LXXXVIII, pp. 289–304.

> A vivid account.

PAGE, WALTER H. The Rebuilding of Old Commonwealths. New York, 1902.

> Contains the address entitled "The Forgotten Man."

PIKE, J. S. The Prostrate State. New York, 1874.

> Shows the misrule of the carpetbaggers and negroes in South Carolina.

ROSE, WYCKLIFFE. "The Educational Movement in the South," Report of the United States Commissioner of Education for 1903, Vol. I, pp. 359–390. Washington, 1905.

TANNENBAUM, FRANK. Darker Phases of the South. New York, 1924.

> A rather gloomy picture of Southern conditions.

THOMPSON, HOLLAND. The New South (The Chronicles of America). Yale University Press, 1919.

> A brief story of social and industrial evolution in the Southern states. Chapter VIII is on educational progress. Contains good bibliographical notes.

WILSON, P. W. An Unofficial Statesman — Robert C. Ogden. New York, 1924.

> Tells, among other things, of Ogden's work through the Conference for Education in the South.

QUESTIONS FOR STUDY AND DISCUSSION

1. List the conditions which made public education such a discouraging problem to the people of the South after 1865.

2. How did the presidential plan of reconstruction differ from the congressional plan? What effect did the political changes of those years have on public education in the Southern states?

3. What was the attitude of Southern leaders toward the education of the freedmen during those years? Give evidence that they would have made provision for the education of the negroes if the presidential plan of reconstruction had been successful.

4. Compare the educational provisions of legislation during congressional reconstruction with those of the ante-bellum period in any Southern state for (1) school support, (2) organization and administration of schools, (3) supervision of schools, (4) training of teachers, (5) examination and certification of teachers, (6) curriculum and textbooks.

5. Why was the question of mixed schools so generally agitated in the constitutional conventions and legislative bodies of reconstruction?

6. Show how public education was promoted in any Southern state during the period of congressional reconstruction. In what ways was it retarded?

7. Show how it was natural that during the years immediately after the close of the war inaccurate statements should have been made concerning the extent of education in the South before 1860.

8. Why was the South looked upon as a promising field for missionary and educational effort after the Civil War? What effect did that attitude have on public education in the South then and later?

9. Should the Federal government have aided the reorganization and development of public education in the South after the Civil War? Give reasons for your answer.

10. Explain the meaning of "the undoing" of reconstruction. Why were public schools involved and subordinated in this process no less perhaps than in the process of reconstruction itself?

11. Make a study of the work and influence of the Peabody Fund for education in the South.

12. Account for the fact that in many parts of the South public educational conditions were less wholesome in the late nineties than they had been at the outbreak of the Civil War.

13. Should an illiterate person be allowed to vote? Why?

14. Can the Southern states attain to national standards in education?

CHAPTER XVI

LATER DEVELOPMENTS

Outline of the chapter. 1. Although some of the obstacles to public education had been removed in part at least, the principles of a democratic educational system had not passed into wide practice by 1860.

2. The abolition of slavery, which had served to keep the public consciousness dull on public educational matters, made brighter the way for public schools.

3. The growth of population, improvements in agriculture and in transportation, the scientific revolution, the rise of cities, the changed status of women, and other forces also had wide social significance.

4. The work of Darwin also had influence on education in the United States.

5. Progress in improving the materials and methods of education was slowly made, but reforms were stimulated by Pestalozzianism, Herbartianism, Froebelianism, the work of John Dewey, and the new psychology.

6. The leaders in the new psychology were Cattell, Hall, James, and especially Thorndike, whose work and influence have been very large in American education. The traditional work of the school was changed by the influence of these workers and by that of Huxley, Spencer, and Eliot.

7. In the meantime, interest in the professional study of education was stimulated by research in the historical foundations of education, which was definitely encouraged by Monroe.

Before the Civil War, as was pointed out in earlier chapters, education in the United States was not generally looked upon as a public obligation. But encouraging progress had been made in some directions. The sectarian controversy which had been troublesome for so many years had grown less and less bitter, and the suggestion that a system of denominational schools be established to meet the educational needs of the time had been rejected. Public support of education had slowly increased through the use of permanent public-school endowments, or so-called literary funds, and by local and state taxation, the idea that public

499

education was public charity had gradually lost some of its earlier repute, and the idea of free education had slowly gained in almost all parts of the country. Localism in educational management had likewise weakened, although here and there it was still holding on tenaciously in 1861. Its hold was still felt in the control of the courses of study and of teachers, in the location and building of schoolhouses, and in the financial support of schools. City superintendents were developing slowly, but county superintendencies were nominal only, and state superintendents were still generally financial and statistical officers, often ex officio, who at the same time played as best they could the rôle of educational evangelists and crusaders. Agencies for the training of teachers were found in occasional institutes and academies and in a few normal schools which were little more than secondary schools. Public high schools were not numerous. Higher education, especially under private and denominational support and control, had greatly expanded, and state universities were slowly developing. Opportunity for graduate instruction had not yet been provided to any appreciable degree, and technological and professional education was also undeveloped. In general the idea of education as a public responsibility was gaining.

Conditions in 1860. The gains which had been made in extending the principles of public support and public control of education, in the training of teachers, in extending public educational effort upward, and in other features of a so-called democratic school system have been pointed out in earlier chapters. Although some if not most of the difficulties and obstacles in the way of a public-school system free and open alike to all had been solved (at least in part) and removed here and there during the closing years of the ante-bellum period, the principles of a democratic educational system had not passed into wide practice. Elementary education was not yet entirely free. State aid by general taxation was still scanty, and state supervision of instruction was practically unknown. Compulsory-attendance legislation was only a theory and when considered at all, was generally viewed as undemocratic. In 1852 Massachusetts had passed what is generally classified as a compulsory-attendance act, which provided that children between the ages of eight and fourteen should attend school for twelve weeks annually, six weeks of this period to be consecutive. However, the many and very liberal exemptions of the law apparently made it inoperative. An act of New York in 1853 to provide for the care and instruction of idle and truant children was an even feebler gesture toward compulsory-attendance legislation, which for many years to come continued to be considered an invasion of the parental and family functions and rights. Only thirty of the states had enacted laws on the subject by 1897, and it was not until 1918 that all of them had done so. Like many other extensions of public educational effort now common in the United States, compulsory-education laws had to wait on the awakening of a livelier educational consciousness than the American public had yet developed.

The retarding effect of slavery. It is doubtful if any fact or force in American history had served longer and more definitely than the institution of human slavery to make and keep the public consciousness dull on matters of public education. Sanctioned by the centuries, not placed strictly under the ban by the Bible, winked at, if not encouraged, by the conquerors and colonizers of both Catholic and Protestant powers, slavery had become a tremendous social and political influence. It had been lawful in all the colonies, and from its introduction in 1619 the nauseating traffic in blacks snatched and stolen from Africa had grown extensive and strong. Few of the colonists saw irregularities in such a commerce. New England captains and owners of ships had ruthlessly and remorselessly sold slaves to Southern planters, who had worked them profitably and without hurt to conscience. The Northern states, which contained about forty thousand negro slaves at the beginning of the national period as against seven hundred thousand in the Southern states, gave up the institution only after it seemed unprofitable and not from moral scruples.

With many preachers and other reformers pliant in the presence of profits in slavery, moral objections to it could not deepen so long as so many men and women shared in and lived by its material benefits. Massachusetts had, by implication in its constitution of 1780, abolished slavery; Pennsylvania, about the same time, had provided for gradual emancipation; the Northwest Ordinance of 1787 had prohibited slavery in the Northwest Territory; and New York had provided for the freedom of all children born of slaves after July 4, 1799, and in 1827 removed slavery entirely. Gradually its importance was reduced in the North, where commercial activities and industry developed; but in the South it grew stronger and stronger, particularly after the cotton gin appeared, although even in that section there was not unanimous agreement upon either the economic or the moral aspects of slavery. But the opportunity for profit which it promised to bring (and often did bring then) served quickly to remove any hatred of slavery and to develop opposition to any attempts to interfere with the institution, just as now somewhat similar conditions serve to perpetuate the system of farm tenancy, which gradually increases the landless multitudes and threatens to fasten peonage and peasantry on many of the rural areas of the United States. Slavery served to prevent the extension of public educational effort in the Southern states, where it helped to strengthen class distinctions, and it retarded the cause of free schools elsewhere. The abolition of the institution removed one of the most stubborn obstacles that the democratic theory of education ever encountered, for schools could not be made fully free and universal in any American state so long as slavery existed.

Other forces favorable to education. By 1876 many of the problems which had their roots in the political reconstruction of the Southern states appeared solved, although, as was noted in Chapter XV, the vices, follies, and crimes of that grotesque burlesque of government, that "hideous orgy of anarchy, violence, unrestrained corruption, undisguised, ostentatious, insulting robbery," remained for many years political, economic, and social afflictions in those states which had formed the Confederacy. Even during the war, however, important economic and social developments had been taking place throughout the country which were widely significant in their effect on the daily lives of the people.

The growth of the population. Between 1870 and 1890 the population increased from about 39,000,000 to about 63,000,000, nearly 25 per cent for each decade, the Southern states showing a little less rapid increase, however, than the country at large. The changes in the economic life of the people appeared in the continuous shifting of the population. Some of the old sections, especially certain rural areas, lost population through the attraction of the rapidly developing cities and also by the expansion of the West. This was hastened by the public-land policy of the national government, which had early encouraged education and transportation, had stimulated settlement in the West, and under the Homestead Act of 1862 had adopted an even more generous system by which millions of acres were taken up by natives as well as by immigrants. Illinois, for example, attracted 1,300,000 people between 1870 and 1890, Kansas more than a million, and Nebraska almost as many. By the latter date almost one fifth of all native Americans were living outside the states in which they had been born.

The growth of agriculture. During these years agriculture was the dominant economic interest in the country taken as a whole, although the Southern states were only slowly recovering from the devastation and stagnation which had followed four years of war and the riot of reconstruction. In the Middle West, however, the growth of agriculture was rapid through increase in population, through the effect of the Homestead Act, and through improvements in transportation and in farm machinery. In the meantime, manufacturing was rapidly developing, cities were growing, and wealth was rapidly being accumulated in the hands of a few. Immigration too was an influential factor during the quarter-century that followed the close of the war, reaching a total of 8,000,000 in the two decades from 1870 to 1890 and 789,000 in the one year of 1882. Its social effects were large and far-reaching. New problems arose which the school was soon called upon to solve. Educational conditions in the Southern states only slowly improved during the three or four decades after the war, but the effect of that struggle was less destructive on education in the Northern and Western states, where recovery was more quickly made through increased wealth, which furnished the economic basis for educational expansion, and through rapid urbanization, which provided the basis of collective action in education. Then as now the cities led the way in demands for better schools, and these were developed, if slowly, during the quarter of a century that followed the close of the war.

The scientific revolution. Achievements in the applications of science to the needs and the comforts of man continued during the years that followed the Civil War. One year after the close of that struggle cable communications were opened with England, and the Associated Press soon afterwards was able to have transmitted, at the cost of the tidy sum of nearly six thousand dollars, the speech which William of Prussia made to his parliament. The first continental railroad, opened in 1869, closed the age of the pony express and the wagon train and made the exchange of goods between the United States and the Orient easy and quick. The telegraph, which Samuel F. B. Morse had made successful in the forties and which had already widely extended, trebled in mileage within a few years after the war. The reaper, invented by Cyrus H. McCormick in piedmont Virginia in 1834, had been greatly improved, and a self-binding model appeared in 1867. Mowers, the improved harrow with adjustable teeth, corn-planters, cultivators, shellers, and other kinds of machinery greatly relieved the farmer's toil. C. L. Sholes, a printer of Milwaukee, working on a device for numbering the pages of a book serially, invented a machine which would write with fair accuracy and speed, and by 1874 Mark Twain was using a typewriter which he said was able to "print faster than I can write" and did not "muss things or scatter ink blots around." In the same year too Alexander Graham Bell was working on a mechanical device destined to transmit the voice by wire and to bring the world closer together. George M. Pullman had built a sleeping car which was immediately successful as a more comfortable means of travel, and George Westinghouse while yet in his early twenties had added to the safety of travelers by inventing the air brake for use on locomotives and railway cars.

The capacity of Americans for invention and increasing control over material forces continued very active. Each year showed an increasing number of patents issued by the Patent Office in Washington. By 1872 Thomas Edison had made it possible to send two messages over the same wire simultaneously. Five years later he had produced the phonograph. Electric lighting was in use by 1876, and electric traction a few years later. The refrigerator car had been built, the linotype machine soon appeared, and concrete and fireproof construction of buildings was being made. Automobiles, flying machines, submarines, wireless telegraphy, dreadnoughts, high explosives, and a host of other mechanical inventions were soon to show how tools were lengthening the hand of man for good or ill.

American cities were growing by leaps and bounds through the rapid increase in material wealth, through the multiplication of mills and factories, and through the development of railways and other means of quick and easy transportation and communication. Almost a million people lived in New York, in 1870, three fourths as many in Philadelphia, nearly a third as many in Chicago, and more than two hundred thousand in Cincinnati. The output of factory-made clothes and shoes was increasing for the rank and file, who also soon "grew used to meats sent from Chicago, canned salmon from Oregon, and canned tomatoes from Maryland." Bread came increasingly from commercial bakeries, and fifty patents for washing machines were taken out in the latter half of 1868. As early as 1866 a thousand sewing machines were being manufactured daily, and shortly afterwards one hundred and eighty thousand were annually going into American homes at a cost of approximately $60 each. Kerosene as a means of illumination brought many styles in lamps, numerous explosions, and much irritation from cracked chimneys. As the anthracite fields of Pennsylvania were developed, stoves for heating and for cooking multiplied. In the best city homes heating by steam or hot water was found, and artificial ice was becoming known. A factory in New Orleans as early as 1871 had a daily output of seventy-two tons, which reduced the price from $40 and $60 to $15 a ton, "to the dismay of Northern ice importers." But not all suggestions of improvements were promptly favored. Even in New York proposals for improved transportation met with fierce opposition from vested interests. Efforts were made to prevent the construction of the first elevated railway by suits at court and by arguments from business interests and those who owned horse cars that the thing was ugly, that horses would be frightened by the trains, and that the noise of the trains would destroy trade. Life everywhere outside the Southern states was marked in general by a prosperity and comfort hitherto unknown in the country. Public well-being was gradually increasing through the increase in material wealth, the applications of science, the increase of foodstuffs, and the development of manufacturing, transportation, and communication. These changes and improvements made the way of the school safer and easier by removing many of the obstacles in its way.

The battle against disease. Control of other forces was slowly gained also. For many years after the close of the Civil War man did not understand the causes of plague, malaria, yellow fever, typhoid fever, cholera, typhus, or dysentery; but within four or five decades he had come to understand how these infections were transmitted, and he was to know more and more about their germs. In a half-century he learned more about how to solve the most important problem in the way of his progress — the problem of his health — than he had learned in many centuries before. Pasteur's work in bacteriology and with serum inoculations and Lister's applications of antiseptics helped to lead the way for effective attacks on disease and made safer the way of surgery through lessening the dangers of blood-poisoning. Slowly Americans began to reap the benefits of advances which were being made in medicine and in surgery, and campaigns against diseases soon followed. Quarantine laws were enacted to stamp out or prevent diseases which threatened the country as a result of immigration. Malaria and ague, and the yellow fever which had so long scourged so many human beings, were traced to the mosquito. The draining of swamps, the oiling of stagnant water surfaces, and the use of screens followed. Serum for smallpox and preventives for hydrophobia and diphtheria were discovered and soon came into use.

Serious questions of health, of sanitation, and of general public safety arose out of the rapid growth of the cities, where poor housing and insanitary conditions and the slums brought new dangers. In 1888 James Bryce had pointed to the government of the cities as "the one conspicuous failure in the United States." Other writers and reformers persistently called attention to the urgent need for improvement. Gradually the progressive urban centers and the national government extended their functions to include sanitation and health activities and the prevention and control of disease. Attention was also drawn to the conservation of the health of children, and slowly the schools came to be used to diffuse information on the prevention and treatment of diseases and the building of health habits. Out of the growth of cities arose the need for recreational opportunities and vacations, and in time "the worthy use of leisure" was added as an objective of the work of the school.

Changed status of women. In addition to the enormous increase in economic wealth, the development of transportation and communication, the rapid growth of industry and the rise of cities, the steady development in agriculture, all stimulated and promoted by the scientific revolution, other factors and forces had social and political as well as economic significance. One of these was the change in the status of women. Opportunities for their higher education gradually increased after the Civil War, and along with those opportunities came demands from the women that they be allowed to enter certain occupations and professions which tradition had long closed to them. An effective means of propaganda for reform developed with the organization in 1890 of the General Federation of Women's Clubs, now the largest organization of women in the world. Before this date the agitation to give the ballot to women had been evidence of a growing interest in a more nearly democratic control of government, and some progress had been made before the close of the century. In general, however, it was the West and not the East that looked with favor on woman suffrage. In the nation at large it was not gained, however, until the ratification of the Nineteenth Amendment in 1920.

Slowly women were made legally more secure in rights to their property and their children. The English common law, which prohibited a married woman's ownership of property, was the rule in most of the states far into the last decades of the nineteenth century. By the close of the century, however, a large majority of the states had modified the laws on the subject in the direction of greater justice for women. The guardianship of children remained the privilege of the father in almost every state until the opening of the present century, and in some states his control was absolute. In 1902 the father and the mother shared equally in the guardianship of their children in the District of Columbia and in only nine states — Colorado, Connecticut, Illinois, Kansas, Maine, Massachusetts, Nebraska, New York, and Washington. Reform came in some of the very conservative states only after public opinion had been rudely shocked by the injustice and danger of the ancient custom. In Massachusetts, for example, a mother, crazed by the declared intention of her husband to exercise his legal right and give away their six children, killed all of them. This tragedy, enacted in 1901, shocked the public conscience and led a year later to the passage of legislation in that state which made the mother equal with the father in the guardianship of their children. As women have come into freedom after freedom through reforms and the softening of laws which had so long discriminated against them, they have become leaders and patrons of education and other civic interests, and more and more have the rights of childhood come to be respected in this country.

Education and the theory of evolution. Probably the most powerful influence on education in the United States in recent years arose out of the work of Charles Darwin. His theory of evolution implied the antiquity of man and the antiquity of the earth on which he lived and died and alleged the mutability of species and development from simple to complex forms by natural causes rather than by divine interference. This theory, which came to be generally accepted before the close of the last century, not only clashed with the Christian Epic and shook faith in the Mosaic explanation of man and the world and all that in it is, but threw much light upon the educative process.

As early as 1860 two important reviews of Darwin's "Origin of Species" had appeared in the *North American Review* and the *New York Times*. Even Emerson had made the suggestion that the light which science was beginning to throw on things was a warning against the traditional view that the social order was fixed and unchanging. Asa Gray, one of the foremost botanists of his time, even before he retired from a professorship in Harvard University in 1873 had given Darwin comfort and courage in publicly championing the theory of evolution. Others followed, among them John Fiske, who wrote and spoke on the subject; E. L. Youmans, who founded the *Popular Science Monthly*, which became an effective means of publicity for the new theories; Charles W. Eliot, the gifted young president of Harvard who was unafraid of his mind; and Andrew D. White, the president of Cornell, whose brilliant work on the warfare of science and theology attracted wide attention in pointing out that advances in knowledge had always been opposed by blind and narrow religionists. In the meantime John W. Draper had surveyed the intellectual development of Europe and pointed bluntly to the dead weight of theological tradition.

Fierce were the attacks against the new theories and theorists and those who bravely or timidly shared their views.

But science gained ground steadily if slowly, more and more triumphantly, and often with increasing arrogance, as it claimed to take from theology and theologians the one real explanation "to the riddle of the universe." In the process of the bitter conflict wider impetus was given to the advancement of intellectual interests. The usefulness of the struggle was in no way greater perhaps or more definite than the change that it was to work in the attitude toward child life and in the emancipation of children, who had so long suffered from the blindness and brutality of a discipline encouraged by the cruel doctrine of original sin. This change, which was made slowly, had wide educational significance.

Methods and materials. Progress in the improvement of methods and materials of instruction was also slowly made. The typical public school as late as 1860 and for many years afterwards probably resembled very closely the typical public school of a much earlier period. Houses were rudely constructed, lacking in comforts and often even the decencies of living. The materials of instruction were narrow and traditional if not medieval in character, and methods of teaching were generally harsh, often brutal, and almost always wasteful. As a rule the teachers were untrained and worked away blindly at their tasks without supervision or direction. Little was known of the nature of child life. Children were looked upon as unregenerated; human nature was considered bad; the "will" of the child must be broken, and discipline, whether formal or informal, was the fashionable doctrine of the time and was sanctioned by theology, by the little psychology that was known, and by ancient scholarship. The more disagreeable and difficult the school task, the more dismal the surroundings of the school, and the sterner the teacher, the better for the child, who was not allowed either in school or out to know the joys of living. The relation between the school and life outside was not yet recognized, and the conception of education as growth or development, had not yet appeared. The doctrines of education considered sound today had to wait on forces that had not yet made themselves felt.

Pestalozzianism. During the latter part of the nineteenth century educational reforms were advanced in large part by influences from Europe. One of these was the work of

JOHANN HEINRICH PESTALOZZI

Johann Heinrich Pestalozzi (1746–1827), who had been inspired by Rousseau's "Émile," one of the most influential books of the eighteenth century. Pestalozzi, probably more than any other educational reformer, laid the basis for the modern elementary school and helped to reform elementary-school practice. He held that education, which he defined as the "natural, progressive, and harmonious development of all the powers and capacities of the human being," is the chief means of social reform and human improvement, that it is a natural process and not an artificial one, and that instruction should be based upon the natural development of the instincts, capacities, interests, and activities of the child. A knowledge of the nature of child life and of the development of the child's mind he believed to be of fundamental importance in instruction. He maintained that the education of the child can be aided or retarded by the methods employed in teaching. Pestalozzi was a strong advocate of universal education, and urged the use of the immediate

PESTALOZZI'S SCHOOL AT STANZ

The lower picture is probably nearer to the reality

environment or experience of the child as the most valuable means and materials of his instruction. Observation and investigation instead of memorizing and class discussion, and thinking instead of reciting, characterized his work, which contained many suggestions for present-day pedagogy and educational reform. He also placed much emphasis upon strict but kind discipline, a "thinking love," which was one of the most prominent principles of his educational theory.

EDWARD A. SHELDON

Pestalozzi conducted experimental schools in Switzerland which attracted educational leaders in both Europe and America for twenty-five years. Pestalozzianism was first introduced into the United States through early American educational journals and reports on European schools (see Chapter VIII), as well as through the work of Joseph Neef, one of Pestalozzi's instructors, who came to this country in the early years of the nineteenth century and taught in Philadelphia, Louisville (Kentucky), and New Harmony (Indiana); but it was most widely diffused after 1860, largely through the work of Superintendent Edward A. Sheldon of the Oswego, New York, schools, whose methods and materials of instruction, based on Pestalozzi's principles, were widely advertised, popularized, and imitated. The Oswego Board of Education invited a group of prominent educational leaders to examine the schools of that city in 1862, and they made a favorable report at the meeting of the National Teachers Association the following year. Sheldon read a paper on the subject of object-teaching. In 1864 the association named a committee to investigate, and in 1865 it made a favorable report upon the Oswego system. Normal schools, which developed rapidly after the Civil War, often adopted the Pestalozzian principles and helped to spread them throughout the country.

The principles which Pestalozzi advocated had a wide influence on industrial education for juvenile reform and the manual-labor school (see Chapter XIII) and on object teaching and oral instruction in arithmetic, geography, language, drawing, writing, reading, elementary science, and music. This new method of object teaching soon led definitely to instruction in elementary science, one of the earliest courses in the subject being organized and published in 1871 by Superintendent William T.

WILLIAM T. HARRIS

Harris of the schools of St. Louis. Instruction in geography was also greatly improved as a result of Pestalozzianism and the work of Colonel Francis W. Parker, who, as principal of teacher-training institutions in Chicago, was an aggressive advocate of better methods in elementary education. His book "How to Teach Geography," which appeared in 1889, had a wide influence.

But not all Pestalozzi's principles and methods were universally approved in the United States, and some of them were attacked here in a manner resembling, if more vigorous, that of Herbert Spencer, who described the Pestalozzian verbal formalism in England as "the well-conceived but ill-conducted system of *object lessons*." Pestalozzianism also ran to seed in the so-called Grube method of teaching arithmetic, which carried "objective illustration to an extreme" according to Professor David Eugene Smith's smashing criticism of the method in 1900, which helped to turn the teaching of arithmetic back to the best ideas of Pesta-

FRANCIS W. PARKER

lozzi. The absurdity of the Grube method, which was widely fashionable in this country in the latter part of the nineteenth century, had also been pointed out by Professor John Dewey as early as 1895. But Pestalozzi's principles had a wide and useful influence in helping to develop in this country, as in Europe, a better conception of child life and to provide more sensible materials and methods for the instruction of children.

Other influences which helped to change educational theory and practice in the United States came from the work of two of Pestalozzi's disciples, Johann Friedrich Herbart (1776–1841) and Friedrich Wilhelm August Froebel (1782–1852), whose traditions and training were more intellectual and scientific than those of their celebrated master.

Herbartianism. Herbart spent most of his life as student, tutor, and university professor; he gave lectures on pedagogy and published books on the subject. He also conducted a pedagogical seminary for the scientific study of educational problems, in connection with which he maintained a practice school at the University of Königsberg. With Herbart the chief purpose of education was to develop personal character and to prepare for social usefulness. He maintained that interest was the most important element or means in good teaching; and building upon Pestalozzi's theory, that the duty of the teacher is to provide new and real experiences for the pupil, he elaborated a teaching method which emphasized interest, the adaptation of instruction to the past experiences and the present attitude of the pupil, systematic and methodical treatment of facts or subject matter, and correlation, or the unification of subjects or studies. The principle of correlation was greatly emphasized by his followers, who developed it further into what came to be known as concentration. Out of Herbart's method, which

JOHANN FRIEDRICH HERBART

was based upon a strange psychology worked out by himself, grew the culture-epoch theory (formulated by Tuiskon Ziller, a professor in the University of Leipzig, and others) and the five formal steps of instruction. Like many other worthy principles of pedagogy, stated before and since his time, the principles of Herbart have tended toward rather extreme formalism and often even toward exaggeration in the hands of his followers and interpreters. This formalism or exaggeration has been more or less evident in a degeneracy in the applications of the doctrine of interest in the schools of the United States, which, next to the land of its birth, has witnessed a larger influence by Herbartianism than any other country.

Here a wide and even a fervid enthusiasm began to develop for the Herbartian principles during the last decade of the nineteenth century. The wave of interest gained force largely through a few eager Americans who had studied at the University of Jena in the eighties before opportunities for graduate instruction in the universities of this country had been provided to any attractive extent. Among these students was Charles de Garmo, who was at Jena in 1886. Dr. Garmo served as professor of education in Cornell University for many years, published "The Essentials of Methods" in 1889, and served as the first president of the National Herbart Society (organized in 1892), and as editor of its publications, which, during the early years of the organization, gave space almost exclusively to strictly Herbartian subjects. Other influential Herbartians who were active in the work of this society, in publication, and in lecturing, and who helped to spread the principles of Herbart were Charles A. McMurry, of the Illinois State Normal University, who had studied at Jena in 1887, and his brother, Frank M. McMurry, a student at Jena in 1889. In 1897 the two brothers published their "Method of the Recitation," and Charles A. McMurry followed his "General Method," published in 1892, with many other books which treated of method in connection with most of the elementary subjects.

The Herbartian influence enriched the elementary-school curriculum by the introduction of historical, story, and literary material and literary classics. It brought a broader conception of history than had yet been current, which is reflected in the reports of important committees representing educational and historical organizations. It led to the substitution of real literature for the conventional readers which had so long dominated the elementary curriculum, and it encouraged correlations between geography and history, between arithmetic and geography, and between arithmetic and constructive work. The application of psychology, imperfect as it was, to educational practices was one of Herbart's important contributions.

Although Herbart began a valuable movement for the improvement of educational theory and practice, not all his principles have continued to enjoy full approval. Some of them have been revised or rejected. For example, John Dewey in 1896, in a significant paper before the National Herbart Society, made so effective an attack upon the Herbartian doctrine of interest as to drive the word "Herbart" from the name of the organization, which was changed in 1902 to the National Society for the Scientific Study of Education. Out of the controversy which in the meantime had waged over the doctrine of interest developed the concept of motivation. This word, which implies purpose on the part of the child, has since had many synonyms, some of them as much misunderstood perhaps and often as formal as Herbart's doctrine of interest that led to the academic warfare which still rages and in which abstract ghost continues to just with abstract ghost.

Froebelianism. The educational principles of Froebel, another enthusiastic follower of Pestalozzi, expressed themselves most definitely in the kindergarten movement. The influence of his educational theories, which were based upon a vague philosophy of symbolism, just as those advocated by Herbart were built upon a strange psychology, appeared also in the manual-training movement and the use of constructive activities in the school, activities encouraged by foreign exhibits at the Centennial Exposition in Philadelphia in 1876. His doctrines of "self-activity," "creativeness," "motor activity," and "self-expression" (terms which suggested Rousseau's influence), the idea of self-realization through social participation, or coöperation, and the principle of learning to do by doing had rather wide popularity in the United States. "To learn a thing in life and through doing is much more developing, cultivating, and strengthening, than to learn it merely through the verbal communication of ideas," maintained Froebel, who emphasized the social aspects of education as fully as he emphasized the principle of self-expression.

© 1898 by Eugene A. Perry

FRIEDRICH FROEBEL [1]

Notwithstanding the superficial faults of his educational theories, many of which lay in the mystic symbolism of his philosophy, Froebel has had a very important influence upon education in this country. Many types of present-day practice and some of the recent educational experiments reveal his principles, which appeared in the work of Francis W. Parker and may be seen in the work of John Dewey's experimental school set up in connection with The University of Chicago. The kindergarten, however, is probably the most definite and concrete contribution made by Froebel to the United States, where it has been developed more widely and thoroughly than in any European country. This type of school work was early encouraged by Superintendent William T. Harris of St. Louis, and by school authorities in Boston and some other cities. First established mainly by philanthropy and private associations, the kindergarten was encouraged as a

[1] Perry Picture Company, Malden, Massachusetts.

part of public-school systems in many cities between 1880 and 1900. But modern psychologists and educators have tended to reject Froebel's symbolism, however, and as a result the Froebelian kindergarten theories and practices have been modified in recent years. Dewey pointed out in the *Elementary School Record* in 1900 that it is impossible for the child to experience the mystic symbolism of a thing as Froebel believed and expected that he could, and in 1903 Thorndike, in "Notes on Child Study," asserted that there was no valid evidence whatever "to show any such preposterous associations in children's minds between plain things and these far-away abstractions." For a later development in educational procedure, originating in the work of Maria Montessori at Rome, rather extravagant claims were

JOHN DEWEY

once made. Her method emphasized the individual freedom of the child and the use of practical activities, but in most respects it was similar to the method advocated by Froebel and did not advance beyond him.

Work and influence of Dewey. The work of Professor John Dewey (now of Columbia University), through his writings and through the experimental school which he conducted at The University of Chicago from 1896 to 1903, has probably had wider influence upon educational theory than any other single factor. For many years he has been among the foremost interpreters of the social and industrial changes which the world has recently witnessed, and probably more definitely than anyone else he has formulated and stated an educational philosophy that seems best suited to the needs of a changed and changing civilization.

Dewey has pointed out the necessity of connecting the work and other activities of the school with the work and other activities of life outside the school and of giving children and youth an intelligent understanding of the world in which they live. He has held throughout his conspicuously influential career as philosopher and educational leader that real education must be based upon the nature of the child; that knowledge is a part of one's intellectual equipment and resources, a means of interpreting life and an instrument of control; that the mind is a process, a growing affair, and that its development depends upon the exercise of its function and requires constant stimuli from social agencies; that one learns to do by doing — to swim by swimming in water, to talk by talking to people about subjects which interest him and them, and to think by seeking to solve real problems and not by stupid and formal exercises in logic. In "How We Think" (1909) Dewey gave almost classic expression to the principle that all learning takes place in attempts to remedy or remove the inadequacies in past experiences, and that it should become the process of making use of past experiences as resources in developing the future; and in "School and Society" (1899) and in other writings he insists that "the school cannot be a preparation for social life except as it reproduces the typical conditions of social life." This and other principles which he set forth have served to modify and improve school practices not only in this country but in many other countries as well. Dewey's own account of the work of his experimental school, which has stimulated similar experiments elsewhere and has had a wide influence upon educational practice, shows how an effort was there made "to carry into effect certain principles which Froebel was perhaps the first consciously to set forth. Speaking in general, these principles are: 'That the primary business of the school is to train children in coöperative and mutually helpful living. . . . That the primary root of all educative activity is in the instinctive, impulsive attitudes and activities of the child, and not in the presentation and

AFTER LUNCHEON IN DEWEY'S KINDERGARTEN IN 1900[1]

application of external material. . . . That these individual tendencies and activities are organized and directed through the uses made of them in keeping up the coöperative living already spoken of, taking advantage of them to reproduce on the child's plane the typical doings and occupations of the larger, maturer society into which he is finally to go forth; and that it is through production and creative use that valuable knowledge is secured and clinched.'" By making a study of industries an important part of the elementary curriculum

[1] From the *Elementary School Record* (University of Chicago Press).

Dewey sought to provide the opportunities for social participation, for motor expression, and for self-expression.

The new psychology. Pestalozzi expressed the desire and aim "to psychologize education." He did what he could, little as it may have been, to satisfy his desire and to reach his aim; and his influence upon educational materials and methods in the United States cannot be questioned, although he knew little psychology. Herbartianism and Froebelianism extended beyond him, and in this country stimulated wide interest in the improvement and reform of the materials and methods of instruction. But the science of psychology had not yet appeared, and many years were to pass before such techniques were devised as permitted any degree of that accuracy and objectivity which modern psychology now claims for itself. In fact, as late as 1879, when Wilhelm Wundt set up in Leipzig, Germany, the first psychological laboratory, the fashions in psychology were set from the armchairs of metaphysician, the philosopher, the theologian, and other pleasant literary ramblers. Through Wundt's effort, however, detailed and more nearly accurate studies began to be made of the psychological processes and mechanisms found in the hearing, taste, smell, and vision, memory, reasoning, judgment, and learning of the so-called normal individual.

Among Wundt's early students were two young Americans, James McKeen Cattell and G. Stanley Hall, who returned to the United States and in the early eighties established psychological laboratories. Far-reaching has been the influence of this pioneer work, out of which developed the movement that has given this country a creditable place in experimental psychological research. Few are the American colleges that do not now have departments of psychology and fewer still are those that are not respectable and modish enough to boast of a laboratory. In 1890 William James, a professor in Harvard University, published his "Principles of Psychology," which immediately became a great success, served to increase the fame of the brilliant author, and pointed the way to many problems for study in the field. Among other subjects in which his work stimulated research was that of the original, unadulterated, unalloyed, and undecorated nature of man, which is still a fertile region for exploration or gleanings, although it has been worked into increasingly since 1913, when Edward L. Thorndike, a professor in Teachers College, Columbia University, published, after several years of ingenious and careful experiments with animals and children, his "Original Nature of Man."

This book contained a rather impressive list of "original tendencies," inborn capacities, or instincts, as they had been called by James, under whom Thorndike had studied at Harvard and to whose memory Thorndike dedicated the significant work. But both James's list of instincts and Thorndike's list have seemed a trifle long to some of the psychologists who have followed. William McDougall, a professor at Harvard (now at Duke University), published a shorter list which attracted notice, and in more recent years others have tried to make the list of instincts still shorter. As a result of this combat of scholarship and research the word "instinct" is not so fashionable as it was in earlier days, and the word "drive" is occasionally substituted for impulses with which human beings are believed to be born. But, whatever the name given to these innate tendencies and whatever innate tendencies these may be, man now knows infinitely more than ever before why he does as he does, and the study of his nature has led most parents, teachers, and other educational workers more definitely to the belief that human behavior can be modified by nurture and the influences of environment, and for this reason, if no other, education has come to be accepted as a more useful social agency than it was ever before considered. Psychology, throwing light upon the manner by which habits are formed and broken, has also given the American public an increased faith in the wonder-working power of good schools.

G. Stanley Hall. The name of Hall, who was professor of psychology in Johns Hopkins University from 1881 to 1888, and president of Clark University from 1888 until 1920 and professor of psychology there, is associated with a type of

G. STANLEY HALL

psychological work which is somewhat metaphysical in attitude and Herbartian in assumption. Hall's studies and those of his students were generally conducted in part through the questionnaire method and often neglected the use of observation and experimentation as a basis of evidence, and frequently invited severe criticisms of his approach to the field of child study, of his interpretation of original tendencies, of his application of his theories to teaching, and of his defense of the culture-epoch and recapitulation theory. Some of his doctrines were mercilessly attacked by critics who were more scientific in their procedure and relied less on speculation and more on fact to support their own views. However, Hall helped to break down the old scholastic psychology which had so long held sway. He was one of the earliest scholars to connect psychology with the evolutionary theory and one of the first to bring the scholarship of German psychologists to bear upon the subject in this country, and he was probably the first American psychologist of repute to countenance some of the theories of the young Viennese physician Sigmund Freud, around whose views a bitter controversy has raged. Hall's published studies of children began in the early eighties and came to most significant expression in the publication of "Adolescence" in 1904. This work stimulated numerous investigations in the psychology of children and adolescents and opened up many important questions which continue to receive attention. Among Americans his work increased the belief, which is probably stronger here than in any other country, that education must be based upon psychology, and that psychology is a field worthy of scientific study.

WILLIAM JAMES

William James. William James also attacked scholastic psychology. The contribution of his "Principles of Psychology" to education as well as to general psychology lay in its rejection of the old faculty psychology and in the objective treatment of the educational significance of instincts, or natural tendencies, the meaning of habit, and such topics as interest, imitation, discipline, the transfer of training, and others which bear the marks of the modern approach to these subjects. Although some critics reproached James for a "planless and unnatural" order of the chapters, he stoutly maintained that he followed what seemed to him "a good pedagogic order" in consequence of what seemed to be "pedagogic necessities." In 1892, in response to the request of the Harvard Corporation, James gave to the teachers of Cambridge, Massachusetts, "a few public lectures on psychology." These were given later to other audiences of teachers. In 1899, when he came to publish the lectures under the title of "Talks to Teachers," he weeded out the "analytical technicality," which experience had taught him that his audiences had relished least, and left unreduced the "concrete practical application," which they had cared for most, thus again revealing the objective point of view. This work has since had a tremendous influence on schoolroom practice. Throughout there is emphasis upon, or suggestion of, the necessity for experimentation and study, work that has been advanced more definitely by Thorndike — perhaps the most influential name connected with modern psychology — than by any other worker in the field.

E. L. Thorndike. Author of thirty or more books and more than three hundred articles since 1898 — when he published "Animal Intelligence," his doctor's dissertation, a scholarly work of prime importance because it marks the real beginning of the science of animal psychology, established "the technique for comparative psychology," opened up many new problems and indicated methods for their solution, and gave to general and educational psychology a new point of view — Thorndike's contribution to education and to psychology has been so large that the history of either subject could not be written, as James McKeen Cattell has said, without giving prominence to his name.

After listening to one of Thorndike's class exercises in Western Reserve University (to which he had migrated after receiving the doctorate at Columbia University) Dean James E. Russell promptly offered the young scholar an instructorship in Teachers College, Columbia University. The position was as promptly accepted. At that time "neither the term nor the subject of educational psychology had been created," says Russell, to whom Thorndike was known principally "as a student who had made a study of the behavior of monkeys," a work which seemed to the distinguished administrator (who was to become in no small degree responsible for Thorndike's notable contributions to the scientific study of education) to be good preparation for

E. L. THORNDIKE

"a study of the nature and behavior of children." Thorndike's subsequent influence and career are now acknowledged by all students of education. "No school is uninfluenced and no humanistic science is unaffected by his labor," says Dean C. E. Seashore of the University of Iowa; and Russell himself says of the interview which brought Thorndike back to New York: "No hour of my life has been more profitably spent."

As early as 1901 Thorndike "hinted that we ought to turn our view of human psychology upside down. . . . When this is done we shall not only relieve human mentality from its isolation and see its real relationships with other forms; we may also come to know more about it, may even elevate our psychologies to the explanatory level and connect mental processes with nervous activities without arousing a sneer from the logician or a grin from the neurologist." His labors have led psychology to such a place among the sciences. His contributions have been made not in the field of animal intelligence only; they have been large in the fields of heredity, in the process of learning, child psychology, individual differences, statistics, mental tests and educational measurements, curriculum construction, adult learning, education in general, and educational administration.

Early in his work Thorndike expressed courage and confidence in the ultimate effect of studies of heredity upon human welfare. "Surely it would be a pitiable thing," he said, "if man should forever make inferior men as a by-product of passion, and deny good men life in mistaken devotion to palliative and remedial philanthropy. Ethics and religion must teach man to want the welfare of the future as well as the relief of the cripple before his eyes; and science must teach man to control his own future nature as well as the animals, plants, and physical forces amongst which he will have to live. It is a noble thing that human reason, bred of a myriad unreasoned happenings, and driven forth into life by whips made æons ago with no thought of man's higher wants, can yet turn back to understand man's birth, survey his journey, chart and steer his future course, and free him from barriers without and defects within. Until the last removable impediment in man's own nature dies childless, human reason will not rest."

The wide movement of thinkers and workers in all fields of human effort toward acceptance of the principles of individual differences has received impetus from the experiments of Thorndike, who has continued, however, to advocate the improvement of the instruments of measurement and to warn against any of their "unreliabilities," which must be removed "by vigorous experimentation." A tireless and zealous exponent of intelligence tests and measurements, he has never denied their defects, and would probably be the last to claim that sound criteria of intelligence exist. Certainly he would maintain that what such tests measure is often unknown. And he would probably not deny that their revelations are too often not understood by hundreds of school-teachers and administrators and other social workers, notwithstanding their glibness in the use of the language of tests and their facility in administering them.

Thorndike's interest in and contribution to American education is significantly revealed in improved school administration, the real basis for which he laid in psychology. Reforms and improvements in the classification and progress of children and youth in elementary, secondary, and higher education, the homogeneous grouping of children, provisions for the exceptional child, differentiated courses of study, and many other progressive administrative practices, including the financial support of schools, have their roots (in part at least) in the results of his work. The application of the statistical method to problems in the field of educational administration has increasingly widened since the publication of his "Mental and Social Measurements" in 1904. Surveys of city, county, and state school systems — a movement which continues to grow — may also be traced in part to his influence.

His researches in the psychology of learning have led to critical appraisals of the values of subject matter in the curriculum and to a more scientific choice of materials of instruction. Largely through his work the old theory of mental discipline and the transfer of training fell into general disrepute. He is chiefly responsible for the statement of the principles of learning which today have such wide application in sound schoolroom practice. Out of his work have developed methods and devices for measuring achievement and for encouraging improvement in learning, principles for the organization of materials of instruction, and the idea that science can and should undertake to determine objectives in education. Not only has he arrived at and stated principles, but he has been diligent in his effort to translate them into actual practice.

Thorndike's first scientific research was in animal psychology. His work as a student at Harvard, where he was encouraged by James, and at Columbia, where he was aided by Cattell, was "a decided innovation" in the field of animal intelligence and learning. Both the methods which he used and the conclusions which he reached in his early as well as his more recent studies aroused wide interest. The experimental devices which he introduced soon became standard equipment in the study of animal psychology and have been employed in numerous studies. Laboratories have been established in colleges and universities, programs of psychological meetings have been crowded with papers on the subject, special magazines have been founded to publish the results of experiments, and interest in the subject has led to feverish activity throughout this country and in parts of Europe. His open-mindedness, his passion for accuracy, and his respect for truth make him "sit down before fact as a little child" and follow humbly "to whatever abysses Nature leads," as Thomas Henry Huxley once advised Charles Kingsley. This attitude, without which one can learn nothing, has served to save the scholar and the fruits of his scholarship from absurdity. Although Thorndike has some imitators who shine for the most part only by reflection and who sometimes fill the educational house with smoke and not light, and numerous interpreters who in attempting to apply to schoolroom practice the laws which he has formulated have often enslaved where he would emancipate, the results and methods of his work have so far stood the test of time and controversy.

His contribution to American education is not confined to his scientific studies, however, conspicuous as these have been for distinction. The educational principles which he has announced are likely to stand until scientific ingenuity devises subtler instruments than he has employed to pry into the secrets of nature. Thorndike is conspicuous in the optimism of his philosophy. Throughout his scientific studies he exhibits faith in the improvability of man and in the idea of progress. To him education is the art of human life, and that art "is to change the world for the better: to make things, animals, plants, men, and one's self more serviceable for life's ends." He maintains that the aims of education should be "to make men want the right things, and to make them better able to control all the forces of nature and themselves that they can satisfy these wants. . . . The study of human life teaches that the world is more than a place where you eat and sleep and endure for the sake of a few cheap, animal pleasures, that it is full of great issues, unselfish motives and heroic deeds." Men in whom "service for truth and justice has become the law of life need not despair of human nature, nor pray for a miracle to purge man of his baser elements. They are the sufficient miracle; their lives are the proof that human nature can change itself for the better — that the human species can teach itself to think for truth alone and to act for the good of all men."

Change in the content of education. Long before psychology had become the master science in education, demanding materials and methods suitable to the varying abilities and needs of children and changing much that had long been traditional in the work of the school, the tendency to introduce the natural sciences into the content of education had been apparent. This movement had been encouraged by scientific discoveries and inventions in the latter part of the nineteenth century and by other forces discussed in preceding chapters. The practical results of science made a knowledge of natural sciences appear necessary to modern life, and as these became more systematized there was an increased demand that they be included in the curriculum. Advocates of science urged, in answer to the arguments of those who held to the prevailing doctrine of formal discipline, that emphasis in education should be upon content rather than upon method.

When Americans were hearing of Darwin for the first time they were also hearing of Herbert Spencer, Thomas Henry Huxley, and John Tyndall, all three of whom visited and lectured in the United States in the seventies and eighties and gathered many disciples. Their books had wide sale here. In "What Knowledge is of Most Worth" Spencer raised in such a fresh fashion the question of the purpose of education as to bring wide influence to his work. "Before there can be a rational curriculum, we must decide which things it most concerns us to know. How to live? — that is the essential question for us. Not how to live in the mere material sense only, but in the widest sense. To prepare us for complete living is the function which education has to discharge; and the only rational mode of judging of any educational course is, to judge in what degree it discharges such function." He held that the sciences furnish as preparation for complete living the knowledge of most worth. In "Science and Education" Huxley also pointed out the educational values of the sciences. He maintained that "education is the instruction of the intellect in the laws of Nature," under which term he included "not merely things and their forces, but men and their ways; and the fashioning of the affections and of the will into an earnest and loving desire to move in harmony with those laws." The claims of the sciences as materials of instruction in the schools were urged also by Edward L. Youmans, Charles W. Eliot, and many others. Through his advocacy of the elective system and the use of modern subjects in the curriculum of the schools and colleges Eliot had a very large and direct influence upon American education. The study of agriculture, the mechanic arts, and the natural sciences was prompted generally also by the Morrill Act of 1862 and the second Morrill Act, of 1890, which provided for the establishment and aid of the land-grant colleges. This scientific movement shows close relation to the psychological movement which has become the basis of so many important changes in educational theory and practice in recent years. But it has not solved all the educational problems; in the "new education" movement itself appear the roots of some which are noted in the concluding chapter.

The historical approach. Interest in the professional study of education has been increased by research and publication in the historical foundations of modern education during the last quarter of a century. Although the history of education was generally found in the course of study for the professional training of teachers in the latter part of the nineteenth century, the materials of instruction in that subject were scanty and some of them, measured by present-day standards, were of doubtful scholarship. Franklin V. N. Painter's "History of Education" had appeared in 1886 and Samuel G. Williams's "History of Modern Education" six years later, but both books were for the most part accounts of educational theories and were based chiefly on the work of the German Karl von Raumer and on materials which Henry Barnard had translated into English. Gabriel Compayré's "History of Pedagogy" had been published in English in 1886, but it gave considerable emphasis

CHARLES W. ELIOT

From a painting by Charles Hopkinson.
By courtesy of Harvard College

to conditions and needs in France. There had been published by the United States Bureau of Education between 1887 and 1902, under the editorship of Professor Herbert B. Adams of Johns Hopkins University and under the title "Contributions to American Educational History," accounts of educational development in many of the states, but most of these were dissertations for the doctorate at Johns Hopkins.

In 1888 Professor Richard G. Boone of Indiana University published his "Education in the United States." In 1904 Professor Edwin Grant Dexter of the University of Illinois published his "History of Education in the United States," which was "offered more as a report of progress than as a final word upon the subject." Although the book contained a mass of information, it was written principally from secondary materials and was defective in its neglect of the economic and political forces in social development and in the lack of organization and interpretation. Few of these early materials were especially valuable as guides in the study of social and educational history.

The work of Paul Monroe. Interest in the historical foundation of education was first stimulated most definitely by Professor Paul Monroe of Teachers College. In 1901 Monroe published his "Source Book in the History of Education for the Greek and Roman Period," in 1904 his "Thomas Platter and the Educational Renaissance of the Sixteenth Century," and a year later his "Textbook in the History of Education." In these books, in The Cyclopedia of Education (a work of five large volumes which he edited and published between 1910 and 1913, by far the best of its kind that has ever appeared), and in his courses at Teachers College, Monroe applied to the study of education the rigid principles of historical research and demonstrated the value of the historical approach to contemporary educational problems. He set a high standard for graduate study and helped to establish for students of education an ideal of accurate investigation which encouraged respect for high standards in other fields of educational work. The fruits of his own scholarship have appeared in the work of many students in whom he stimulated energetic interest in research and publication. The dissertations of forty-six of the one hundred and ninety one persons who received the doctorate at Teachers College between 1899 and 1921 were in "the field represented by the work of Professor Monroe," writes Dean Ellwood P. Cubberley of Stanford University, whose "Syllabus of Lectures on the History of Education," which was first published in 1902, "owed something of its value to the teaching of Monroe." Cubberley's "Public Education in the United States," published in 1919, and his "History of Education" and "Readings in the History of Education," which appeared in 1921, are valuable additions to the materials of instruction, in the history of education. Other contributions that reveal Monroe's direct or indirect influence include books by Dr. Frank P. Graves, now Commissioner of Education in New York State, who has written widely on the subject; the writings of Professor Edward H. Reisner of Teachers College, especially his "Nationalism and Education since 1789" — a social and political history of modern education published in 1922 — and his "Historical Foundations of Education," which appeared in 1927; and numerous monographs and less pretentious studies by many other scholars. Much of the solid knowledge now available to students of the historical development of American schools is the fruit of researches stimulated and encouraged by Monroe, whose scholarship could not be confined or restrained in Teachers College, which he has helped so notably to make and which in a large sense has helped to make him. He has served to give to the historical and comparative study of education a fresh significance in the professional training of school teachers and administrators and to remove the suspicion that it is a pretender in the field of teacher-training by helping to make it an ally of science rather than a competitor.

This chapter has indicated some of the forces which have had a significant effect upon education since the Civil War. Among these influences were the abolition of slavery, the growth in population, developments in agriculture and in industry, the rise of cities, the changed status of women, and increased scientific knowledge. Other influences upon education came from abroad through Pestalozzianism, Herbartianism, and Froebelianism. Dewey's work, the work of the leaders in the new psychology, and interest in the professional study of education have also served to change the work of the schools. As a result of the forces and facts of history described in this chapter American education has taken new directions in recent years. Significant tendencies have appeared and new problems have arisen. A brief consideration of some of these tendencies and problems is given in the final chapter.

REFERENCES AND READINGS

BEARD, CHARLES A., and MARY R. The Rise of American Civilization. 2 vols. New York, 1927.

> Chapters XX–XXII of Volume II are valuable as supplementary reading for this chapter.

BOWEN, H. C. Froebel and Education through Self-activity. New York, 1893.

> A good historical and interpretative account.

CUBBERLEY, E. P. Public Education in the United States. Boston, 1919.

> Chapters IX, X, and XI are good as supplementary reading for this chapter.

DE GARMO, CHARLES. Herbart and the Herbartians. New York, 1895.

> A good account of the Herbartian movement.

GRAVES, F. P. Great Educators of Three Centuries. New York, 1912.

> Contains chapters on Pestalozzi, Herbart, and Froebel.

GRAVES, F. P. A History of Education in Modern Times. New York, 1913.

> Chapters II, V, VII, X, and XI contain discussions of Pestalozzianism, Herbartianism, Froebelianism, Spencer, Huxley, Dewey, and Thorndike.

KANDEL, I. L. (Editor). Twenty-five Years of American Education. New York, 1924.

> Contains, among others, chapters on the university study of education, tendencies in educational philosophy, and the development of educational psychology, with considerable material on the work of James, Dewey, and Thorndike.

KNIGHT, EDGAR W. "Presentation to Professor Monroe," *Teachers College Record*, Vol. XXIV, No. 3 (May, 1923), pp. 249–252.

> A brief appraisal of Monroe's work and influence.

LINGLEY, CHARLES R. Since the Civil War (Revised Edition). New York, 1926.

> Chapters III, IV, and XIX deal with economic, political, and intellectual foundation and background, and conditions at the close of the last century. Contains valuable bibliographical notes.

MOORE, ERNEST C. Fifty Years of American Education. Boston, 1917.

> A fairly accurate summary of the progress of education in the United States from 1867 to 1917.

PARKER, SAMUEL CHESTER. A Textbook in the History of Modern Elementary Education. Boston, 1912.

> Chapters XIII–XVI (Pestalozzianism), Chapter XVII (Herbartianism), and Chapter XVIII (Froebelianism, Dewey, James, Thorndike, and others) are good discussions. Contains very useful bibliographical notes.

QUICK, R. H. Essays on Educational Reformers. New York, 1890.

> Chapter XVI interprets Pestalozzi's life and work. Contains chapters on Pestalozzi, Froebel, and Spencer.

RATNER, JOSEPH. The Philosophy of John Dewey. New York, 1928.

> Extracts from Dewey's writings, without critical exposition or comment, which give his philosophy.

REISNER, EDWARD H. "General Historical Background, 1897–1922," in Twenty-five Years of American Education (I. L. Kandel, Editor). New York, 1924.

> An excellent and suggestive summary of the background of the period.

REISNER, EDWARD H. Nationalism and Education since 1789. New York, 1922.

> Chapters XVII and XVIII throw light upon topics treated in this chapter.

SUZZALLO, HENRY. "Paul Monroe — An Appreciation," in Twenty-five Years of American Education (I. L. Kandel, Editor). New York, 1924.

> The introduction to this book, inscribed to Professor Monroe by his former students, appraises his fruitful activities and influence.

THORNDIKE, E. L. Notes on Child Study. New York, 1901.

> Presents the reliable findings of child study at that time, and puts to rest the "current twaddle of opinion" on the subject.

Teachers College Record, Vol. XXVII, No. 6 (February, 1926). New York, 1926.

> Devoted entirely to Thorndike's life and works and in his honor, this number of this educational journal contains articles by James E. Russell, J. McKeen Cattell, Robert S. Woodworth, and Henry Suzzallo, and other students of Thorndike's. Contains a valuable annotated chronological bibliography of Thorndike's publications from 1898 to 1925, which run to nearly three hundred titles.

Teachers College Record, Vol. XXIV, No. 3 (May, 1923). New York, 1923.

> Addresses in honor of James Earl Russell on his twenty-fifth anniversary as dean of Teachers College, Columbia University. Contains, among other interesting discussions, an account of the development of education as a university subject.

QUESTIONS FOR STUDY AND DISCUSSION

1. Describe public education in the United States in 1860 in (1) organization and administration, (2) means of support, (3) materials and methods of instruction, (4) training of teachers, (5) compulsory-attendance and child-labor legislation, (6) public high schools, and (7) higher institutions of learning.

2. In what way had slavery prevented the growth of the democratic principles of education?

3. What economic changes and scientific developments took place in the United States after the Civil War which had definite influence upon education? Show how education was affected by such changes.

4. Consider the relation between the control and the prevention of disease and enlarged educational opportunity. Point out the relation.

5. What was the social and educational significance of the changed economic and political status of women?

6. Show how the theory of evolution threw light upon the educative process. What has been the influence of Spencer and Huxley on American education?

7. List the principles of Pestalozzianism. How did Pestalozzi define the aim of education? In what respect is the definition adequate for the educational needs of the present? In what respect is it inadequate?

8. Show the channels through which Pestalozzianism came into this country.

9. Criticize the principles of Herbartianism. Show how Herbartianism was spread to the United States.

10. What contribution did Froebelianism make to American education?

11. State the educational principles of John Dewey.

12. What do you understand by the "new psychology"? How does it differ from the old psychology?

13. Point out the contributions made to psychology and education by Hall, Cattell, James, and Thorndike.

14. Show how schoolroom practice has been affected by the work of Thorndike.

15. Discuss the educational influence of Monroe. What is the value of the historical approach to education?

CHAPTER XVII

TENDENCIES AND PROBLEMS

Outline of the chapter. 1. Recently proposed extensions of public educational effort show new tendencies and also give rise to new problems in American education, with the result that facilities and opportunities for the scientific study of education are now made throughout the country.

2. School surveys for determining accurately the effectiveness and needs of school systems have greatly increased in recent years and have been widely applied in American education.

3. Educational research and discussions are encouraged by professional associations and educational journalism, and the use of standard tests and measurements of mental ability and educational achievements has also greatly widened and become a significant movement.

4. Although the United States has not made conspicuous progress in the field, interest in adult education is increasing.

5. One of the significant phenomena in American educational history appears in the creation and use of educational foundations or trusts, representing about $800,000,000 of private wealth.

6. Interest has recently increased also in the movement to gain national aid for general education in the states, a movement which has many advocates as well as opponents.

7. Education in the strictly rural areas, the education of the negro, the education of foreign-born citizens, and the inequalities in American education present perplexing problems.

8. The last two decades have witnessed many experiments and proposed reorganizations of elementary, secondary, and higher education, and public concern for the care of physical, moral, and mental defectives, delinquents, and dependents has become keener in recent years.

9. Probably the most conspicuous features of public education in the United States at the present time are its organization and administration, which have assumed the proportions of a huge machine.

10. Although the American school system reveals many weaknesses, it continues to hold the confidence of the people, whose increased efforts for public education are tributes to their robust faith.

The principles of American education — free and universal, publicly supported and controlled, compulsory, and

542

nonsectarian — were defined in Chapter I, and the practical arrangements that have been established upon them were also described there. In succeeding chapters the story has been related of the controversies and struggles which were waged over those principles in an effort to have them practically applied. Similar, if not always so bitter, are the controversies and struggles now waged over proposed public educational extensions. These not only reveal new tendencies in American education but also fresh problems.

Recent extensions of educational effort. Out of the industrial and electrical revolutions and the recent phenomenal growth of the factory system new industrial problems have arisen, and the school, called upon to help in their solution, has undertaken to give industrial training. This type of educational work had begun under private agencies before the close of the last century, but more recently it has found a place in public-school systems. Evening schools, part-time schools, and continuation schools have also developed rapidly, especially in the urban communities. Commercial education has expanded: business schools and colleges, high schools and colleges of commerce, have multiplied. Emphasis has been given to agricultural education, which first received particular attention under the provisions of the Morrill Act of 1862, which set the land-grant colleges on the way of their development, and to vocational education, which has been rather generously encouraged by the national government since the passage of the Smith-Hughes Bill in 1917. This legislation created a Federal Board for Vocational Education and provided for Federal aid to promote instruction in agriculture, trades, home economics, and industrial subjects, and to encourage investigations and reports on the needs in these fields. More and more is attention being given to the care of physical, mental, and moral defectives, delinquents, and dependents. There is a growing tendency also to throw safeguards around the children of selfish or irresponsible parents by strengthening child-labor and compulsory-school-attendance legislation, and by providing aid for poor widows whose children should be in school. Citizenship classes for foreign-born adults and efforts to remove the menace of illiteracy among the native-born are other recent extensions of the principles of public education, made for the purpose of increasing the happiness and elevating the character of the people.

The study of education. Rather wide provision of facilities and opportunities for the scientific study of education is now made through the organization of schools and departments of education in the colleges and universities and through other means. Only slight attention had been given to the subject before the close of the nineteenth century, and the chairs or departments of pedagogy which had been established by that time were often frowned upon by the older departments and were generally grudgingly recognized. But with its establishment in 1889 Clark University began to give considerable attention to psychology and education, and Teachers College, organized in 1898 as a professional school of Columbia University, was given rank with the schools of law, medicine, and applied science in that institution. These developments, together with the creation of the School of Education of The University of Chicago and of the Graduate School of Education of Harvard and the organization of schools and departments of education in many other public and private colleges and universities, are evidences of the increasing attention that the professional study of education is now attracting throughout the country.

From humble professorships, the original purpose of which was largely to give some undergraduate instruction in methods of teaching and managing schools, the institutional study of education has developed more and more into graduate agencies for research and investigation and for the publication, diffusion, and interpretation of the results of scientific studies in education. The development of educational administration, the establishment of educational standards, and the construction of standard tests and measurements and of curriculum, or courses of study, and educational engineering (commonly known as school surveys) have grown out of this movement during the last three decades. In many other ways is the college and university study of education justifying itself, even though its work and often the professors who direct it are sometimes held under suspicion by other members of the academic household. However, schools of education are likely to grow in academic respectability and in public esteem as they increase their standards of work and their own demands for thoroughness and excellence.

The school survey. School surveys, for the purpose of determining accurately the effectiveness and needs of city, township, county, and state school systems, have also greatly increased in recent years and are widely used. This procedure in educational administration, which has demonstrated its practical usefulness by leading to reforms and improvements in the organization, administration, supervision, support, and control of schools, is not, however, entirely new. The "personal-estimate type of survey report," usually made by one or two people, and general investigations of school conditions had been used in this country before the Civil War. Even state educational commissions were created for purposes of survey during the ante-bellum period. Some of the surveys which have been made even in recent years are of a very general nature; but as more objective standards of educational measurement have been established, a more nearly scientific form of educational engineering has developed and increased in importance. Although the recommendations of surveys are not always accepted and promptly acted upon by governing educational authorities, nevertheless the survey method is increasingly used by both public-school systems and private institutions as an intelligent guide for the diagnosis and treatment of educational weaknesses.

Surveys have been very numerous since 1911, when Professor Paul H. Hanus of Harvard University made a brief and general report on the conditions and needs of the schools of Montclair, New Jersey. A report on educational conditions in Baltimore, made in the same year by Elmer Ellsworth Brown, Commissioner of Education of the United States at that time, Professor Ellwood P. Cubberley of Stanford University, and Superintendent Calvin N. Kendall of the schools of Indianapolis, with the assistance of Dr. Milo B. Hillegas and Dr. Harlan Updegraff, who were then of the staff of the United States Bureau of Education, was the first "descriptive and comparative type of school survey." A study of the public-school system of Boise, Idaho, was made in 1912 by Professor Edward C. Elliott of the University of Wisconsin, Professor George D. Strayer of Teachers College, Columbia University, and Professor Charles H. Judd of The University of Chicago. In 1911–1912 an extensive statistical study of the New York City school system was directed by Hanus, with the assistance of many educational experts, and a survey of the Cleveland, Ohio, school system was made in 1915–1916 under the direction of Dr. Leonard P. Ayres, who was at that time director of the departments of education and statistics for the Russell Sage Foundation. In later years Abraham Flexner of the General Education Board directed a study of the school system of Gary, Indiana. These early surveys, although experimental, were important not only for the immediate use made of them, but because out of them came valuable suggestions for future surveys. The report of the schools of East Orange, New Jersey, by Professor Ernest C. Moore of Harvard University in 1911 ; the survey of the schools of

Bridgeport, Connecticut, made in 1913 under the direction of James H. Van Sickle, who was then superintendent of the schools of Springfield, Massachusetts; a study of the schools of Portland, Oregon, by Cubberley and a staff of experts in 1913; a study of the schools of Springfield, Illinois, by Ayres in 1914, — treated the strong and the weak features of school administration in these cities in such ways as to afford direction for many similar subsequent surveys. Techniques for surveying city school systems had become fairly well developed by 1916, and since that time the survey has come into very wide use.

The application of the survey method has also been applied increasingly to many county and state school systems through the aid of such organizations as the Carnegie Foundation, the General Education Board, and the United States Bureau of Education, schools of education in public and private colleges and universities, and other agencies. A survey of educational conditions and needs in Vermont was made as early as 1913 by Elliott, Hillegas, and Dr. William S. Learned (a member of the staff of the Carnegie Foundation) at the request of an education commission of that state. Three years later Flexner and Dr. Frank P. Bachman, of the General Education Board, made for a state commission of Maryland a study of public education in that state, which resulted in marked improvements. Since the Maryland study and report, surveys have been made of educational conditions in many states, including Delaware, North Carolina, Kentucky, Indiana, Virginia, and Florida. Numerous educational surveys have been made by the Institute of Educational Research, Division of Field Studies, under the direction of Strayer, since its establishment at Teachers College in 1921. Bureaus or departments of research are now being established in city and state school systems, in schools and departments of education in colleges and universities, and in teachers' colleges. This development led in 1916 to the organization of the National Association of Directors of Educational Research (now known as the Educational Research Association) for the purpose of promoting research in educational administration, supervision, and teaching. The survey movement has helped to change school administration from a business of guesswork to one that is at least approximately scientific in theory if not always so in actual practice.

Professional associations and journals. Educational research and discussions are being widely encouraged also by many professional associations which have developed rapidly during the last quarter of a century. In the changes that have taken place in the philosophy, or the science, or the practice of teaching and managing schools, the National Education Association has had considerable influence. This organization was chartered by Congress in 1906, after having been organized in 1871 as the National Educational Association; it grew out of the National Teachers' Association, which had been established in 1857. Through the activity and discussion of this association a department of education was established in the national government in 1867; since that time it has urged the establishment of a national university, has initiated important investigation, and has published valuable reports on subjects dealing with many forms of educational effort — elementary and secondary education, teacher-training institutions, teachers' pensions, rural-school problems, college-entrance requirements, libraries, and hosts of other subjects. It is now a vigorous advocate of Federal aid to general education in the various states through the transformation of the United States Bureau of Education into a department, with rank in the president's cabinet. The services of the organization to the cause of education continue to be made by its numerous departments, the strongest of which is the department of superintendence.

Other associations which promote the study and discussion of educational problems include the National Society of College Teachers of Education, the National Society for the Study of Education, the Educational Research Association, the National Association of State Universities, the National Conference on Educational Method, the National Council of Education (a section of the National Association for the Advancement of Science), and numerous state and local organizations, all of which are devoted to the study and improvement of education. Of the making of journals and publications representing the work of these and other educational organizations and associations, and already running into the hundreds, there is no end. These agencies are increasing interest in the scientific study of education and are promoting the professionalization of teaching and school administration.

Tests and measurements. The use of standard tests and measurements of mental ability and of educational achievement has greatly widened during the last two decades and has become one of the significant movements in American education. This attempt to solve educational problems by the application of the statistical method had its origin in the work of Francis Galton (1822–1911), an Englishman whose studies of heredity and allied subjects between 1869 and 1889 developed important statistical principles and suggested the measurement of human traits. It was further stimulated by the work of two Frenchmen, Alfred Binet and Thomas Simon, who published in the early part of the present century a series of standardized mental tests and a scale for the measurement of intelligence. In this country the subject had engaged the attention of Professor James McKeen Cattell of Columbia University in the last decade of the nineteenth century, and he soon won recognition for his studies. It also excited the interest of Thorndike, who, as early as 1895, in a course on measurements under Professor

Franz Boas of Columbia, had struggled with statistical methods and had found them "new and hard . . . to learn." But the mastery of the matter by Thorndike, who has been called "the father of the movement," has never been seriously questioned. By 1902 he was offering at Teachers College a course on the "application of psychological and statistical methods to education," probably the first course of its kind given in the United States. In the catalogue description was the promise to deal, among other things, "with means of measurement of physical, mental, and moral qualities, including the abilities involved in the school subjects, and rates of progress in various functions." Similar courses appeared at The University of Chicago in 1908–1909, at Leland Stanford Jr. University a year later, and at some other universities during the next decade. Since the introduction of the Binet scale into this country several important revisions and adaptations have been made by Professor Lewis M. Terman of Stanford and others. A great advance in the use of intelligence tests was made during the World War, when they were so constructed as to be easily administered to groups instead of to individuals one at a time. Since the impetus thus given to this means of measuring intelligence the number of intelligence tests has greatly increased and their use has widely extended; and since the publication of Dr. C. W. Stone's "Reasoning Test in Arithmetic" (1908) and Thorndike's scale for the measurement of handwriting (1910), educational or achievement tests have so greatly multiplied that they are now counted by hundreds. They are of all kinds and descriptions and cover practically all school subjects. The literature on the subject of tests and measurements is voluminous and continues to grow.

But when the movement began it aroused a storm of protest. Not only did the work of Dr. Joseph M. Rice, who is considered the real inventor of the comparative test in America, not meet with the approval of the educators of the time, but the results he presented made him the target of their vigorous attacks. He had tested the spelling ability of thirty-three thousand school children, and his findings appeared in 1897 in *The Forum*, which he edited between 1897 and 1907. They revealed, among other things, that children who had spent thirty minutes a day on spelling for eight years did not spell any better than children who had spent only half that time on the subject. Educators and the educational press denounced as "foolish, reprehensible, and from every point of view indefensible, the effort to discover anything about the value of the teaching of spelling by finding out whether or not the children could spell. They claimed that the object of such work was not to teach children to spell, but to develop their minds!" The report of Dr. Rice's findings in spelling and other investigations was received with derision by the Department of Superintendence of the National Education Association, and at its meeting in 1912 that body of educational leaders voted by a small majority, after a heated discussion, against the measurement movement. Two years later, however, a committee on tests and standards made to the organization a favorable report which was adopted by a majority vote. In the meantime Thorndike's interest in the subject continued to grow, and the subsequent development of the movement has been due in large part to his own work and that of many able students whom he has guided.

By the aid of the scientific method in education, of which tests and measurements are important parts, school administration has undergone radical changes in recent years. Through this method attempts are made to apply the mathematical attitude to the study of education. Efforts are made to measure with an irritating exactness and certitude differences in native abilities, character, and conduct, and to substitute the objective and precise methods of measurement of ability and achievement for the subjective and inexact methods. Increased efforts are also made to adapt courses of study to the needs of children and to make teaching effort and supervisory control more effective. The purpose of the movement is to replace opinion and guesswork in education by knowledge and evidence.

The movement has had rapid and feverish growth and has led to extensive "testing programs" throughout the country. Every properly organized city school system now has its research division, and it is a very backward provincial county school system which does not periodically turn upon the children, even in the remote rural regions, "batteries" of tests, which annually multiply in number. The programs of the meetings of psychologists have probably given to the discussion of intelligence tests more space than has been permitted any other single topic. Tests and measurements have also had a peculiar fascination for schoolmen and teachers. The superintendent of schools who does not know or who neglects to make use of these devices is considered quite out of date, and his usefulness as an educational leader is generally questioned. The teacher or supervisor whose vocabulary lacks such cryptic words or terms as "mean," "median," "mode," "coefficient of correlation," "probable error," "mean deviation," "standard deviation," and "I.Q." is rapidly becoming a relic of an earlier and unscientific age. The movement has widened, its productivity has increased, and through it have come into education greater general clearness and definiteness of purpose. However, even their most enthusiastic supporters admit the crudeness and imperfection of the tests and measurements and dare not predict their limits.

Adult education. Compared with certain European countries, among them Denmark, England, and France, the United States has not made notable progress in adult education, although something more than a beginning has been made. Agencies for guiding youth through the period between the time of leaving school and the time, a few years later, when they become fairly definitely fixed in the courses which they are likely to follow throughout life, include public free evening schools, vocational and technical schools, continuation schools, coöperative schools, and numerous educational agencies provided by such organizations as the Young Men's Christian Association, the Young Women's Christian Association, the Knights of Columbus, and the Young Men's Hebrew Association. Public libraries are also widening their educational influence. Under the leadership of the American Library Association, an organization made up of the librarians of the nation, with an energetic and effective executive office, the library is rapidly becoming "a dynamic institution of education," and books are more and more considered the agencies of learning and the library an integral part of the educational organization of the community.

Through university-extension work adult education is also widely extended. Study centers are organized, lecture courses are provided, traveling exhibits and traveling libraries are established, correspondence study is conducted, and in many other ways the usefulness of the university is extended beyond the campus. Since the beginning of this work by the University of Wisconsin about 1892 and the organization of an extension division in that institution about 1906, the university-extension idea has made its way into most of the large institutions, in which scores of thousands of adult students are annually enrolled.

The many recent developments in adult education are evidences that in this as in many other fields of educational effort time-honored theories have been upset. Until recently it was generally believed that old people did not learn; but within the last few years the traditional assumption that one's years of learning pass with the years of adolescence has been scientifically tested by Professor Thorndike in extended experimental studies which he conducted in connection with the American Association for Adult Education, which was created in 1926 and sponsored by the Carnegie Corporation of New York. Thorndike's conclusions that one may at least double the years of learning, "that persons under fifty should seldom be deterred from trying to learn anything which they really need to learn by the fear that they are too old," and that lack of opportunity or desire rather than lack of ability is the chief reason "why adults so seldom learn a new language or a new trade" or reach any extensive achievement of knowledge or skill, were reported to a meeting of the association in 1927 and a year later his findings were published in a nontechnical form in his "Adult Learning." The evidence increases that adults can learn and that they are eager to do so. Probably 175,000 people register annually in university-extension classes. It is estimated that more than 3,000,000 are trying to improve their education beyond the training which they originally received. Private correspondence schools, which have reached such astonishing proportions in the United States, annually carry on their books 2,000,000 men and women who pay every year fees that aggregate $70,000,000. Approximately 1,500,000 new students are enrolled every year by these agencies, which seek quick and easy profits from gullible men and women whose needs should be met by more reliable and sincere agencies of adult education. The extension of effort into the field of adult education is an important matter and should be considered a legitimate function of the state.

Educational foundations or trusts. One of the most significant phenomena in all American educational history is the creation of large private funds to supplement and assist institutions and agencies engaged in educational and public-welfare work. Since 1867, when George Peabody, a native of Massachusetts but then a resident of London, established a fund which was later increased to more than $2,000,000 and wrote, "This I give to the suffering South for the good of the whole country," more than a score of trusts have been created representing about $800,000,000 of private wealth and dedicated to the promotion of education and public well-being. All except $8,000,000 of these huge sums have been given since 1900.

The work of five of these foundations has been confined principally to the Southern states. The Peabody Fund, established for the purpose of encouraging and promoting public schools in "those portions of our beloved and common country which have suffered from the destructive ravages, and not less disastrous consequences, of civil war," as the donor expressed it, was not only the earliest manifestation of a spirit of reconciliation on the part of a Northern man toward the Southern states, but it was also one of the largest educational blessings which ever came from the outside to that section of the country. It aided in the establishment of complete state school systems, in removing hostility to the public education of the negroes or prejudice against it; it encouraged the work of training teachers, and in its final dissolution the fund became a part of the endowment of the George Peabody College for Teachers, which was chartered in 1909 and opened four years later. It also became a source of assistance in the establishment of schools of education in universities in the Southern states.

The Slater Fund of $1,000,000 was created in 1882 by John F. Slater, a New England manufacturer, "for the uplifting of the lately emancipated people of the Southern states and their posterity, by conferring on them the blessings of Christian education." Normal schools and industrial education for the negroes in the South have been aided materially from this foundation. In 1908 Miss Anna T. Jeanes of Philadelphia left the sum of $1,000,000 to Swarthmore College, located near that city, on condition that the institution should abandon intercollegiate football forever. The college refused a bounty tied with such strings, and through that circumstance still another means of education was brought to the negroes of the Southern states. Under the provisions of the bequest, if the fund was refused by Swarthmore it was to be used for the development of education and better living conditions among negroes in the rural sections of the South. The following year Miss Caroline Phelps Stokes left by will the sum of $1,000,000 as a fund, which was incorporated in 1911 as the Phelps-Stokes Fund, to promote, among several other worthy objects, "the education of negroes, both in Africa and the United States." The fund has been used to prepare and publish a study of the facilities for education of the negro, to support fellowships at the University of Georgia and the University of Virginia for the study of the negro, and to provide grants to encourage other activities in the interest of the negro and of better race relations. In 1915 Julius Rosenwald of Chicago created a fund which bears his name to aid in the construction of modern schoolhouses for the negroes in the rural sections of the Southern states.

Useful as these foundations have been, they do not compare in the extent of their influence with the large endowments created by John D. Rockefeller, Andrew Carnegie, Mrs. Russell Sage, and Mrs. Stephen B. Harkness. The Rockefeller foundations include the Rockefeller Institute for Medical Research, the General Education Board, the Rockefeller Foundation, established between 1901 and 1914 and richly endowed, and the Laura Spelman Rockefeller Memorial created in 1920 in memory of Mr. Rockefeller's wife and also given large sums. The amounts which constitute these endowments total almost $400,000,000 and "represent the greatest individual gifts the world has ever known." Sound business principles are employed in their administration, and the value they have rendered to the causes of medical research, education, the welfare of women and children, public health, and to multitudes of other worthy objects is beyond calculation. Immensely valuable also have been the Carnegie endowments (the Carnegie Institution of Washington, the Carnegie Foundation for the Advancement of Teaching, the Carnegie Endowment for International Peace, and the Carnegie Corporation of New York), which were created between 1902 and 1911 and provided with rich resources "to encourage, in the broadest and most liberal manner, investigation, research, and discovery, and the application of knowledge to the improvement of mankind," to provide retiring allowances for college and university professors, to promote the cause of world peace, and to promote the advancement and diffusion of knowledge and understanding among the people of the United States by aiding technical schools, institutions of higher learning, libraries, scientific research, hero funds, useful publications, and the like. Before he created these endowments Carnegie had given much money to establish libraries in this country and in the British Empire. He also established and liberally endowed the Carnegie Library and the Carnegie Institute at Pittsburgh and contributed in many other ways to the advancement of human welfare. To the foundations and other agencies which he established and aided he gave approximately $300,000,000.

The Commonwealth Fund, created in 1918 by Mrs. Stephen B. Harkness and endowed with $40,000,000 or more, engages in many useful activities, including work for children's health and welfare, prevention of delinquency, the promotion of mental hygiene, and educational research ; it undertakes also to promote international good will through the support of fellowships for British students at American universities. Other very important trusts include the Russell Sage Foundation, established in 1907 by Mrs. Russell Sage in memory of her husband and endowed to the extent of $15,000,000 or more, which is concerned chiefly with the improvement of social and living conditions; the Milbank Memorial Fund, representing approximately $10,000,000 and designed "to improve the physical, mental, and moral condition of humanity, and generally to advance charitable and benevolent objects," which was created in 1905 by Elizabeth Milbank Anderson in memory of her parents; and the John Simon Guggenheim Memorial Foundation, established in 1925 by Mr. and Mrs. Simon Guggenheim in memory of their son and endowed with $3,000,000 to be used "to improve the quality of education and the practice of the arts and professions in the United States." The Duke Endowment was established by James B. Duke in December, 1924, with the sum of approximately $40,000,000, to which the provisions of his will added considerable resources upon his death in October, 1925. One of the aims of this endowment, the assets of which are estimated at nearly $80,000,000, was the transformation of Trinity College at Durham, North Carolina, which the Duke family had already generously supported, into Duke University. Other purposes included subsidies to Davidson College in North Carolina, Furman University in South Carolina, and the Johnson C. Smith University, an institution for negroes, at Charlotte, North Carolina; aid to orphanages for white children and for colored children in the Carolinas and to hospitals in those states; provision for the care and maintenance of retired ministers of the Methodist Episcopal Church, South, in North Carolina, and their widows and orphans; and the construction and support of Methodist churches in the rural sections of that state.

The usefulness of educational foundations in the past and their opportunities for further service in the advancement of learning and in the increase of human welfare are not often questioned, but fears of the dangers which are said to lurk in the size and power of such huge sums are frequently expressed. It has been said that gifts from such sources tend to stop those from individual philanthropists and perhaps even make legislatures indifferent to their responsibility to provide liberally for the support of education. The fear is sometimes expressed that the funds of the foundations may be used to limit freedom of thought and action. Among other fears are those which seemed to be in the minds of the regents of the University of Wisconsin in 1925 when they voted nine to six to reject thereafter any gifts, donations, or subsidies "from any incorporated educational endowments or organizations of like character." By refusing to make the resolution retroactive, however, the regents saved to the institution a gift of $12,500 from one of the Rockefeller endowments, to be used for medical research, — a donation which had brought severe criticism from certain interests in the state, including the State Federation of Labor, and had led to this action. Previously the university had also accepted $218,000 from one of the Carnegie endowments for teachers' retiring allowances. Charges were made during the argument on the resolution that the funds of some of the large foundations were acquired by methods that should be condemned, that the money was therefore tainted, and that the Standard Oil Company had spent money for lobbying during a recent session of the Wisconsin legislature. In the history of foundations, moreover, support may be found for such disquietude. However, the governing bodies of most of these trusts are usually conservative. They are chosen because of their fiduciary responsibility and are allowed large freedom in the use of the funds for worthy objects. The funds of most of the large endowments are not held in perpetuity, and the trustees may use the principal as well as the income from it.

Although some of the foundation funds, whether good money or tainted, have been wasted through unintelligent

administration or through the incompetency of those selected to use them, there are a great many more examples
of intelligent administration and competent use. To cite
one case, a grant of $8000, used through the University of
Toronto, enabled experts to attack the baffling problem of
diabetes and to develop insulin; and to cite another, the
campaign in behalf of medical education, begun by one
foundation and continued by another for a decade or more,
has been of incalculable value to public welfare. Examples
of assistance given to other good causes run into the thousands. The amount of aid which goes from these foundations
to the general purposes of colleges and universities is steadily on the decrease, but that which goes to support special
projects is gradually increasing. Any important research
problems which are indorsed by representative scholars are
likely to receive aid from the resources of one or another
foundation, no matter what the source of the projects.
These projects may originate anywhere: in the alert mind
of an individual scholar or an organization of scholars, in
a college or a university, or in a foundation itself. The
primary consideration with the foundations, which have
developed rather skillful techniques in giving, is that the
need that the project is intended to meet be real rather than
fanciful. The educational foundations have afforded to
ripe scholars and research workers such opportunities as
could not be provided otherwise and have been the means
of encouragement and training to prospective scholars.
About fifteen hundred scholars and research workers are
supported every year by aid from these sources. When the
public comes to understand more fully the purpose of these
agencies — to advance knowledge and not to mold opinion —
the fear of their unsocial use is likely to disappear.

National aid to education. The high illiteracy rate and
educational backwardness of the Southern states, due in part
to the large negro population, their economic desolation,

their rural isolation, and the alleged uncertainty of proper educational sentiment in that section of the country, aroused rather wide interest in national aid to education shortly after the Civil War. As early as 1870 attempts were made in Congress through the Hoar Bill to establish a national system of educational support and control, but the proposed measure failed to pass. Another somewhat similar attempt was made through the Blair Bill, which was introduced in 1881, passed the Senate in 1884, 1886, and 1888, but never gained sufficient support to pass the House, although the division of votes on the bill did not follow sectional or party lines.

Not until recently were attempts again made toward national aid to education in the states. But the extent of illiteracy disclosed by the census of 1920, the problems of negro education and of immigrant education, the backwardness of education in the strictly rural areas, and the unwholesome conditions revealed by the army draft during the World War were pointed to as national educational liabilities. One in every six men examined during the World War was rejected as unfit for military service, making a total of more than 1,340,000 who had physical defects, most of which were preventable. These men were under thirty-two years of age and supposedly in the prime of life. The census of 1920 revealed 5,000,000 confessed illiterates, three million of whom were native-born. In the army draft it had been shown that one man in every four could not write a letter home or read a newspaper in English. This menace of illiteracy, which resulted in immense economic waste, came to be considered a national problem, to be met successfully only by national effort. Studies showed that the yearly economic loss through preventable disease and death was nearly two billion dollars. The census of 1920 also showed that child laborers between the ages of ten and fifteen years numbered above a million. It was learned that three out of every five teachers in the United States had less training than is generally required of teachers by advanced nations, and that in 1920 nearly a million and a half children between the ages of seven and thirteen years were not attending school of any kind. It was also disclosed that of the 14,000,000 foreign-born citizens of the United States 8,000,000 had come from countries in which from 25 per cent to 80 per cent of the population were illiterate.

Education of the negro. The census of 1920 showed that nearly 10 per cent of the total population of the United States, or 10,463,131 persons, were negroes who had been a part of the national citizenship since the adoption of the Fourteenth Amendment to the Constitution of the United States in 1868. Most of these negroes were living in the Southern states; these states had been devastated by war and humiliated by congressional reconstruction, which had given the negroes (who were for the most part in a state of sheer illiteracy) civil and political rights that they were unprepared to use properly and safely. Since that time the difficult problem of the education of the negroes has been largely a responsibility of the Southern states, in which they are found in such large numbers, and those states were for many years unable to provide adequately for the education of either the white children or the negro children. With the adoption of separate schools, which was an imperative necessity and became the policy in seventeen of the Southern states, an additional educational burden was laid on the slender educational resources of that section of the country. Although progress has been made in the solution of this problem, achievements in negro education have not been distinguished, and in it many inequalities and discriminations still appear. According to the census of 1920 nearly 23 per cent of the negro population of the United States was unable to read and write. In five of the Southern states the number of negro illiterates ranged from 29 per cent to

38 per cent, and in no one of those states was the rate less than 16 per cent. The problem of negro illiteracy constitutes about two fifths of the entire problem of illiteracy in the United States.

Rural education. Education in the strictly rural areas also presents perplexing and persistent problems. In these places are found irregularities, inconsistencies, and inequalities by which scores of thousands of rural children are discriminated against and are denied the educational opportunities the constitutions of their states guarantee to them. Few features of public education in the United States furnish sources of such depressing and humiliating reflection as the rural schools. Many of the buildings are unsightly, insanitary in their surroundings, and poorly equipped, and too often they are in charge of teachers who are very deficient in training and educational outlook — spiritless, uninspired, and uninspiring — and who grope their way clumsily and aimlessly through the routine of giving and hearing lessons without any professional guidance or supervisory assistance whatever. Improvement is being made slowly in the progressive states, but the roots of the problems of education in the rural sections run back to the ancient and persistent devotion to and confidence in localism in education. The old district system, which has been so long maintained by law and strengthened by tradition, still commends itself to wide popular approval because of the deep democratic color it is believed to wear. It persists, too, by means of the continued chaos of county government, which is probably the least creditable institution in many states, the least efficient and the most wasteful — the jungle of American democracy.

In the existence of such conditions and in the unequal needs and unequal abilities of different states, the advocates of national aid to education see a national responsibility. It is argued that only by such assistance can equality of educational opportunity be provided. In the Morrill Act of 1862, the second Morrill Act of 1890, the Smith-Lever Bill, the Smith-Hughes Bill, the Smith-Sears Vocational Rehabilitation Act of 1918, and the Sheppard-Towner Act of 1921 (see Chapter I) precedents are seen by many people prominent in educational and other public affairs for the proper participation of the national government in general education in the states. The opponents of the movement, on the other hand, view Federal aid to general education as a sinister menace to democratic institutions.

Experiments and reorganizations. The attempt of the American people to provide universal and free education by public support and under public control has filled the schools with children. Since 1900 attendance has increased more than 11 per cent in the elementary schools, about 66 per cent in the secondary schools, and more than 75 per cent in the higher educational institutions; more and more are the doors of educational opportunity being opened to the masses. The lengthening of the school term, the strengthening of compulsory-school-attendance and child-labor laws (which have not, however, yet reached in all the states a high level of proper enforcement), and the increase in economic wealth, whereby children and youth are enabled to remain longer in school, have started new and pressing problems in elementary, secondary, and higher education. The new education and its doctrine of individual differences, and the conception that real education must be based upon the nature and needs of the child, have recently brought some of these problems into prominence. Old assumptions have given way to new aims in the educational process, and in an effort to solve the problems that have arisen out of these changes much experimentation has been done and new plans and schemes continue to be offered.

In Gary, Indiana, a reorganization appeared some years ago for the purpose of developing into one scheme a variety of activities, including work, study, and play, so as to provide for better teaching, for improved administration and supervision, and for better care of the children. The Gary plan, or platoon system, is being adopted or copied by many cities throughout the country. Plans for the more flexible grading and promotion of children, experiments to break the "lockstep" which seems inevitable in the rigidly graded system and to enable children of exceptional ability to move more easily and safely through school work, and plans by which laggards could be coached by assistant teachers have also been made here and there. Among other experiments which have attracted more or less notice in recent years are the Pueblo plan, the Cambridge plan, the Winnetka plan, the Batavia plan, and the Dalton plan. Reorganizations and novel methods appear in differentiated and parallel courses of study, supervised study, the "socialized recitation," the "problem method," the "project method" (which has been widely popularized through the writings and teaching of Professor William H. Kilpatrick of Teachers College, Columbia University, and others), and in other unconventional applications of the doctrines of "interest," "freedom," and "creativeness," which sometimes tend toward shadowy and even bizarre if alluring devices. But the most vocal advocates of these reorganizations and methods (which have their opponents also) see in them the means of adjusting the work of the school to the abilities and interests of the pupils.

Novel arrangements have made their way into secondary and higher education. The high-school curriculum has been reorganized, new courses have been introduced, eliminations and substitutions have been made, optional and elective courses have been provided, new types of high schools have been established, the junior-high-school movement has gained wide acceptance, extracurricular activities of wide variety have become the vogue, and experiments in student self-government have been made after the manner of many colleges. In these higher institutions also, as was mentioned in Chapter XIII, many new remedies are being prescribed, and some are being used, for ills which have become alarming. One of the most serious of all the problems of higher education is the loss by the end of the first year of one fifth or more of the three hundred thousand freshmen who now annually enter college, and the loss of from 50 per cent to 60 per cent between the freshman and senior years. Faulty standards and methods of admission, the inability of students to adjust themselves to the college environment because of their own limitations or the imperfections of college life and methods, and perhaps also the fads which have appeared out of the "new education" and its doctrine of "freedom," are listed among the causes of the present plight. Improvement of these distressing conditions is being attempted by experiments varying in degrees of hopefulness all the way from the orientation and "freshmen week" program of recreation and good fellowship — one purpose of which is to "reduce the pangs of homesickness and create a wholesome grown-up feeling" — to thoughtful effort made here and there to improve the instruction of the freshmen. The purpose of these and other reorganizations, methods, and devices is to effect an economy in time and to prevent such waste as results from faulty grading, inflexible organization, ineffective supervision, and indifferent instruction, and to give proper attention to the individual pupil.

The work of repair. Public concern for the care of defectives, delinquents, and dependents — physical, moral, and mental — has also become keener in recent years. Industrial and reformatory schools have been established to take care of juvenile delinquents; the deaf, the blind, the feeble-minded, the tuberculous, the incorrigible, and the crippled are discovered by the state, which undertakes to care for and to educate them. The medical examinations made in connection with the draft during the World War disclosed an alarming amount of physical defects among the young men of the nation, and since then a new emphasis has been given to medical inspection and health supervision in the schools. Thus new burdens have been placed upon the educational and welfare agencies of the American public, which seems to be growing more humanitarian and benevolent toward the unfortunate. The noble movement to catch up and repair the dropped stitches in the social fabric constantly gains strength throughout the country, but there is also encouragement in the nobler signs, which occasionally appear, of interest in the prevention of weakness.

The huge machine. Probably the most conspicuous features of public education in the United States at the present time are its organization and administration. The sums which the various states expend annually on the support of schools are enormous, but by no means out of proportion to the economic ability of the wealthiest nation the world has ever seen. The phenomenal development of physical plants and equipment for schools cannot be matched in all educational history. Every year hundreds of millions go into the construction and maintenance of schoolhouses. Millions are spent in experimentation on curriculum construction and on materials of instruction. Scores of millions are invested in the preparation, publication, manufacture, and distribution of textbooks, which are naturally of vast commercial importance in a country with low standards for the preparation and reward of its teachers. But in the immense enterprise of public education, which bears so many mechanical features, appear some of its weaknesses.

Whether American educational leaders are primarily interested in bigger and better schoolhouses, in tests and measurements, in the revision, alteration, and enlargement of curricula, in finding new and catchy names for methods of teaching, in the latest fashions in textbooks, or in any other externalities of education, it does appear that they too frequently overlook the most persistent and probably the most difficult problem of all — that of securing, training, and retaining excellent teachers for the schools. The problem of improved instruction has been long persistent and difficult, largely because of conditions pointed out in Chapters XI and XII; that it now continues to be stubborn is at least partly because school-teaching has been subordinated to school management.

An influence of industry. The interest of the average American school manager in the machinery, the organization, and the administration of education grows largely out of his eagerness to imitate the methods employed by captains of industry. The organization of mammoth private corporations, with their immense capitalizations, their intricate administrative and supervisory machinery, and their vast armies of employees, has characterized the growth of industry; and in education, which has come to be the largest public business in the country, it is now the fashion to copy closely the methods of business. Mass production and standardization are becoming as characteristic of the American school as of the American factory; volume and velocity of output are almost as conspicuous in the realm of education as in the field of machine-made materials. Although fads and spasms of experimentation are often reported as attempts to emancipate education from the suffocation with which an imitation of the forces of machine industry threatens to stifle it, the mechanical practices of the factory and the countinghouse are coming more and more to be the practices of the schools and colleges. Few features of American educational life escape the monotonous routine of the machine of which the school, the college, and the university are parts and in whose wheels children and youth are more and more made to revolve. Education is becoming increasingly standardized and mechanical, graded by years, by points, by credits, by majors, by courses, and wearing the veneer of finality. Even now there are signs that American education tends to encourage a uniformity of mind and manners that makes for superficiality, and as it becomes more and more mechanical, more and more are the American people likely to mistake its shadow for its substance.

Robust faith in education. Notwithstanding its weaknesses, however, public education continues to hold the confidence of the American people. Probably no other theory, or doctrine, of democracy has for them such fascinating interest as the theory, or doctrine, that relates to the equality of educational opportunity. Probably no other principle of democratic government has had so much claimed for it. It is comforting in its almost romantic promise of an educational Utopia. The validity of many of the claims of the democratic school system finds encouraging support in actual practice. The public school has played and continues to play a most vital part in the spiritual advancement of the American people as well as in their material advancement, and it has served to guide them toward high-mindedness as well as to increase their material riches and power. The principle of universal education, although far from complete in practical application, has uplifted and enriched them and quickened and refined their life.

The increased and constantly increasing economic wellbeing of the average citizen of the United States — the widespread material prosperity of the country at large — is largely due to the extension and application of this principle. Comparative statistics dealing with the increase in per capita wealth, bank resources, savings accounts, and other evidences of economic power in the last sixty years make a very impressive showing. During that period public education has had its most effective development. And along with the personal and corporate accumulations of material wealth has gone also a rapid rate of progress in public welfare generally, promoted largely by the public school, which has served to give the average American citizen an appreciation of public services and has led him to demand many others. Not only has his faith in education increased, but increasingly does he appear to view it as necessary to personal and public well-being. Increasingly also does he express faith not only in the school but in other forms of collective action : police, fire, and health protection, hospitals, improved roads, and agencies for the care of the delinquent, dependent, and defective members of society. Increasingly is he demanding for his community such agencies of enlightenment as libraries and museums and other things which promise to add to the sum total of human happiness. Perhaps the most competent evidence of his faith in education appears in his endeavors and often in his sacrifices for the support of the school and other cultural and civilizing agencies. These endeavors and sacrifices are impressive tributes to the belief of the American people in the effectiveness of public education. Sometimes, indeed, they seem to see in it the panacea for the ills and weaknesses inevitable in a democratic society. But even when the public school, like other theories or dreams of democracy, falls short in reality or practical application and fails to fulfill its promises to the masses for whom it was established, their faith remains robust. They refuse to see comedy in the democratic theory of education or to decry it, as opponents and cynics so often do.

This chapter has treated in a rather general way some of the principal tendencies and problems in American education at the present time. It has pointed out the recently enlarged provision of facilities and opportunities for the scientific study of education, the significance of the school survey and the testing and measurements movement, and the means by which educational research and educational discussion are encouraged. Attention has also been called to the increased interest in adult education, to the place of educational foundations and trusts, and to the movement to secure from the national government financial aid for general education in the states.

The chapter has also drawn attention to the problems of rural education, the education of the negro and of foreign-born citizens, and to certain new problems that have appeared recently in elementary, secondary, and higher education. The interest of the public in the care of defectives, delinquents, and dependents has also been noted; and attention has been called to the recent rapid development in the organization and administration of education. The chapter shows also that although the American school system has many defects it continues to hold the confidence of the American people, who are constantly increasing their efforts to support the schools.

In this chapter as well as in the other chapters of the book it may be seen that underlying the American public school is a great philosophy, and behind it a sublime idea. Its history is the story of struggles with selfishness, with vested rights, and even with mediocrity in management. There was never a time in all its history when it did not need reformation and improvement. Even now it resembles the field full of wheat and tares, or the giant "never perfectly well all over." Nevertheless the public school has served and continues to serve a noble purpose. Much of its strength is in its aim. And despite the obstacles which have obstructed and continue to obstruct the effectiveness of public education, it has served to provide the American people with many worthy opportunities which they could not have equally known by any other means.

REFERENCES AND READINGS

AYRES, LEONARD P. Seven Great Foundations. New York, 1911.

> Tells of the origin, purposes, and activities of the more important educational foundations at that time.

BAGLEY, W. C. Determinism in Education. Baltimore, 1925.

> Discusses the "relative influence of inherited and acquired traits in determining intelligence, achievement, and character." An analysis of some assumptions made upon the theory of fixed intelligence and the findings of intelligence tests.

BITTNER, W. S. The University Extension Movement, *Bulletin No. 84*, United States Bureau of Education, Washington, 1920.

> Definition, history, and conditions of the movement at that time.

CUBBERLEY, E. P. Public Education in the United States. Boston, 1919.

> Chapters XII–XV supplement the material of this chapter. Contains very good references.

CUBBERLEY, E. P. State School Administration. Boston, 1927.

> Chapter X on problems of education in rural areas, Chapter XIV on extension education, Chapter XVIII on Federal aid, and Chapter XXVIII on endowments and foundations (each with good references), and Chapter X, giving a selected list of rural school surveys, form good supplementary reading for this chapter.

DU BOIS, W. E. B. The Souls of Black Folk. Chicago, 1907.

> Here, as in his other writings on the subject, Du Bois is somewhat bitter.

FISHER, DOROTHY CANFIELD. Why Stop Learning? New York, 1927.

> This book, which deals with "the new stretch of road leading toward an educated citizenry," describes the new conception of adult education, with a glance at possibilities and tendencies in that field. Contains chapters on libraries, lyceums, Chautauquas, correspondence schools, university extension, and the like.

GROVES, E. R. The Rural Mind and Social Welfare. The University of Chicago Press, 1922.

> Shows that rural welfare is a national concern "because it influences for good the country as a whole."

KANDEL, I. L. (Editor). Twenty-five Years of American Education. New York, 1924.

> Covers the developments of a quarter of a century from 1897, with discussions of topics treated in this chapter: Chapter II, "University Study of Education," by I. L. Kandel; Chapter III,

"Tendencies in Educational Philosophy," by William H. Kilpatrick; Chapter V, "Development of Tests and Measurements," by Daniel B. Leary; Chapter VII, "Public School Administration," by E. P. Cubberley; Chapter VIII, "Public School Finance," by F. H. Swift; Chapter XI, "Vocational Education," by W. T. Woody; Chapter XII, "Education of Exceptional Children," by John F. Reigart; Chapter XIV, "Education in the South," by Edgar W. Knight; and Chapter XV, "Education of the Negro," by S. G. Noble.

KEITH, JOHN A. H., and BAGLEY, W. C. The Nation and the Schools. New York, 1920.

> A careful study of Federal aid to general education. "The Federal government can, by subventions, realize educational ends as truly as if its sovereignty included education."

QUICK, HERBERT. The Fairview Idea. Indianapolis, 1919.

> A delightfully written story of the new rural life.

SEARS, J. B. The School Survey. Boston, 1925.

> Shows the contribution of the survey movement to education. Contains excellent references.

STRAYER, GEORGE D. Standards and Tests for Measuring the Efficiency of Schools or Systems of Schools (Report of the Committee of the National Council of Education by the chairman), *Bulletin No. 13*, United States Bureau of Education, Washington, 1913.

SULLIVAN, MARK. Our Times. 2 vols. New York, 1926, 1927.

> A history of the United States from 1900 to 1925, written in a breezy, gossipy, and occasionally somewhat jazzy style, but plentifully documented, largely from newspaper and other periodical materials. Volume I, chaps. i–iii, viii, x, xiv, xvi, xviii, xix, xxii, and Volume II, chaps. i–vii, xi, xxvii, make interesting supplementary material for this chapter.

THOMAS, WILLIAM H. The American Negro. New York, 1901.

> A rather pessimistic view of the future of the negro people because of their moral delinquencies.

TRABUE, M. R. Measuring Results in Education. New York, 1924.

> Chapters I and II, on the nature of measurements and the development of standard tests, bear on this chapter.

WASHINGTON, BOOKER T. The Story of the Negro, the Rise of the Race from Slavery. 2 vols. New York, 1909.

> Emphasizes achievements and not delinquencies and deficiencies and is more optimistic than the book by Thomas, listed above.

QUESTIONS FOR STUDY AND DISCUSSION

1. Make a study of the recent extensions of educational effort in your state, listing the various forms which such extensions take.

2. Why were the colleges and universities slow to provide facilities and opportunities for the scientific study of education? List the various institutions and agencies in your state which now provide such facilities and opportunities.

3. What is the significance of the school-survey movement? Consider some of the surveys which have been made in your state and note any reforms or improvements which have resulted.

4. Make a list of the more important professional associations and journals which help to promote education in your state.

5. Point out the significance of the use of standard tests and measurements of mental ability and of educational achievement.

6. What are the conventional arguments often heard against the testing and measuring movement in education? What are the arguments made in support of the movement? Point out any dangers you see in the movement.

7. Why is the United States making less progress in adult education than certain European countries? List all the agencies promoting adult education in your state.

8. List the advantages and disadvantages of the large private funds (foundations or trusts) which are used to promote educational and public-welfare work. Study the work of any of these foundations in your state.

9. The Southern states do not now reach to national standards in education. Point out the causes.

10. Point out the arguments for and against the proposal before Congress in recent years for national aid to general education in the state.

11. Why does education in strictly rural areas present such perplexing and stubborn problems? Indicate a solution of those problems.

12. Make a study of negro education in the South and offer a solution for the problem.

13. Report on any significant experiments now being made in your state in (1) elementary education; (2) secondary education; (3) higher education.

14. What is the purpose of the junior high school? of the junior college? of orientation courses and "freshman week" in the colleges?

15. Make a study of the agencies now operating in your state for the care of physical, moral, and mental defectives, delinquents, and dependents. To what extent is this work one of repair rather than of prevention? What effort is your state making to prevent these weaknesses?

16. It is sometimes said in criticism of the American school system that emphasis is more upon organization and administration than upon teaching. Discuss the criticism.

17. Point out any evidence which you see that the American people have an increasing faith in the idea of public education.

INDEX

"ABC shooters," 56
Abbott, Edwin, 463, 474
Abbott, Jacob, 328
Abelard, 47
Academical Herald and Journal of Education, 196
Academies, 373 ff.; characteristics of, 373–376; extension of, 376; humble origin of some, 377–379; influence of, 376, 377; number of, 376; variants of, 380–384
Academy and College of Philadelphia, 71, 114, 116
Adams, Herbert B., 536
Adams, James Truslow, 419
Adams, John Quincy, 137, 218
Administration expensive, 14
"Adolescence," 527
Adult education, 30, 31, 552, 554
Adult illiteracy, 30
"Adult Learning," 554
Agassiz, Louis, 333, 337, 338, 340, 400
Age requirements of teachers, 22
Agencies for training teachers, 24
Agricultural and mechanical colleges, 28
Agricultural machinery, 505
Agriculture, growth of, 504; instruction in, 32
Akron, Ohio, school budget of, 13
Alabama, educational convention in, 206
Alabama Educational Association, 206
Alabama Educational Journal, 206
Alcott, William A., 194
Alderman, Edwin A., 476
Allston, R. E. W., 205, 325
American Annals of Education, 194, 207
American Association for Adult Education, 554
American Association for the Advancement of Science, 400
American Association of Teachers Colleges, 23
American education, principles of, 2 ff.
American Education Society, 382
American Institute of Instruction, 156, 318
American Journal of Education (Barnard's), 195, 220, 227, 427
American Journal of Education (Russell's), 194
American Library Association, 31, 553; reading courses of, 31
American Literary, Scientific, and Military Academy, 384

American Lyceum, 207
American Peace Society founded, 186
American Philosophical Society, 146, 390
American Quarterly Register, 382
American Quarterly Register and Journal of the American Education Society, 194
American Sunday School Union, 169
American Temperance Union founded, 186
American Weekly Mercury, 125
"A New and Complete System of Arithmetic" (Pike's), 421
"An Experiment in Education," 163
Anæsthetics, use of, 401
Anderson, Elizabeth Milbank, 558
Andover Academy, 72
Andover Theological Seminary, 227
"Animal Intelligence," 528
Annual cost of education, 2
Antioch College, 218, 333, 334, 403
Antiseptics, 507
Apprenticeship and poor laws, 72, 99 ff., 102 ff.
Aristotle, 46, 116
Arithmetics, 427–429
Arkwright, Richard, 173
Army draft, 561
Arnold, Thomas, 47
Arthur, Timothy Shay, 186
Association of American Universities, 23
Association of Colleges and Preparatory Schools of the Middle States and Maryland, 18, 23
Attendance, compulsory, 3; irregular, 18
Audubon, John James, 400
Awakening, educational, in second quarter of nineteenth century, 192 ff.
Awakening of labor, 173 ff.
Aycock, Charles B., 489, 494
Ayres, Leonard P., 546, 547

Bache, A. D., 315; report of, 201
Bachman, Frank P., 547
Ballard, Edward, 321
Ballot, restriction of, 75 ff.
Baltimore & Ohio Railroad, 172
Barnard, F. A. P., 334
Barnard, Henry, 107, 156, 195, 208, 218–221, 233, 249, 272, 315, 320, 332, 333, 380, 472, 535; his *American Journal of Education*, 195; in Rhode Island, 220; on education in Europe, 201
Barnard College, 403

Bassett, John Spencer, 380
Batavia plan, 565
Bathing prohibited, 413
Bathtubs, opposition to, 413
Beecher, Catherine Esther, 178, 420
Beecher, Henry Ward, 208
Bell, Alexander Graham, 505
Bell, Andrew, 66, 163, 194
Beresford, Richard, 117
Berkeley, Governor William, 64, 97
Bethesda Orphan House, 119, 120
"Biglow Papers, The," 175
Bill of Rights of England, 57
Binet, Alfred, 549
Bingham, Caleb, 444
Bishop, Nathan, 304
Black Death, 54
Blackboards, 444
Blair, James, 87
Blair Bill, 561
Blind, schools for, 33
"Boarding around," 247, 248, 456, 457
Boas, Franz, 550
Books, private collections of, among colonists, 89
Boone, Richard G., 536
Boston News-Letter, 125
Boston Patriot, 317
Bradford, William, 52, 60, 85
Bray, Thomas, 65
Breckinridge, Robert J., 233
British and Foreign School Society, 66
Brooks, Charles, 199, 201, 319
Brown, E. E., 546
Brown, Goold, 435
Brown, Governor Joseph E., 206
Brown University, 71, 81, 116, 334, 378, 397
Bryce, James, 182, 508
Bryn Mawr College, 340, 403
Buildings and equipment, 413, 414
Byrd, William, 86, 87

Caldwell, David, 221, 379
Caldwell, Joseph, 222, 353; advocate of teacher-training, 322, 323; letters of, 222–223
Calvinism, epic of, 107; wane of, 108
Cambridge plan, 565
Carey, Matthew, 178
Carnegie, Andrew, 556
Carnegie Corporation of New York, 27, 554, 557
Carnegie Endowment for International Peace, 557
Carnegie Foundation for the Advancement of Teaching, 27, 302, 547, 557
Carnegie Institute of Pittsburgh, 557
Carnegie Institution of Washington, 27, 557
Carter, James G., 107, 199, 209, 210, 317, 318, 319
Catholics excluded from suffrage, 76
Cattell, James McKeen, 524, 529, 532, 549

Causes of increased school costs, 13 ff.
Cavaliers, 61
Centennial Exposition, 519
Centralization in education, 43, 44, 281
Certification of teachers, 22; early practices in, 356, 357
Chadsey, Charles E., 364
Chandler School of Science (Dartmouth), 397
Channing, William Ellery, 178
Chantries Act, 56
Characteristics of early teachers, 347, 348
Charity in education, 180; in rate bill, 264 ff.; survivals of, 265, 266
Charles I, 59, 60, 61
Charlotte Democrat, 227
Chautauqua, 31, 207, 338
Chavis, John, 380
Cheever, Ezekiel, 113, 357, 364
Chicago, Milwaukee and St. Paul Railway Company case, 392
Child laborers, 561
Child-labor legislation, 235, 482, 544, 564; in Southern states, 482
Chipman, Nathaniel, 146
Ciphering books and slates, 429–431
Cities, growth of, 506, 508
Citizenship classes, 544
City school superintendency, 303 ff.; beginnings of, 304; recent development of, 305
City school systems, progressive character of, 10
City unit of educational administration, 10
Clark University, 526, 544
Class distinctions in colonial period, 74 ff.
Claxton, P. P., 476
Clermont, 171
Clinton, DeWitt, 161, 167, 187, 316
Clio's Nursery and Science Hall, 379
Coeducation, 5
College of Philadelphia, 389
College professors imported from Europe, 73
Colleges, 14, 78, 114–116, 234, 389, 392, 393, 403–407; appropriations for, 404, 405; attendance in, 405, 406; colonial, 114–116; denominational interest in, 393; increased enrollment in, 14; number of, 392, 393; number in 1860, 234; rapid rise of private, 393; recent development in, 403–406; social distinctions in, 78 ff.; tendencies and problems in, 406, 407
Colonial education, background of, 50 ff.
Colonial life restricted, 70, 71
Colonies, class distinctions in, 74 ff.; economic interests in, 89; extent of education in, 89 ff.

Colonists, democracy frowned upon by, 90, 91; enslaved to superstition, 91, 92; medical notions of, 92; motives of, 63 ff.

Colonization, purpose of, 63 ff.

Columbia University, 71, 82, 116, 334, 339, 399, 403

Columbian Magazine, 178

Committee of Five, 388

Committee of Ten, 388

Common School Assistant, 194

Common School Journal, 194, 212, 435

Commonwealth Fund, 27, 557

Compayré, Gabriel, 535

Compulsory-attendance legislation, 3, 234, 235, 482, 501, 544, 564; in 1897, 501; in Southern states, 482

Compulsory education in apprenticeship practices, 104

Condorcet, 143, 197, 198

Confederate textbooks, 446–448

Conference for Education in the South, 463, 464, 474 ff.

Confidence of public in education, 569, 570

Connecticut, work of Henry Barnard in, 219

Connecticut Common School Journal, 195, 219

Connecticut Gazette, 125

Connecticut Observer, 314

Consolidation and transportation, 26

Constitution of the United States, 4, 139, 143, 282; silent on the subject of schools, 4, 143

Constitutional provisions for schools, early state, 138 ff.

Content of education, change in, 533

Contests, over principles of public education, 4

Continuation education, 31

Contrasts, colonial, 85 ff.

"Contributions to American Educational History," 536

Control of education, 3

Cooper, Thomas, 396

Copy slips, 444

Coram, Robert, 146, 147, 351

Cornelius, Elias, 382

Cornell University, 338, 403, 518

Correspondence courses, 341, 553, 554

Correspondence schools, 31, 554

Cotton, influence of, in the Southern states, 468 ff.

Cotton, John, 128

Cotton gin, 174, 401

County library service, 32

County superintendent of schools, 302, 303

County unit of educational administration, 7

Courses of study, expansion of, 14

Cousin, Victor, 195, 198, 199, 233, 315

Crane, Ichabod, 248, 348

Crary, Isaac E., 199, 233

Craven, Braxton, 225, 324

Criticisms of early teachers, 350 ff.

Crompton, Edmund, 173

Cromwell, Oliver, 61

Cubberley, E. P., 537, 546, 547

Culture, colonial, inherited from Europe, 71 ff.

Culture-epoch theory, 517

Cumberland College, 314

Cumberland Road, 171

Curriculum construction, 567

Curry, J. L. M., 475, 476

Curtis, George William, 208

Curtis-Reed bill, 273

Cutler, Manasseh, 144

Cyclopedia of Education, 536

Dabney, C. W., 476

Dalton plan, 565

Dame schools, 72, 120, 121

Dana, J. D., 400

Dartmouth College, 71, 81, 116, 227, 399

Dartmouth College case, 117, 391, 392

Darwin, Charles, 510, 534

Davidson College, 558

Davie, William R., 394

Davies, Charles, 333

Davis, John, 377, 378, 379, 415

"Day of Doom, The," 126

Deaf, schools for, 33

Death penalty, abolition of, advocated, 185

Debt, imprisonment for, 175, 180, 181

Defectives and delinquents, 566; schools for, 33

Defoe, Daniel, 373

De Garmo, Charles, 518

"Degradation" in colonial colleges, 79, 81

Degrees, college and university, 29

"De la Educación," 216

Delaware, early constitutional provisions for schools in, 139; early schools in, 111

Delaware College, 251

Democracy frowned upon by the leading colonists, 90, 91

Dentistry, early instruction in, 398–400

Denver, Colorado, school budget of, 13

Department of superintendence, 551

Departments of pedagogy, 544

Dewey, John, 516, 519, 520, 521 ff.

Dexter, Edwin G., 536

Dimitry, Alexander, 234

Diphtheria, serum for, 507

Discipline, severity of, 126–128, 422

Discoveries, before 1860, 401

Disease, battle against, 507; extent of, 412; view of, 235, 412

Dismal Swamp Canal, 171

Dissenters, Virginia law against, 82

District school, beginnings of, in Massachusetts, 108 ff.; legalized, 109

District unit of educational administration, 11
Dix, Dorothea, 413
Doherty, W. H., 333
Draper, John W., 510
Dudley, Bishop T. U., 474
Dudley, Governor Joseph, 246
Duke, James B., 558
Duke Endowment, 27, 558
Duke University, 324, 558
Dunster, Henry, 357
Du Pont de Nemours, 146
Dwight, Edward, 319
Dwight, Henry E., 313

Early national period, population in, 135, 136
East Florida Seminary, 325
Eaton, Nathaniel, dismissed from Harvard, 127, 357
Eaton, Thomas, 112, 113
Eaton School, 72
Economic interests in colonies, 61 ff., 89
Edison, Thomas, 505
Education, annual cost of, 2; colonial, 73, 74; conservative character of, 39; early courses in, 334; function of government, 4, 5, 186, 187; history of, 38 ff.; religious motive in, 98, 99; subject to fads, 40
"Education in Europe," 201
Educational associations, 548, 549
Educational conventions and memorials, 202–206
Educational foundations, 27, 554–560
Educational journals, 195, 196, 548
Educational leaders of ante-bellum period, 208 ff.
Educational Research Association, 548, 549
Edwards, Jonathan, 116
Edwards, Ninian, 233
Eggleston, Edward, 455
Eggleston, J. D., Jr., 476
Elective offices, increase of, 185
Elementary School Records, 521
Eliot, Charles W., 47, 399, 510, 534, 535
Elliott, Edward C., 546, 547
Elliott, Stephen, 205, 325
Elmira College, 402
Emerson, Ralph Waldo, 208, 407, 510
"Émile," 512
Endowments, early educational, 117
England, economic conditions in, during colonial period, 53 ff.; public education established in, 67; theory of education in, 64 ff.
England during American colonization, 51 ff.
English Church, 58, 59, 61, 65, 66, 82, 84, 115
English Humanists, 58
English Poor Law, 100, 104
Enrollment, increase in, 14, 21

Entail and primogeniture, rules of, 82; abolished, 148, 149, 153
Erie Canal, 171, 172
"Essay on the Principle of Population, An," 142, 143
Established churches, 83 ff.; disestablished, 148, 153
Eton College, 72
Ettinger, William L., 364
European conditions, reports on, 196 ff.
European influence upon American educational journals, 195, 196
Evening schools, 122, 123
Everett, Edward, 207, 215
"Evils Suffered by American Women and Children," 420
Evolution, theory of, 510
Exeter Academy, 72
Expenditures for education, 2, 567
Experiments and reorganizations, 564 ff.
Extension courses, 24, 31, 341

Factory system, rise of, 173; social problems produced by, 174–176
Farm tenancy, 469, 470
Farmers' High School, 397
Federal Board for Vocational Education, 32, 543
Fellenberg, 193, 315, 380, 381
Finegan, Thomas E., 364, 489
Fiske, John, 510
Five formal steps, 517
Flexner, Abraham, 546, 547
Force of economic interest in colonies, 61
Foundations, educational, 27, 554–560
Fourteenth Amendment, 392, 562
Fowle, William B., 435
Franklin, Benjamin, 89, 146, 147, 311, 373, 389, 390; academy of, 114, 116, 119, 120; on taxation, 244; proposal for academies, 72
Free School Society of New York, 423
Free textbooks, 5
Freedom, of the press, 153; of speech, 153
French and Indian War, 182
"Freshman week," 406, 566
Freud, Sigmund, 527
Frissell, H. B., 476
Froebel, Friedrich Wilhelm August, 329, 516, 519 ff.
Frontier, social influence of, 182, 183
Fulton, Robert, 171
Furman University, 558

Gallatin, Albert, report on roads, 170
Gallaudet, Thomas H., 208, 314, 333, 334
Galloway, Samuel, 233
Galton, Francis, 549
Gary plan, 564
General Education Board, 27, 302, 386, 474, 477, 478, 546, 547, 556

General Federation of Women's Clubs, 508

Genesee College, 403

Geographical jingles, 441–443

Geography, 437; early texts in, 438 ff.; influence of, 73, 86 ff.

George Peabody College for Teachers, 555

Georgia, 71; apprenticeship legislation in, 101; constitutional provisions for schools, 139, 140; early schools in, 112; educational convention in, 206

Georgia Gazette, 126

"Georgia Scenes," 378, 379

Girard, Stephen, 201

Girard College for Orphans, 201

Goodrich, Samuel C., 415, 420, 440

Graduate instruction, 500

Graduate school, first, 404

Grammar, early methods in, 433, 434; early texts, 431–436; teachers deficient in, 434, 435

Grand Remonstrance, 57

Graves, Frank P., 298, 537

Gray, Asa, 400, 510

Great Charter, 57

Greeley, Horace, 208, 398

Green, Samuel S., 304

Gregory, John M., 334

Grimké, Thomas S., 208

Grissom, John, 208, 315

Grube Method, 516

Guggenheim Memorial Foundation, 27, 558

Guggenheim, Simon, 558

Guyot, Arnold, 333, 441

Habersham, James, 119

Hall, G. Stanley, 524, 526, 527

Hall, James, 379

Hall, Samuel R., 309, 313, 316, 328

Hamilton, Alexander, 177

Hampton Academy, 113

Hanus, Paul H., 546

Hargreaves, James, 173

Harkness, Mrs. Stephen B., 556, 557

Harris, William T., 515, 520

Hartford Ministerial Association, 265

Harvard, John, 115

Harvard University, 71, 78, 79, 80, 81, 113, 115, 117, 127, 390, 399, 400, 403, 510; expenses at, 245; social distinctions in, 78 ff.

Harvey, William, 92

Hawley, Gideon, 219, 288, 289, 488

Henry VIII, 55, 56, 58, 59

Herbart, Johann Friedrich, 516 ff.

High Commission, 59

High schools, 17, 18, 21, 384 ff.; present problems of, 389

Higher institutions, admission to, 28; characteristics of, 29; enrollment in, 29; types of, 28

Hillegas, Milo B., 546, 547

Hiram College, 334

"Hire-and-fire" policy, 25

History, 436; early texts in, 437

History of education, 38 ff., 535–538

Hoar Bill, 561

Holbrook, Josiah, 207

Holmes, Oliver Wendell, 208, 399

Home economics, instruction in, 32

Home Missionary, 227

Homestead Act, 503, 504

Hornbook, 120, 124

"How We Think," 522

Howe, John de la, 381

Hubbard, M. G., 194

Humanitarian movement, 185, 186

Hutch, Aaron, 355

Huxley, Thomas Henry, 532, 534

Illinois Common School Advocate, 195

Illinois Educational Convention, 203

Illiteracy, 30, 464, 544, 560, 562, 563

Immigration, 504

Imprisonment for debt, 175, 180, 181

Inclosures and sheep-raising, 54

Increasing cost of education, 274

Independents, 59

Indiana, work of Caleb Mills in, 227–233

Individual differences, doctrine of, 151, 564

Industrial Revolution, 173

Industry, influence of, 568

Infant schools, 162, 163

Insane, treatment of, 413

Institute of Educational Research, 547

Insulin, development of, 560

Interest, doctrine of, 517

Internal improvements, mania for, 171

Inventions before 1860, 401

Inventories in seventeenth century, 90

Irregular attendance, cost of, 18

Jackson, Andrew, 175, 182 ff., 186

Jacksonian democracy, 182 ff.

James I, 51, 53

James, William, 524, 525, 527 ff., 532

Jamestown, settlement of, 53

Jay, John, 141

Jeanes, Anna T., 555

Jeanes Fund, 555

Jefferson, Thomas, 109, 141, 148, 151, 152, 156, 186, 260, 352, 377, 395; anticipated doctrine of individual differences, 151; civic oath of, 152; quoted on education, 141; reform program of, 148–153; school bill of, for Virginia (1779), 109, 149–152, 156, 197, 198, 260, 261, 282

Jess, Zachariah, arithmetic of, 428

Jews excluded from suffrage, 76

Johns Hopkins University, 404, 526

Johnson, Andrew, 205

Johnson, Samuel, 250

Johnson, Walter R., 313

Johnson C. Smith University, 558

Journal of Education, 312, 315
Judd, Charles H., 546
Julius, H., 201
Junior colleges, 27
Junior high school, 18, 565
Junto, 389, 390

Kalamazoo case, 386
Kendall, Calvin N., 546
Kent, Chancellor James, 183, 219
Kilpatrick, William H., 565
Kindergartens, 16, 163, 519, 520
King Philip's War, 108
King's College, 71, 116, 250
Kingsley, Charles, 532
Kingsley, James L., 312
Knights of Columbus, 31, 553
Knox, Samuel, 146

Labor, awakening of, 173 ff.; early
    conditions of, 175–177; hostile atti-
    tude toward, 177
Labor journals, 175
Labor unions, rise of, 175
Lafitte du Courteil, 146
Lancaster, Joseph, 66, 163, 164, 166,
    194, 197
Lancasterian schools, 66, 163–166, 167
"Land-grant colleges," 28
Lane Theological Seminary, 199
Latin grammar schools, 71, 112 ff.
Law, case method in, 400; early in-
    struction in, 398–400
Lawrence Scientific School, 397
Learned, William S., 547
"Lectures on Schoolkeeping," 309, 316,
    328
Legislative gestures for schools, 154,
    155
Lehigh University, 398
Leisure, worthy use of, 508
Length of school term, 5, 20
Lewis, Samuel, 233
Libraries in colonies, 89, 90, 553
Library service, 32
Licenses of teachers, 22
"Life in the Argentine Republic," 218
Lighting, electric, 505
Lincoln, Abraham, 187, 208
Lindsley, Philip, 208, 313, 314
Linotype invented, 505
Lister, work of, 507
Local supervision and control, 302, 303
Local taxation, 273
Localism in education, 43, 274, 275; in
    Massachusetts, 109 ff.
London Company, 53, 61
Longstreet, A. B., 378, 379
Lotteries used for schools, 250–252
Lowell, Francis C., 174
Lowell, James Russell, 175
Luther, Martin, 127, 310
Luxuries, expenditures for, 276
Lyceum courses, 31

Lyceum movement, 206–208
Lyon, Mary, 402

McAndrew, William, 364
McCorkle, Samuel, 315, 316, 379
McCormick, Cyrus H., 505
McDougall, William, 525
McEwen, Robert H., 234, 256, 290
McIver, Charles D., 245, 476
McLaughlin, Judge Chester B., 297, 298
McMurry, Charles A., 518
McMurry, Frank M., 518
Machinery, introduction of, 173
Madison, James, 142
Malthus, Thomas Robert, 142, 143
Mania, for internal improvements, 171;
    for organizations, 181
Mann, Horace, 47, 107, 178, 179, 194,
    199, 208, 210 ff., 221, 233, 266, 272,
    291; achievements, 216–218; con-
    troversy with Boston schoolmasters,
    215, 216; influence in South America,
    216–218; later career, 218; report
    of, on education in Europe, 201, 202;
    seventh report of, 215, 318, 333, 334,
    364, 403, 472
Mann, Mrs. Horace, 218
Manual-labor schools, 380–384, 515
Manual-training movement, 519
Manufacturing, growth of, 174, 506
Marion, General Francis, 141
Maryland, early schools in, 111
Maryland Gazette, 125
Mass production in education, 568
Massachusetts, apprenticeship legisla-
    tion in, 100; beginnings of district
    school in, 108 ff.; early constitu-
    tional provisions for schools in, 139,
    140; compulsory-attendance laws in,
    501; educational decline in, 108;
    exemptions of schoolmasters in, 107;
    Latin grammar schools in, in 1700,
    113; legalized district school, 109;
    "old deluder" act of, 85, 104 ff.;
    work of Horace Mann in, 210 ff.
Massachusetts Institute of Technology,
    398, 403
Massachusetts Magazine, 311
Materials and methods of teaching,
    123–125, 423 ff., 511
Maury, Matthew F., 400
Mayflower Compact, 90
Mayhew, Ira, 321
Medical education, 398–400, 560
Medical notions among the colonists, 92
Mental discipline, theory of, 531
"Mental and Social Measurements,"
    531
Milbank Memorial Fund, 558
Military schools, 384
Miller, Lewis, 207
Mills, Caleb, 208, 222, 227–233, 266, 272;
    addresses to legislature of Indiana,
    229 ff.

Minimum standards fixed by the state, 5
Missionary societies formed, 186
Mississippi College, 326
Mitchel, Ormsby M., 400
Monasteries destroyed by Henry VIII, 56
Monitorial schools, 66, 163–166
Monroe, James, 82, 177
Monroe, Paul, 536–538
Montessori, Maria, 521
Moore, Ernest C., 546
Morrill Acts, 384, 397, 398, 534, 543, 563, 564
Morse, Jedidiah, 438, 439
Morse, Samuel F. B., 505
Motives of settlers, 59 ff.
Mount Holyoke Seminary, 402
Murphey, Archibald D., 167, 196–198, 272
Murray, Daniel, 80, 81
Murray, Lindley, 432

National aid to education, 560, 561
National Association for the Advancement of Science, 549
National Association of State Universities, 549
National Conference on Educational Methods, 549
National Congress of Parents and Teachers, 31
National Council of Education, 549
National Education Association, 548
"National Education in Europe," 201
National government and education, 32, 33
National Herbart Society, 518, 519
National land grants for schools, 253, 254
"National Pike," 171
National Society of College Teachers of Education, 549
National Society for Promoting the Education of the Poor, 66
National Society for the Scientific Study of Education, 519, 549
National Teachers Association, 514
Neef, Joseph, 514
Negro, education of, 562, 563; illiteracy of, 563; slavery of, 74, 154
New England College Entrance Examination Board, 17
New England Primer, 73, 125, 426
New Hampshire, early constitutional provisions for schools in, 139, 140
New Hampshire Gazette, 126
New Jersey, early schools in, 111
New Jersey Gazette, 126
New York, compulsory-attendance law in, 501; cost of education in, 13; early schools in, 110
New York City Board of Education, 162, 213

New York Gazette, 125
New York Mercury, 250
New York Public School Society, 161, 162, 166
New York Times, 510
New York Tribune, 398
New York University, 334
Newspapers, colonial, 125, 126
Niles' Weekly Register, 179
Nineteenth Amendment, 509
Noble, Governor Patrick, 205
Noisy schools, 414
Nonsectarian character of American education, 3
Normal College, 225
Normal schools, 16
North American Review, 312, 510
North Carolina, apprenticeship legislation in, 101; early constitutional provisions for schools in, 139; early schools in, 111, 112; school fund of, 13; value of school property in, 13; William Byrd's comments on, 86, 87; work of Calvin H. Wiley in, 221 ff.
North Carolina Gazette, 125
North Carolina Institute of Education, 203
North Carolina Journal of Education, 195
"North Carolina Reader," 225
North Central Association of Colleges and Secondary Schools, 18, 23
Northwest Association of Secondary and Higher Schools, 18, 23
Northwest Ordinance, 144–146, 502

Oberlin College, 402
Ogden, Robert C., 475
Ogden Movement, 474
"Old Blue Back" speller, 424, 425
"Old deluder" act of 1647 (Massachusetts), 85, 104 ff.; text of, 105; unpopular, 106; theological purpose of, 107
Olmsted, Denison, 208, 311, 350
Oneida Manual Labor Institute, 382
One-teacher schools, 26
Open letter against schools, 243
Orange County Sunday School Union, 169
Oregon case, 3
Organizations, mania for, 181
Orientation courses, 406, 566
"Origin of Species," reviews of, 510
"Original Nature of Man," 525
Oswego movement, 328, 514
Oswego Normal School, 317
"Our Times," 442
Owen, Robert, 162
Oxford Mercury, 221
Oxford University, 71, 78, 79, 114

Page, David, 328
Page, Walter H., 462, 463, 464, 474, 483

Paine, Tom, 142
Painter, Franklin V. N., 535
Panic of 1837, 172
Parker, Francis W., 441, 515, 516, 520
Partridge, Captain Alden, 384
Pasteur, work of, 507
Patents, number of, 505
Pauperism, dangers of, in England, 54
Peabody, George, 554
Peabody Fund, 333, 378, 386, 555
Pears, B. O., 208
Pedagogy, early courses in, 334; reluctantly admitted by colleges, 335; under prejudice, 336
Penal code in colonial period, 91, 127
Penn, William, 63
Pennsylvania, early constitutional provisions for schools in, 139; early schools in, 110; struggle for free schools in, 267 ff.
Pennsylvania Society for the Promotion of Public Schools, 203
Pennsylvania State College, 397
Pensions for teachers, 15, 362
Per capita cost of schools, 13
Permanent public-school funds, 5, 253 ff., 285
Permissive taxation for schools, 261–263
Perry, William F., 206, 234
Pestalozzi, Johann Heinrich, 194, 197, 315, 380, 512 ff.
"Pestalozzi and Pestalozzianism," 220
"Peter Parley," 415, 440, 441
Petition of Right, 57
Pharmacy, early instruction in, 398–400
Phelps-Stokes Fund, 556
Philanthropy, motive for schools, 72
Phillips, Samuel, 80, 81
Phillips, Wendell, 208
Phonograph invented, 505
Pickard, J. L., 321
Picket, Albert and John, 193
Pierce, Cyrus, 272, 320
Pierce, John D., 199, 233, 321
Pike, Nicholas, arithmetic of, 421, 427, 428, 429
Plato, 46, 151, 195
Political conditions in England during colonial period, 57 ff.
Polytechnic Institute of Brooklyn, 397
Poor, education of, 66
Poor-law and apprenticeship practices, 72, 99 ff., 102 ff.
Popular Science Monthly, 510
Population, in early national period, 135, 136; growth of, from 1870 to 1890, 503
Practices, organization and administrative, 5 ff.; school, 97 ff., 411 ff.
Present conditions, 1 ff.
Price's "Thrashing Machine," 422
Primers and readers, 426
Primogeniture and entail, rules of, 82; abolished, 148, 149, 153

Princeton University, 71, 82, 116, 221, 222, 313, 379, 380, 403, 441
Principles of American education, 2 ff.; contests over, 4
"Principles of Psychology," 524, 527
Printing press, 64, 89; in colonies, 125
Private libraries in colonies, 89, 90
Privy Council, 59
"Problem method," 565
Professional education, 500
Professional schools, 30; characteristics of early, 398–400
"Project method," 565
Property qualifications for suffrage, 75 ff.; removed, 77, 78, 183, 185
Psychology, the new, 524 ff.
Public control of education, 3, 280 ff.
Public funds for schools, 242
Public high schools, in 1860, 234
Public libraries, 553
Public School Society, 161, 162, 166, 251
Public-school support, 241 ff.; tendencies in, 272 ff.
Publicity and propaganda agencies, 193 ff.
Pueblo plan, 565
Pullman, George M., 505
Puritans, 58, 59, 60

Quakers, 84
Qualifications for voting, 75 ff.
Quarantine laws, 507
Quincy, Josiah, 215

Racial conflict in the Southern states, 470
Radcliffe College, 403
Radio, educational use of, 31
Raikes, Robert, 168
Railroad-building, 172, 173
Raleigh Academy, 166
Raleigh Standard, 227
Rate bills, 109, 156, 264 ff.
Raumer, Karl von, 535
Reaping machine, 505
Recent extensions of educational effort, 543 ff.
Reconstruction, educational influence of, 503; effect of, on Southern states, 468; undone, 470, 471
Reformation, 73
Reisner, Edward H., 537
Religion not a subject of instruction, 3
Religious conditions in England during colonial period, 58 ff.
Religious interests in American colonies, 82 ff.
Religious motive in colonial education, 98, 99
Rensselaer, Stephen Van, 396
Rensselaer Polytechnic Institute, 396, 397
Restriction of the ballot, 75 ff.

Rhode Island, 105, 110; work of Henry Barnard in, 220
Rhode Island Gazette, 125
Rhodes scholars, appraisal of teachers by, 367, 368
Rice, Joseph M., 550, 551
"Rights of Man," 142
Ritter, Carl, 440, 441
Rockford College, 402
Rockefeller, John D., 242, 556
Rockefeller Foundation, 27, 556
Rockefeller Institute for Medical Research, 27, 556
Rockefeller Memorial, Laura Spelman, 27, 556
Rosenwald, Julius, 556
Rosenwald Fund, 556
Rousseau, J. J., 512, 519
Ruffner, Henry, 203, 324
Ruffner, William H., 203, 324
Rules, school, 448 ff.
Rural education, 25–27, 563, 564
Rush, Benjamin, 146, 147
Russell, James E., 529
Russell, William, 194, 312, 315, 333
Russell Sage Foundation, 27, 546, 557
Rutgers College, 71, 82, 116

Sage, Mrs. Russell, 556, 557
St. Clair, General Arthur, 228
St. John's College, 220
St. Paul's doctrine of good works, 72
Salaries of teachers, 19, 25, 26
Sale, Captain William H., 463, 464
Sargent, Thomas, 127
Sarmiento, Domingo Faustino, 216–218
"School and Society," 522
School of Mines, 398
School discipline, colonial, 126–128
School expenditures, 2
School practices, 97 ff., 411 ff.
School property, value of, 2
School rules, before 1860, 448 ff.
School societies, 161, 162
School support, 2, 11, 12, 245, 246, 259
School surveys, 33, 545 ff.
School terms, 5, 20, 21
Schoolhouses, early, 415 ff.; in 1860, 412; log, 414, 418
Schoolmasters, exemptions of, in Massachusetts, 107; the passing of, 364, 365
"Schools, Basis of the Prosperity and of the Republic in the United States," 218
Schools, types of, 16 ff.
Schools of education, 24
Science, early advances in, 400; effect upon schools, 400, 401
"Science and Education," 534
Scientific revolution, 504–507
Scientific study of education, 544
Scopes case, 488
Scrooby group of Pilgrims, 60

Sears, Barnas, 378
Seashore, C. E., 529
Sectarian teachings not allowed, 3
Sectarianism in Massachusetts, 213
Secular Sunday schools, 167–170
Separate schools, 5, 480
Separatists, 59
Servants, white indentured, introduced into Virginia, 88
Sessions, colonial school, 123
Settlers, motives of, 59 ff.
Sheep-raising and inclosures, 54
Sheffield Scientific School, 397
Sheldon, Edward A., 514, 515
Sheppard-Towner Maternity Aid Act, 32, 33, 564
Sholes, C. L., 505
Silliman, Benjamin, 400
Simon, Thomas, 549
Sims, J. Marion, 421, 455
"Single salary schedule," 19
Skidmore, Thomas, 177
Slater, John F., 555
Slater, Samuel, 174
Slater Fund, 555
Slates and ciphering books, 429–431
Slaughterhouse cases, 392
Slavery, 63, 74, 87, 154, 400, 462, 489, 501, 502
Smallpox, serum for, 507
Smith, Adam, 142
Smith, David Eugene, 516
Smith, John, 61
Smith, Samuel H., 146
Smith, Sydney, 244
Smith College, 403
Smith-Hughes Bill, 32, 273, 543, 564
Smith-Lever Act, 32, 273, 564
Smith-Sears Vocational Rehabilitation Act, 32, 564
Smith-Towner Bill, 273
Smithson, James, 400
Smithsonian Institution, 398, 400
Social distinctions in colonies, 74 ff.
Society for the Promotion of Christian Knowledge, 65
Society for Promoting Manual Labor in Literary Institutions, 382
Society for the Propagation of the Gospel in Foreign Parts, 65, 66, 112
Sources of school support, 11, 12, 259
South America, Horace Mann's influence in, 216–218
South Carolina, apprenticeship legislation in, 101; early schools in, 111; early school surveys in, 205
South Carolina Agricultural Society, 205
South Carolina College, 325, 472
South Carolina Gazette, 125
Southern Association of Colleges and Secondary Schools, 18, 23
Southern Central Agricultural Society, 206

Southern Commercial Convention, 446
Southern Education Board, 474, 476, 477
Southern Educational Journal, 445
Southern Pacific Railway Company cases, 392
Southern states, child-labor legislation in, 482; colleges in, 466; complacency of, 491 ff.; compulsory-school legislation in, 482;· education in, before 1860, 471, 472; education in, in 1897, 464 ff.; educational problems of, 461 ff., 480; educational rank of, 479; evolution fight in, 487, 488; facilities for graduate instruction in, 487; high-school attendance in, 486; illiteracy in, 464, 486, 487; libraries in, 488; national standards in, 483 ff.; needed reforms in, 481 ff.; present problems in, 490, 491; recent progress in, 478 ff., 489, 490; separate schools in, 5; textbooks in, 445–448
Southern Weekly Post, 221
Spelling books, 424–426
Spencer, Herbert, 195, 515, 534
Standard Oil Company, 559
Standard tests and measurements, 549 ff.
Standards, minimum, fixed by the state, 5
Star Chamber, 59
State Agricultural Society, 325
State boards of education, 6, 298, 299, 300, 301
State constitutions, early educational provisions of, 138 ff.
State control of education, 284
State Journal, 229
State superintendency of schools, 6, 285 ff.
State taxation for schools, 272
Steamboat, 401
Sterling-Reed Bill, 33
Stevens, Thaddeus, speech of, in Pennsylvania legislature, 268–271
Stokes, Caroline Phelps, 556
Stone, C. W., 550
Stone, J. F., 452
Stowe, Calvin, 195, 199, 200, 203; report of, 199–201, 315
Strayer, George D., 546, 547
Stroughan, William, 86
Student self-government, 565
Submarine cable, 401
Suffrage, property requirements for, 75 ff.
Sullivan, James, 146
Sullivan, Mark, 442
Summer schools, 24, 337 ff.
Sumner, Charles, 215
Sumner, Henry, 205, 325
Sunday schools, 66, 72, 167–170, 338, 340
Superintendent of schools, city, 303 ff., 500; county, 302, 500; state, 500

Superstition of colonists, 91, 92
Surgery made safer, 507
Surplus revenue of 1837, 257
Surveys, school, 205, 531, 545 ff.
Survivals of charity in education, 265, 266
Swarthmore College, 555
Swett, John, 233
Symms, Benjamin, 98, 112, 113, 117
Symms School, 64, 72
Syracuse University, 403

"Talks to Teachers," 528
Talleyrand, 143
Taxation for school support, 3; authorized slowly, 263, 264; bitterly fought, 266, 267; difficult to secure, 249 ff.; dread of, 245; objection to, 242 ff.; permissive, 261–263
Teachers, age requirements of, 22, 364; agencies for training, 24; boarded around, 456, 457; certificates of, 22; characteristics of early, 347, 348; colonial, 124; criticisms of, 350 ff.; early requirements of, 357, 358, 419 ff.; effect of poor pay on, 358; hire-and-fire policy concerning, 363, 364; influence of the church on, 349; influence of good, 367, 368; number of, 2; queer requirements of, 359–361; salaries of, 19, 419; tenure of, 361, 362; training of, 23, 309 ff.; turned out, 129, 454–456; under close public scrutiny, 358, 359.
Teacher's Guide and Parent's Assistant, 194
Teachers' colleges, 16, 334, 339, 544
Teachers' institutes, 332–334
Teacher-training, agencies for, 24; beginnings of, in the South, 322 ff.; conditions of, in 1870, 326–328; early advocates of, 311 ff.; early attempts at, 315 ff.; present problems of, 341, 342; present tendencies in, 330, 331; recent reorganization in, 329 ff.; standards of, 331, 332
Teaching, increase in dignity of, 365, 366; not a regular occupation, 355
Teaching personnel, frequent changes in, 24, 25
Teaching profession, instability of, 361
Technological education, 396, 500
Technological schools, 30
Telegraph, 401, 505
Telephone invented, 505
"Ten Nights in a Barroom," 186
Tendencies and problems, 542 ff.
Ten-hour working day recognized, 179
Tennent, William, 116
Tennessee, educational convention in, 205
Tenth Amendment, educational implication of, 4
Terman, Lewis M., 550

Tests and measurements, 549 ff.
Textbooks, after Revolutionary War, 423, 424; free, 5; in slave states, 445–448
The Academician, 193
The Common School Journal, 417
The Connecticut Common School Journal, 315
The Educator, 196
"The Forgotten Man," 462, 463
The Forum, 551
The Society for Establishing a Free School in the City of New York, 161, 162, 166
"Theory and Practice of Teaching," 328
Thomas, Evan, 172
Thomason, James, 227
Thorndike, E. L., 521, 525, 528 ff., 532, 549, 550, 554
Thornwell, James H., 205, 325
Tice, James H., 304
Tobacco, influence of, 61, 62; in Virginia, 87
Town, unit of educational administration, 7, 8
Township, unit of educational administration, 8
"Tractate on Education," 373
Traction, electric, 505
Training of teachers, 23, 309 ff., 562
Transfer of training, 531
Transportation and communication, 170–173; in early national period, 136
Transportation of school children, 26, 27
Trinity College, 324, 558
Troy Seminary, 402
Turner, J. B., 398
Tutorial instruction, 72
Twain, Mark, 505
Tyndall, John, 534
Types of schools, 16 ff.
Typewriter invented, 505

"Uncle Tom's Cabin," 200
Union College, 397
Union Institute, 323, 324
United States Bureau of Education, 31, 32, 302, 334, 547, 548
United States Coast Guard School, 32
United States Commissioner of Education, 220, 284
United States Department of Agriculture, 477
United States Military Academy, 32, 384
United States Naval Academy, 32
Universal education, principle of, 3
University extension courses, 31, 553, 554
University of Alabama, 394
University of California, 405
University of Chicago, 403
University of Georgia, 394, 556
University of Illinois, 405

University of Indiana, 394, 403
University of Iowa, 334, 403
University of Jena, 518
University of Königsberg, 517
University of Maryland, 399
University of Michigan, 394, 403
University of Missouri, 334
University of Nashville, 314
University of North Carolina, 221, 338, 394, 472, 487
University of Paris, 92
University of Pennsylvania, 71, 82, 114, 389, 399, 403
University of Texas, 487
University of Toronto, 560
University of Utah, 403
University of Vermont, 394
University of Virginia, 153, 340, 394, 395, 399, 400, 472, 556
University of Wisconsin, 220, 328, 403, 553, 559
Updegraff, Harlan, 546

Van Sickle, James H., 547
Vance, Governor Zebulon B., 227
Vassar, Matthew, 401
Vassar College, 402, 403
Vermont, early constitutional provisions for schools in, 139
Vincent, John H., 207, 338, 340
Virginia, apprenticeship legislation in, 101; educational conventions in, 203, 204; entail and primogeniture abolished in, 148, 149; negro slavery introduced into, 87; school plan of 1779, 149–152; white indentured servants introduced into, 88
Virginia Company, 112
Virginia Educational Convention, 204
Virginia Gazette, 125
Virginia Military Institute, 384

Wabash College, 228
Waddell, Moses, 379
Wars of the Roses, 55
Washington, George, 140, 141, 171, 203, 207, 324
Washington and Lee University, 203, 324
Watts, Isaac, 126
"Wealth of Nations," 142
Webster, Daniel, 117, 183, 187, 218, 391
Webster, Noah, 125, 146, 437; spelling book of, 424, 425
Weld, Theodore D., 382
Wellesley College, 403
Wesley, Charles, 119
Wesleyan College, 402
West Florida Seminary, 325
Western Academic Institute and Board of Education, 203
Western Reserve University, 529
Westinghouse, George, 505
Westminster School, 72

"What Knowledge is of Most Worth," 534
Whipping posts, 127
White, Andrew D., 510
Whitefield, George, 119, 120
Whittier, John G., 215
Wickersham, James P., 333
Wigglesworth, Michael, 126
Wiley, Calvin H., 195, 206, 208, 221–227, 233, 272, 323, 364, 414, 472
Willard, Emma, 402
William and Mary, College of, 71, 82, 87, 115, 151, 261
Williams, Samuel G., 535
Wills in seventeenth century, 72, 90
Wilmington Courant, 126
Wingfield, Edward Maria, 84
Winnetka plan, 565
Winyaw Indigo Society, 117–119
Wise, Henry A., 204, 272, 427
Witchcraft, belief in, 84, 91
Withers, John W., 364
Woman suffrage, 509
Woman's rights, convention on, 401, 402
Women, changed status of, 508, 509;

education of, neglected, 72, 121, 377, 401–403; rights to their children, 509; rights to their property, 509
Woodbridge, William C., 194, 208, 315
Woods, Alva, 208
Worcester Polytechnic Institute, 398
Writing, place of, in schools, 443–445
Wundt, Wilhelm, 524

Yale, Elihu, 116, 390
Yale University, 71, 78, 79, 80, 81, 116, 379, 390, 399, 400, 403, 404, 472; social distinctions in, 78 ff.
Youmans, Edward L., 510, 534
Young Men's Christian Association, 31, 553
"Young Child's Catechism," 126
Young Men's Hebrew Association, 31, 553
Young Women's Christian Association, 31, 553
Ypsilanti Normal School, 321

Ziller, Tuiskon, 517
Zion Parnassus, 315, 316, 379